Bert van D

Microcontroller Systems

45 projects for PIC, AVR and ARM

Microcontroller Systems Engineering

45 projects for PIC, AVR and ARM

Bert van Dam

Elektor International Media BV
Postbus 11
6114 ZG Susteren
The Netherlands

All rights reserved. No part of this book may be reproduced in any material form, including photocopying, or storing in any medium by electronic means and whether or not transiently or incidentally to some other use of this publication, without the written permission of the copyright holder except in accordance with the provisions of the Copyright, Designs and Patents Act 1988 or under the terms of a licence issued by the Copyright Licensing Agency Ltd, 90 Tottenham Court Road, London, England W1P 9HE. Applications for the copyright holder's written permission to reproduce any part of this publication should be addressed to the publishers.

The publishers have used their best efforts in ensuring the correctness of the information contained in this book. They do not assume, and hereby disclaim, any liability to any party for any loss or damage caused by errors or omissions in this book, whether such errors or omissions result from negligence, accident or any other cause.

British Library Cataloguing in Publication Data
A catalogue record for this book is available from the British Library

ISBN 978-0-905705-75-0

Prepress production: Autronic, Blaricum
First published in the United Kingdom 2008
Second edition April 2009
Printed in the Netherlands by Wilco, Amersfoort
© Elektor International Media BV 2008

089023/UK

Content

	Prologue	9
1	What you will need	12
2	Tutorial	17
2.1	Concept	17
2.2	Hardware	17
2.3	Software	22
2.4	Simulation	29
2.5	Downloading	31
2.6	Operational	32
3	Basic	33
3.1	LCD display	33
3.2	Running light	39
3.3	Secret doorbell	45
3.4	Serial communication	51
3.4.1	RS232	51
3.4.2	USB	58
3.5	Analog to Digital Conversion	62
3.6	Dark activated switch	66
3.7	Youth deterrent	70
3.8	Sound activated switch	77
3.9	Air to fuel ratio	80
3.10	Digital clock	87
3.11	Debugging	91
3.11.1	Simulation	93
3.11.2	Serial connection	94
3.12	Bootloader	96
4	Advanced	100
4.1	Vref+	100
4.2	Record short sounds	105
4.3	Cricket	111
4.3.1	High quality version	111
4.3.2	Low cost version	116
4.4	Custom Characters	119
4.5	Animation	123

4.6	Random	124
4.7	A fan on PWM	128
4.8	Persistence of vision	135
4.9	Flash memory	139
4.10	USART connection	144
4.11	GPS tracking	149
4.12	Use PPP to access EEPROM	155
4.13	Poetry box	159
4.14	Voice command	163
5	Sensors	169
5.1	Infrared object detection	169
5.2	Photometer	172
5.3	Ultrasonic range finder	178
5.4	Digital thermometer	184
5.5	Data sampling the fridge	189
5.6	Heat loss in a residential building	197
5.7	Capture sound frequency	202
5.8	Tow away alarm	212
6	Cell phone	217
6.1	Send a text message	217
6.2	Receive a text message	221
6.3	Remote control	225
7	CAN bus	232
7.1	Remote LEDs	232
7.2	Monitor	240
8	Internet	248
8.1	Ping (Are you there?)	248
8.2	Webserver	258
8.3	Send an alarm e-mail	265
8.4	UDP remote control	276
9	Design your own E-block	282
9.1	Analog test signal	282
9.2	Microphone pre-amplifier	284
10	Migration between PIC, AVR and ARM	288
10.1	Software	288
10.2	Hardware	289
10.3	Example	293

11	Going into production	296
11.1	Youth deterrent (continued)	296
12	Appendix	302
12.1	ASCII table	302
12.2	Visual Basic communications	303
12.3	Tips and tricks	305
12.4	Microcontroller Mathematics	314
12.5	E-block connections	320
	Index	327

Prologue

You have to do what others won't,
to achieve what others don't.
(Anonymous)

When I was young my dad taught me how to program a large mainframe computer. First you need to think through what you want the program to do. Then draw a flowchart, which is a graphical representation of the program flow. It consists of symbols connected by lines with arrows. The program will flow from symbol to symbol following the arrows. Each symbol of the flowchart has a specific meaning. The rectangle for example is an operation, the diamond is a decision, the circle a connector to a different part of the program.

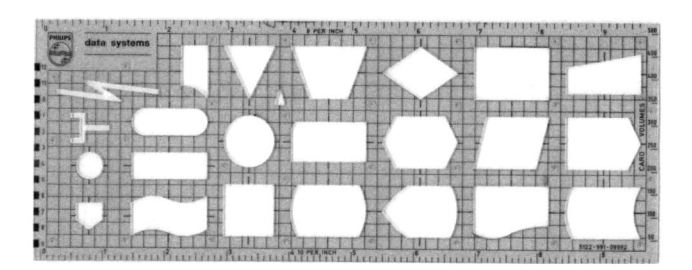

Figure 1. Flowchart template.

Flowcharting is an ideal way to develop a program, because it allows anyone, not just programmers, to understand what the program will do. Once everyone involved is satisfied that this is indeed the program they want, the flowchart must be transformed into lines of code. Then each line is copied onto a cardboard card with a kind of typewriter that punches holes in the card. The stack of cards is fed into a punchcardreader because that was the only way to get the program into the computer. The computer itself was in a different room, in fact it *filled* an entire room, and controlled by people in white lab coats. No one was allowed to get near it, let alone touch it. The results of the program would be printed on large sheets of tractorfed paper. And often there would only be one sheet with one line, such as: Error in line 2816, execution aborted.

We have come a long way. State of the art tools allow you to draw a flowchart directly on your computer screen, and enter in each symbol details of what you want the program to do at that location. With a press on a button the program is simulated allowing for very easy debugging. And with another button the whole program is compiled and downloaded into a microcontroller, a computer the size of a fingernail. You can get a program up and running in a matter of minutes.

Prologue

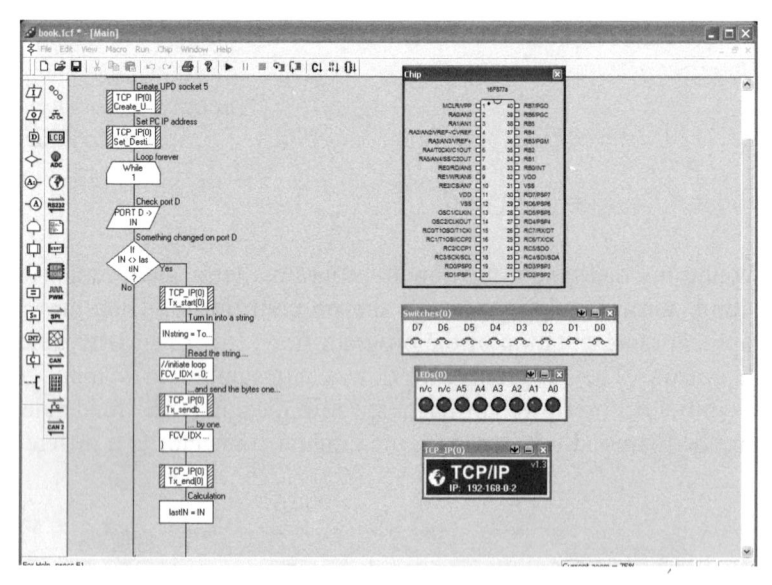

Figure 2. Flowcode state of the art software design.

This book is about such a state of the art tool, Flowcode®, and how you can use Flowcode to develop microcontroller applications. The book starts very simply with a tutorial project and step-by-step instructions. As you go along the projects increase in difficulty and only the new concepts are explained. Each project has a clear description of both hardware and software with pictures and diagrams, which explain not just how things are done but also why. All sources are available for free download, including the support software[1].

E-blocks® will be used as hardware for the projects in this book. This way hardware can be put together quickly and reliably. Fully tested units simply connect together using connectors or short flat ribbon cables to form completed projects. No soldering is required.

Since Flowcode is a high level language the intricacies of microcontroller programming are hidden from view. For that reason it doesn't make much difference whether the program is meant for a PIC, AVR or ARM microcontroller. On a high level the programs for these microcontrollers, although vastly different in internal structure, are identical. For that reason this book is on microcontroller systems engineering in general, not just for one type of microcontroller. If you don't own the microcontroller described in a project you can usually convert it to another microcontroller quite easily, as explained in chapter 10.

---

[1] Flowcode is not included and must be purchased separately.

Prologue

This book covers a series of exciting and fun projects such as a secret doorbell, a youth deterrent, GPS tracking, cell phone remote control, persistence of vision and an Internet webserver. You can use it as a projects book, and build the projects for your own use. Or you can use it as a study guide to learn more about Flowcode systems engineering and the PIC, AVR and ARM microcontrollers.

I would like to thank Ben Rowland, Sean King, Steve Tandy and John Dobson for their help and support while writing this book, and Alan Dobson for his help with the final editing.

Bert van Dam
Roosendaal, 2008

1 What you will need

1 What you will need

1. Flowcode

First of all you need to decide which microcontroller to work with: PIC, AVR or ARM. Due to the structure of Flowcode and the design of the E-blocks the projects are almost the same for either of these microcontrollers. In fact a project described for a particular microcontroller can usually be converted to the other types quite easily. See chapter 10 for more information on migration. If this is all new to you and you have no preference I suggest PIC for this is the easiest type to work with. It is readily available at low cost, and the PDIP package makes it easy to solder[2]. If you have experience with microcontrollers and are comfortable with the use of datasheets I would recommend ARM because it is the fastest and most powerful, up to 50 times faster than PIC or AVR.

With the exception of the tutorial all PIC microcontroller projects in this book use the 16F877A microcontroller and not the 16F88 which is supplied with the programmer. This microcontroller must be purchased separately.

Figure 3. Flowcode V3 for ARM and E-blocks bundle, courtesy Matrix Multimedia LTD.

---

[2] PDIP is an acronym for Plastic Dual Inline Package. It means the microcontroller has "large" pins that fit in the holes of a breadboard or experimental circuit board.

1 What you will need

To get started the "Flowcode for PIC and E-blocks bundle" (or AVR or ARM) will get you Flowcode professional, a programmer board with a microcontroller, power supply and LCD board, a LED board and a Switch board. Do make sure you choose the professional version.

2. E-blocks (in addition to the bundle)

A very useful, and in fact highly recommended, extension to the bundle would be the EB016 Proto board. This is an E-block with a small breadboard to allow custom peripherals to be connected to the microcontroller of your choice. Use 22 gauge, or 0.5 mm^2 Cu wire on the breadboard. There is a small patch area for more permanent extensions. See section 9.1 for a very convenient expansion to this board.

Figure 4. EB016 Proto board.

If you are interested in specialty projects such as the Internet, cell phone or CAN bus you need at least the appropriate E-blocks as shown in the next table:

Internet	EB023 Internet board
Cell phone	EB015 RS232 board
	EB186 Mobile phone module
CAN bus	EB018 CAN bus board (2x)
	An additional programmer board

1   What you will need

If you want to build all projects in this book you will need the following E-blocks in addition to the bundle and the previous suggestions.

EB013	SPI memory and D/A board
EB014	Keypad board
EB017	Patch board
EB022	Motor driver board
EB037	MMC board
EB038	Relay board
EB039	USB board
EB061	Application board
ECIO40	USB bootloader 18F4455 unit

In some cases you need to connect E-blocks using cables. The easiest way to do this is use a 9 wire flat ribbon cable and press-on D9-plug connectors. Take care when installing the press-on the parts: when you press too hard the pins ever so slightly bend rendering the connector useless. By connecting multiple female plugs to one cable you can connect multiple E-blocks to a single microcontroller port, see project 7.2 for an example.

Figure 5. Flat ribbon cable with press-on D9 connector.

3. Miscellaneous

A few projects use special software for the PC. You will find this software in the free download file at www.boekinfo.tk. This download also includes the sources and HEX or BIN files for all projects in this book. The support website features a FAQ (Frequently Asked Questions), the Errata and links to suppliers of Flowcode, E-blocks and other parts you may need. Visiting this website is highly recommended, and all downloads are free!

Included in the download are two tools that come in handy when debugging microcontroller applications: a software Oscilloscope and a Spectrum Analyzer.

1   What you will need

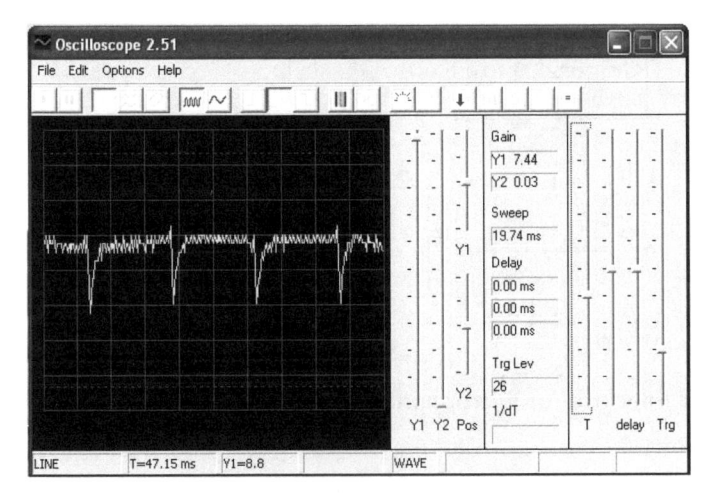

Figure 6. Software Oscilloscope.

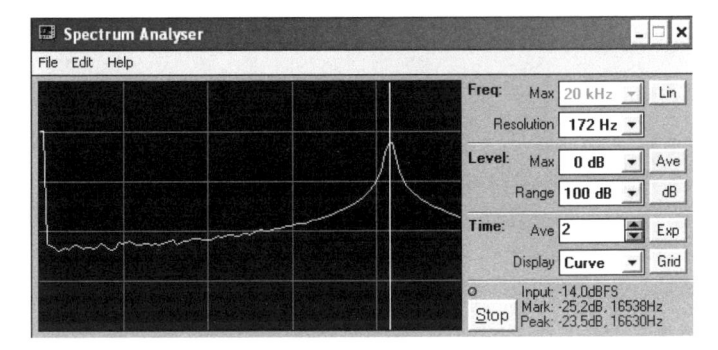

Figure 7. Spectrum Analyzer.

The software oscilloscope and the spectrum analyzer use the soundcard of a PC to convert the signals. One of the limitations is that the frequency that these tools can measure depends on the maximum frequency that your soundcard can handle. Another limitation is that you need to make a small interface to protect the soundcard.

1   What you will need

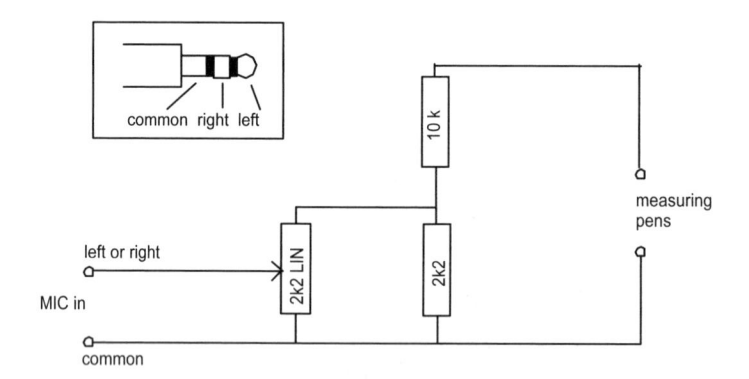

Figure 8. Interface for microphone or line input of a soundcard on a PC.

The interface in the previous Figure is used to reduce the maximum voltage on the microphone or line input of the soundcard from 5 volts to 0.9 volts. Do not use this tool with voltages over 5 volts without changing the values of the 10k and 2k2 resistors accordingly.

2 Tutorial

This tutorial will take you through the steps required to get a Flowcode application up and running. It is highly recommended that you read this chapter before building one of the other projects in this book.

It is assumed that you have installed Flowcode and the appropriate drivers for the programmer of your choice. If you haven't now would be a good time to do so. Closely follow the Getting Started Guide that came with Flowcode.

Before you can design and built anything you need to know what you want to accomplish. In real life the section "Concept" would contain the project description and design specifications (if any) that you need to follow.

2.1 Concept

In order to cut energy cost the lights in common stairways in multistory residential buildings are often controlled by timers. You press a pushbutton switch and the light will come on for a fixed period of time. In this tutorial project we will build a small application where an LED (Light Emitting Diode) is switched on for three seconds.

2.2 Hardware

At this point we will need to decide which microcontroller to use. Normally you would select the smallest and cheapest one that can just handle the requirements. An advantage of using Flowcode is that you have a wide range of PIC, AVR and ARM microcontrollers at your disposal. During the development phase it is often easier to use a relatively large microcontroller so you don't run out of ports or memory. The final stage of the design process would be to reduce the size of the microcontroller to the bare minimum, see chapter 11 for an example.

This tutorial is applicable for PIC, AVR and ARM users, the only difference is in the hardware section. So select the part in this hardware section that applies to your microcontroller and when you are done continue with the software in section 2.3.

2.2 Hardware

I own the EB006 PIC programmer with a 16F88.

The programmer can draw its power from the USB connection to the PC, but it is strongly recommended always to use an external power supply. This is the only way to get power to the +14V terminal required in some projects in this book, and it allows you to disable low voltage programming meaning you gain an extra pin.

Board EB004 will provide an LED and board EB007 the switch. In fact each board contains seven LEDs/switches, but we will use only one in this project. Connect the LED board to port A and the Switch board to port B. Note that the Switch board needs positive power, so you need to connect the +Vin terminal to one of the +V terminals of the programmer board. Take care not to use the +14V terminal!

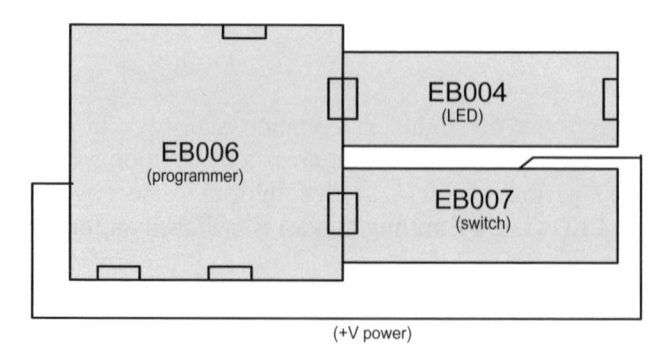

Figure 9. Schematic of the tutorial project (PIC).

Connection summary:

Programmer	Switches to XTAL and Fast, LVP jumper on I/O port, J29 to PSU, J12-14 to USB, use external power supply.
Port A	EB004 LED board.
Port B	EB007 Switch (or button) board

When you start Flowcode it immediately asks for a target microcontroller. Select the 16F88. Next select Chip from the menu, and then Configure. Click on the button called Expert Screen and make sure the settings from the next figure match your settings.

2 Tutorial

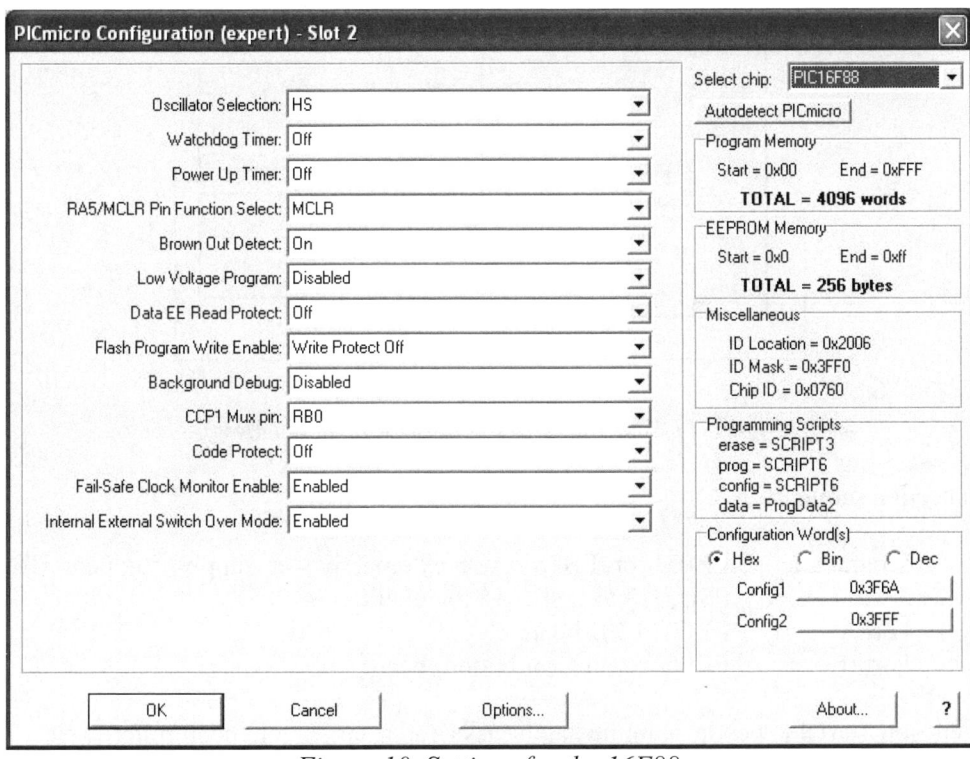

Figure 10. Settings for the 16F88.

Continue reading with section 2.3 (Software).

I own the EB031 or EB185 [3] ARM programmer with an AT91SAM7S128.

The programmer can draw its power from the USB connection to the PC, but it is strongly recommended always to use an external power supply. This is the only way to get power to the +PSU V terminal required in some projects in this book.

Board EB004 will provide an LED and board EB007 the switch. In fact each board contains seven LEDs/switches, but we will use only one in this project. Connect the LED board to port A and the Switch board to port B. Note that the Switch board needs positive power, so you need to connect the +Vin terminal to one of the +V terminals of the Programmer board. Take care not to use the +PSU V terminal!

---

[3] EB185 is a combination of the EB031 programmer board and an EB034 daughter board with an AT91SAM7S128 ARM processor. In all other projects we will refer to this board as the EB185.

19

2.2 Hardware

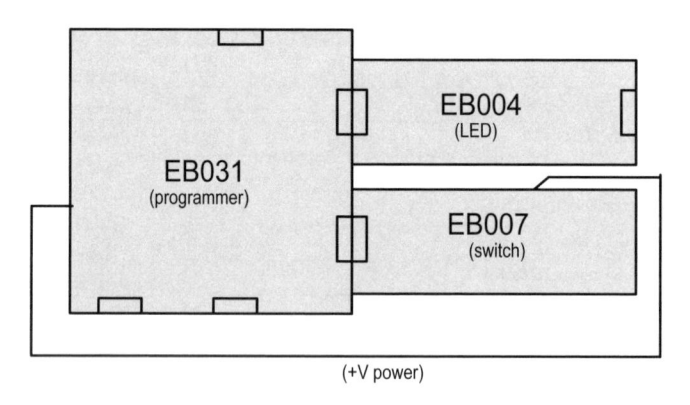

Figure 11. Schematic of the tutorial project (ARM).

Connection summary:

> Programmer   EB031 or EB185, use external power supply, jumpers J16 to PSU, J18 to USB, J15 to default.
> Port A   EB004 LED board.
> Port B   EB007 Switch (or button) board.

When you start Flowcode it immediately asks for a target microcontroller. Select the AT91SAM7S128. Make sure the clock speed in the Chip menu is set to 47923200 Hz.

Continue reading with section 2.3 (Software).

I own the EB194 AVR programmer with an ATMEGA32.

The programmer can draw its power from the USB connection to the PC, but it is strongly recommended always to use an external power supply. This is the only way to get power to the +14V terminal required in some projects in this book.

Board EB004 will provide an LED and board EB007 the switch. In fact each board contains seven LEDs/switches, but we will use only one in this project. Connect the LED board to port A and the Switch board to port B. Note that the Switch board needs positive power, so you need to connect the +Vin terminal to one of the +V terminals of the Programmer board. Take care not to use the +14V terminal!

2 Tutorial

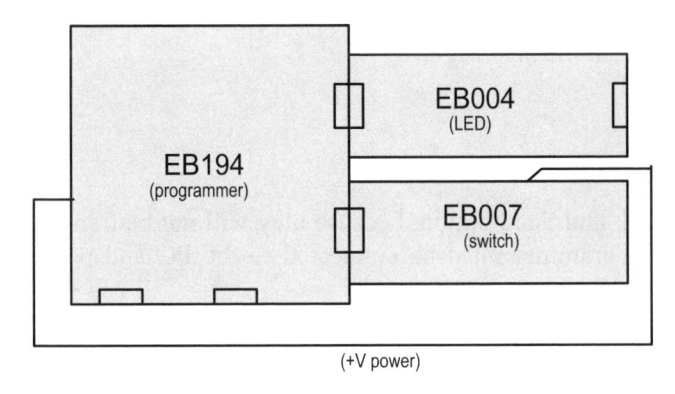

Figure 12. Schematic of the tutorial project (AVR).

Connection summary:

> Programmer   EB194, jumper to default, use external power supply.
> Port A   EB004 LED board.
> Port B   EB007 Switch (or button) board.

Make sure the notch on the programmer cable is on the outside of the programmer board, so the flat ribbon cable folds over the board.

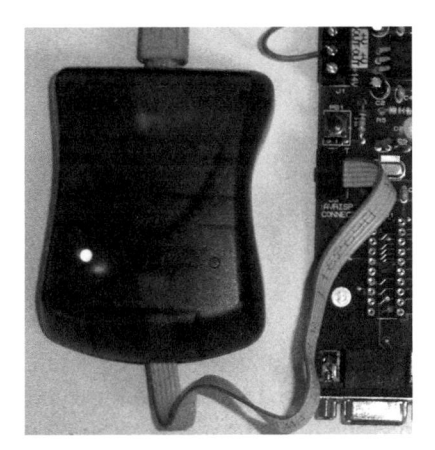

Figure 13. Connection of the programmer to the board.

When you start Flowcode it immediately asks for a target microcontroller. Select the ATMEGA32.

21

2.3 Software

Select the "Chip" menu and "Configure" to set the fuses. Enter these settings (copy these lines exactly, as seen in the next Figure).

    0x0,0xdf
    0x1,0xff.

Then click on the Ok and Send button, because they will not be transferred by default. Of course the AVR programmer must be connected to the PC and powered on for this to work.

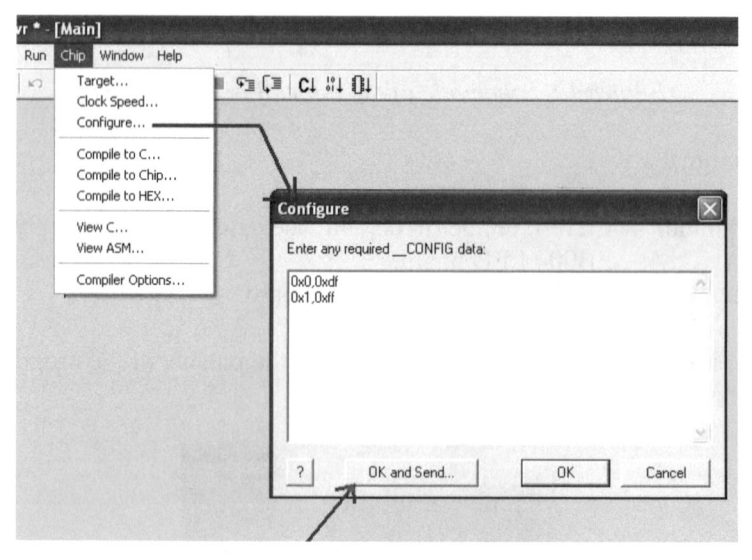

Figure 14. Set the fuses on the ATMEGA32.

2.3 Software

We will start designing the software in pretty much the same way as you would do with a pencil and a piece of paper. Except this time we use Flowcode. When you start Flowcode and select the appropriate microcontroller you are presented with an empty program as seen in the next Figure.

2 Tutorial

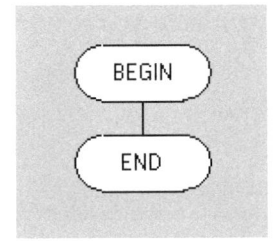

Figure 15. Empty program at Flowcode start-up

The timer switch that we want to design is not supposed to work just once, but every time one of the residents wants to use the stairway. So we will start with a loop. Click with the left button of the mouse on the loop symbol on the left-hand side, and drag it with the left button engaged, onto the flowchart. When you get near the program itself a small arrow appears to indicate where the loop will be inserted. If you are satisfied with the location the arrow is pointing to simply let go of the mouse button. At this point there's not much choice for placing the loop.

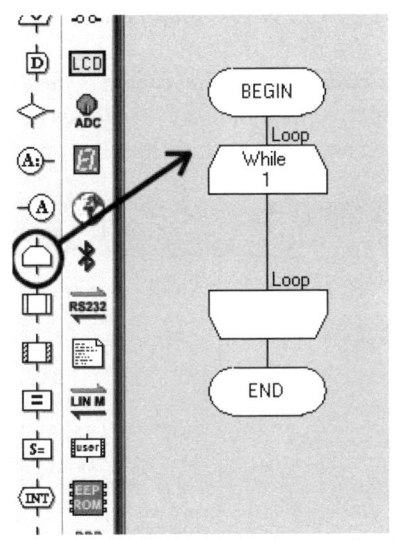

Figure 16. Drag the loop symbol onto the flowchart.

The next step is to set the loop conditions that determine when and how often the loop should be executed. Double click with the left mouse button on any of the two symbols that make up the loop in the flowchart. A properties window opens up. At this point it says "Loop while 1", Flowcode language for "loop forever". This is exactly what we need. To help remember that the loop is executed "forever" we will change the comment from "Loop" to "Loop forever". When a program is small and simple you don't need many comments, but as they grow bigger and more complex it is a good habit to keep the comments updated. In the event of future maintenance of the program by you or one of

23

2.3 Software

your co-workers these comments will help you remember why certain design decisions were made.

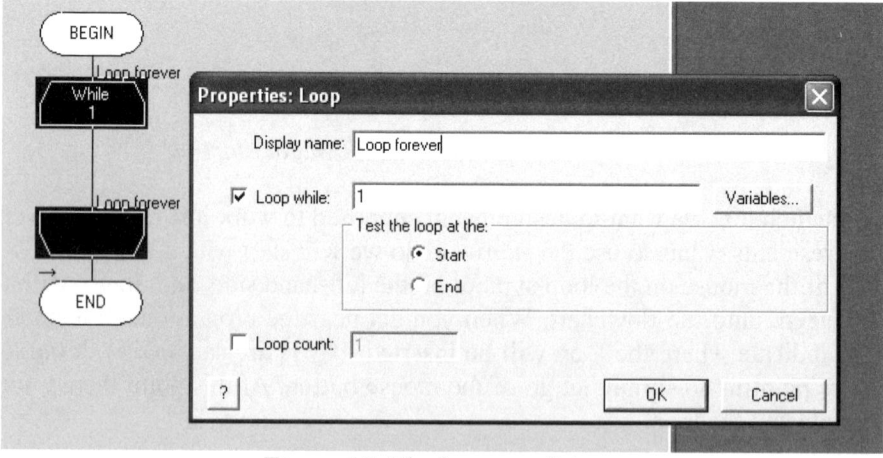

Figure 17. The loop conditions.

The next step is to check the condition of the switch. Click on the switch component on the left-hand side. A graphical representation of the switches is displayed next to the flowchart. Press the little down arrow to specify to which port the switches are connected.

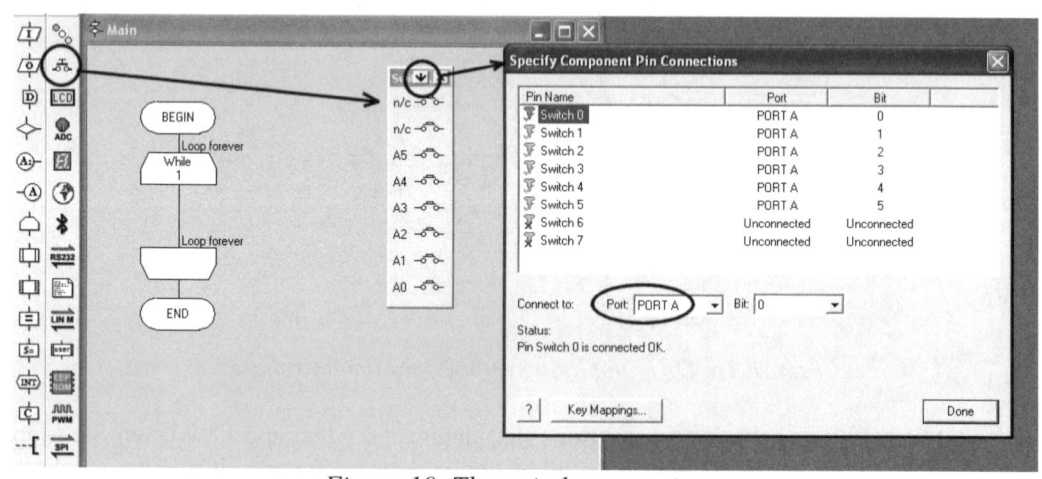

Figure 18. The switch connections.

Change the port from port A, the default, to port B, since this is the port the switches are connected to. While we are at it let's add the LED by pressing the LED component on the left-hand side. Check to see if the LEDs are connected to the right port (A). If not use the little down arrow to change the port settings.

2   **Tutorial**

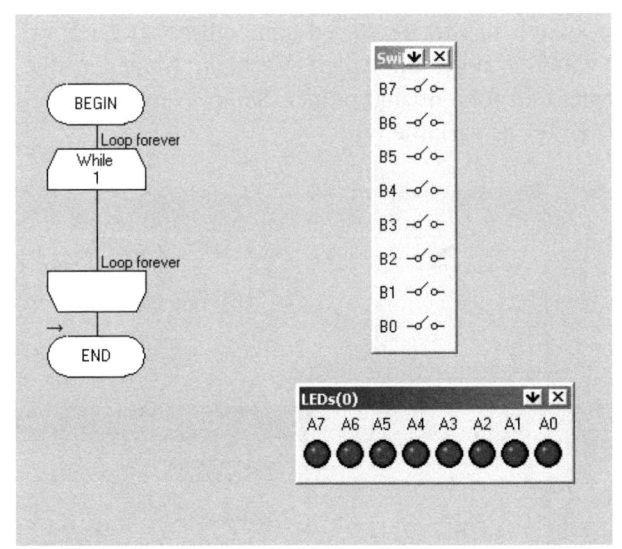

Figure 19. All hardware has been added to the workspace.

Your workspace should now look as shown in the previous figure. We started adding the hardware components because we wanted to check the condition of the switch. A switch is input, so drag an input symbol onto the flowchart, and open it by double clicking on it. Change the comment to "Wall pushbutton". Since we only want to use one switch select Single bit, number 1. On the Switch board the switches are labeled SW0 to SW7, bit number one represents switch SW1. Change the port to B since the Switch board is connected to that port.

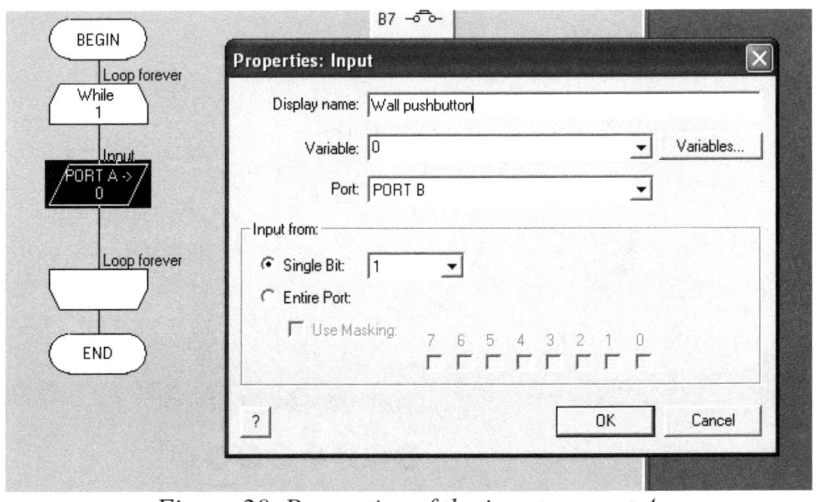

Figure 20. Properties of the input on port A.

25

2.3 Software

The position of the switch has to be stored somewhere so click on the button labeled Variables. A new window pops up called Variable Manager that lists all variables declared in our project (so none at this point). Select New Variable. Name the variable "Button" and select "Byte" as variable type.

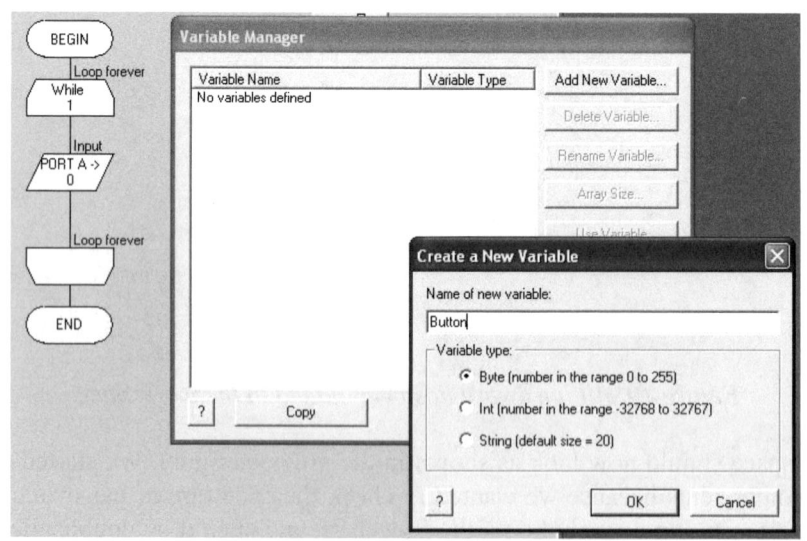

Figure 21. Declaring a new variable.

Now click the ok button to get back to the Variable Manager window. Double click on the variable we just made ("button") to select it. Then click on Ok to close the Input Properties window. The workspace should now look like this:

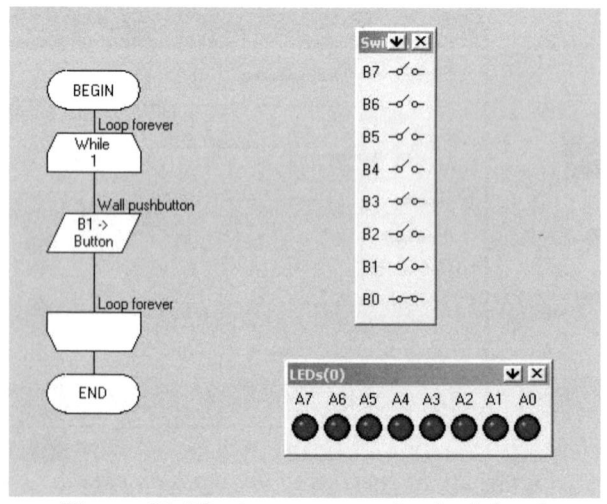

Figure 22. The input is completely defined.

2 **Tutorial**

When the button is pushed the LED needs to go on. That would be an output so drag an Output symbol to a location slightly below the input symbol of the flow chart. Open it by double clicking on it, and make the following entries:

    Display name   Stairway light
    Variable or value   Button
    Port   Port A
    Output to   Single Bit 1

Note that you do not need to enter the variable name, simply click on Variables to open the Variables Manager and double click on the variable you want to use.

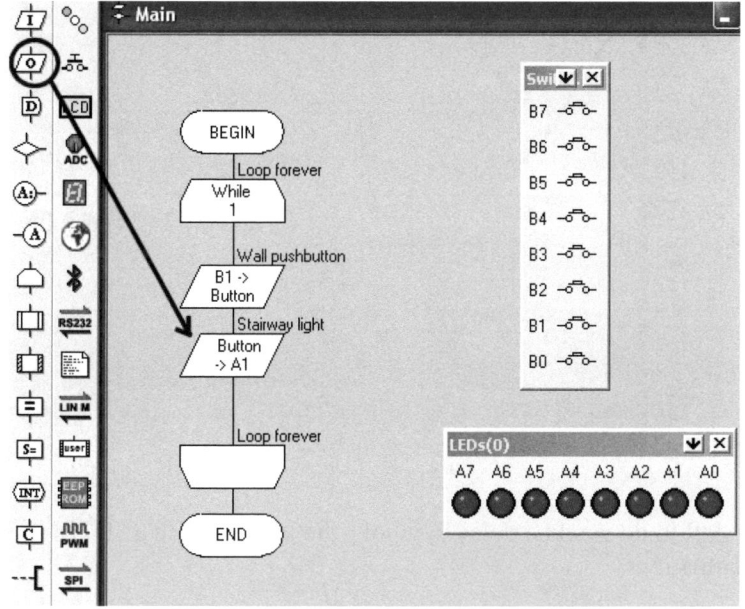

Figure 23. A fully functional program.

Based on the input a choice has to be made. If the button is open, which means variable "button" is 0, no action needs to be taken. But if the button has been pushed, which means variable "button" is 1, the program has to wait three seconds. Since at this point the LED is on, this means that the LED will stay on for three seconds as well; exactly in line with the assignment.

Click on a decision symbol (diamond shaped) and drag it to a location below the output symbol on the flowchart.

27

2.3 Software

Open it by double clicking and enter the following information.

        Display name   Button pushed?
        If: Button = 1

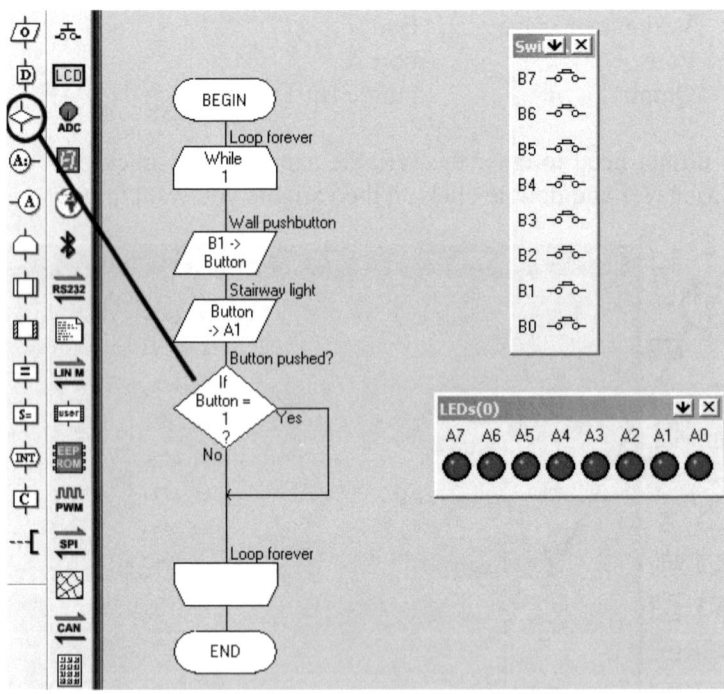

Figure 24. A decision has been added.

Now all that's left to do is add a delay symbol (the symbol with a "D" in it), and enter the following information:

    Display name   Light on
    Delay value or variable   3
    Select   Seconds

The completed program should look like this:

2   Tutorial

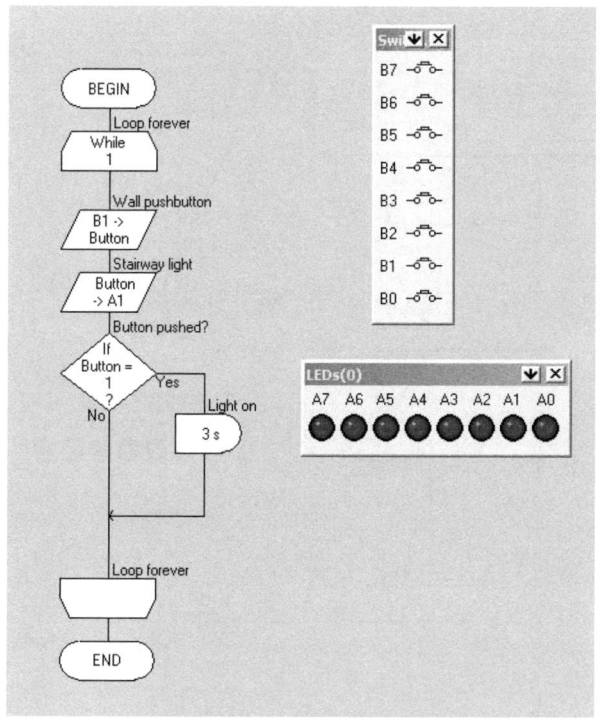

Figure 25. Completed program

2.4   Simulation

At any point during the development process the Flowcode program can be simulated. Click the blue triangle at the top of the screen, and move the two windows that pop up (Call Stack and Variable) out of the way for the time being.

The program is now running. So if you close the switch, by clicking on B1, the LED connected to A1 will go on, and a timer will be shown that counts down three seconds.

This is a very powerful feature in the development process: at any given time can you simulate the programs behavior without downloading it into a microcontroller, in fact without as much as owning a microcontroller!

2.4 Simulation

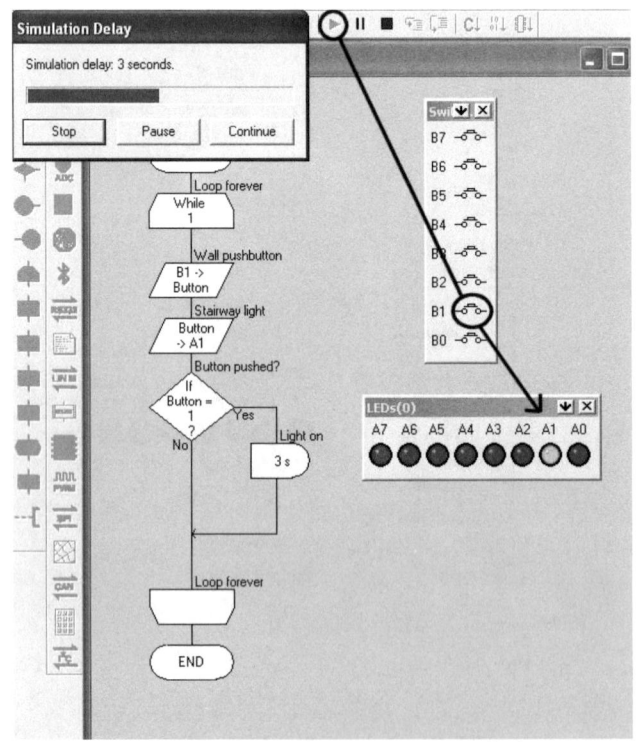

Figure 26. Simulation in progress: the light is on!

The speed of the simulation can be changed. In the menu select Chip and then Clock Speed. Adjust the value in the Simulation Speed box to for example 10 Hz (do not change the clock speed itself!). Start the simulation again by clicking on the blue triangle. The simulation runs much slower, which gives you a clear view of what is going on. At this speed[4] the Variables Window displays the content of all variables, in this case "button". If you close the switch (by clicking on B1) you can see that the variable button now gets value one.

Another nifty simulation trick is a breakpoint. This is an instruction to the simulator to stop the simulation at a certain point so you can examine the value of the variables at your leisure. To make a breakpoint click with the right mouse button on a symbol on the flowchart and select "Toggle breakpoint". A red dot will appear next to the symbol to indicate this breakpoint. When you run the simulation it will stop at that breakpoint. Press the Run button again to continue. You can have multiple breakpoints in a program.

---

[4] In fact at any speed except the "As fast as possible" speed.

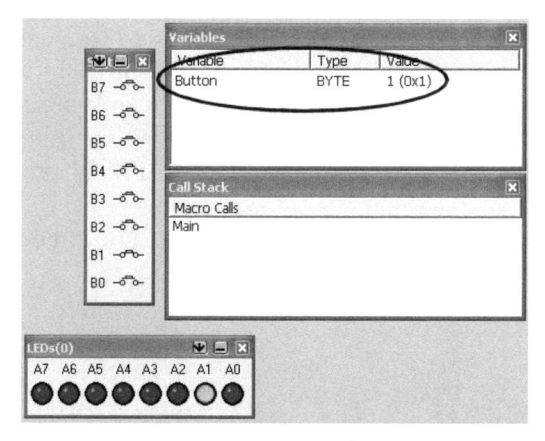

Figure 27. The value of variable Button is shown (1).

Another way to simulate is a step by step approach. Instead of the blue triangle click on the Step Into button. Each time you click this button the next command is executed. Alternatively the Step Over button allows you to skip the next command. While stepping through this program the Variables Window always displays the content of all variables.

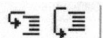

Figure 28. Step Into (left) and Step Over (right).

It's impossible to click on the Step Into button and the switch at the same time, so for step debugging it is best to change the switch from pushbutton to toggle switch. Use the little down arrow on the switch component to access the Switch Properties, and change the type from Push to Make to Toggle. Remember to change this back when you're done testing.

2.5 Downloading

This would be a good time to save the program if you haven't done so already. Make sure the hardware is connected as described in section 2.2, and that the programmer is connected to a USB port on your computer. Switch on the power and click the "Compile to Chip" button. As small window appears with a lot of messages which eventually end with Return Code = 0. Meaning the download was successful[5].

---

[5] If you use the ARM programmerboard EB185 you will at some point get a message on the PC screen to press the programming button on the board and shortly tap the reset button. At this point the LEDs will light softly and programming will continue automatically. After a fraction of a second a message will instruct you to press the reset button to start the program.

31

2.6 Operational

If the download fails, scroll up in the Compiler Messages to identify the problem. If the simulation ran ok it is either a hardware problem, or a problem with the settings. Make sure your power supply meets the requirements in terms of voltage and stability. Check to see if the installation has been run on the computer you are using, and if the USB cable is connected between the USB programmer and the PC. Fix the problem and try again.

Try the program by pushing button SW1. As a result LED1 will come on, and stay on for three seconds.

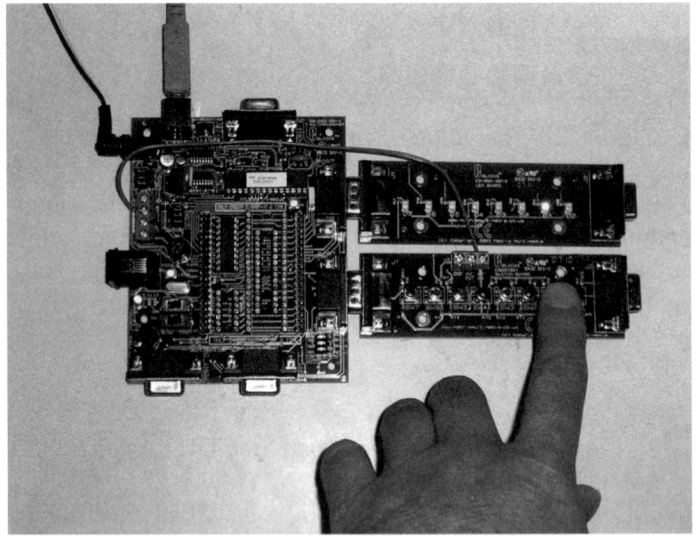

Figure 29. The tutorial program in use on the 16F88 PIC microcontroller.

2.6 Operational

All projects in this book will stop at this point, since both hardware and software are operational. But since you're not going to sell your USB programmer and E-blocks to your customer the next step would be design a printed circuit board (PCB) for your project. See chapter 11 for an example of how to turn a prototype into a production model.

In the next chapters the projects will be described in much less detail. It is assumed that you understand the basic operation of Flowcode, and how to simulate and download programs. If in doubt you can refer back to this tutorial.

3 Basic

A selection of projects that handle basic Flowcode and microcontroller properties, such as interrupts, tables, pulse width modulation etc. If you are new to programming, microcontrollers or Flowcode it is highly recommended that you at least read these chapters before starting with the more advanced projects.

3.1 LCD display

Concept

Use an LCD to display a simple message and learn how to use a component macro.

Hardware

For this project we will use the ATMEGA 32 AVR microcontroller, in combination with an LCD screen. Note that the LCD board needs power so you need to connect the +Vin terminal to one of the +V terminals of the Programmer board. Remember that if you don't own an AVR microcontroller, chapter 10 will show you how to migrate a project such as this to another microcontroller such as PIC or ARM.

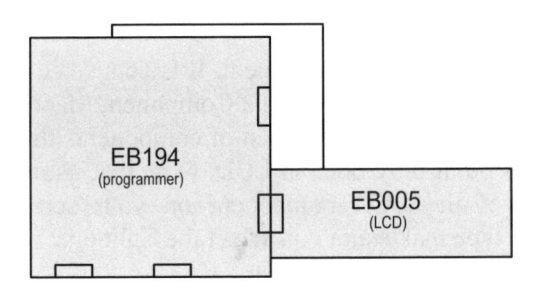

Figure 30. LCD on an ATMEGA 32.

Connection summary:

    Programmer   EB194, jumper to default.
    Port B   EB005 LCD, jumper to default.

Software

If you haven't done so already first of all make sure that the fuses of the ATMEGA 32 are set correctly to 0x0,0xdf and 0x1,0xff. Select the "Chip" menu and "Configure". Enter the

3.1 LCD display

settings and remember to click on the Ok and Send button, because they will not be transferred by default. Of course the AVR programmer must be connected to the PC and powered on for this to work.

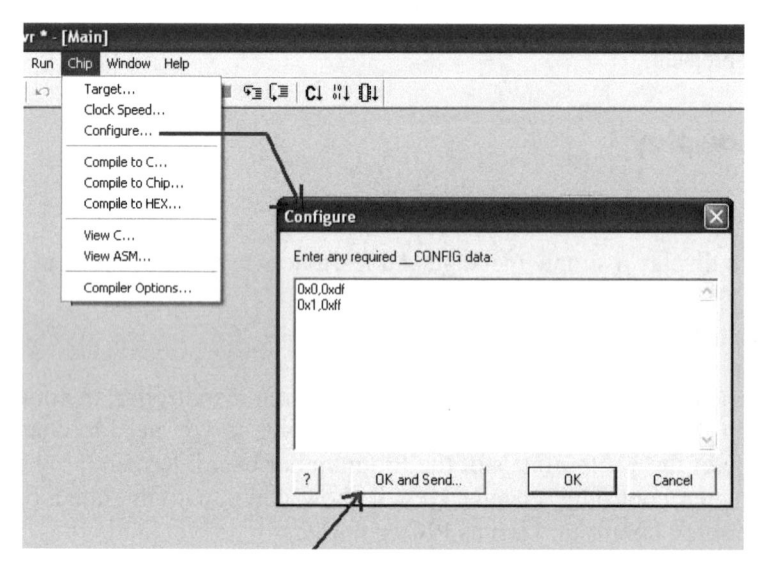

Figure 31. Set the fuses on the ATMEGA32.

The next step is to click on the LCD component. It is connected to port B by default, so you don't need to change anything. Then drag a Component Macro into your program and double click on it. When it opens you see a list of components that are currently attached to your program. At this point only one: an LCD. Note that its name, LCDDisplay(0), is identical to the name of the LCD component on your screen. If you have more components of the same type make sure you select the right one.

3   Basic

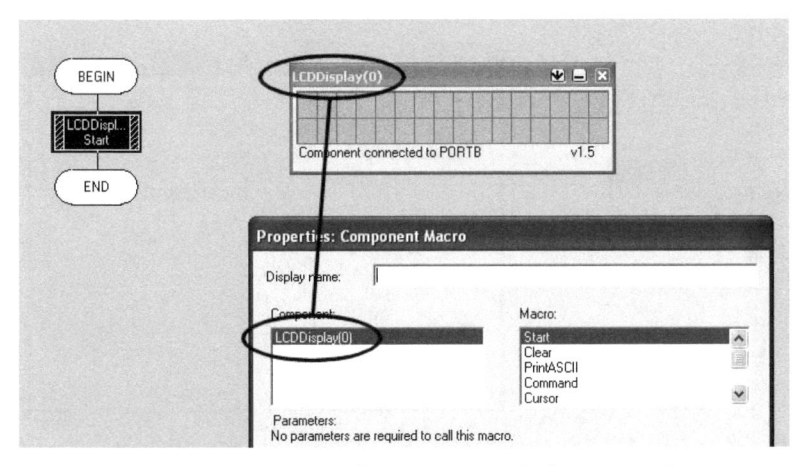

Figure 32. Macros and components belong together.

Once you click on the LCD a list of macros associated with this component appears. These macros all belong to the LCD component that you have previously added. You only have access to these macros if you have selected a component first! So even if you don't plan on simulation you still need to add all components in order to get access to the component macros.

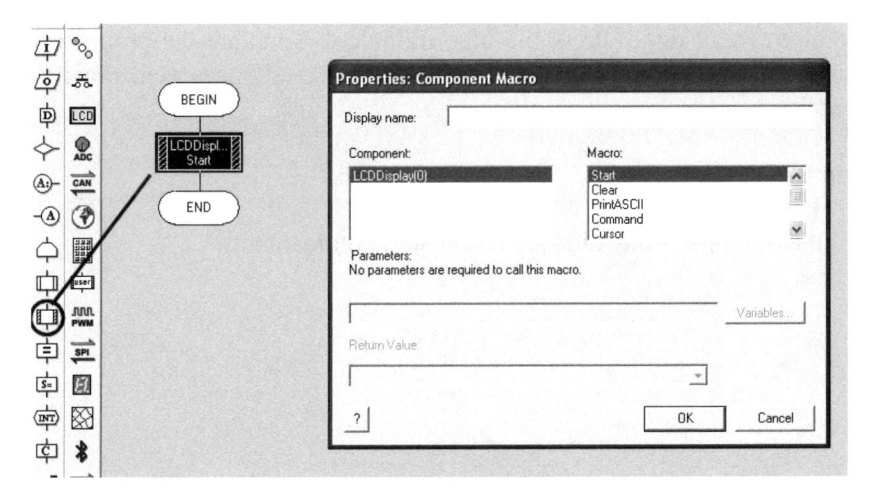

Figure 33. LCD Start.

The LCD needs to be initialized in order for it to work, so select the "Start" macro. Some LCDs may need a bit of time to initialize. In that case add a delay of, for example, 200 ms right behind the Start macro.

35

3.1 LCD display

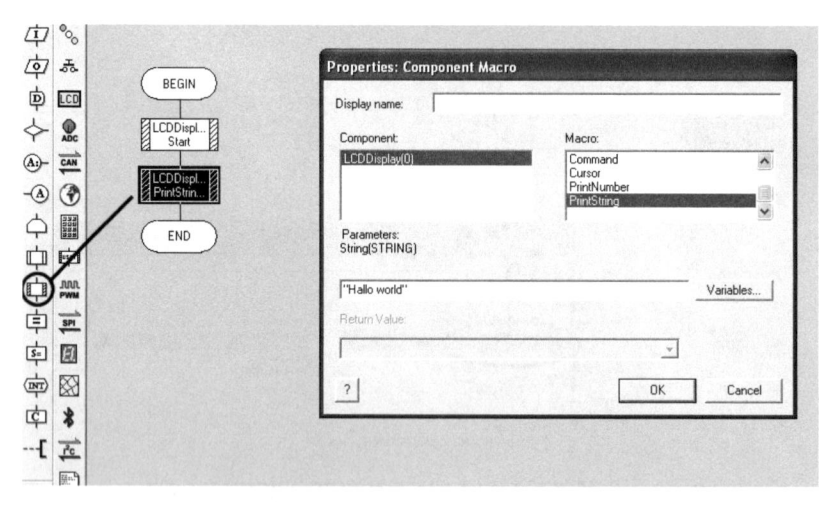

Figure 34. The actual message.

Now drag another Component Macro into your program and double click on it. This time select the macro PrintString. In the parameters section you can either enter the name of a (string) variable, of simply type a string. In an utter lack of creativity enter the string "Hello world" including the quotation marks.

At this point we're all done. Press the blue triangle to simulate the program. The LCD display on the screen should now read Hello world. If all goes well download to the microcontroller.

Operational

As soon as the program is downloaded it will start automatically[6].

---

[6] If you use the EB194 the programmer needs to be either disconnected (with the plug at the EB194 board itself) or completely connected to the USB port on the PC. In other configurations, for example connected to the board but with an unplugged USB connector, the microcontroller will not start.

Figure 35. Hello world.

The next Figure shows the available characters. Note that the simulation uses the ASCII characters of the PC. In some cases these differ from the characters that the actual display will show. For example ASCII 223 will show a beta sign in the simulation but a degree sign on a real LCD.

3.1 LCD display

Figure 36. Character set of the LCD display.

To determine the ASCII code of a character, combine the top and left bits to get one single byte. For the capital M for example this would yield 01001101 which is 77 in decimal.

If you want to know how to scroll the display take a look at project 3.4 in the USB section.

3 Basic

3.2 Running light

Concept

Make a small light display using an LED board and learn how to use arrays.

Hardware

For this project a 16F877A PIC microcontroller is selected with an LED board connected to port B.

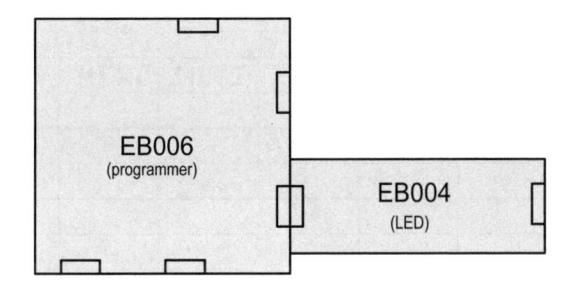

Figure 37. Running light schematic.

Connection summary:

    Programmer   Switches to XTAL and Fast, LVP jumper on I/O port, J29 to PSU, J12-14 to USB, use external power supply.
    Port B   EB004 LED board.

Software

The LED board contains eight LEDs numbers 0 through 7. Each of these LEDs is connected to a pin on the port to which the board is connected. So LED0 for example is connected to pin B0, if the LED board is connected to port B. An LED is on if the pin that it is connected to is made high, and this is done by making it 1. The LED can be switched off by making the pin low, and that is done by making it 0.

3.2 Running light

You can make any pin high if you know its position in the port. The next Figure shows which number you need to send to a port to make a particular pin high.

pin	B7	B6	B5	B4	B3	B2	B1	B0
number	128	64	32	16	8	4	2	1

So if you want to make pin B6 high, or 1, you need to send 64 to port B. If you want to make pin B6 and also pin B0 high you need to send 64 + 1 = 65 to port B. And since each of the pins has a LED connected to it this means LED6 and LED0 will be on.

By sending a row of numbers one by one to the port a simple light display called running light can be made, A small matrix can be used to design the display:

LED7	LED6	LED5	LED4	LED3	LED2	LED1	LED0	number
x							x	129
	x					x		66
		x			x			36
			x	x				24
								0

Figure 38. Light display design (x means the LED is on).

Start a new program for the 16F877A microcontroller. In the menu select Chip, then Configure and then switch to Expert Config Screen. Make sure the following settings are made:

Description	Setting
Oscillator	HS
Watchdog timer	Off
Power up timer	Off
Brown out detect	Off
Low voltage program	Disabled
Flash program write	Write protection off
Background debug	Disabled
Data EE readprotect	Off
Code protect	Off

Figure 39. Configuration settings for the 16F877A microcontroller.

A faster way to achieve the same thing: In the section Configuration Word(s) make sure HEX is selected and then click on the Config1 button and enter: 0x3F3A.

3   Basic

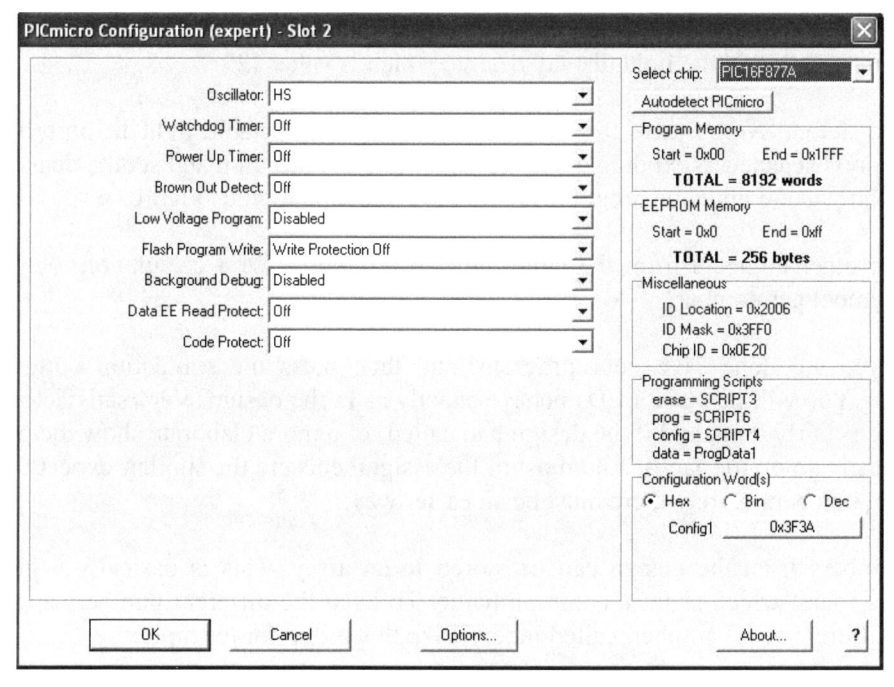

Figure 40. Expert screen for the 16F877A.

Click on an LED component and connect it to port B using the little down arrow. Drag a Loop symbol onto the program and a calculation symbol.

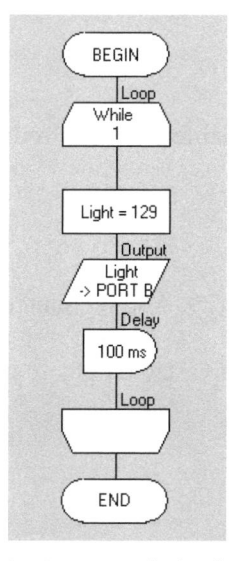

Figure 41. Running light, first step.

41

3.2 Running light

Open the calculations symbol and make a new variable called light. Give light the value of the first number in the light display design, which is value 129.

Drag an output symbol into the program and send the variable light to port B, leave "entire port" selected. Next drag a delay symbol into the program and set the delay to 100 ms. When you are done the program should look like the previous Figure.

Add the other numbers from the table into the program. Use a calculation, output and delay symbol per number.

When you are done save your program, and then press the simulation button (blue triangle). You will now see LEDs behave exactly as in the design. Very satisfactory. The program is fairly long, and if the design had called for a more elaborate show the program could easily go on for pages. And most of the assignments are the similar, expect they use different numbers. Surely there must be an easier way.

The numbers from the design can be stored in an array. This is basically a group of numbers (data) which share a common name. To keep the different numbers apart each gets a different serial number, called index. Take this group for example:

> 129, 66, 36, 24, 0

The number 129 will get index zero (computers start counting at zero). That means that for example 36 will get index 2. If we call the group "light" the index will be added between square brackets. For example:

> light[0] = 129

The advantage is that a second variable can be introduced, called for example "counter", which allows us to do this:

> light[counter]

If counter is 0 then light[counter] =129. And if counter = 3 then light[counter] = 24.

Let's make a new program. Define a variable light as an array with 5 items (0 through 4).

3   Basic

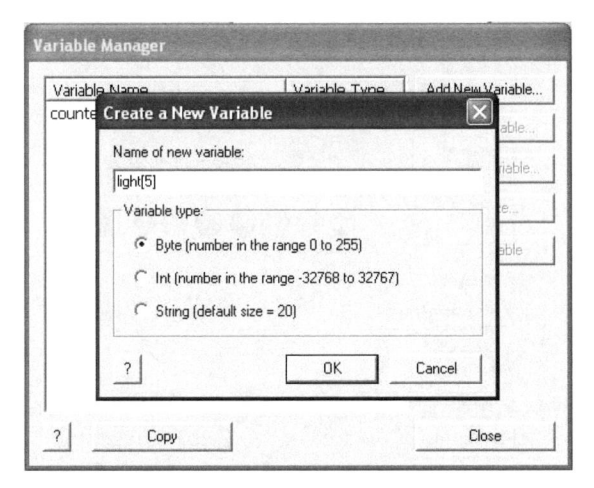

Figure 42. Define an array by adding [5] to the variable name.

At the start of the program the counter is set to zero and the array is filled with the numbers from the design table in a calculation symbol:

    counter = 0
    light[0] = 129
    light[1] = 66
    light[2] = 36
    light[3] = 24
    light[4] = 0

Add a loop symbol, and send the value light[counter] to port B and thus to the LEDs.

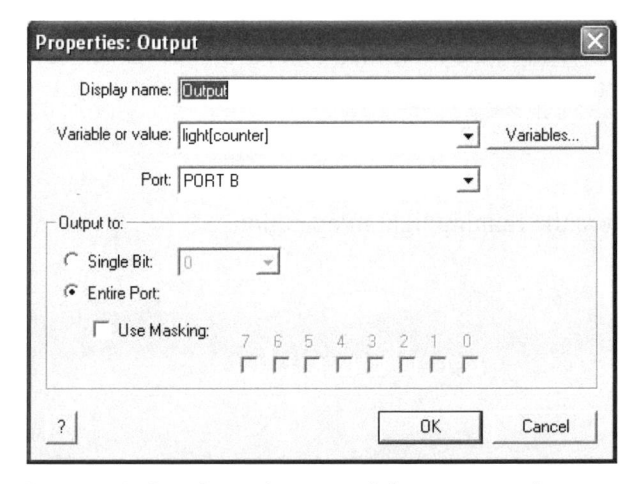

Figure 43. Send an element of the array to the port.

43

3.2 Running light

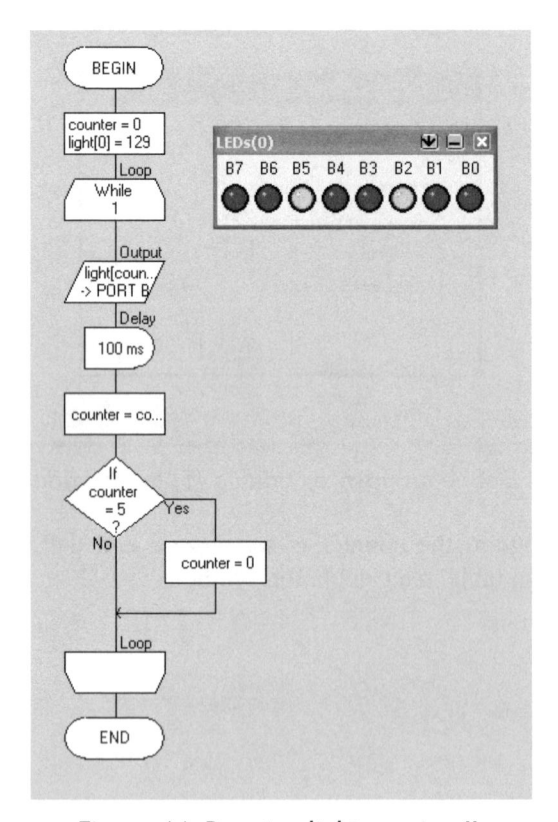

Figure 44. Running light, version II.

Add a short 100 ms delay, increment the counter, and if the counter is greater than five make it zero again. If you are not sure how to do this consult the previous Figure. This is the version that is included in the download file. Now start the simulation. The LEDs will do the same thing, but the program looks much nicer.

Operational

The next Figure shows the running light in operation.

3   **Basic**

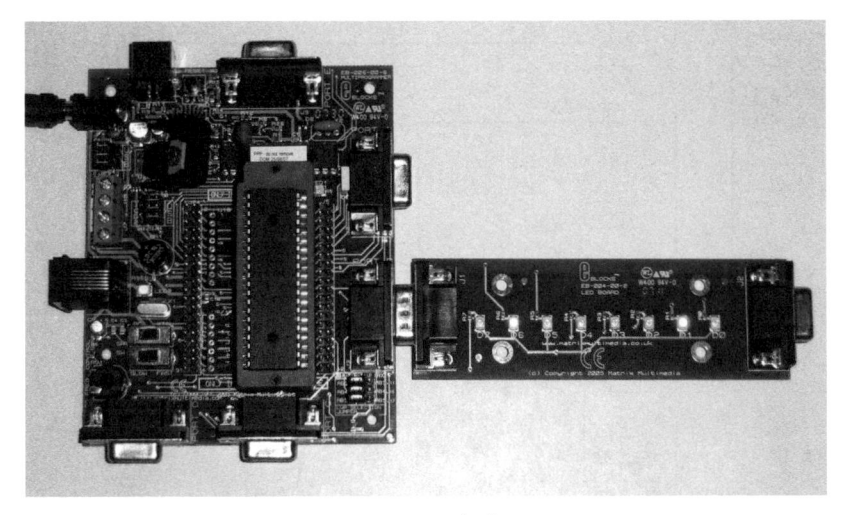

Figure 45. Running light in action.

3.3   Secret doorbell

Concept

Make your life a bit quieter. Design a doorbell that will only ring if the visitor knows a four digit secret code.

Hardware

For this project a 16F877A PIC microcontroller is selected. A keypad board EB014 is used to allow the user to enter a code, a relay board EB038 is used to operate the actual doorbell and an LCD board EB005 is used for visual feedback during debugging. Note that the LCD board needs power so you need to connect the +Vin terminal to one of the +V terminals of the Programmer board. The relay board needs an elevated voltage to operate: 14 volts, so you need to connect it to the +14V connection on the Programmer. It is recommended to use a different color wire to prevent mixing it with the 5 volt power connections.

3.3 Secret doorbell

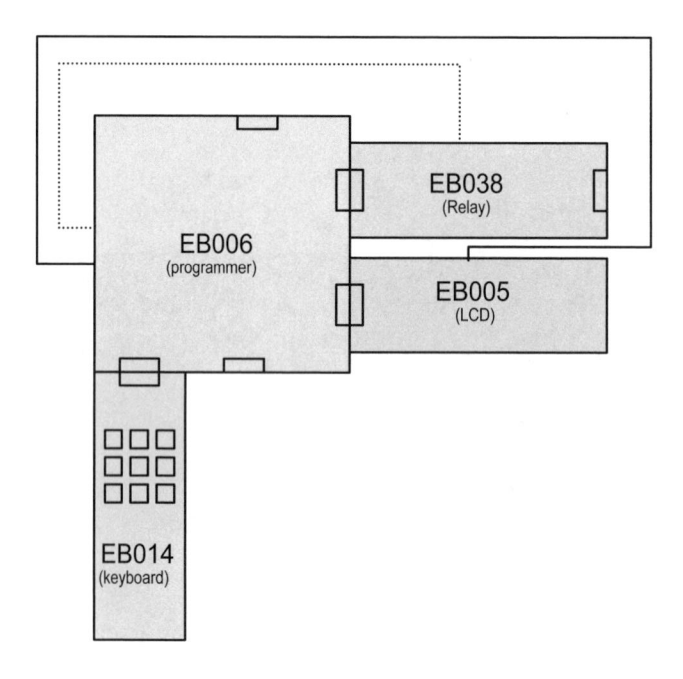

Figure 46. Schematic secret doorbell.

Connection summary:

Programmer	Switches to XTAL and Fast, LVP jumper on I/O port, J29 to PSU, J12-14 to USB, use external power supply.
Port A	Relay board EB038, jumper on low.
Port B	LCD EB005, jumper to default.
Port D	Keypad EB014.

According to the documentation of the relay board the relays can handle mains, but it recommends not to exceed 24 volts. The relays on my board are stamped 7A / 250 V (Song Chuan, type 812BH-1C-CE)[7]. Your doorbell will most likely be 12 volts, check this to make sure. The voltage is usually stamped on the transformer that connects your doorbell to mains. Cut one of the wires between the transformer and the doorbell and connect Relay D1 in between.

---

[7] Should you decide to use mains remember that high voltages can kill. Take all necessary safety precautions and follow local safety rules and guidelines. Proceed at your own risk.

3   Basic

Software

In the menu select Chip, then Configure and then switch to Expert Config Screen. In the section Configuration Word(s) make sure HEX is selected and then click on the Config1 button and enter: 0x3F3A.

The secret code to let the doorbell ring is four digits long, in this example 5578. First an array needs to be set up to contain this code. An array is a row of characters that all have the same name. The different characters in the array are addresses by their position. This is the definition for the code array, in a calculation symbol:

code[0] = 5
code[1] = 5
code[2] = 7
code[3] = 8

Note that the first position in the array is zero! An array is created the same way as a "regular" variable, except the length is added between square brackets, for example doorbell[4] will create an array with four characters, numbered.... 0 to 3.

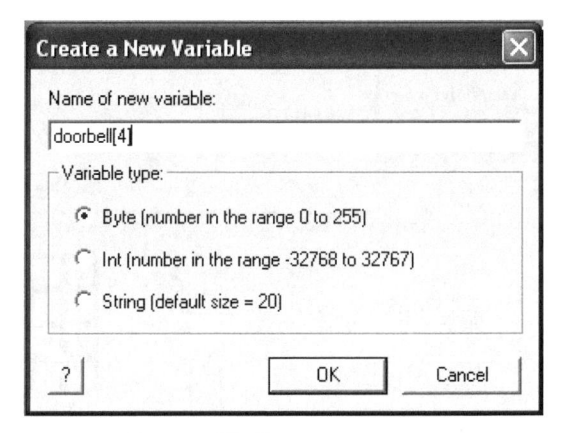

Figure 47. Create an array.

The characters, or numbers in this case, in the code array need to be compared with the numbers that are entered into the keypad into the doorbell array. Every time a new number is entered on the keypad this is inserted in doorbell at position 4, so doorbell[3]. Prior to that all digits currently in the array move one position to the left. So if the array contained the values 1,4,7,3 and the user enters an 8 on the keypad the array then contains the values 4,7,3,8. The next step is to compare the new content of the array and compare it with the correct code. The number of correct digits is counted and if this number is four

3.3 Secret doorbell

the doorbell will ring. The next Figure shows this comparison for someone who entered 4,7,3,8 on the keypad.

	[0]	[1]	[2]	[3]	
code	5	5	7	8	
doorbell	4	7	3	8	
	wrong	wrong	wrong	correct	so 1 correct

Figure 48. Comparing code with keypad entry.

In order to use the keypad add a keypad component to the program. Use the little down arrow to connect the keypad to port C. Add a component macro symbol and call the GetKeypadAscii macro.

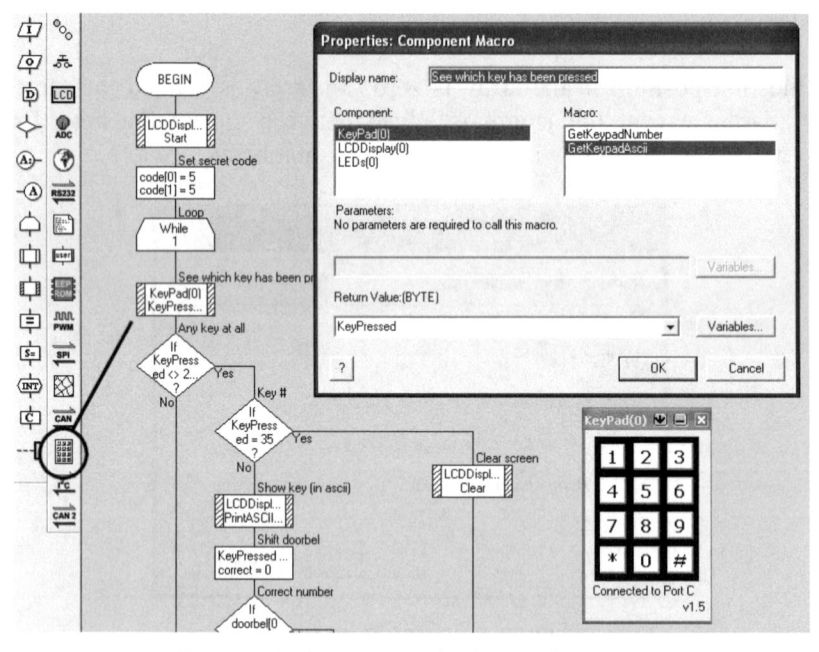

Figure 49. Setting up the keypad macro.

This macro will return the ASCII codes of the keys rather than the actual key numbers. So in stead of 0 it will return 48, see the appendix for an ASCII table. The macro GetKeypadNumber would have been more convenient because there would be no need to convert from ASCII to decimal numbers, which means subtracting 48. We do want to display the numbers on the LCD however and this needs to be in ASCII. So either way we would need to convert.

The program is much faster than the user, so if a user pressed a key just once the program will have recorded this dozens of times. So before a new entry is accepted the program will wait for the user to release the key. If contact bouncing is a problem is small delay, say 100 ms, might be added at this point.[8]

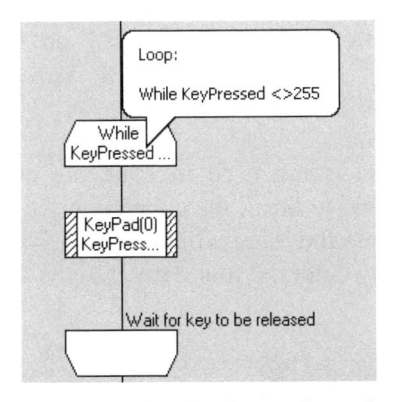

Figure 50. Wait for the key to be released.

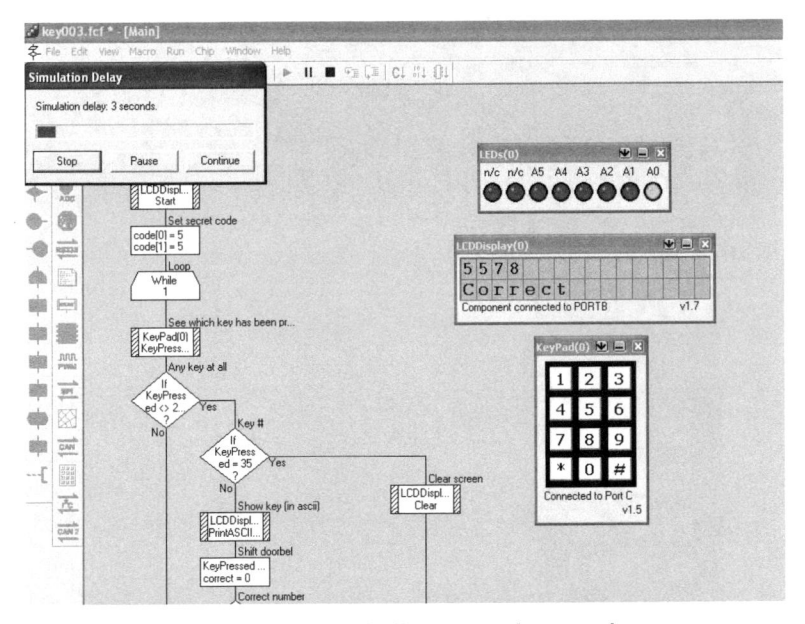

Figure 51. The doorbell rings in this simulation.

---

[8] When you press the switch the metal contacts inside approach and then glide over each other. During this time contact is made and lost, back and forth many times. You won't see any of this, but the microcontroller will. It will see this as a series of on/off switching.

3.3 Secret doorbell

Flowcode doesn't have a Relay component, so use an LED component instead. This program is great for simulation. Press the "Run" button (blue triangle) and try different codes. If you reduce the speed of the simulation in the Chip Clockspeed menu the contents of the variables is shown (press the buttons long enough for the simulation to actually see them if you did indeed lower the simulation speed). Note that # will clear the LCD screen, but for the operation of the program this is not required.

Operational

In normal operation the LCD is not used to eliminate any visual feedback. Without feedback it is almost impossible to break the code simply by using trail and error. If you enter the correct four digit code the relay will switch on. Should you make a mistake do not do anything special, simply enter the four correct digits again.

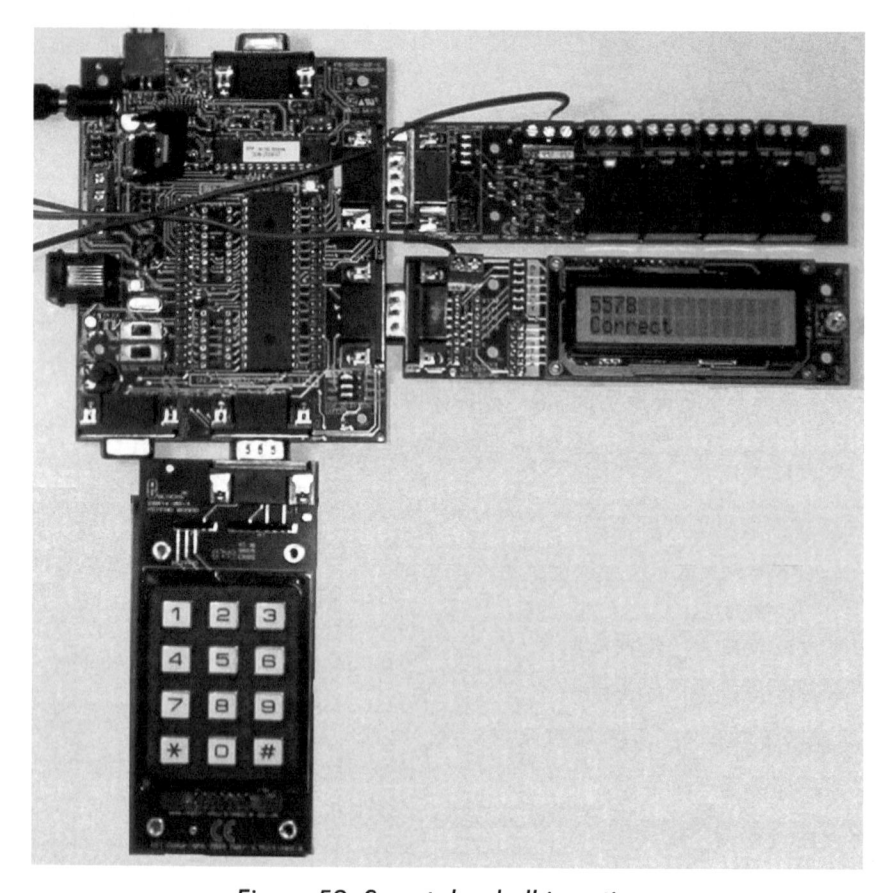

Figure 52. Secret doorbell in action.

3 Basic

3.4 Serial communication

Serial communication is the most commonly used form of communication between computers and microcontrollers. In traditional computers and industrial applications RS232 is the most used technique, in portable computers and handhelds USB is the technique if choice. Both RS232 and USB will be discussed.

3.4.1 RS232

Concept

Set up a serial communication between a microcontroller and a PC using the RS232 protocol.

Hardware

For this project we will use the ATMEGA 32 AVR microcontroller, in combination with a keypad, LCD screen and an RS232 E-block.

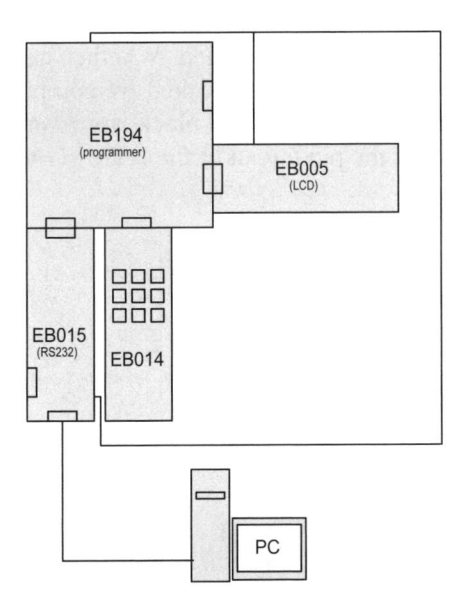

Figure 53. Schematic of an RS232 connection to a PC.

51

3.4 Serial communication

Connection summary:

Programmer	EB194, jumper to default.
Port B	EB005 LCD, jumper to default.
Port C	EB014 keypad.
Port D	EB015 RS232 board (jumpers on D and 2, and route wires from pin 0 to RX and Pin1 to TX).

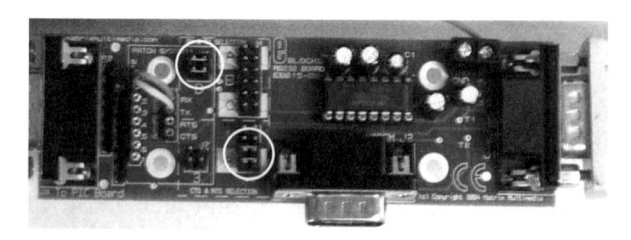

Figure 54. RS232 patch panel for ATMEGA 32 port D.

Connect an RS232 cable to the D9 connector at the end of the EB015 and plug it into a serial port on the PC.

Patch

In this project the RS23 board has to be patched. Whether patching is needed, and if so what needs to be patched to what, can be checked by comparing the pin layout of the microcontroller you intend to use and the E-block you want to connect to it. As an example the next Figure shows the pin layout of the ATMEGA 32 AVR microcontroller:

PDIP

```
(XCK/T0) PB0  1      40  PA0 (ADC0)
(T1)     PB1  2      39  PA1 (ADC1)
(INT2/AIN0) PB2 3    38  PA2 (ADC2)
(OC0/AIN1) PB3 4     37  PA3 (ADC3)
(SS)     PB4  5      36  PA4 (ADC4)
(MOSI)   PB5  6      35  PA5 (ADC5)
(MISO)   PB6  7      34  PA6 (ADC6)
(SCK)    PB7  8      33  PA7 (ADC7)
         RESET 9     32  AREF
         VCC  10     31  GND
         GND  11     30  AVCC
         XTAL2 12    29  PC7 (TOSC2)
         XTAL1 13    28  PC6 (TOSC1)
(RXD)    PD0  14     27  PC5 (TDI)
(TXD)    PD1  15     26  PC4 (TDO)
(INT0)   PD2  16     25  PC3 (TMS)
(INT1)   PD3  17     24  PC2 (TCK)
(OC1B)   PD4  18     23  PC1 (SDA)
(OC1A)   PD5  19     22  PC0 (SCL)
(ICP1)   PD6  20     21  PD7 (OC2)
```

Figure 55. Pin layout of the ATMEGA 32 AVR microcontroller.

3   Basic

And this is a section from the datasheet of the EB015 RS232 E-block.

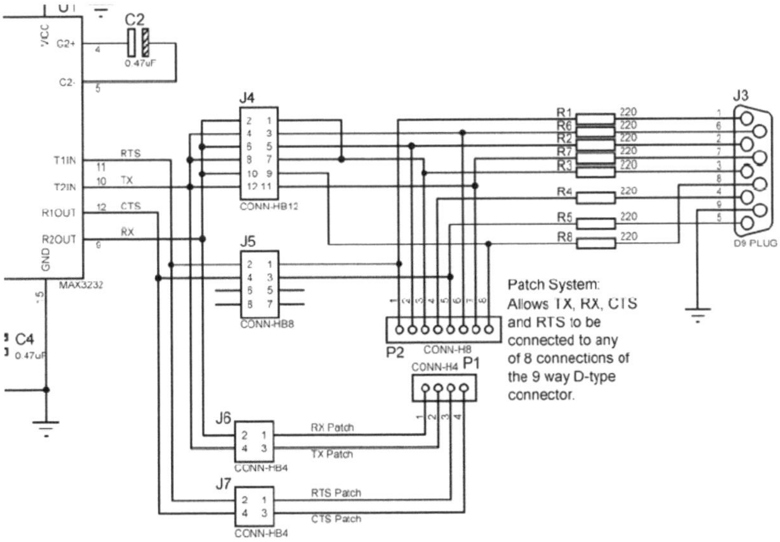

Figure 56. Section of the EB015 datasheet.

If the pin connections are put in a table it is immediately apparent which connections have to be patched to what (if you prefer not to follow the lines in the diagram simply always use the patch panel). Both RTS and CTS are not needed but must be disabled by setting the jumper to 2 and not patching them. Both TX and RX need to be moved, so jumper to D and route wires from pin 0 to RX and Pin1 to TX.

EB015 RS232 E-block pin D9	description	ATMEGA 32 port D	description
1	RTS	D0	RX
2		D1	TX
3		D2	
4		D3	
5	CTS	D4	
6		D5	
7	TX	D6	
8	RX	D7	
9		GND	

Figure 57. Determine patch requirements.

53

3.4 Serial communication

See sections 10.2 and 12.5 for more information on pin lay-outs of microcontrollers and E-blocks. If you haven't done so already it is highly recommended that you download the datasheets of all microcontrollers, E-blocks and other components that you own or intend to use from the Matrix Multimedia website[9]. These datasheets also contain important information on power requirements and examples on how to verify that your E-blocks are functioning properly. Check the website regularly for updates, upgrades and new E-blocks.

Software

If you haven't done so already first of all make sure that the fuses of the ATMEGA 32 are set correctly to 0x0,0xdf and 0x1,0xff. Select the "Chip" menu and "Configure". Enter the settings and remember to click on the Ok and Send button, because they will not be transferred by default. Of course the AVR programmer must be connected to the PC and powered on for this to work.

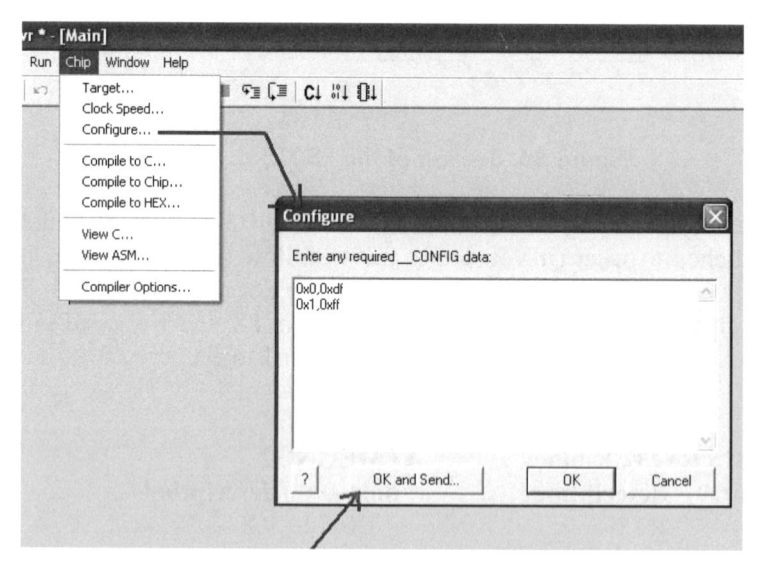

Figure 58. Set the fuses on the ATMEGA32.

Click on an RS232 component and set the BAUD rate[10] to 38400 and check SendCharacters. Leave the other options unchecked. The first part of the program is to actually receive data. Use a Component Macro symbol and select RS232 and then

---

[9] www.matrixmultimedia.com/

[10] The BAUD rate is a measure for the communication speed. Technically it is the number of times per second that the carrier signal changes state. Roughly this translates to bits per second, or 1/8 of a byte per second. Since 38400 is used in this program the application on the other side must be set to the exact same speed.

ReceiveRS232Char. Next enter a Timeout value. If you use 255 as a time out the program will wait forever, literally, for incoming data. Any other value represents the time in milliseconds. A good value is 10 ms. After a timeout the variable in which the incoming data is to be collected gets value 255. So if the value is 255 ignore it, otherwise send it to the LCD.

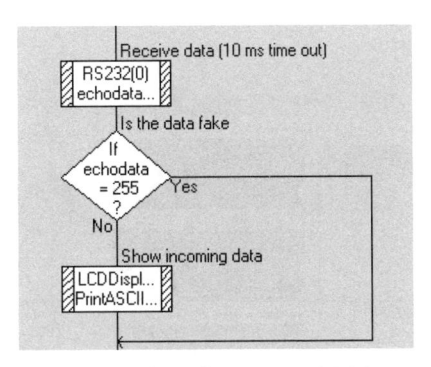

Figure 59. Receive data from an RS232 connection.

Note that this means that you cannot receive number 255, unless you use an infinite timeout.

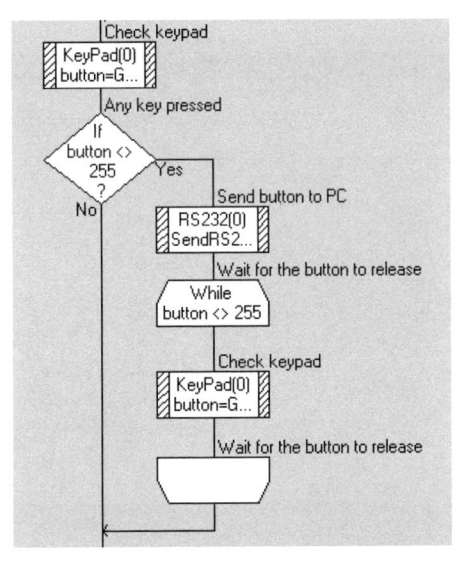

Figure 60. Send data using RS232.

3.4 Serial communication

Next check the keypad, in ASCII. If no buttons are pressed the keypad value is 255. In all other cases send the keypad value to the PC. Just as in project 3.3 the program has to wait for the user to release the button.

The RS232 component allows simulation of the receipt of data over the RS232 connection, as if the data came from the PC. Click the plus button on the RS232 component and enter the data for the simulation. Then enter the OK button. The data will now be sent into your simulation.

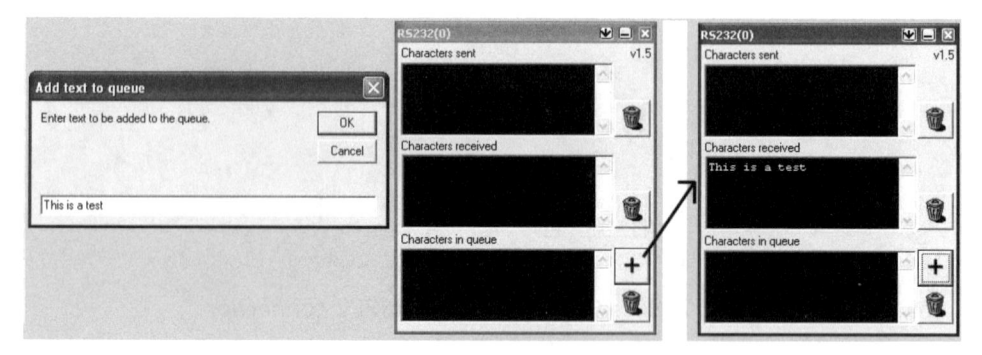

Figure 61. Simulate receipt of data.

Operational

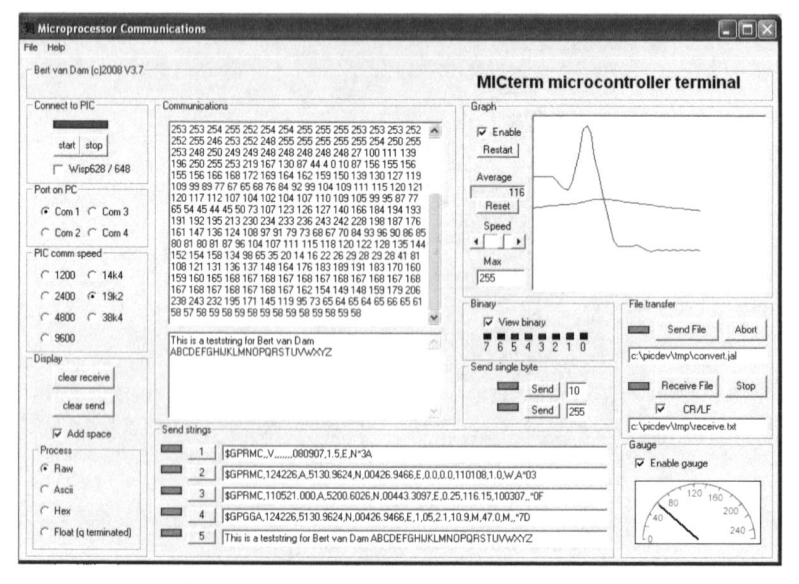

Figure 62. MICterm terminal program.

3   Basic

On the PC you can use any communications package you like. Part of the download package is MICterm that is specifically designed for use with microcontrollers. Select the COM port the microcontroller is connected to, set the speed at 38k4 and select "ASCII" in the "Display" area, then press the Connect button.

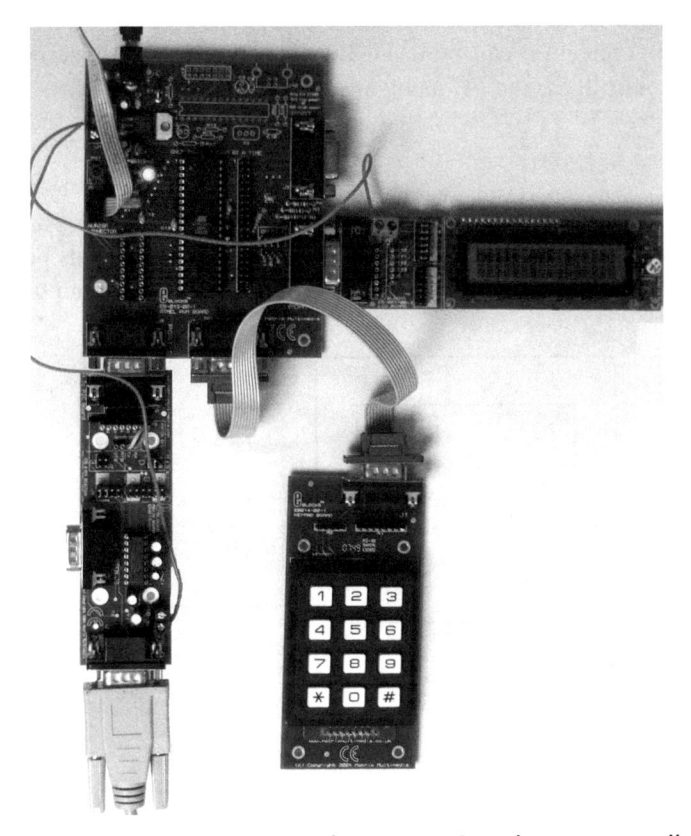

Figure 63. RS232 connection between PC and microcontroller.

Anything you type on the keyboard of your computer will be displayed in the lower window of MICterm and sent to the microcontroller that will display it on the LCD screen. Anything you type on the small keypad will be send to the PC and displayed in the upper window.

57

3.4 Serial communication

3.4.2 USB

Concept

Many computers, particularly portables, do not have a serial or RS232 port anymore. In that case an USB connection can be used. In this project set up a serial communication between a microcontroller and a PC using an USB connection.

Hardware

For this project a 16F877A PIC microcontroller is selected, with an LCD on port B and an USB-RS232 board on port C. Note that both the LCD board needs power so you need to connect the +Vin terminal to one of the +V terminals of the Programmer board

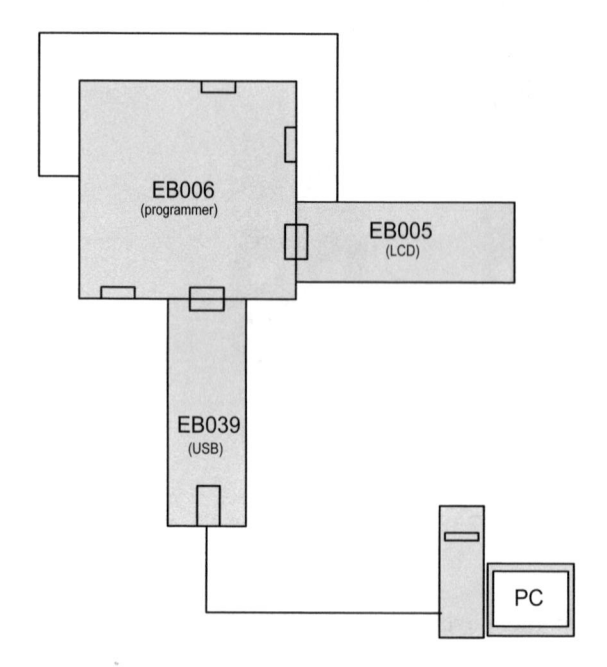

Figure 64. Schematic of the USB serial connection.

Connection summary:

Programmer	Switches to XTAL and Fast, LVP jumper on I/O port, J29 to PSU, J12-14 to USB, use external power supply.
Port B	EB005 LCD, jumper to default.
Port C	EB039 USB-RS232, jumpers on C and 1.

3 Basic

Software

In the menu select Chip, then Configure and then switch to Expert Config Screen. In the section Configuration Word(s) make sure HEX is selected and then click on the Config1 button and enter: 0x3F3A.

If this is the first time the EB039 is used the diver needs to be installed first. Follow the excellent instructions in the EB039 Driver Installation PDF that comes with the board, or can be downloaded from the Matrix Multimedia website. Note that an administrator account or administrator privileges are required for the installation itself.

Once the installation is completed a virtual COM port is assigned to the EB039. That means that software on the PC can use the USB connection by communicating with this virtual COM port. In reality this port doesn't exist and the driver will relay all data to the USB connection. This ensures that legacy PC software can use this USB connection. Windows XP users can run devmgmt.msc on their PC using Start, Execute, devmgmt.msc, to check what number is assigned to the virtual COM port, see next Figure.

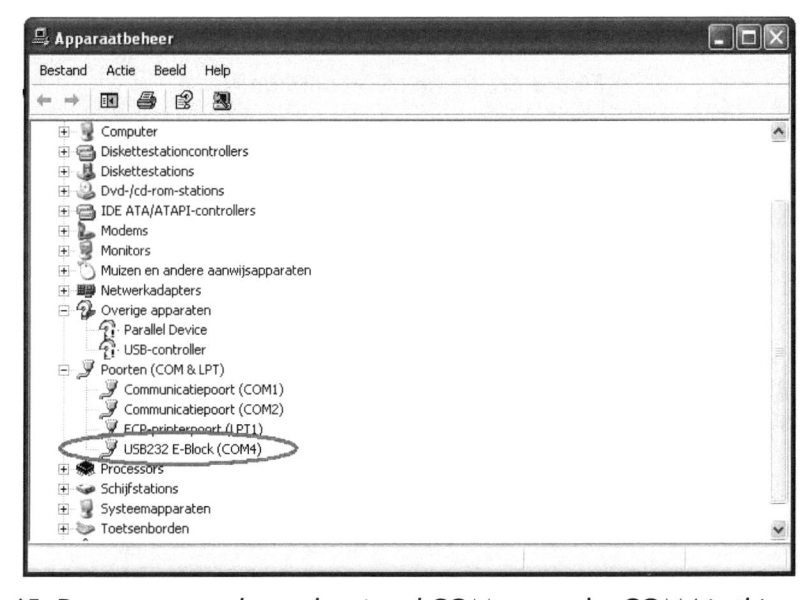

Figure 65. Devmgmt.msc shows the virtual COM port to be COM4 in this example.

The EB039 is in fact an RS232 to USB converter. That means that on the microcontroller side it behaves just like a regular RS232 connection. So an RS232 component has to be used in the program, exactly the same as with a normal RS232 connection.

3.4 Serial communication

That shows all you have to do to convert a Flowcode project from RS232 to USB is to change the EB015 for the EB039!

The program listens to incoming data with a time-out of 10 ms. After a timeout the variable in which the incoming data is to be collected gets value 255. So if the value not equal to 255 it is shown on the LCD screen, and echoed back to the computer.

Note that the LCD messages are scrolling to the left[11]. This is handled by a special LCD command 0b00011000 that can be found in the datasheet of the LCD display.

Description	Command
clear display	0b00000001
return home	0b00000010
display on/off	0b00001000
cursor shift right	0b00010100
cursor shift left	0b00010000
display shift right	0b00011100
display shift left	0b00011000

Figure 66. Some LCD commands.

This command shifts the entire display 1 position to the left. Unfortunately that also applies to the cursor. So for example position 16,0 (writing starts at the far right to have plenty of room for scrolling) now becomes 15,0, and eventually the cursor will move outside the visible display area on the left. So after each left shift the cursor position has to be incremented just to stay in the same location

The maximum allowable cursor position on most LCD screens is 39. After that the display wraps around and starts at zero again, or moves to the next line in some LCDs, so incrementing the cursor position needs to roll over at 39 too. This is handled by the MOD command:

locate = (locate + 1) MOD 40

MOD is short for modulo and means "remainder after number is divided by divisor". So as long as (locate + 1) is smaller than 40 nothing will happen, but as soon as (locate + 1) is equal to 40 then mod 40 is 0 and the counting starts all over.

---

[11] This doesn't work in simulation, only on a real LCD because the simulation doesn't allow direct commands.

locate	(locate + 1) MOD 40
38	39
39	0
0	1

Figure 67. MOD 40.

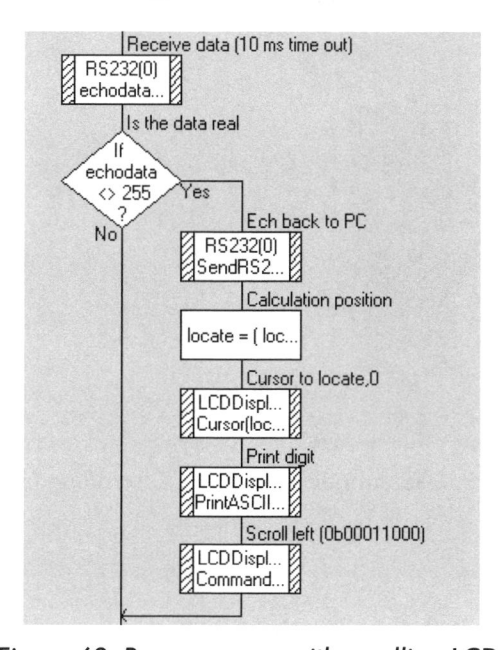

Figure 68. Program core with scrolling LCD.

Operational

Connect the EB039 with the USB cable to the computer, use the same port you used when installing the driver. Start the program. On the PC start a terminal program, for example MICterm. Use the virtual COM port number and a 38k4 as BAUD rate. Any data you enter on the keyboard should appear in the send window, and on the LCD, and be echoed back to the PC.

3.5 Analog to Digital Conversion

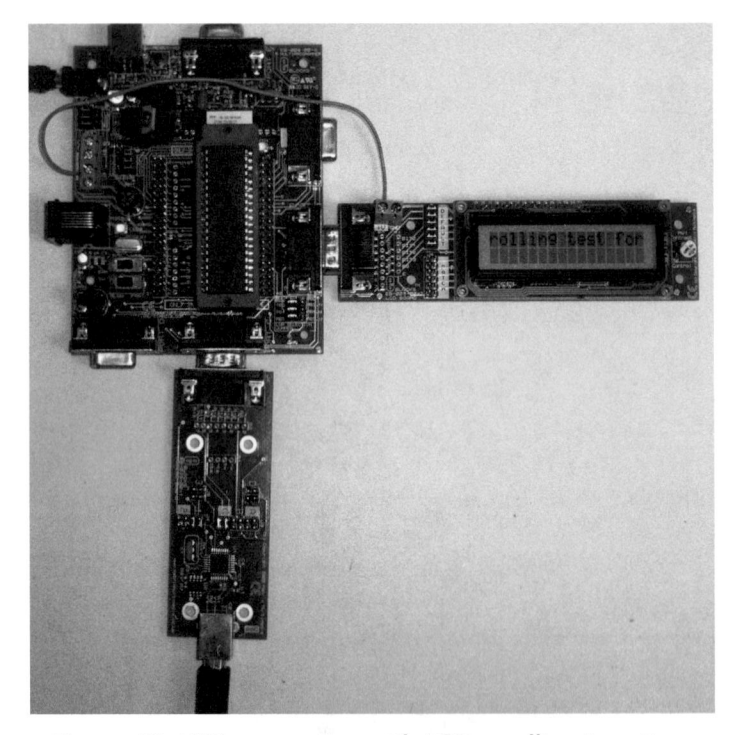

Figure 69. USB connection with LCD scrolling in action.

3.5 Analog to Digital Conversion

Concept

Read an analog signal (voltage) and show the value in a digital format on an LCD.

Hardware

For this project a 16F877A PIC microcontroller is selected, with a Proto board on port A and an LCD on port B. The Proto board has a 10k variable resistor with one end tied to the GND and the other end to +V. The center contact is connected to A0. Note that both the Proto board and the LCD board need power so you need to connect the +Vin terminals of both boards to one of the +V terminals of the Programmer board. There is not enough room for the Proto board so you need a flat ribbon cable to connect it.

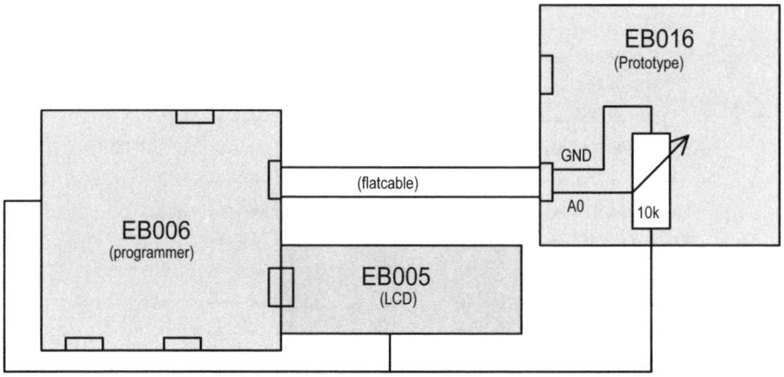

3 Basic

Figure 70. Schematic of the ADC project.

Connection summary:

Programmer   Switches to XTAL and Fast, LVP jumper on I/O port, J29 to PSU, J12-14 to USB, use external power supply.
Port A   EB016 Proto board with a 10k variable resistor between GND and +V, center contact to A0.
Port B   EB005 LCD, jumper to default.

The software

In the menu select Chip, then Configure and then switch to Expert Config Screen. In the section Configuration Word(s) make sure HEX is selected and then click on the Config1 button and enter: 0x3F3A.

The 16F877A is capable of converting a voltage on a pin of the A and E ports into a digital value. This digital value is in the range 0 to 255 where 0 stands for 0 volt on the pin, and 255 for +V volt on the pin. In this project the microcontroller runs on 5 volts, so +V is 5 volts too[12]. Note that if you convert this project to the ARM microcontroller then +V is 3.3 volts.

If for example the digital measurement is 34 that means that the voltage on that pin is:

$$\frac{34}{255} \times 5 = 0.7 \text{ Volt.}$$

---

[12] It is possible to reduce this voltage range and increase the accuracy, see project 4.1.

3.5 Analog to Digital Conversion

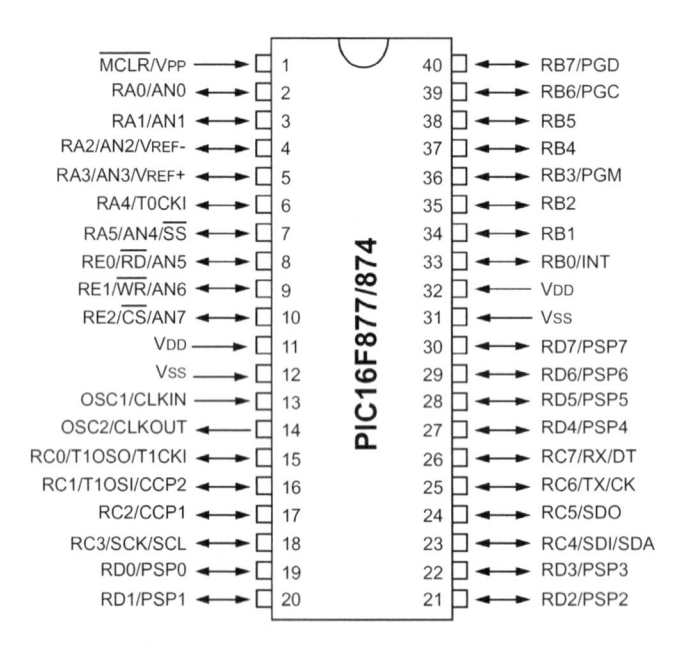

```
MCLR/VPP      → □ 1        40 □ ↔ RB7/PGD
RA0/AN0       ↔ □ 2        39 □ ↔ RB6/PGC
RA1/AN1       ↔ □ 3        38 □ ↔ RB5
RA2/AN2/VREF- ↔ □ 4        37 □ ↔ RB4
RA3/AN3/VREF+ ↔ □ 5        36 □ ↔ RB3/PGM
RA4/T0CKI     ↔ □ 6        35 □ ↔ RB2
RA5/AN4/SS    ↔ □ 7        34 □ ↔ RB1
RE0/RD/AN5    ↔ □ 8        33 □ ↔ RB0/INT
RE1/WR/AN6    ↔ □ 9        32 □ ← VDD
RE2/CS/AN7    ↔ □ 10       31 □ ← VSS
VDD           → □ 11       30 □ ↔ RD7/PSP7
VSS           → □ 12       29 □ ↔ RD6/PSP6
OSC1/CLKIN    → □ 13       28 □ ↔ RD5/PSP5
OSC2/CLKOUT   ← □ 14       27 □ ↔ RD4/PSP4
RC0/T1OSO/T1CKI ↔ □ 15     26 □ ↔ RC7/RX/DT
RC1/T1OSI/CCP2 ↔ □ 16      25 □ ↔ RC6/TX/CK
RC2/CCP1      ↔ □ 17       24 □ ↔ RC5/SDO
RC3/SCK/SCL   ↔ □ 18       23 □ ↔ RC4/SDI/SDA
RD0/PSP0      ↔ □ 19       22 □ ↔ RD3/PSP3
RD1/PSP1      ↔ □ 20       21 □ ↔ RD2/PSP2
```
(PIC16F877/874)

Figure 71. Pin layout of the 16F877A.

First of all click on an ADC component which looks like a red knob with ADC printed underneath, and use the down arrow to select an ADC unit. The 16F877A has seven ADC units distributed over port A and E as can be seen in the previous Figure marked as AN0, AN1 etc. Note that pin A4 has no ADC unit.

Since the variable resistor is connected to pin A0 select ADC0. The component itself is called ADC(0). This zero has nothing to do with the converter that we just selected, it is simply a component reference.

Taking an actual measurement is a two step process.

1. First take a sample of the particular ADC channel by dragging a component macro into the program. Select the macro SampleADC.
2. Then put the sampled value into a variable with another component macro symbol. Select the macro ReadAsByte.

Should you want to sample more than one channel than these steps will both have to be repeated for each channel.

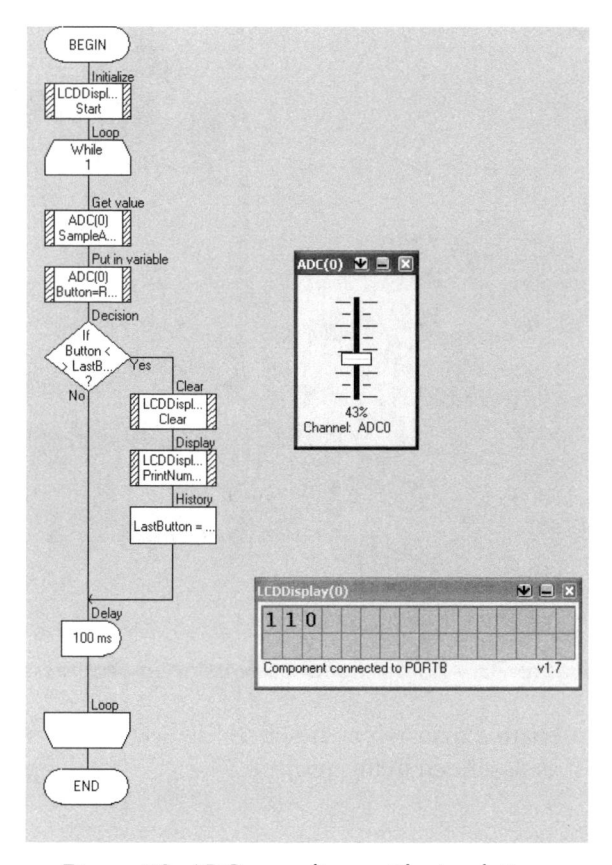

Figure 72. ADC sampling, with simulation.

In between ADC measurements the channel needs to restore itself. If the program is very short, such as this project, a small delay will do the trick. Without this the measurements will vary a bit and thus be unreliable.

The variables button and lastbutton make sure that the LCD display doesn't flicker because only changed values are written to it.

Operational

If you turn the knob on the variable resistor the LCD screen will display the converted value.

3.6 Dark activated switch

Figure 73. Analog digital conversion in progress.

If you built the Proto board expansion as described in section 9.1 set the jumper to the first pin and connect it as described in this project.

3.6 Dark activated switch

Concept

In the evening street lights go on automatically. In this project measure the light level and switch on a relay, which could for example be used for a porch or garden light.

Hardware

For this project we will use the ATMEGA32 AVR microcontroller, in combination with a Proto board and a relay board. The Proto board is extended as described in section 9.1. Note that the Proto board needs power so you need to connect the +Vin terminal to one of the +V terminals of the Programmer board. The relay board needs an elevated voltage to operate: 14 volts, so you need to connect it to the +14V connection on the Programmer. It is recommended to use a different color wire to prevent mixing it with the 5 volt power connections.

3   Basic

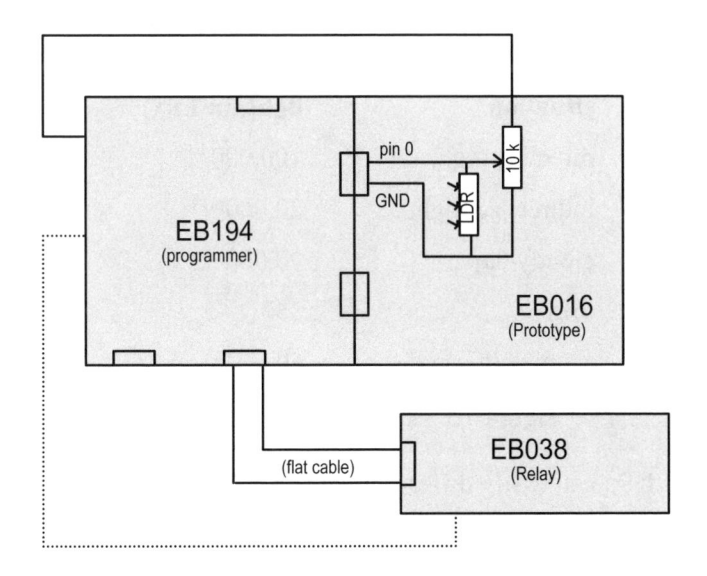

Figure 74. Schematic of the light dependent switch.

Connection summary:

    Programmer   EB194, jumper to default.
    Port B   EB016 Proto board, with a 10k linear variable resistor mounted between +V and GND, with an LDR mounted between GND and the center pin of the variable resistor.
    Port C   EB038 Relay board, jumper on low.

According to the documentation of the relay board the relays can handle mains, but it recommends not to exceed 24 volts. The relays themselves are stamped 7A / 250 V (Song Chuan, type 812BH-1C-CE)[13].

The amount of light can be measured using an LDR (Light Dependent Resistor). This is a resistor whose value is dependent on the amount of light that hits it. The relationship between the resistance and the amount of light is not linear and is usually something like this:

$$R = \frac{500}{L}$$

---

[13] Should you use mains remember that high voltages can kill. Take all necessary safety precautions and follow local safety rules and guidelines. Proceed at your own risk.

3.6 Dark activated switch

With R in k ohm and L in Lux. To get a feel for the meaning of Lux:

situation	light (in Lux)
direct sunlight	100,000
indirect sunlight	20,000
cloudy day	10,000
office	350
room with candle	50

Figure 75. Examples of Lux values.

Even "identical" LDRs can easily differ as much as 50%, so you'll need to calibrate it or use a variable resistor for fine adjustment. Keep in mind that the more light falling on the LDR the lower its resistance is.

If you are interested in measuring the light in Lux take a look at project 5.2 in the sensor section of this book.

An LDR will normally consume about 50 to 80 mW of power, which at 5 volts equals a current of 10 to 16 mA. This means the LDR can be connected directly to the microcontroller without damage.

Software

If you haven't done so already first of all make sure that the fuses of the ATMEGA 32 are set correctly to 0x0,0xdf and 0x1,0xff. Select the "Chip" menu and "Configure". Enter the settings and remember to click on the Ok and Send button, because they will not be transferred by default. Of course the AVR programmer must be connected to the PC and powered on for this to work.

The program measures the ADC value on pin 0 of port A in a continuous loop and compares it with a threshold value of 125. If the measured value is higher this means the light has dropped to a "low" level so the relay will be switched on. In all other cases the relay will be switched off.

The exact value of the threshold is not important because the variable resistor is used to set the actual threshold.

3 Basic

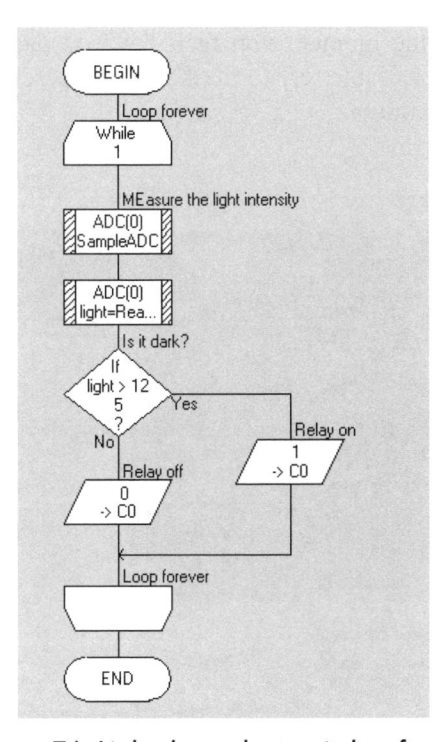

Figure 76. Light dependent switch software.

Operational

The LDR is connected to the project using the hardware described in section 9.1. Alternatively both the 10 k linear variable resistor and the LDR could be mounted on the breadboard part of the Proto board with exactly the same result.

Figure 77. Connection of the LDR.

3.7 Youth deterrent

Switch on the power. At the moment you feel that it is dark enough for the relay to engage carefully adjust the variable resistor to the point where the relay just engages. The project is now ready for operation.

Figure 78. Light dependent switch.

With a few adaptations to the program the other relays on the board could be switched on at different light levels. So the darker it gets, the more lights are switched on.

3.7 Youth deterrent

Concept

Many people find groups of teens hanging about annoying and look for non-violent ways to keep their doorsteps empty. One solution is to emit a high pitched whistle at a frequency that only teenagers can hear. Adults are oblivious to the sound, as seem pets. Another application using the same sound, but emitted more softly, could serve as a warning signal between youths. One such application would be a ring tone that could be used while in class, or a secret doorbell. The target frequency is 16 to 20 kHz.

3 Basic

Hardware

For this project a 16F877A PIC microcontroller is selected. To emit the sound you obviously need a loudspeaker. Since there are no demands other than the correct frequency, it is meant as a deterrent after all, he sound can be made by flipping a pin of the microcontroller high and low. So we will connect the speaker directly to a pin using the Proto board, with a variable resistor to control the volume.

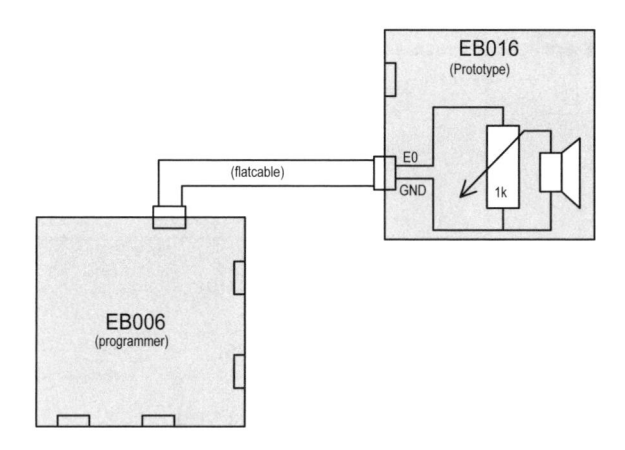

Figure 79. Youth deterrent hardware.

Connection summary:

Programmer	Switches to XTAL and Fast, LVP jumper on I/O port, J29 to PSU, J12-14 to USB, use external power supply.		
Port E	E0	Variable resistor	
	GND	Variable resistor and a tiny loudspeaker	

Software

In the menu select Chip, then Configure and then switch to Expert Config Screen. In the section Configuration Word(s) make sure HEX is selected and then click on the Config1 button and enter: 0x3F3A.

In order to flip the pin at a very regular pace an interrupt will be used. This is a mechanism that interrupts a running program at preset intervals, and runs a small separate routine, or macro. After this macro has finished the main program continues. Using interrupts requires a bit of planning. If the interrupt routine is too long the main program will not get enough time to run. So interrupt routines must be kept short. The main program must be doing a task that can actually be safely interrupted. If for example you

71

3.7 Youth deterrent

interrupt a communications routine chances are some information may get lost. In general interrupts are to be avoided if possible.

To set up an interrupt drag the interrupt symbol into your program and double click on it.

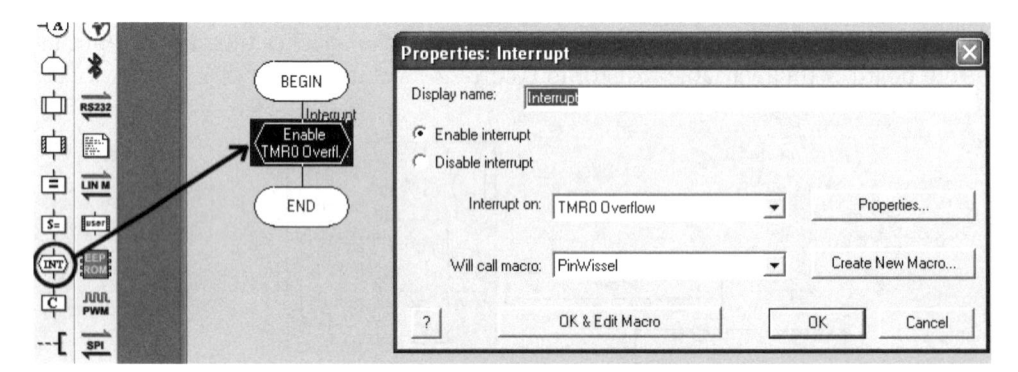

Figure 80. Enable an interrupt.

Select Enable interrupt and make the following selections:

    Display name   Interrupt or anything else you fancy.
    Interrupt on   TMR0 overflow.

TMR0 is an abbreviation of Timer 0, a counter that increments from 0 to 255 and then starts again (roll over) at 0. Now click properties.

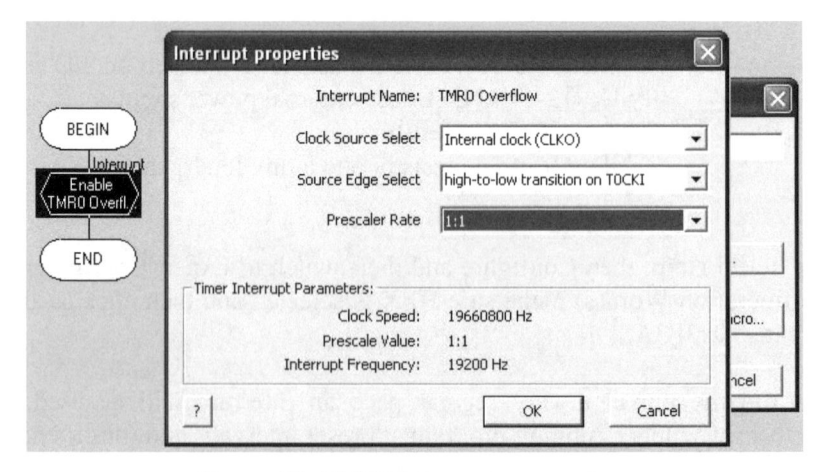

Figure 81. TMR0 interrupt properties.

3 Basic

Make the following selections:

Clock source select	Internal clock (CLKO)
Source edge select	High to low transition on T0CKI
Prescaler rate	1:1

The prescaler rate is where the actual interrupt frequency is set. These are the possibilities when using a 16F877A PIC with a clock speed or crystal at 19660800 Hz:

Prescaler	Interrupt frequency (Hz)
1:1	19200
1:2	9600
1:4	4800
1:8	2400
1:16	1200
1:32	600
1:64	300
1:128	150
1:256	75

Figure 82. TMR0 interrupt frequencies.

In order to make a sound wave a pin has to be made high and then low. The high and low combined produces one wave. That means that if the interrupt, and thus the pin frequency is 19200 Hz the frequency of the sound produced by this pin is half of that value, so 9600 Hz. This is far below our target sound frequency range of 16 to 20 kHz.

tmr0 start value	Sound frequency (kHz)
0	9.5
120	9.3
150	11.2
180	14.5
190	16.0
195	16.5

Figure 83. Measured sound frequencies with TMR0 offset.

Normally timer 0 starts at 0 and then increments up to 255. The interrupt occurs at the roll over from 255 back to 0. If the counter would not start at 0 but at a higher value the roll over point would be reached sooner so the interrupt frequency would go up. The exact

3.7 Youth deterrent

effect is hard to predict because of program overhead, so the previous Figure shows actual measurements of the sound frequency for different starting values of TMR0:

So a starting point of 195 would result in the target sound frequency. Flowcode does not offer direct access to TMR0 so a C-box needs to be used containing the text (note the semi colon at the end of the statement):

>   tmr0=0x195;

Anyway, continuing with the interrupt settings, close the window by clicking on OK.

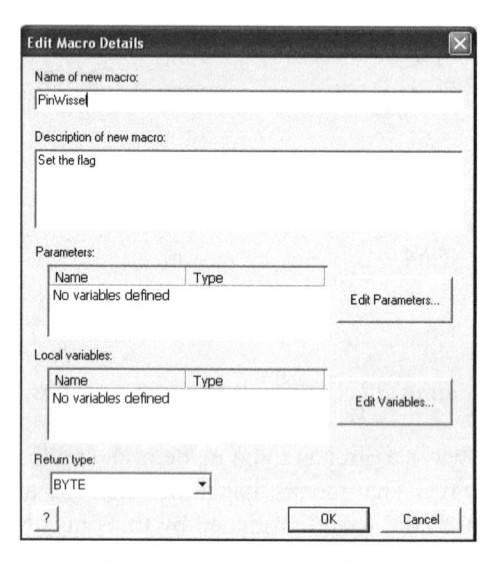

Figure 84. Macro settings.

Then click on "Create new macro". Enter a name, for example "PinWissel", and short description. Make return type a BYTE, see the previous Figure, and ignore the other fields.

You will now be presented with a new program, which is in fact the macro that is called by the interrupt. Use a calculation box to change a variable called flag:

>   flag = NOT flag

3   Basic

Output the variable to port D. So whatever the signal was on port D it is now the exact opposite[14]. Note to ourselves: in the main program the variable flag must be set to 0. The next step is to set the TMR0 starting value with the c-statement previously discussed, which concludes the macro routine.

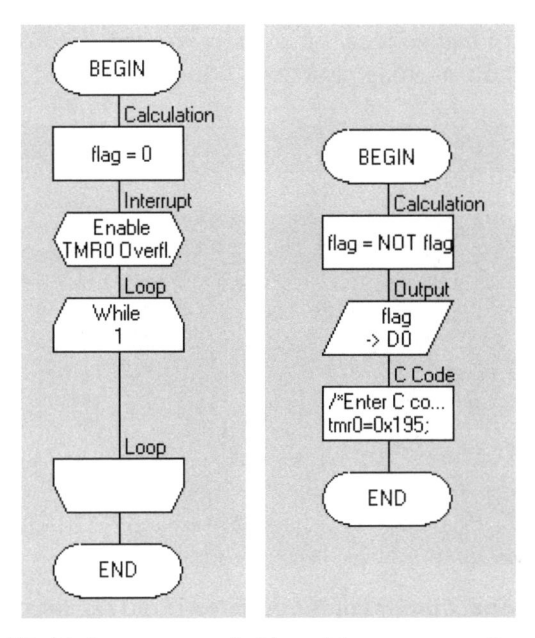

Figure 85. Main program (left) and interrupt routine (right).

Use the Macro menu and the View main to get back to the main program. Before the interrupt settings add a calculation box and set flag to 0. Then enter an empty forever loop. This program is basically doing nothing at all, it is simply waiting for an interrupt to occur.

In general having an output routine in an interrupt is "not done" amongst programmers, because outputs tend to take a long time. And since interrupt routines should be as short as possible it is considered desirable to restrict the use of outputs to the main program. In this case however that means the main program needs an additional loop where the program waits for the flag to change. So in effect this program is faster than the more

---

[14] In Boolean logic NOT 1 equals 0. In this case however flag is defined as a byte, which contains 8 bits. So in reality 0 is 00000000 in binary so NOT 0 is 11111111 in binary, which equals 255. In this case that doesn't matter. We are only interested in bit 0 (which is connected to D0), and that single bit does indeed flip from 1 to 0. That the other bits flip as well is irrelevant because they are not connected to anything. Check section 12.4 for more information on microcontroller mathematics.

75

3.7 Youth deterrent

formal program would be. Check project 4.2 for a program that uses the formal programming methodology and waits for a flag.

Operation

When I built this project I had no idea if it actually worked, because I couldn't hear it. The spectrum analyzer did show a strong peak at 16.6 kHz, but would it be annoying enough?

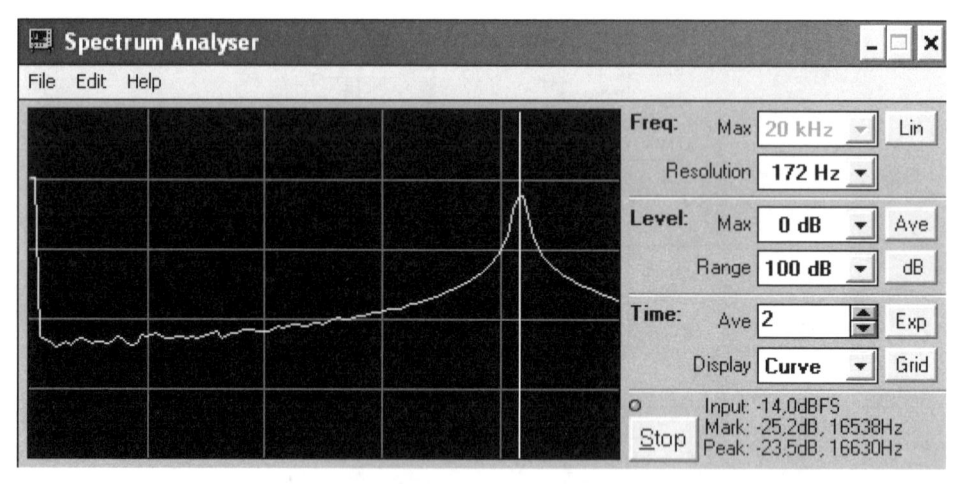

Figure 86. Spectrum analyzer data for TRM0 starting point 195.

So when my teenage daughter happened to walk into my office I switched it on and I was just about to ask "Can you hear anything?" when she jumped back, covered her ears, and said "What is that horrible noise!?"

So I guess it works just fine.

Note that in several countries outdoor use in public or semi-public places as youth deterrent may not be legal.

In chapter 11 this project will be used as an example how to convert a prototype into a production unit.

3 Basic

Figure 87. Youth deterrent in operation.

3.8 Sound activated switch

Concept

Sound operated equipment such as automatic recording devices or burglar alarms need a mechanism to measure sound levels and respond to them by switching something on or off. In this project a microphone will be used to detect the sound of clapping hands. Each time the sound is detected a row of LEDs is switched on and off repeatedly.

Hardware

For this project a 16F877A PIC microcontroller is selected. You will need the microphone board from section 9.2 to detect the sound. If you didn't build the board you can use the schematic given in that chapter to build the project on a Proto board. The EB004 LED board provides the LEDs.

Note that the Microphone pre-amplifier needs power so you need to connect the +Vin terminal to one of the +V terminals of the Programmer board.

3.8 Sound activated switch

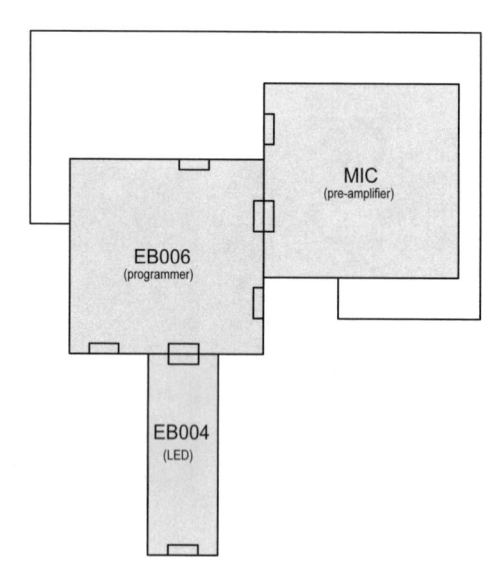

Figure 88. Schematic of the sound switch.

Connection summary:

Programmer	Switches to XTAL and Fast, LVP jumper on I/O port, J29 to PSU, J12-14 to USB, use external power supply.
Port A	A0 Microphone pre-amplifier
	J1 first position
	J2 right (pre-amplifier)
Port C	EB004 LED board

Software

In the menu select Chip, then Configure and then switch to Expert Config Screen. In the section Configuration Word(s) make sure HEX is selected and then click on the Config1 button and enter: 0x3F3A.

The microphone pre-amplifier will produce a voltage depending on the volume of the sound that hits the microphone. This voltage is lead to pin A0, where an ADC (Analog to Digital Converter) turns it into a digital value.

3 Basic

The program then compares this value to a threshold level. If the voltage is above the threshold the status of port C is flipped from 0 to 1 and vise versa. After this a 500 ms delay is used to prevent a single short sound from repeatedly flipping the port.

The current threshold limit is 50, so 0.98 volts, which at the lowest amplification level of the microphone pre-amplifier is high enough to ignore ambient noise such as conversations, yet low enough to pick up the sound of clapping hands.

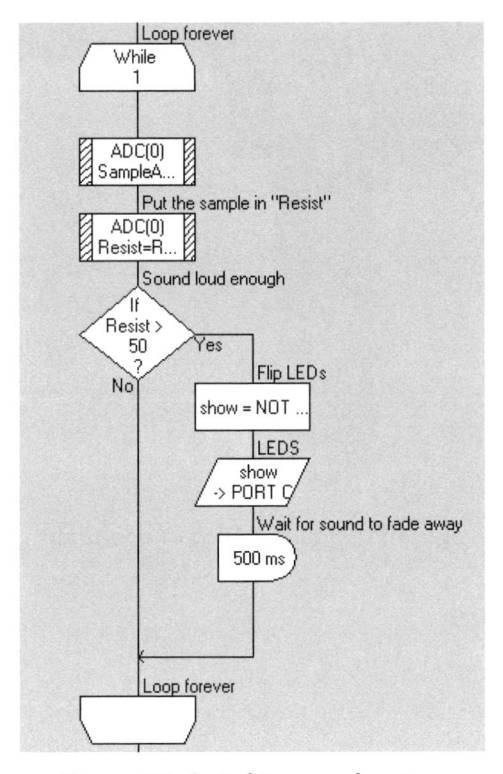

Figure 89. Switching mechanism.

The full source of this program is part of the download package and listed under the project number.

Operation

If a timer replaces the flipping mechanism the microphone can be mounted on a object that intruders are likely to break, such as a window, and used as a intruder alert. Loud banging on the window, or breaking it, would result in the alarm going off. Note that in several countries it is mandatory that alarms switch off automatically after a preset time.

3.9 Air to fuel ratio

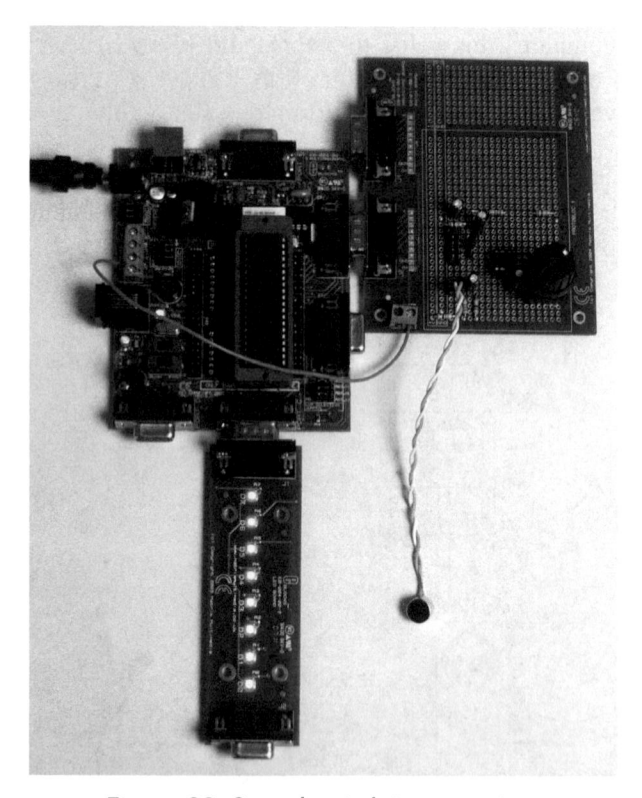

Figure 90. Sound switch in operation.

3.9 Air to fuel ratio

Concept

Use a Lookup Table (LUT) to store and retrieve two dimensional data. The data in this project is the relationship between torque or motor strength[15] and air to fuel ratio (how much air is fed into the motor in relationship to the fuel). Data like this is used in motor management systems in automobiles to optimize fuel consumption and performance.

---

[15] Torque is the amount of force acting on the motor axle causing it to rotate. The power output is torque multiplied by the rotational speed.

3 Basic

Hardware

For this project a 16F877A PIC microcontroller is selected, with an LCD on port B and a Keypad on port D. Note that the LCD board needs power so you need to connect the +Vin terminal to one of the +V terminals of the Programmer board

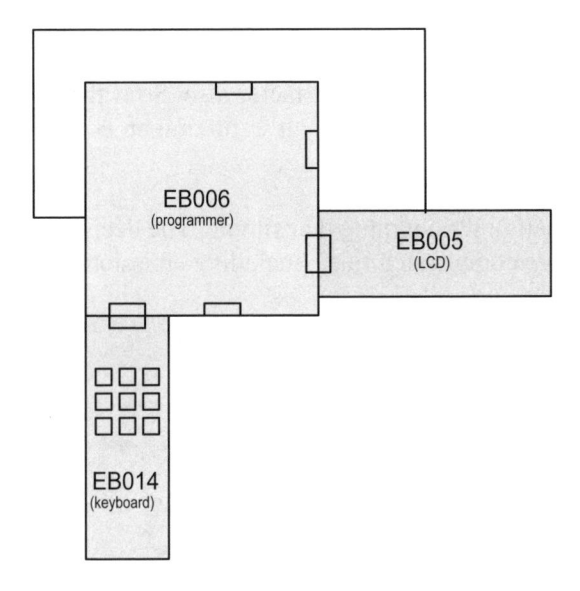

Figure 91. Schematic of the ADC project.

Connection summary:

Programmer	Switches to XTAL and Fast, LVP jumper on I/O port, J29 to PSU, J12-14 to USB, use external power supply.
Port B	EB005 LCD, jumper to default.
Port D	Keypad EB014.

Software

In the menu select Chip, then Configure and then switch to Expert Config Screen. In the section Configuration Word(s) make sure HEX is selected and then click on the Config1 button and enter: 0x3F3A.

If data is two dimensional this means that two numbers have a relationship. If the relationship for example is "multiply by eight" then 2 and 16 would be an example of two

3.9 Air to fuel ratio

dimensional data. If the relationship is a known formula then one of the data set can be used to calculate the other[16].

In this project we will look at motor torque in relationship to the air and fuel mixture that is fed into the engine. The relationship between these two data sets is known as a series of measurements, but not as a formula, see next Figures. There is a mixture at which the torque is the highest. This is the optimum if all we care about is torque.

In reality fuel consumption is an important factor also. So if the car needs less torque but the speed needs to remain constant the air ratio might be increased to reduce fuel consumption.

Of course in a real situation it's not quite that simple. The decision process involves many more variables and more complicated rules, including emissions.

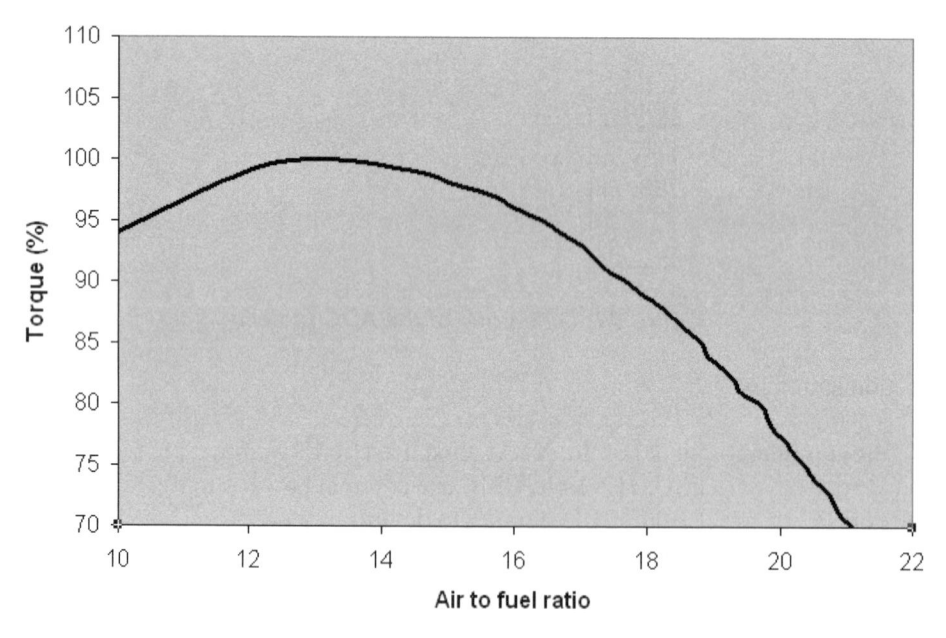

Figure 92. Torque against air to fuel ratio in motor performance.

The graph is based on the measurements shown in the table in next Figure. If we need to know the fuel to air ration to reach for example a torque of 75% we can simply look it up in this table and find 20.4. Hence the name: Lookup Table, or LUT.

---

[16] In some cases even relationships with a known formula are put in Lookup tables because calculating them on the spot often takes too much time, for example trigonometric and logarithmic functions.

In this project we are only interested in the right hand part of the graph, because the further to the right we adjust the mixture the less fuel the car uses. So based on the torque needed the right mixture must be found.

Torque	Air to fuel ratio	Torque	Air to fuel ratio
94	10	85	18.8
99	12	84	18.9
100	13.2	83	19.1
99	14.5	82	19.3
98	15.1	81	19.4
97	15.7	80	19.7
96	16	79	19.8
95	16.4	78	19.9
94	16.7	77	20.1
93	17	76	20.2
92	17.2	75	20.4
91	17.4	74	20.5
90	17.7	73	20.7
89	17.9	72	20.8
88	18.2	71	20.9
87	18.4	70	21.1
86	18.6		

Figure 93. Air to fuel ratio and torque relationship measurements.

Lookup table must be defined in the Definitions section of the Supplementary Code box:

rom char* ATF = {132,145,151,157,160,164,167,170,172, 174,177,179,182, 184, 186,188,189,191,193,194,197,198,199,201,202,204,205,207,208,209,211};

The name of the Lookup Table is ATF (Air To Fuel) and the numbers between the curly brackets are the data from the right columns of the previous table. Decimals are not possible so all values are multiplied by 10. When printing them to the LCD the decimal point must be inserted again. Retrieving a value from the LUT is done using:

FCV_FROMTABLE = ATF[FCV_POSITIONINTABLE];

in a C-code component. Note that in C the Flowcode variables are preceded by FCV_ and they need to be in capitals.

3.9 Air to fuel ratio

The first number in the LUT is position 0, the second one position 1 etc.

So if for example the number on position 0 has to be retrieved and put into Flowcode variable AirToFuel the statement would be:

FCV_AIRTOFUEL = ATF[0];

Since the first torque percentage is 70 and the first position in the table is 0 we need to subtract 70 from the torque to get the location in the table.

torque = torque - 70

If the torque is for example 90 then the fuel to air ratio is in position 20. After retrieving the number is needs to be "divided by 10" again before being displayed.

One way to do this is to convert the number into a string, then separate the left and the right part, and put them back together with a decimal point in between in a string manipulation symbol. The table shows the Flowcode commands in the left column and the result in the right column. The variables tolcd, part1 and part2 are only temporary variables.

Operation	Result
	211
tolcd = ToString$(airtofuel)	211
part1 = left$(tolcd, 2)	21
part2 = right$(tolcd, 1)	1
tolcd = part1 + "." + part2	21.1

Figure 94. String operations.

Since we don't have an actual motor management system connected to our project the required torque percentage can be entered using a keypad. A small loops checks which number is entered on the keypad, and multiplies this with a factor to represent its location, a variable called "multiplier". If for example you enter 123 the first digit (1) needs to be multiplied by 100 to get the actual value. The second needs to be multiplied by 10 and the last digit by 1.

This is handled by a variable called "Multiplier", see the next Figure. This variable starts at 100 and is divided each loop by 10. Interestingly enough the program exits the loop when multiplier is 0. Which you'd think it never will be if all you do is divide by 10. Multiplier however is defined as a byte, so 1/10 = 0. This will take place after the third digit, which means that if you want to lookup 73 you will have to enter 073.

3   Basic

The program checks for the * key (10) and # key (11) at the same time when it checks for a valid key entry, meaning an entry not equal to 255[17]:

(entry <> 255) AND (entry <> 10) AND (entry <> 11)

Note that the brackets are needed. Without them the line can be read in multiple ways, and the compiler will undoubtedly pick the wrong one[18].

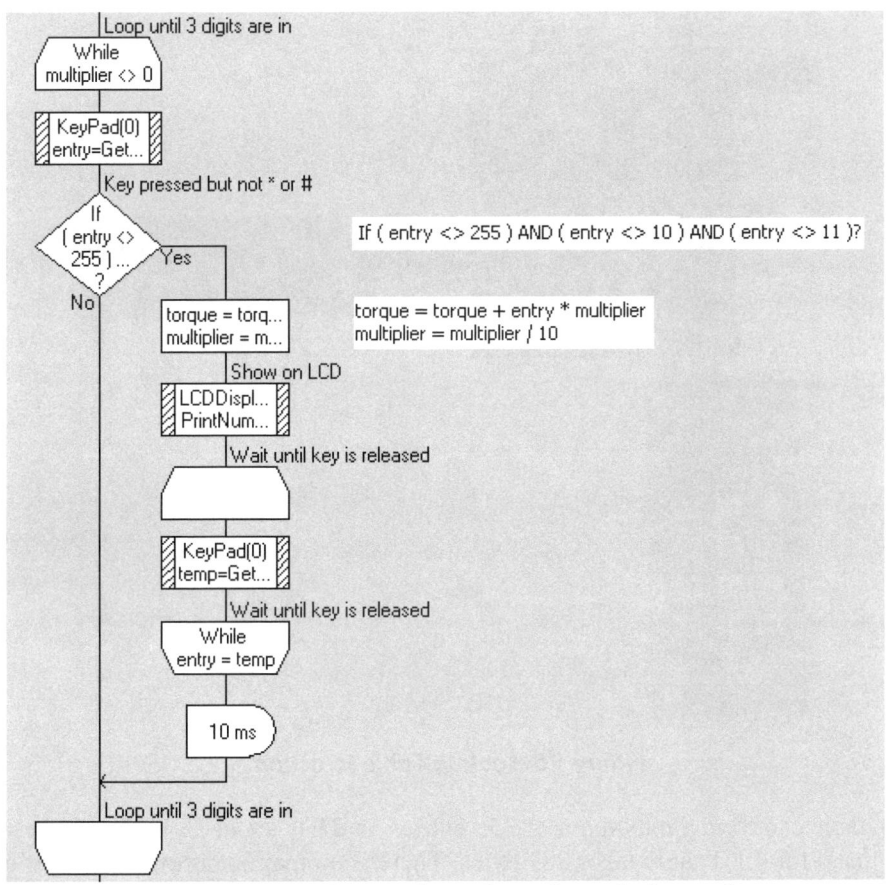

Figure 95. Gathering three digits from the keypad.

Operational

Enter a torque value in three digits, for example 073. The program will show your entry on the first line. Once the third digit has been entered the result from the lookup table, in

---

[17] The keypad returns 255 if no key is pressed when the program checks the keypad.
[18] For example entry <> (255 AND entry) <> (10 AND entry) <> 11

85

3.9   Air to fuel ratio

this case 15.7, is shown on the lower line. After one second the LCD is cleared and you can enter the next torque.

The LCD display will show the corresponding Air to fuel ratio. Of course this is just a demonstration of how Lookup Tables work. See for example project 4.3 for a more practical application.

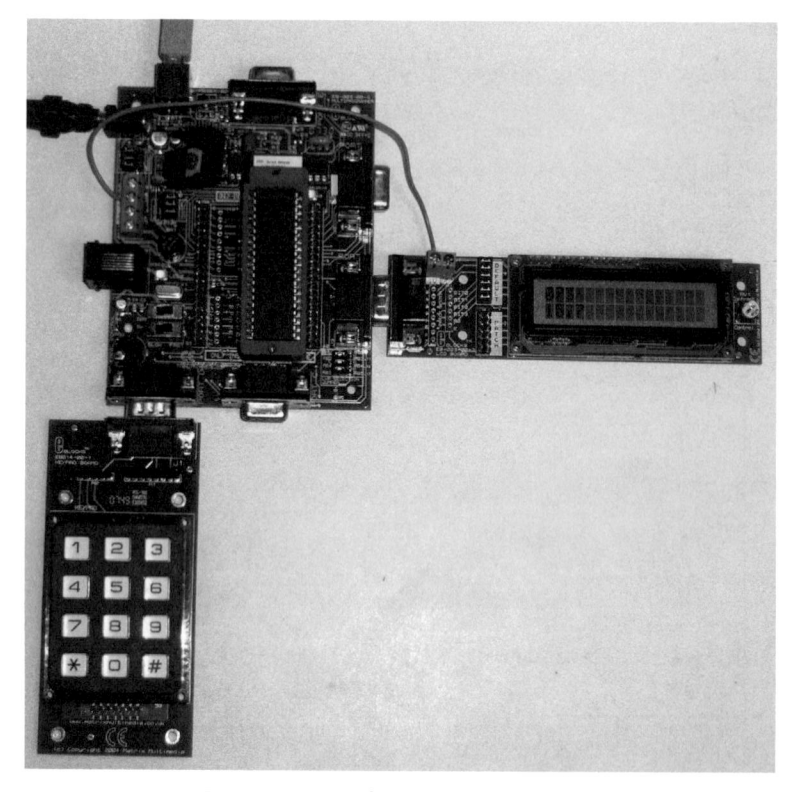

Figure 96. Lookup Table in action.

A LUT table can have a maximum of 255 entries, and has about 28 bytes overhead. This means that a full LUT table takes 283 bytes. There is no maximum to the number of LUT tables, except of course the amount of Flash memory. The easiest way to find out how many LUT tables your program can have is to compile it and download it to the microcontroller. Flowcode will tell you how much memory was used, in this case 2012 bytes.

Finished reading PICmicro contents
Program sent and verified OK

2012 out of 8192 program words used
0 out of 256 data bytes used
That took 3,281 seconds

Subtract this from the available memory and divide by 283. The program in this project could for example additionally hold (8192-2012)/283 = 21 additional fully loaded (255 bytes) LUT tables. See project 4.3 for an example with 11 LUT tables.

3.10 Digital clock

Concept

Design a simple digital clock with a three button operation to set the time.

Hardware

For this project we will use the ATMEGA32 AVR microcontroller, in combination with an LCD screen and a Switch board. Note that both boards need power so you need to connect the +Vin terminals of the boards to the +V terminals of the Programmer board.

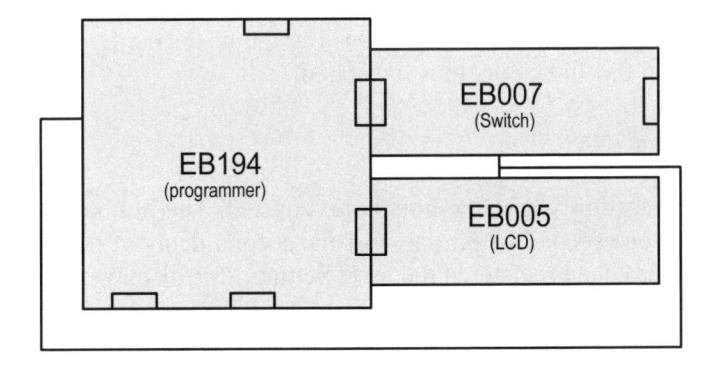

Figure 97. Schematic of the digital clock hardware.

3.10 Digital clock

Connection summary:

>Programmer   EB194, jumper to default.
>Port A   EB007 Switch board.
>Port B   EB005 LCD, jumper to default.

Software

If you haven't done so already first of all make sure that the fuses of the ATMEGA 32 are set correctly to 0x0,0xdf and 0x1,0xff. Select the "Chip" menu and "Configure". Enter the settings and remember to click on the Ok and Send button, because they will not be transferred by default. Of course the AVR programmer must be connected to the PC and powered on for this to work.

The structure of this program is a bit unusual. In the main loop the program checks the button on A0, and displays the time (hours, minutes and seconds) on the LCD screen. Depending on the number of times that button A0 has been pressed the program will execute one of the following side loops.

1. Button pressed zero times

>This is the actual clock. Every second the variable Second is incremented by one. If second reaches 60 it is reset to zero and variable Minute is incremented. If minute reaches 60 then it is reset and variable Hour is incremented. If variable hour reaches 25 then it is reset. Note that this is the European way of displaying time. Should you prefer the American way the hour counter must roll over at 12, and AM and PM indicators must be added.

2. Button pressed one time

>This is the section where the hours are adjusted. The button needs to be pressed for at least one second to get past the one second delay of the actual clock. Once the button has been registered the text "Setting..." is displayed on the lower line.

>In this section pressing the Up button A1 will increment the hours. If the hours are above 24 they will roll over, if they are below 0 they will roll back to 23.

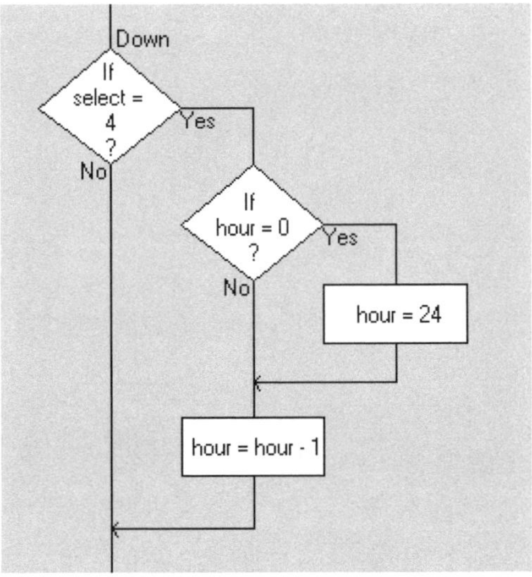

3   Basic

Figure 98. Down button.

When the down button is pressed, see the previous Figure, it is not possible to subtract first and then check to see if hours is less than zero, in which case a roll back to 23 must be made. Hour is defined as a byte and can thus never be negative: 0 - 1 = 255. See section 12.4 for more information on microcontroller mathematics.

3 Button pressed twice

This is the section where the minutes are adjusted. This time the 1 second delay is not in the loop so the program will respond quickly with "Setting...". Technically the loop is similar to the hour loop.

4. Button pressed three times

The button counter (Selected) is reset so the button now appears to have been pressed zero times, which means that the clock starts running again. Note that whenever the time is being adjusted debouncing takes place in the main program loop. This way one debouncing loop takes care of four button operations, see the next Figure.

89

3.10 Digital clock

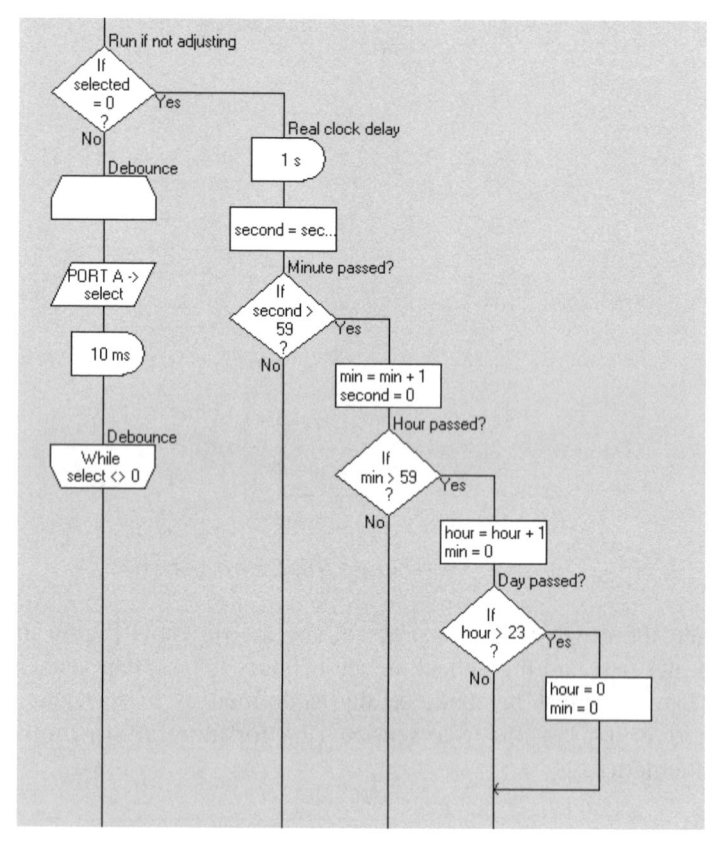

Figure 99. Debouncing in the main loop.

Operational

Figure 100. Digital clock in operation.

Start the clock and set the correct time using the buttons:

    A0   Set / select hours / select minutes / continue
    A1   Up
    A2   Down

3.11 Debugging

Concept

Your program compiles and can be downloaded into the microcontroller. Unfortunately however it doesn't do what you want it to do. This project shows how to fix problems like this.

Hardware

For this project we will use the AT91SAM7S128 ARM microcontroller, in combination with an RS232 board and a Switch board. Note that both boards need power so you need to connect the +Vin terminals of the boards to the +V terminals of the Programmer board.

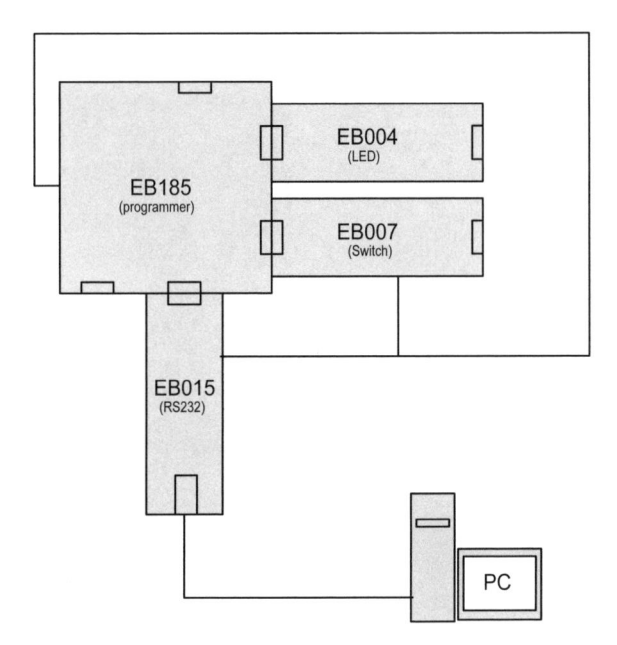

Figure 101. Hardware for the debug project.

3.11 Debugging

Connection summary:

    Programmer   EB185, jumpers J16 at PSU, J18 at USB, J15 at default.
    Port A   EB004 LED.
    Port B   EB007 Switch board.

Do not connect the RS232 board on port C yet.

If you don't own the ARM microcontroller but instead the PIC or AVR check out chapter 10 on how to migrate this project to your microcontroller.

Software

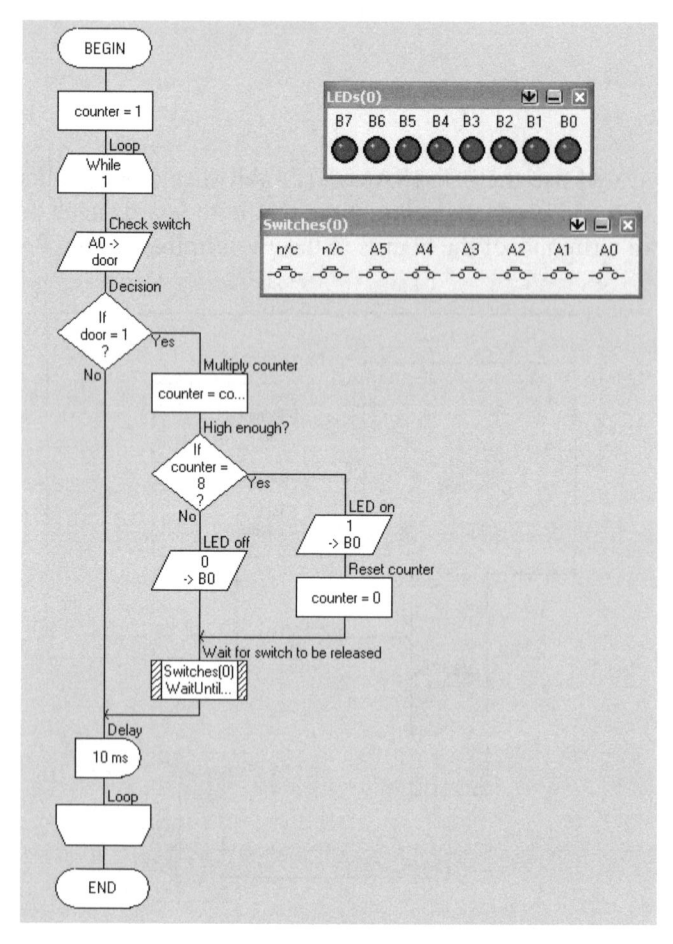

Figure 102. A program with two errors.

In this project you must use the program in the download package. Note that this program contains two errors, it will not run correctly! Two debugging techniques will be used to find the errors.

Button SW0 represents a contact on a shop entrance door. Every time the door opens a counter is multiplied by two. When the counter hits eight LED D0 will light. The next customer to open the door will switch the LED back off and reset the counter. So every third customer the LED should go on. The WaitUntil macro combined with the 10ms delay takes care of debouncing the switch.

Compile the program and download it into the project. Press button SW0 ten times. After three, six and nine times LED D0 should light. Note that this does not happen.

3.11.1 Simulation

Run the simulation by pressing the "run" button in Flowcode (the blue triangle[19]). Repeat the previous test: press SW0 ten times. At the third time LED D0 will light up as it should, but after 6 and 9 times nothing happens. Stop the simulation.

If you simulate step by step you cannot click on the next step button and on the switch at the same time. So change the setting of the Switch board from "push to make" to "toggle". Now step through the simulation by clicking with the mouse on the "Step Into" button. Toggle switch SW0 before the program hits the "check switch" symbol, and "Step Into" again to continue. Note that the counter value is shown in the Variables window. It correctly increments from one to two, and if you loop (remember to toggle the switch off at the lower WaitUntil symbol) it will increase further to four and eight at which point the LED will go on, and the counter is reset to 0. Loop again, and at that point you will notice that the counter doesn't increase anymore because zero multiplied by two will remain zero.

So the error is that the counter is reset to zero, while it should have been reset to one. Which incidentally is the value it got at the very beginning of the program, and that is why it worked fine the first time but not thereafter.

You can test this in the simulation. Double click on the counter in the Variables window. A small window pops up allowing you to change the value of counter. Change the reset to one and you will see that the program runs perfectly in simulation.

---

[19] Note that you can change the speed of the simulation in the Chip and then Clock Speed menu. Any speed other than "As fast as possible" will result in variable content and macro calls to be shown.

3.11 Debugging

Download the corrected program into the microcontroller. If you try the program in the microcontroller it unfortunately still will not light the LED.

3.11.2 Serial connection

The difference between theory and practice is that in theory there is no difference but in practice there is, as someone once said to me. This is exactly the problem: in theory (simulation) the program works but in practice it doesn't.

The key variable is the counter. Since this is a simple program with just one variable we could use an LCD to display the value of counter to see what is going on. Instead we will use an RS232 connection to a terminal program on the computer to examine the value of counter. This has three advantages:

1. You can send as many variables as you like to the PC without the screen ever overflowing.
2. You can make the microcontroller wait for you while you analyze the data on the screen. This is particularly important if the program is running in a loop without waiting for anything.
3. You can make a graph or view the data in a different format.

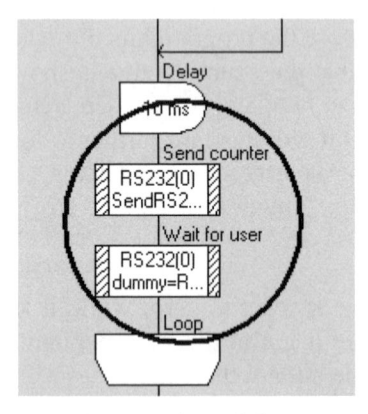

Figure 103. Stop and go debugging point..

Connect the EB015 RS232 board (jumpers to C and 1)[20] to port C. Add an RS232 component to your program, set it at 9600 BAUD, send Bytes. Now somewhere in the main loop, for example after the 10ms delay add an RS232 component macro to send the counter. Right behind it use an RS232 component macro to receive a variable called

---

[20] Note that these are the jumper settings for the AT91SAM7S128 ARM microcontroller.

3 Basic

dummy. Important: enter 255 as a time out value. This means that there is no time out. So the program will wait indefinitely for you to send some data, any data in fact, to the microcontroller. If your program is complex you can add multiple points like this and step through your program in real life, almost like in the simulation.

Start a terminal program on your PC, for example MICterm, at a speed of 9600 BAUD. then power up the microcontroller. A 1 will appear in the receive window. At that moment the programs stops, waiting for input. Press space on the keyboard. Another 1 appears. So far so good. Now press button SW0 and then press space, and then let go of SW0. This time the program should see the pressed button during its loop and multiply the counter, so the result should be 2. But the result is still 1. In fact you will see this result even before you let go of the pushbutton. That means the program doesn't see button SW0. Otherwise it would have multiplied the counter, and it would have waited for you to release the button. This can only mean one of two things:

1. The Switch board is malfunctioning.
2. The Switch board is on the wrong port in the Flowcode program.

The easiest way to check this is leave the program as it is but exchange the Switch and LED board on the microcontroller.

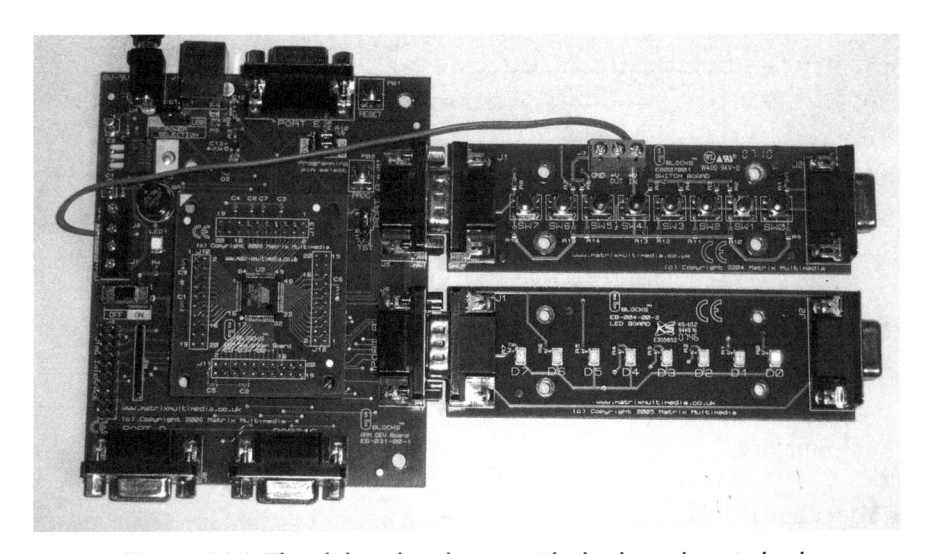

Figure 104. The debug hardware with the boards switched.

Power up again and this time the program runs perfectly. So the problem was number 2: the Switch board was on the wrong port.

3.12 Bootloader

It is assumed that you installed the drivers and software that are required for the ECIO boards. If you haven't done this now would be a good time to do so[21].

Concept

You need a programmer to get a program from the PC into a microcontroller. Some microcontrollers however are capable of programming themselves. Apart from the obvious advantage to the hobbyist, no need to buy an expensive programmer, the advantage for businesses is even greater. Customers can upgrade equipment without the need for a programmer. Just e-mail an HEX file and a small PC loader program.

Hardware

For this project the ECIO40 is selected. The ECIO40 is a 18F4455 PIC microcontroller with an USB connection and a bootloader. A bootloader is a tiny program that is pre-installed on the ECIO and can take care of programming itself. So no programmer is required for this project. To enable connection to the E-blocks an EB061 application board is used that basically just has a power connection and 5 ports. An EB004 LED board is connected to port B. Note the unusual configuration of ports on the application board!

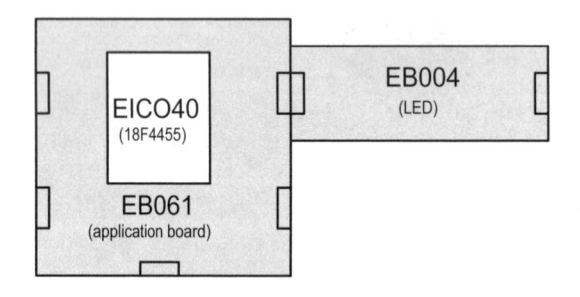

Figure 105. Schematic EICO bootloader.

Connection summary:

    Programmer   None.
    Microcontroller ECIO40, jumper to EXT, on an EB061 application board.
    Port B   EB004 LED board.

---

[21] You can download the required files from the Matrix Multimedia website http://www.matrixmultimedia.com/ECIO-X.php

3 Basic

Software

If you select the ECIO40 as target in Flowcode the configuration will be set automatically and cannot be changed by the user. Since this is a project on bootloading a simple program will be used that alternates two flashing LEDs. The program will write value 1 to port B, wait one second, then write value 2 to the port, and again wait one second. This will repeat forever.

Since 1 in 8 bit binary is 00000001 and 2 in 8 bit binary is 00000010 this program flips bits 0 and 1 alternating. And since LEDs D0 and D1 are connected to these bits the LEDs will flash.

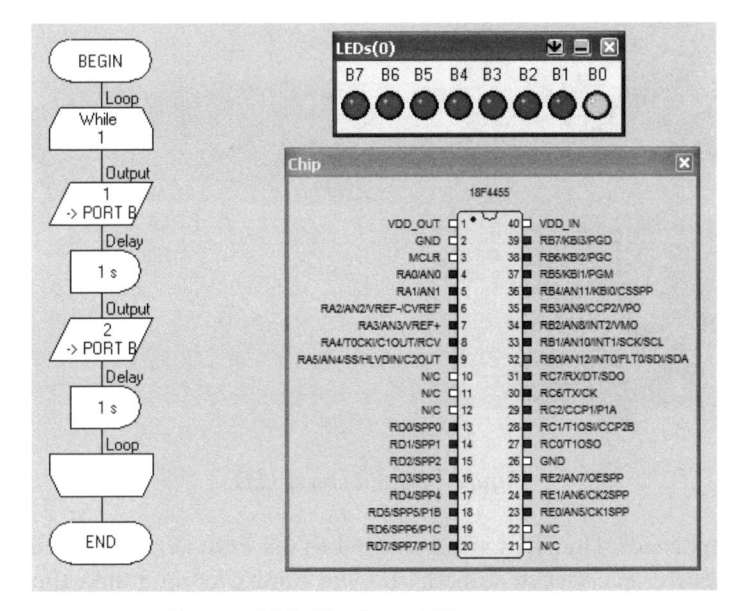

Figure 106. Flashing LED program.

Operational

Save the program and use compile to chip to download the program to the ECIO40. Make sure the USB cable is connected and the application board has power. After a few seconds an alert will pop up, see the next Figure.

97

3.12 Bootloader

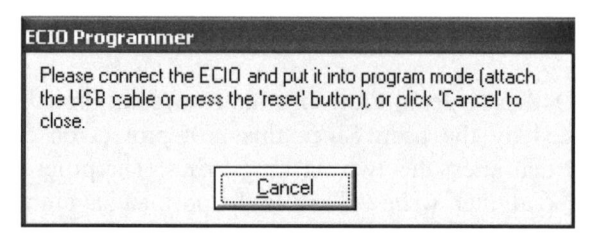

Figure 107. Connect ECIO or press reset button.

Press the little rest button on the ECIO40. The window will disappear again and the ECIO will program itself.

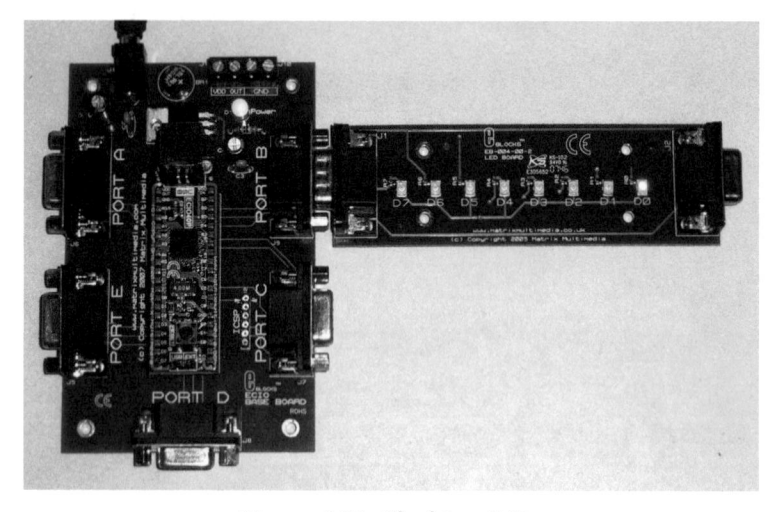

Figure 108. Flashing LED.

So what just happened? The HEX file was send to the ECIO40. When the reset button is pressed, or the power is connected, the ECIO will run a tiny program called a bootloader. This program will look at the USB connection to see if any HEX data is coming in. If there is no data the program will quickly time-out and start the normal program that is in program memory. But if there is a HEX file the tiny bootloader program inside the microcontroller will erase program memory, except the place where it resides itself, and then take the HEX file and write that into the just erased space. Then it will start the program that is contained in the HEX file.

Note that the ECIO does not contain any programmer hardware, just a few components for the USB connection, and a crystal as a clock.

Bootloading a HEX file

Change the program in Flowcode a bit, for example make the delays shorter, and save it. This way the new flashing rhythm will indicate if the next procedure was successful. Then compile to HEX but not to the ECIO (so use the Compile to HEX button with the zero's and one's on it). Then take the following steps:

1. Close Flowcode.
2. Start the program ECIOprog.exe. Ignore the warning "ECIO not found!"
3. Locate the HEX file that we just made, the one with the changed delay times. In the download package this file is called "ECIO book2.HEX. The ECIO programmer will now report "Program has been loaded".

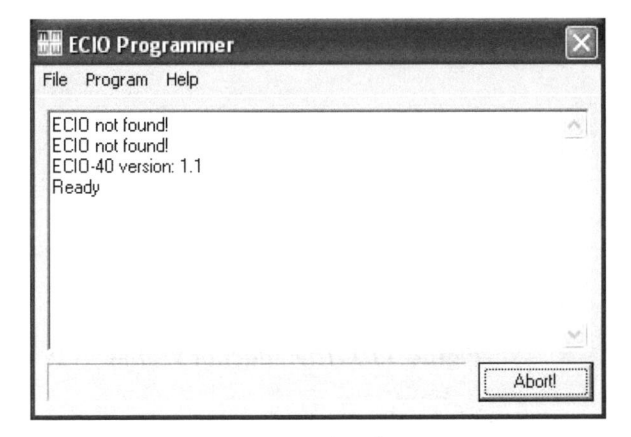

Figure 109. ECIO loader program.

4. Press the reset button on the ECIO40. The ECIO programmer should now report "ECIO-40 version 1.1".
5. Now select Program and then Send program from the menu. The program will now be sent to the ECIO40 which will program itself with it.
6. When the progress bar has reached the end take one of the following steps:
   1. Click on Program and then Reset the ECIO.
   2. Remove the USB cable, power the project down and then back up.

Both options will start the program. For a hobbyist method one would be most appropriate. In an industrial environment you may not want your program to start while it is still connected to a PC so method two might be better.

4.1 Vref+

4 Advanced

The projects in this chapter are more difficult than those in the previous chapter. It is assumed that the reader understands the basics of Flowcode and microcontrollers.

4.1 Vref+

Concept

Use the Vref+ to reduce the maximum voltage that the ADC channel will convert, and thus increase the accuracy. So rather than a scale from 0 to +5 volt the new scale is 0 to Vref+ volt as shown in the next Figure.

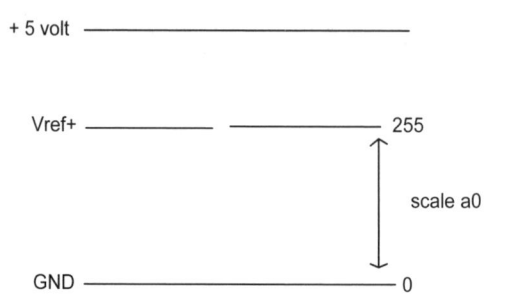

```
+ 5 volt  ─────────────────────

Vref+ ──────────   ────────── 255
                       ↑
                       │
                       │ scale a0
                       │
                       ↓
GND   ──────────────────────── 0
```

Figure 110. The effect of Vref+.

Note that if the voltage exceeds Vref+ the ADC value will remain at 255. Take care not to exceed the +V voltage (5 volts in this project) otherwise you will damage the microcontroller.

Hardware

For this project a 16F877A PIC microcontroller is selected, with a Proto board on port A and an LCD on port B. The Proto board has two 10k variable resistors with one end tied to the GND and the other end to +V. The center contact of one variable resistor is connected to A0, the center contact of the second one is connected to A3. Note that both the Proto board and the LCD board need power so you need to connect the +Vin terminals of both boards to one of the +V terminals of the Programmer board

4 Advanced

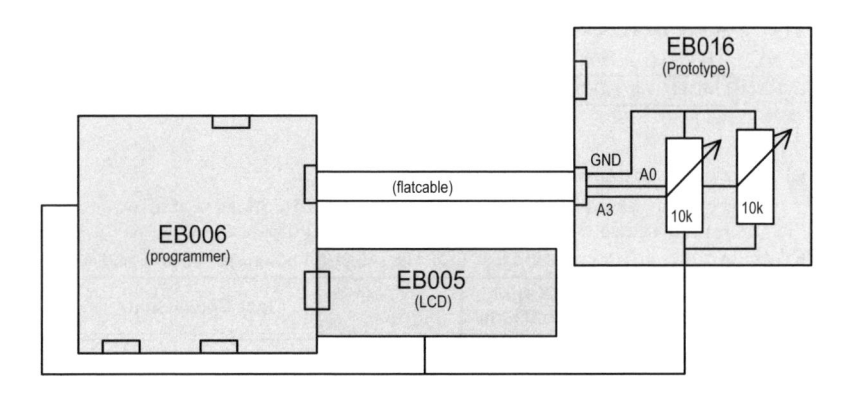

Figure 111. Schematic of the Vref+ hardware.

Connection summary:

Programmer	Switches to XTAL and Fast, LVP jumper on I/O port, J29 to PSU, J12-14 to USB, use external power supply.
Port A	EB016 Proto board. Two 10k variable resistors between GND and +V, Center contact of the first to A0. Center contact of the second to A3.
Port B	EB005 LCD, jumper to default.

Software

In the menu select Chip, then Configure and then switch to Expert Config Screen. In the section Configuration Word(s) make sure HEX is selected and then click on the Config1 button and enter: 0x3F3A.

In order to use a Vref+ signal the ADCON1 register must be set. There are multiple options as can be seen in the next Figure which is copied from the 16F877A datasheet.

In this project we will select the one with the arrow in the next Figure, like this in a C-box, note the semicolon at the end of the statement:

adcon1 = 0x01;

4.1 Vref+

REGISTER 11-2: ADCON1 REGISTER (ADDRESS 9Fh)

R/W-0	R/W-0	U-0	U-0	R/W-0	R/W-0	R/W-0	R/W-0
ADFM	ADCS2	—	—	PCFG3	PCFG2	PCFG1	PCFG0
bit 7							bit 0

bit 7 **ADFM:** A/D Result Format Select bit
1 = Right justified. Six (6) Most Significant bits of ADRESH are read as '0'.
0 = Left justified. Six (6) Least Significant bits of ADRESL are read as '0'.

bit 6 **ADCS2:** A/D Conversion Clock Select bit (ADCON1 bits in shaded area and in **bold**)

ADCON1 <ADCS2>	ADCON0 <ADCS1:ADCS0>	Clock Conversion
0	00	Fosc/2
0	01	Fosc/8
0	10	Fosc/32
0	11	FRC (clock derived from the internal A/D RC oscillator)
1	00	Fosc/4
1	01	Fosc/16
1	10	Fosc/64
1	11	FRC (clock derived from the internal A/D RC oscillator)

bit 5-4 **Unimplemented:** Read as '0'

bit 3-0 **PCFG3:PCFG0:** A/D Port Configuration Control bits

PCFG<3:0>	AN7	AN6	AN5	AN4	AN3	AN2	AN1	AN0	VREF+	VREF-	C/R
0000	A	A	A	A	A	A	A	A	VDD	VSS	8/0
0001	A	A	A	A	VREF+	A	A	A	AN3	VSS	7/1
0010	D	D	D	A	A	A	A	A	VDD	VSS	5/0
0011	D	D	D	A	VREF+	A	A	A	AN3	VSS	4/1
0100	D	D	D	D	A	D	A	A	VDD	VSS	3/0
0101	D	D	D	D	VREF+	D	A	A	AN3	VSS	2/1
011x	D	D	D	D	D	D	D	D	—	—	0/0
1000	A	A	A	A	VREF+	VREF-	A	A	AN3	AN2	6/2
1001	D	D	A	A	A	A	A	A	VDD	VSS	6/0
1010	D	D	A	A	VREF+	A	A	A	AN3	VSS	5/1
1011	D	D	A	A	VREF+	VREF-	A	A	AN3	AN2	4/2
1100	D	D	D	A	VREF+	VREF-	A	A	AN3	AN2	3/2
1101	D	D	D	D	VREF+	VREF-	A	A	AN3	AN2	2/2
1110	D	D	D	D	D	D	D	A	VDD	VSS	1/0
1111	D	D	D	D	VREF+	VREF-	D	A	AN3	AN2	1/2

A = Analog input   D = Digital I/O
C/R = # of analog input channels/# of A/D voltage references

Figure 112. The ADCON1 register of the 16F877A.

Unfortunately when Flowcode takes an ADC sample it will set ADCON1 itself thus overwriting our setting. Flowcode uses C as intermediary code, and if you take a look at

4 Advanced

the C file[22] how the ADC sample is taken you can see that the two bold lines cause the problems:

```
void FCD_ADC0_SampleADC()
{
    char ta, te, cnt;
    adcon1 = 0x00;
    ta = trisa;
    trisa = trisa | 0x2F;
    te = trise;
    trise = trise | 0x07;
    adcon0 = 0x81 | (0 << 3);
    cnt =0;
    while (cnt <40) cnt++;
    adcon0 = adcon0 | 0x04;
    while (adcon0 & 0x04) ;
    trisa = ta;
    trise = te;
    adcon1 = 0x07;
    adcon0 = 0x80;
}
```

The solution is to not use the Flowcode ADCmacro but instead write our own. This is easier than it sounds because we can simply copy the C code above and change

adcon1 = 0x00;

into

adcon1 = 0x01;

Since a C box is in fact a procedure the procedure heading doesn't need to be included.

Once the sample has been taken the normal ReadAsByte ADC macro can be used to put the answer into a variable. The next Figure shows the completed program.

---

[22] Select the menu "Chip" and then "View C code".

103

4.1 Vref+

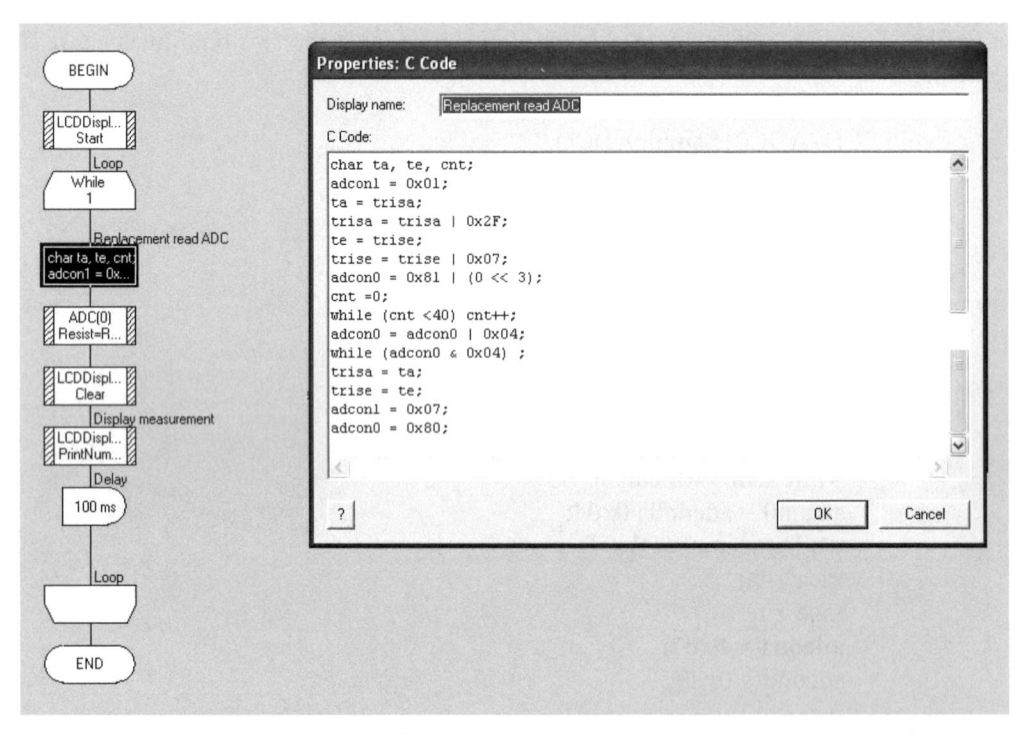

Figure 113. The completed Vref+ program with replacement ADC sampling.

Operational

The lower variable resistor, connected to A3, controls the Vref+ voltage. The upper variable resistor, connected to A0, is the "normal" measurement.

Set the lower variable resistor to a voltage of 2 V (use a multimeter). Now turn the knob of the upper variable resistor. The full ADC scale (0 - 255) is now from 0 to 2 Volt.

Note that you can use the same technique to set a Vref- level, meaning that the bottom of the range, currently zero, can be elevated. If you set Vref+ and Vref- both you could for example make a range from 2 to 3 volts, and still have a resolution of 255 steps!

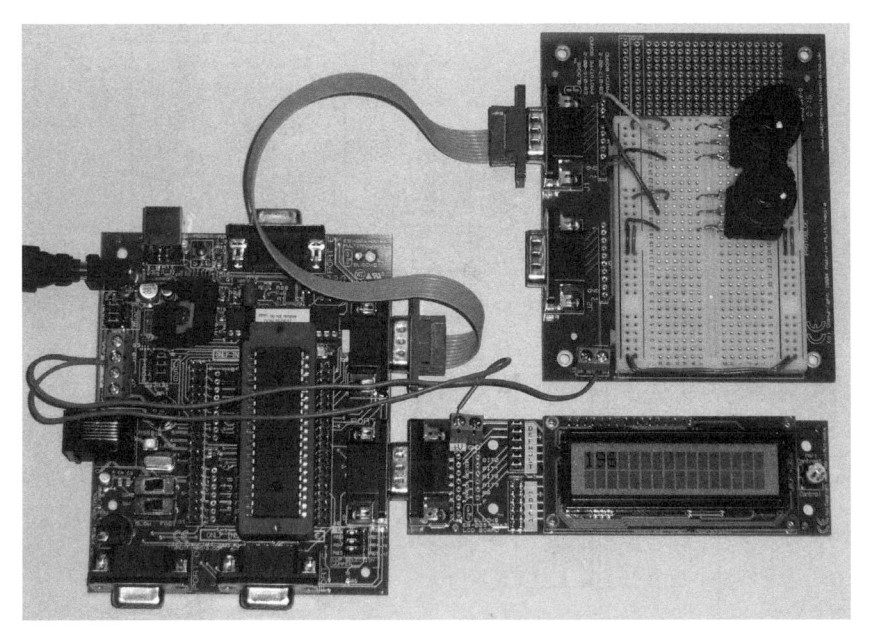

Figure 114. Vref+ measurement.

4.2 Record short sounds

Concept

Record a short sound and store it in FRAM (Fast Random Access Memory) memory, and play back using a DAC (Digital to Analog Converter).

Hardware

For this project a 16F877A PIC microcontroller is selected. You will need the microphone board from section 9.2. If you didn't build the board you can use the schematic given in that chapter to build the project on a Proto board. The EB004 LED board provides the LEDs. A switchboard (EB007) and SPI/DAC board (EB013) are also needed. A tiny loudspeaker (8 ohms, 0.25 W) is connected to the DAC.

4.2 Record short sounds

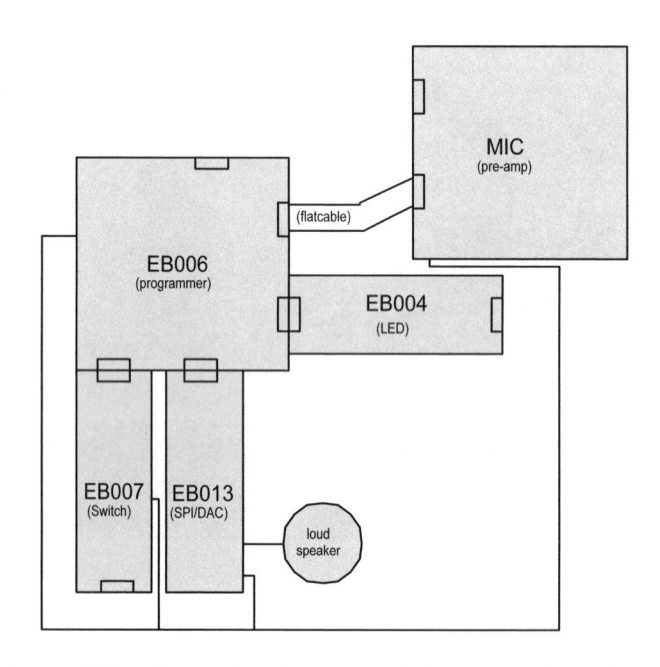

Figure 115. Schematic of the record short sounds project.

Note that the Microphone pre-amplifier, EB007 and EB013 need power so you need to connect the +Vin terminals to one of the +V terminals of the Programmer board

Connection summary:

Programmer	Switches to XTAL and Fast, LVP jumper on I/O port, J29 to PSU, J12-14 to USB, use external power supply.
Port A	A0 Microphone pre-amplifier.
	J1 first position, J2 right (pre-amplifier).
Port B	LED board.
Port C	SPI/DAC board, jumpers at 1 and A.
Port D	Switch board.

Software

In the menu select Chip, then Configure and then switch to Expert Config Screen. In the section Configuration Word(s) make sure HEX is selected and then click on the Config1 button and enter: 0x3F3A.

The SPI/DAC module is equipped with two chips, a 64 kbit FRAM FM25640 chip and a slower EEPROM 25LC640. The only chip fast enough for recording is FRAM, which has

4 Advanced

room for 64000/8 = 8000 bytes. At a sampling rate of 9600 Hz this is less than one second.

Unfortunately the project cannot handle 9600 Hz. The combination of taking an ADC sample and sending it to FRAM takes too long. For that reason recording takes more time than playback, so playback takes place at an increased speed. If you don't want a Donald Duck voice the highest workable speed is 4800 Hz which yields about 1.7 seconds of sound. Surprisingly enough it sounds quite intelligible.

FRAM memory on the EB013 is an SPI device. SPI (Serial Peripheral Interface Bus) is a three wire communications protocol using a input wire SDI, an output wire SDO and a clock wire SCK. The clock controls the communication speed. One of the chips is the master, the other the slave. The master controls the clock wire. Each time the clock toggles a bit is sent. Since there are two data lines the master and slave can talk at the same time. That means the protocol is ideally suited for continuous communication such as streaming audio and video.

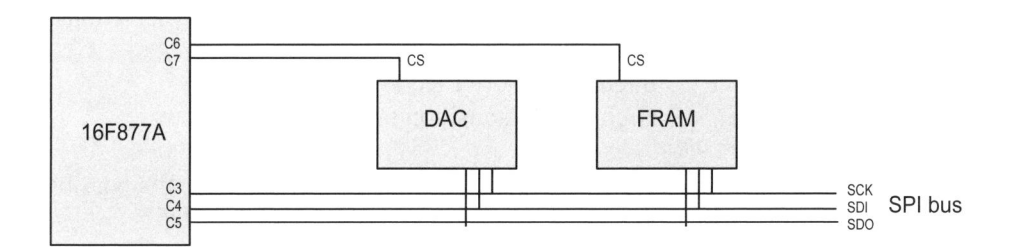

Figure 116. SPI setup for the EB013 with a 16F877A PIC.

If multiple devices are on the same wires a fourth wire is used to select which device is addressed, the Chip Select wire CS.

SPI clock	Fosc/4
SPOI clock polarity	idle_low
SPI clock edge	Data transmit on rising clock edge
SPI sample bit	Input sampled at middle of data output time
NVM enable	pin 6
DAC enable	pin 7
Send characters or bytes	Characters

Figure 117. SPI settings.

4.2 Record short sounds

First of all we need an SPI component for the EB013. In combination with the 16F877A the default settings can be used. Confirm that the settings as shown in the previous Figure are in use. Note that the pin numbers used are the numbers of the pins on port C and not on the D9 connector.

The next step is to initialize SPI, and enable FRAM (DAC does not have to be enabled) using two component macro symbols. A button is used to determine if the user wants to record (D0) or playback (D1) sound. Note that FRAM memory is retained even after the power is switched off.

Recording and playback have to take place at the exact same speed so an interrupt will be used. Select Enable interrupt and make the following selections:

Display name	Interrupt, or anything else you fancy.
Interrupt on	TMR0 overflow.

TMR0 is an abbreviation of Timer 0, a counter that increments from 0 to 255 and then starts again (overflows) at 0. Now click properties and make the following selections:

Clock source select	Internal clock (CLKO).
Source edge select	High to low transition on T0CKI.

The prescaler rate is where the actual interrupt frequency is set. These are the possibilities when using an 16F877A PIC with a clock speed or crystal at 19660800 Hz:

Prescaler	Interrupt frequency (Hz)
1:1	19200
1:2	9600
1:4	4800
1:8	2400
1:16	1200
1:32	600
1:64	300
1:128	150
1:256	75

Figure 118. TMR0 interrupt frequencies.

For this project a speed of 4800 Hz will be used, so the prescaler needs to be set to 1:4.

4 Advanced

For recording a sound the following steps have to be taken:

1. Increment the memory counter
2. Wait for the interrupt
3. Read the microphone signal using ADC
4. Store the value in FRAM
5. Loop back to step 1 until we're out of FRAM memory

In reality you need two loops for counting because FRAM memory locations are in bytes so both a high byte counter and low byte counter need to be incremented.

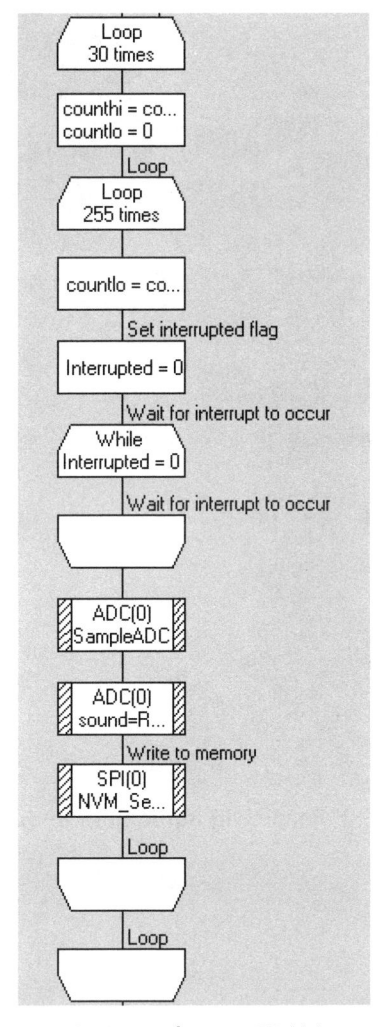

Figure 119. Recording in FRAM memory.

4.2 Record short sounds

Playback of the recorded sound is done similarly. After the interrupt a number is read from memory and sent to the DAC. Flowcode will take care of flipping the chip select lines for you.

Operational

The sound quality is not very good, because the recording frequency is rather low. If you try to speak with a clear voice you will be quite intelligible, but it will still sound like a very old radio transmission.

Figure 120. Recording equipment in operation.

4 Advanced

4.3 Cricket

A short recording of a cricket is prepared on a PC and then stored into Lookup Tables, see project 3.9. A smart randomized playback routine turns this tiny bit into a believable cricket. A DAC will be used to get excellent playback results. In the next chapter a low cost solution using PWM (Pulse Width Modulation) instead of DAC.

4.3.1 High quality version

Concept

This version uses a DAC (Digital to Analog Converter) to convert the data from the WAV file to audible sound waves. Since this is an exact reversal of the recording process that used an ADC (Analog to Digital Converter) this results in an optimum sound quality.

Hardware

For this project a 16F877A PIC microcontroller is selected. A DAC is connected to port C. A tiny loudspeaker of 8 ohms, 0.25 W is connected to the DAC. Note that the EB013 needs power so you need to connect the +Vin terminal to one of the +V terminals of the Programmer board.

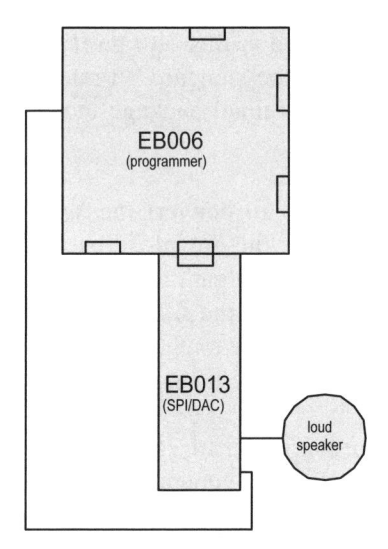

Figure 121. Schematic of the cricket project.

4.3 Cricket

Connection summary:

> Programmer   Switches to XTAL and Fast, LVP jumper on I/O port, J29 to PSU, J12-14 to USB, use external power supply.
> Port C   EB013 SPI/DAC board,
> Jumpers at A, 1 and FRAM.

Software

In the menu select Chip, then Configure and then switch to Expert Config Screen. In the section Configuration Word(s) make sure HEX is selected and then click on the Config1 button and enter: 0x3F3A.

In this project the sound data is stored in Lookup tables and send one by one to the DAC. Playback has to be done at a consistent rate; you will be able to hear the tiniest deviation. The best way to achieve this is to use the Timer 0 interrupt. The faster you can send data to the DAC module the better the sound quality, but also the more room you need (per second of sound you need more data). As a compromise we have opted for 9600 Hz, a frequency that can be easily realized with the Timer 0 interrupt. This frequency is called the bit rate.

So now we need to record a sound on the PC and store it in a WAV file, with a bit rate of 9600 Hz. Many programs can record at this bit rate (sampling rate), but when they store the file they automatically use a more standard bit rate. In this project we have used the sound program Cool Edit. The download package includes a WAV file you can use in case you don't own Cool Edit.

The WAVconvert program is used to convert the WAV file into lookup tables. This Visual Basic program is included in the download package. At the bottom left you enter the name of the WAV file, including the path. Make sure the filename and the path do not contain spaces. Click "view" to display the file. It will also display the bit rate, so if you made the file yourself this is a good time to check if the software you used actually stored the file at 9600 Hz. The length of the file is displayed at the bottom right corner.

A lookup table can contain a maximum of 255 bytes. The cricket sound is some 2500 bytes long so multiple tables will be generated by WAVconvert. Be sure to use the following settings:

> Encoding   Wav
> Output file   Lookup table
> Output Options   Standard

4   Advanced

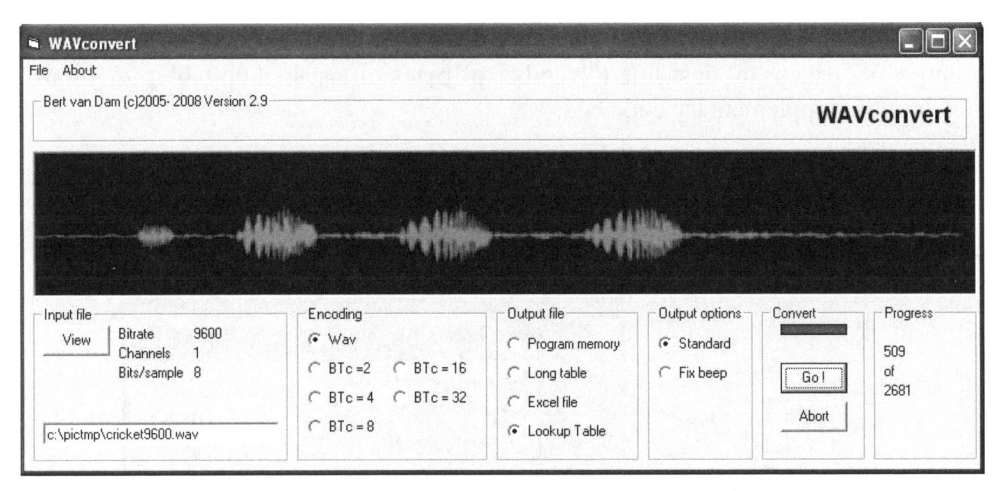

Figure 122. Converting WAV to Lookup table using WAVconvert.

In the same directory where the WAV file is located a file with an identical name but extension .TMP is created. This file contains the Lookup tables. The fragment shown in the next Figure only shows the first and the last table.

```
rom char* MAX0 = {
 128, 123, 125, 124, 125, 124, 124, 123, 126, 123, 124, 124, 126, 123, 125, 124  123, 125, 124,
 124, 126, 123, 124, 125, 124, 125, 123, 125, 124, 124, 125, 124, 125, 125, 124, 126, 127, 125,
 125, 128, 125, 127, 126, 126, 127, 125, 127, 127, 127, 128, 127, 128, 127, 128, 128, 128, 128,
 127, 128, 129, 128, 126, 129, 128, 128, 126, 128, 127, 126, 127, 126, 126, 126, 127, 124,
 125, 127, 126, 125, 123, 125, 125, 124, 125, 124, 124, 125, 124, 124, 124, 126, 124, 126, 124,
 124, 127, 123, 127, 124, 125, 128, 123, 126, 124, 126, 125, 125, 127, 123, 125, 125, 124, 126,
 124, 126, 125, 126, 127, 125, 126, 125, 127, 125, 126, 127, 127, 126, 127, 126, 128, 126, 128,
 126, 128, 128, 129, 128, 128, 126, 128, 127, 127, 128, 127, 127, 126, 129, 128, 125, 128, 126,
 127, 127, 127, 126, 125, 125, 125, 126, 127, 125, 125, 125, 123, 126, 124, 125, 125, 125, 124,
 123, 128, 124, 124, 126, 124, 125, 124, 124, 125, 124, 124, 125, 123, 126, 123, 126, 124, 126,
 124, 126, 125, 125, 126, 124, 125, 125, 127, 126, 126, 126, 127, 126, 127, 129, 127, 128, 126,
 127, 127, 127, 129, 126, 128, 128, 128, 128, 127, 127, 129, 127, 128, 128, 129, 127, 128, 128, 128,
 129, 128, 127, 127, 126, 127, 127, 126, 126, 127, 125, 126, 126, 126, 126, 124, 125, 125, 124,
 125, 125, 123, 124, 125, 125, 124, 125
};

[---- cut ----]

rom char* MAX10 = {
 124, 123, 124, 122, 125, 123, 124, 122, 125, 123, 121, 125, 122, 125, 123, 126  121, 126, 122,
 125, 123, 125, 124, 123, 123, 123, 125, 125, 125, 124, 125, 124, 126, 124, 126, 127, 126, 125,
 127, 125, 127, 125, 129, 126, 127, 128, 128, 127, 128, 129, 126, 130, 126, 129, 127, 127, 127,
 127, 127, 126, 127, 126, 127, 125, 126, 124, 127, 124, 127, 124, 126, 124, 126, 125, 123, 127,
 123, 127, 124, 125, 124, 125, 124, 125, 124, 124, 125, 126, 125, 124, 125, 123, 123, 123, 129
};
```

Number of bytes in last lookup table: 95

Figure 123. First and last Lookup table.

4.3 Cricket

The entire file except the last line ("Number of bytes in last lookup table: 95") must be copied into the supplementary code box.

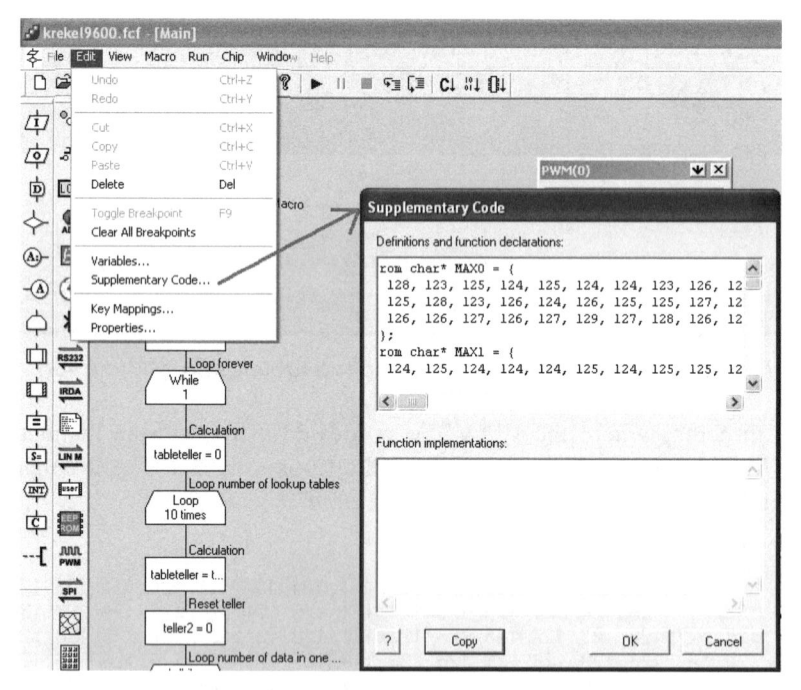

Figure 124. Lookup table in supplementary code box.

Reading data from these Lookup tables is described in chapter 3.9.

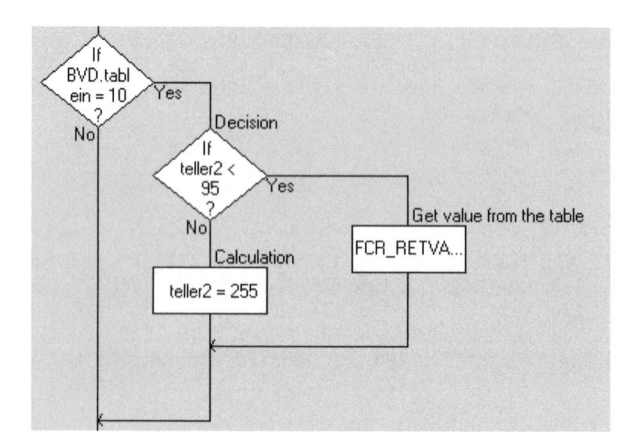

Figure 125. Make sure not to read past the end of the table.

4 Advanced

The 11th table (number 10) only contains 95 bytes (WAVconvert printed this message at the end of the conversion file), so a check is required when reading this table.

Use an SPI component in the program to allow sending data to the DAC. In combination with the 16F877A the default settings can be used. Confirm that the following settings are in use:

SPI clock	Fosc/4
SPOI clock polarity	idle_low
SPI clock edge	Data transmit on rising clock edge
SPI sample bit	Input sampled at middle of data output time
NVM enable	pin 6
DAC enable	pin 7
Send characters or bytes	Characters

Figure 126. SPI settings.

Note that the pin numbers used are the numbers of the pins on port C and not on the D9 connector.

The cricket sound is just one short "chirp". To turn this into a real sound a random number is drawn, see project 4.6. If this number is larger than 200, so in 22% of the cases, the cricket will be silent for two seconds. If the number is smaller than 200 than that will be the number of milliseconds that the cricket will be quiet. This simple mechanism proves surprisingly realistic.

Operational

Since the Lookup tables are in program memory their content is retained when the power is switched off.

Take the following steps to use your own sound recording:

1. Record the sound at a sampling (bit rate) of 9600 Hz.
2. Use WAVconvert to verify the sampling rate.
3. Use WAVconvert to convert the sound to Lookup tables.
4. Enter the Lookup tables into the Supplementary Code box.
5. Modify the "BVD" macro so it contains the right number of tables, and doesn't read past the end of the last table.
6. Modify the randomizer if needed.

4.3 Cricket

Figure 127. The cricket in action.

4.3.2 Low cost version

Concept

Even with the relatively low sampling rate of 9600 Hz the project still has a very good sound quality. By sacrificing some of that quality the total cost of the unit can be seriously reduced. Instead of a DAC we will make use of the built-in PWM (Pulse Width Modulation) module of the 16F877A.

Hardware

For this project a 16F877A PIC microcontroller is selected. A tiny loudspeaker of 8 ohms, 0.25 W is connected to a 1k variable resistor, which is in turn connected to the GND and C2.

4 Advanced

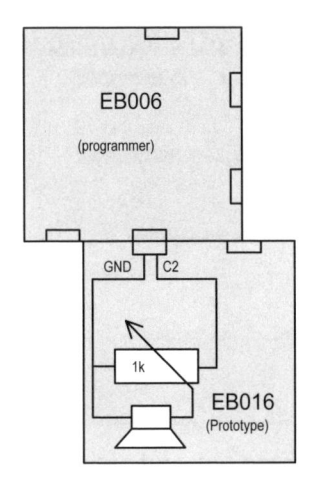

Figure 128. Schematic of the low cost version.

Connection summary:

>Port C   EB016 Prototype
>Variable resistor to GND and c2

If needed the variable resistor can be left out reducing the cost even further.

Software

In the menu select Chip, then Configure and then switch to Expert Config Screen. In the section Configuration Word(s) make sure HEX is selected and then click on the Config1 button and enter: 0x3F3A.

Add a PWM component to de program, and confirm that the following settings are used:

>Period register = 255
>Clock source = clk / 1

See project 4.7 for e detailed description of PWM. Enable PWM unit 1 (this is the unit connected to pin C2), and use the number retrieved from the Lookup table as duty cycle for this unit, as shown in the next Figure.

4.3 Cricket

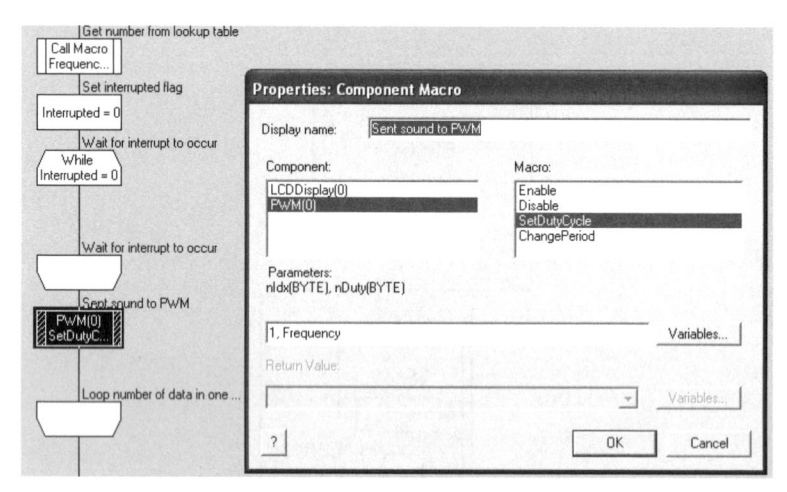

Figure 129. Feed the value to the PWM module.

The remainder of the program is basically identical to the "High Quality Version", see the file in the download.

Operational

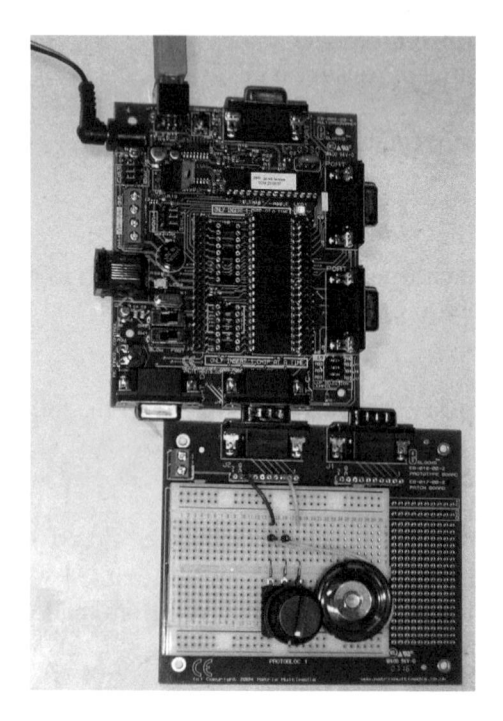

4 Advanced

4.4 Custom Characters

Concept

Design your own character for the LCD screen (a cherry) and display it. Once this project is completed carry on with the next project to make a small animation.

Hardware

For this project we will use the ATMEGA 32 AVR microcontroller, in combination with an LCD screen. Note that the LCD board needs power so you need to connect the +Vin terminal to the +V terminals of the Programmer board.

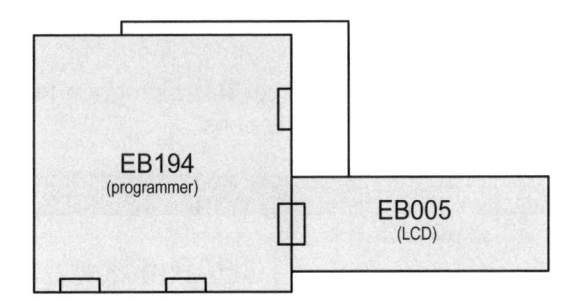

Figure 130. Schematic of the custom character hardware.

Connection summary:

    Programmer   EB194, jumper to default.
    Port B   EB005 LCD, jumper to default.

Software

If you haven't done so already first of all make sure that the fuses of the ATMEGA 32 are set correctly to 0x0,0xdf and 0x1,0xff. Select the "Chip" menu and "Configure". Enter the settings and remember to click on the Ok and Send button, because they will not be transferred by default. Of course the AVR programmer must be connected to the PC and powered on for this to work.

The LCD controller on the LCD board has eight custom definable character spaces. These correspond to the ASCII characters 0 through seven, which normally serve as control codes and were never meant to be printed anyway. See project 3.1 for an overview of the available characters.

4.4 Custom Characters

Characters are 5 columns by 8 rows in size. LCD characters usually leave the lowest row empty to leave room for the cursor. Each row is represented by one byte, so to define a custom character you need eight bytes. The next Figure shows how to draw a custom character (a cherry) and convert it into these eight bytes.

			x		00010 = 2
		x			00100 = 4
		x			00100 = 4
	x	x	x		01110 = 14
x				x	10001 = 17
x				x	10001 = 17
	x	x	x		01110 = 14
					00000 = 0

Figure 131. Cherry as custom character.

In the download package you will find a Visual Basic program to help you define these characters without the binary to decimal conversions.

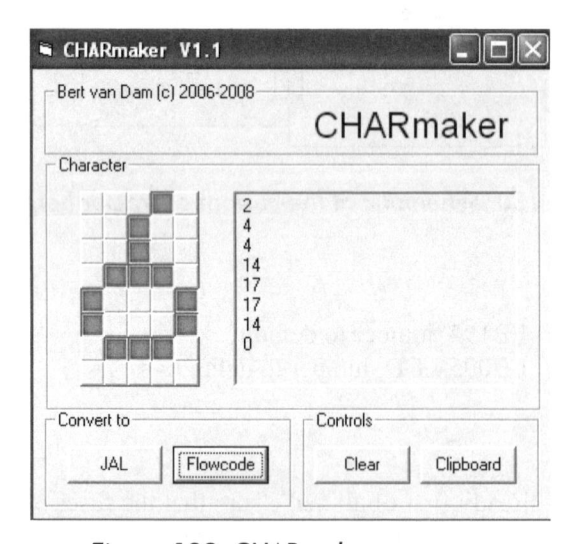

Figure 132. CHARmaker program.

Simply draw the character by clicking the tiny squares on and off. When the character is completed click on the Flowcode button in the Convert to section.

In order to get this new character into the LCD the following steps need to be taken:

4   Advanced

1. Give an LCD command with the memory address.

The following Figure shows the memory address of the eight ASCII signs that can be used for custom characters. The last column shows how to display these characters on the LCD.

ASCII	Memory address	Display on LCD screen
0	64	printASCII(0)
1	72	printASCII(1)
2	80	printASCII(2)
3	88	printASCII(3)
4	96	printASCII(4)
5	104	printASCII(5)
6	112	printASCII(6)
7	120	printASCII(7)

Figure 133. Memory addresses of the custom character spaces.

This program snippet shows how the ASCII 0, at memory address 64, can be opened for transfer.

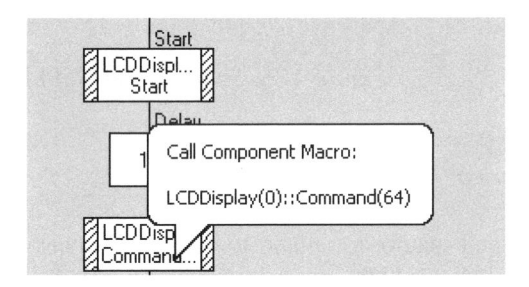

Figure 134. Open ASCII 0 for writing.

2. Send the eight bytes.

This is done by using the PrintASCII() command eight times.

4.4 Custom Characters

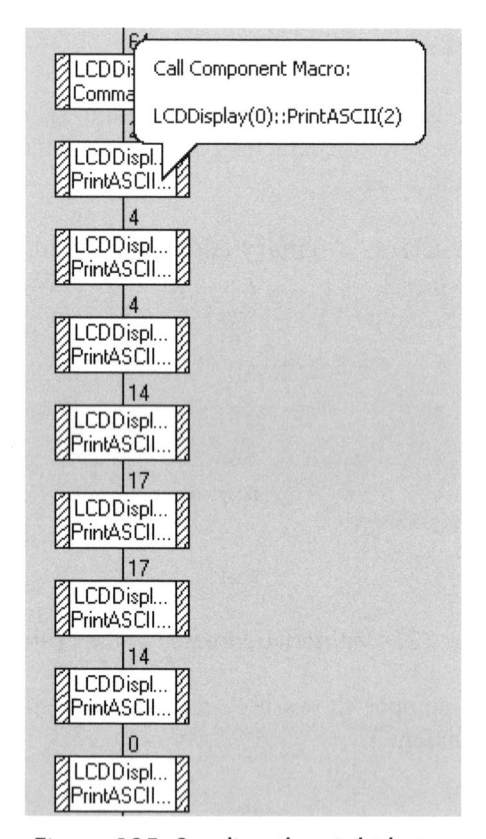

Figure 135. Sending the eight bytes.

3. Close with any normal operation.

Use any normal macro command to restore normal operation, move for example the cursor to location 0,0.

The character is now loaded into the LCD display and can be used by issuing a PrintASCII(0) command. Note that the LCD memory is retained even when the power is switched off. If you want another character at this memory location simply overwrite it.

Operational

As soon as the program is downloaded it will start automatically and show the cherry.

4 Advanced

Figure 136. The cherry on the LCD.

4.5 Animation

Concept

Use the technique of the previous project to display a tiny animation.

Hardware

Use the exact same hardware as in the previous project. In fact if you haven't done so already it is recommended you try that project first.

Software

Normally speaking an animation would be made by first writing a series of custom made characters into LCD memory and then displaying them in the right sequence. This limits the animation to eight frames since there are only eight character spaces.

Interestingly enough a custom character can be modified while it is being displayed, simply by overwriting the LCD memory location with a new character. This means the

123

4.6 Random

number of animation frames[23] is virtually unlimited. When stored for example in a Lookup table, see project 3.9 one could envision that an entire animation movie might be made using a single LCD memory location.

At the end of the program from the previous project write a new character to the same memory location (64) and restore operation by moving the cursor. These two parts are now placed into a Loop forever.

Operational

Due to a stunning lack of creativity the second custom character is a series of horizontal stripes, so the animation changes a cherry into a row of horizontal stripes and back.

Figure 137. The animation changes the cherry into stripes.

4.6 Random

Concept

Generate random numbers, a small exercise in C language.

Hardware

For this project a 16F877A PIC microcontroller is selected, with a Switch board on port A and an LCD on port B. Note that both the Switch board and the LCD board need power so you need to connect the +Vin terminals of both boards to one of the +V terminals of the Programmer board

---

[23] A frame is a single picture in an animation or movie.

4   Advanced

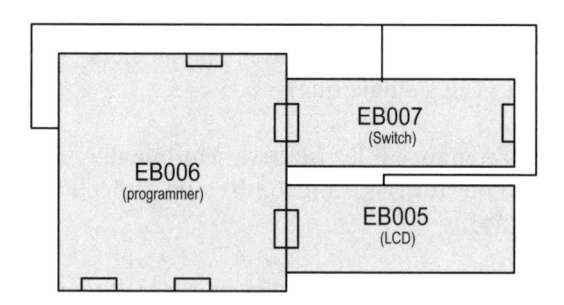

Figure 138. Random numbers hardware.

Connection summary:

    Programmer   Switches to XTAL and Fast, LVP jumper on I/O port, J29 to PSU, J12-14 to USB, use external power supply.
    Port A   EB007 Switch board.
    Port B   EB005 LCD, jumper to default.

Software

In the menu select Chip, then Configure and then switch to Expert Config Screen. In the section Configuration Word(s) make sure HEX is selected and then click on the Config1 button and enter: 0x3F3A.

Obviously real random number generators written purely in software do not exist. Whatever the program is, its outcome is by definition predetermined and thus not random. Pseudo random number generators use complicated calculations that make numbers appear random to humans. Random enough anyway for games and the like.

Flowcode doesn't have a random number generator, but C does. And since Flowcode is basically a graphical layer around C we can mix C code freely with Flowcode, and assembler too for that matter.

First the proper C library needs to be available. The 16F877A PIC is a 16 bit microcontroller, so the library for 16 bit PICs is required: rand.pic16.lib. This is done in two steps:

    1. Firstly go to Edit -> Supplementary code and add the following line to the definitions window.

        #include <rand.h>

4.6 Random

2. Then goto Chip -> Compiler options and add the following to the linker parameter: rand.pic16.lib The Linker parameters should end up looking something like this (on a single line):

-ld "C:\Program Files\Matrix Multimedia\Flowcode V3\BoostC\lib" libc.pic16.lib flowcode.pic16.lib rand.pic16.lib "%f.obj" -t PIC%p -d "%d" -p "%f"

The pseudo random function needs to be seeded (initiated if you like) with a value. If you use the exact same value each time, then you get the exact same random numbers, so we will seed with timer 0[24]. Drag a C-code symbol into the program and add the following code:

srand (tmr0);

Now every time you need a random value use a C-code symbol with the following code:

FCV_RANDOM = rand ();

So how random is this? The next Figure shows a series of random numbers paired up and put in a graph. It would appear that this is random enough for practical purposes.

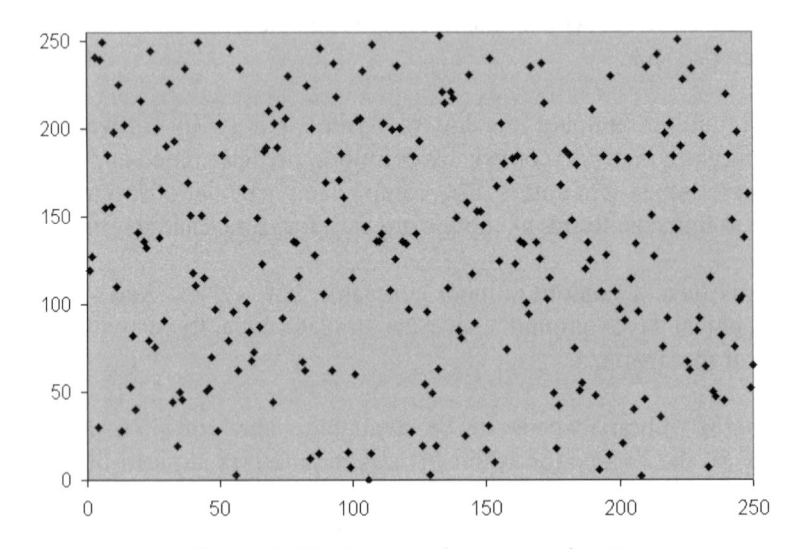

Figure 139. How random is random?

---

[24] When you are comparing two programs it may actually be beneficially to test them against the exact same "random" numbers. In that case seed with a known value.

4 Advanced

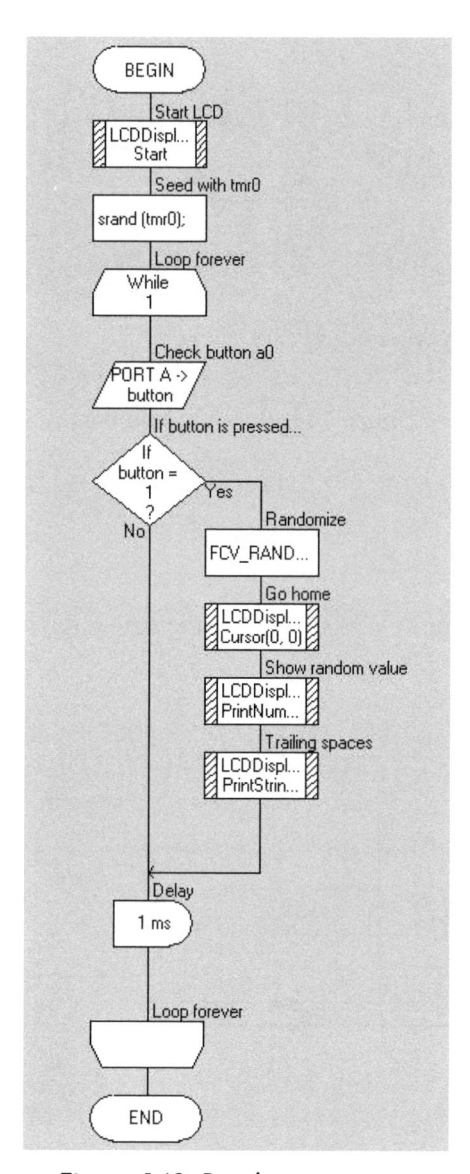

Figure 140. Random program.

Operational

Power the unit. Every time you press button A0 a new random value is shown on the LCD. Linker information is not project dependent but part of the general Flowcode settings. So remember to remove the random library once the project is completed.

4.7 A fan on PWM

Figure 141. Random numbers.

4.7 A fan on PWM

Concept

Use Pulse Width Modulation (PWM) to control the speed of a small fan.

Hardware

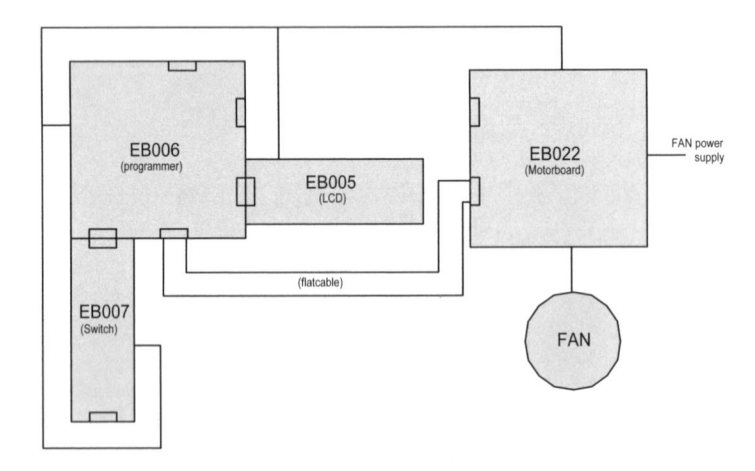

Figure 142. Schematic Pulse Width Modulation.

For this project a 16F877A PIC microcontroller is selected. A small 12 volts 0.15 Amp fan is used. Since the fan consumes more power than the microcontroller can deliver an EB022 Motor board is used.

4 Advanced

Connection summary:

Programmer	Switches to XTAL and Fast, LVP jumper on I/O port, J29 to PSU, J12-14 to USB, use external power supply.
Port B	LCD, jumper to default.
Port C	EB022 motor board, lower D9 plug
Port D	EB007 Switch board

The EB022 is a very flexible board and thus rather complicated. The upper half of the board, with the D9 connectors facing left, is the sensor part, the lower part is the motor part.

Figure 143. EB022 sensor section.

1. D9 connector of the sensor section of the EB022. If the default is used (at 2 the jumpers on A, at 3 the jumpers on default) the pins are connected as follows:

pin	connection
1	consumption motor (A of 1)
2	consumption motor (B of 2)
3	quad (block 5) top screw
4	quad (block 5) center crew
5	quad (block 5) bottom screw
6	open (patch panel)
7	open (patch panel)
8	open (patch panel)
9	GND

Figure 144. Top D9 connector.

129

4.7 A fan on PWM

2. These jumpers route the signal from the quad connector (5) to the D9 connector. The numbers in the table indicate the pin numbers on this D9 connector.

connection	jumper op block		
	A	B	C
quad (block 5) top screw	3	4	patch 1
quad (block 5) center screw	4	5	patch 2
quad (block 5) bottom screw	5	6	patch 3

Figure 145. Jumpers block 2.

3. These jumpers route the motor consumption signals to the pins on the D9 connector.

signal	jumper on default	jumper on patch
motor consumption	1	patch 4
motor consumption	2	patch 5

Figure 146. Jumpers on block 3.

4. These are the feedback connectors. They are connected to the patch panel only.

5. These are the quad connections routed to the D9 pins as described at item 2.

Figure 147. EB022 motor section.

4 Advanced

1. Power connector for the board itself, so +5 Volt.

2. Power connector for the motors, maximum 46 volt.

3. D9 connector to the microcontroller. The "Pin on microcontroller" column assumes a 16F877A as in this project, but it can be connected to any microcontroller (or another port on the 16F877A if you don't want to use PWM). This table is valid with the jumper from item 4 on default.

pin	pin on microcontroller	connection
1	C0	in 1 (motor A or 1)
2	C1 (CCP2)	in2 (motor A or 1)
3	C2 (CCP1)	in 3 (motor B or 2)
4	C3	in 4 (motor B or 2)
5	C4	optional Enable A (see item 6)
6	C5	optional Enable B (see item 6)
7	C6	
8	C7	
9		GND

Figure 148. Lower D9 connector.

4. The jumper to the right (default) yields the connections as shown in the previous Figure, to the left means all connection can be patched at will.

5. Connections to the motor. The terms "A" and "1" are used for the left connector, "B" and "2" for the right connection. Technical data for the motors::

Voltage	max 46 volt
Consumption	max 2 Amp
Peak consumption	max 3 Amp

The peak consumption is allowed for short periods of time such as start-up, as long as the total power consumption is below 4 Amps. For more information consult the datasheets of the L298 and L6210.

4.7 A fan on PWM

6. This jumper routes the motor enable signal.

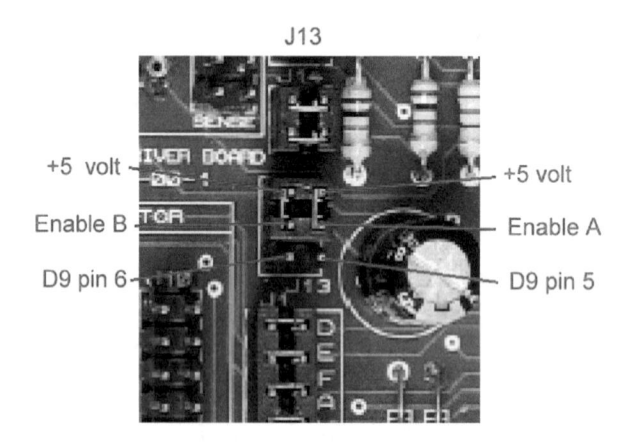

Figure 149. Jumper routing the motor enable signal.

Default the enable contacts of both motors are connected to +5V, so they can always be used. Optionally you can connect the enable signals to pins of the D9 connector so motors can be disabled (switched off) without touching any of the other settings, such as speed. The possible options are shown in the next Figure.

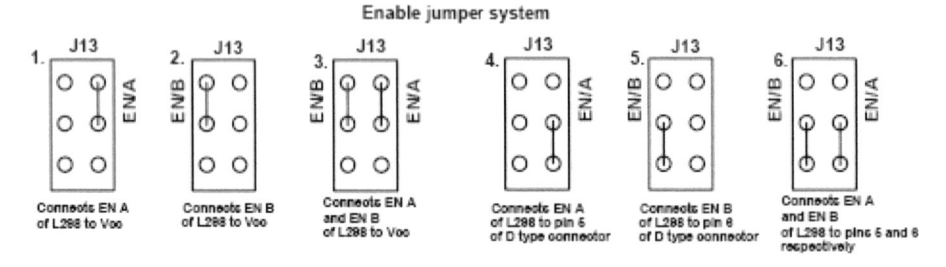

Figure 150. Motor enable jumper options.

So for this application make the following connections:

- Fan on motor contacts OUT1 and OUT2
- Board power to +V
- Fan power to VPWR
- Jumpers on A, default, pos 2 of the previous Figure, default

Note that all boards in this project need power so you need to connect the +Vin terminal to one of the +V terminals of the Programmer board.

4   Advanced

Software

In the menu select Chip, then Configure and then switch to Expert Config Screen. In the section Configuration Word(s) make sure HEX is selected and then click on the Config1 button and enter: 0x3F3A.

The simplest way to control the speed of an electric motor would be to vary the voltage between 0 and the maximum voltage. Unfortunately this doesn't work. First of all, the motor needs a minimum voltage to get started, so it will immediately go from off to relatively fast. Secondly, the torque at low speeds is extremely low. The solution is to keep the voltage constant the maximum - which eliminates starting problems - and simply switch the power on and off. If you do that quickly enough the motor will run very smoothly, even at low revolutions. If the motor needs to run faster keep the power a bit longer on than off. This technique is called Pulse Width Modulation or PWM because the width of the pulses (the time that the power is switched on) is varied, or modulated.

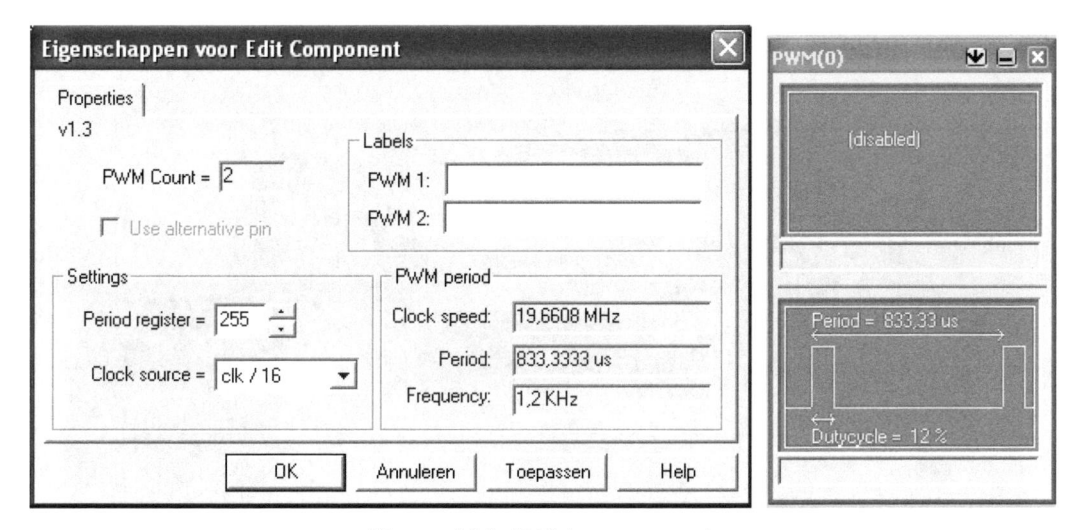

Figure 151. PWM component.

First add a PWM component to your program and press the down arrow. The clock source sets the frequency of the pulses that go to the motor. It may take a bit of trial and error to see which frequency works best for the motor that you are using. High frequencies may cause start-up problems because the pulses are short, low frequencies may cause a beep-like noise at low revolutions.

The period determines how long a period is. Obviously that has an impact on the frequency of the signal too. The particular fan we are using is very difficult to start so we will use these settings:

4.7 A fan on PWM

    Clock source   clk / 16
    Period register   255

Once this is taken care, of add a component macro symbol to the program and set "PWM Enable" with parameter 2. Oddly enough motor 1 is connected to CCP2.

In order to change the speed of the motor use a component macro symbol with parameters 2 and the desired duty cycle.

The rest of the program is straight forward, and can be found in the download package listed under this chapter number.

Operational

Connect the power to both Programmer and the motor board and use the D0 button to increase the speed and the D1 button to decrease the speed. The actual duty cycle will be displayed on the LCD.

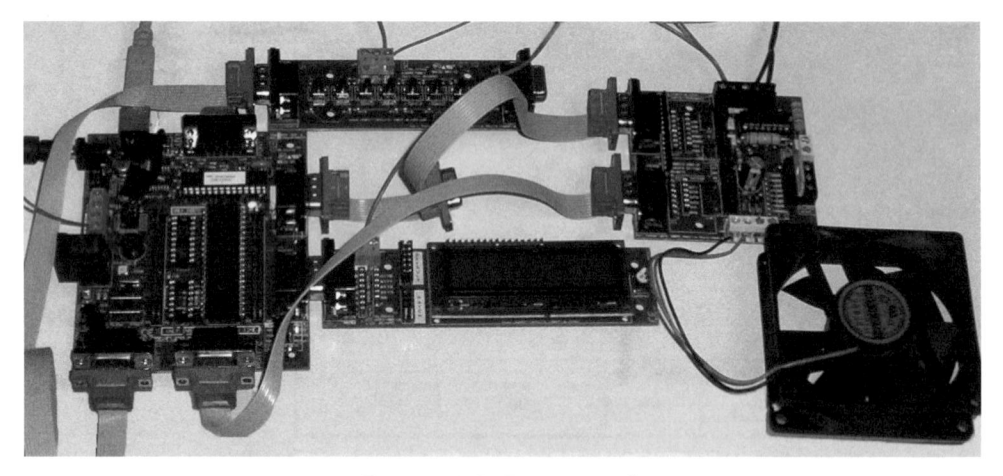

Figure 152. Fan control.

Feedback

The previous Figure has a feedback flat ribbon cable installed from the upper D9 on the motor board to port A of the Programmer board, which is not used in this project. The motor board generates a feedback signal for motor 1 on A0, directly proportional to the power consumption of the connector to motor 1. The fan motor is very small and gives a small reading. At startup the reading is about 7 or 8, but when the fan is running full throttle the value drops to 3 to 4.

4 Advanced

If your motor has a wider range in power consumption read the value on A0 using and ADC component and display it on the LCD.

4.8 Persistence of vision

Concept

Make use of the slowness of the human eye, persistence of vision, to paint text in the air.

Hardware

For this project a 16F877A PIC microcontroller is selected, with a LED board. The LED board is connected to the programmer with a very long flat ribbon cable because you will have to swing it through the air during operation. The recommended length is 2 meters or more.

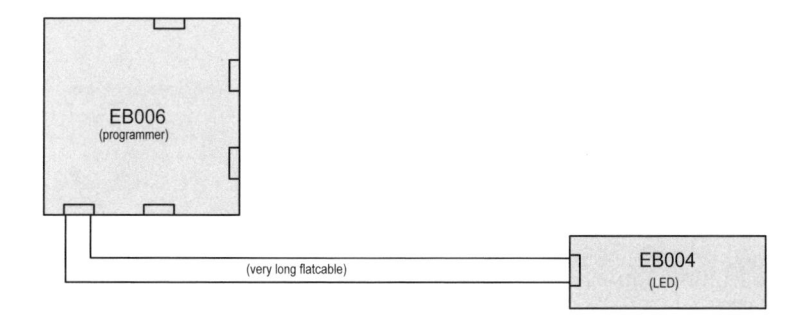

Figure 153. Persistence of vision hardware with extra long flat ribbon cable.

Connection summary:

Programmer	Switches to XTAL and Fast, LVP jumper on I/O port, J29 to PSU, J12-14 to USB, use external power supply.
Port D	EB004 LED board.

Software

In the menu select Chip, then Configure and then switch to Expert Config Screen. In the section Configuration Word(s) make sure HEX is selected and then click on the Config1 button and enter: 0x3F3A.

Persistence of vision means that an image you see remains visible to your brain for a very short time even after the image is gone. In this project we will make use of this

135

4.8 Persistence of vision

"slowness" of your eye. First we show a part of a letter by lighting a series of LEDs. Then we move the LEDs slightly to the right and show the second part of that letter. Again we move the LEDs slightly and show the next part of that letter. If we do this fast enough the first part of the letter is still visible to your eye by the time we are completely done showing that particular letter, or in fact a whole series of letters. So it appears a complete text is written in the air.

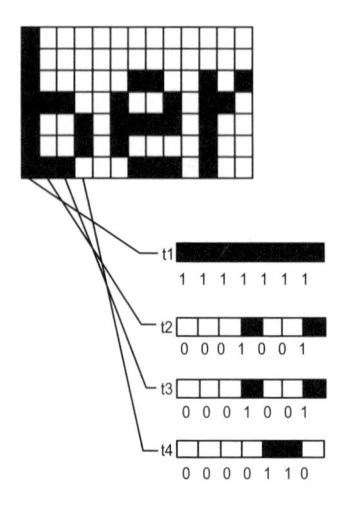

Figure 154. Building the data file.

The previous Figure shows how a text is split up into vertical lines. Each square represents a LED. Black means the LED is lit, white means it is off. At the start (t_1) all LEDs are lit. A very short moment later (t_2) only two of the LEDs are lit. In the meantime the LEDs must have move a bit to the right. Another short moment later (t_3) still two LEDs are lit, et cetera. This way the entire text can be decoded into LED lighting instructions. Doing this manually is rather tedious so a small Visual Basic program is included in the download file to help you.

First enter the name of a file that you want the data to be written to, and click on the "Start lookup table" button. Then draw the letters by clicking on the tiny squares. When you are done select all the lines that need to go into the file and click on the "Add marked columns" button. If the screen isn't large enough clear it and add more columns. You can add as many as you like, but the longer the text is the longer your arm needs to be! When you have added all the text that you want click on the "Finish lookup table" button.

4 Advanced

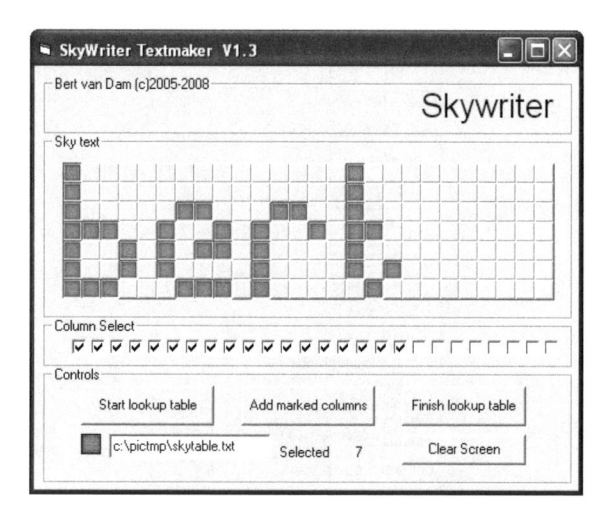

Figure 155. Skywriter data builder

For the example in the previous Figure the file would contain the following information:

> rom char* SKY = { 127 , 72 , 72 , 48 , 0 , 56 , 68 84 , 88 , 0 ,
> 120 , 4 , 4 , 8 , 0 , 63 , 72 , 32 };
>
> -- sweep back 18 times.

These numbers must be fed to the LED board at regular intervals. While displaying the text you must move the LED board swiftly through the air. The "sweep back 18 times" indicates how long the LEDs should remain off to give you enough time to sweep your arm back.

First open the file and copy the Lookup table into a supplementary code box, declarations section. Next make a loop which repeats 18 times (the number indicated in the file). Read the first number from the Lookup and send it to the LED board table, see project 3.9 for more information on Lookup tables. Wait three milliseconds and get the next number.

After the loop add a delay symbol with 18 x 3 ms = 54 ms for the sweep back.

Repeat the whole process indefinitely by using a Loop While 1.

137

4.8 Persistence of vision

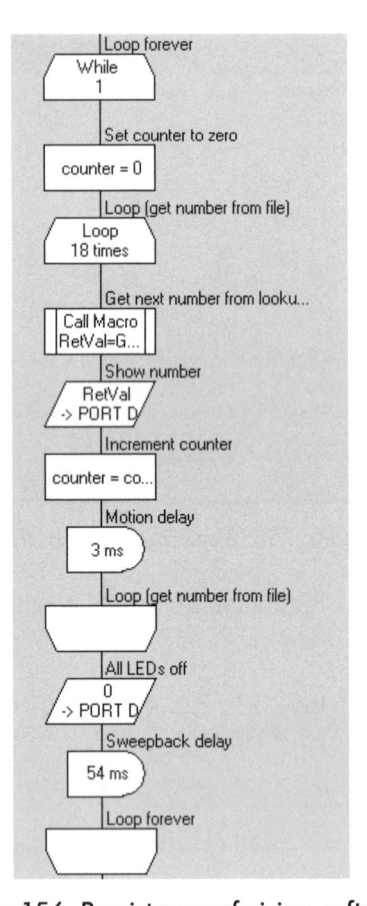

Figure 156. Persistence of vision software.

Operational

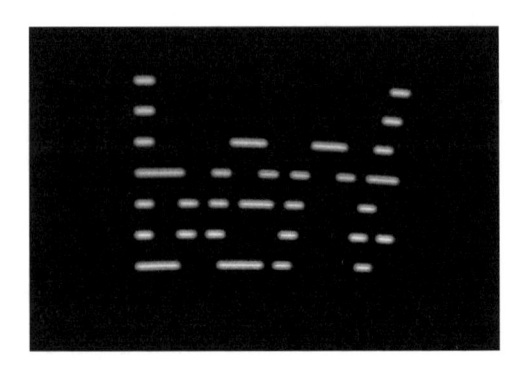

Figure 157. A word painted in the air.

4 Advanced

This project works best in dim light or complete darkness. Switch it on and wave the LED board back and forth in a regular motion. It takes a bit of fiddling to get the motion just right but then suddenly letters appear in the sky.

The previous Figure shows this project in the dark. Don't hold the LED board by the flat ribbon cable otherwise the D9 connector will come loose and catapult the board into the nearest expensive object.

Figure 158. Not much to see without waving it in the dark.

Note that you cannot run this program in simulation because Flowcode is unable to simulate Lookup tables.

4.9 Flash memory

Concept

Flash memory would be an interesting place to store data, assuming the program itself, which also lives in Flash, is not too large. The normal way to use flash for data storage would be to use Lookup tables, see project 3.9. This requires however that the data to be stored is known at programming time and doesn't change. In this chapter a technique is discussed to store and retrieve data on the fly. This means that data could be recorded or sampled and stored in the process.

4.9 Flash memory

This is the memory overview for the 16F877A microcontroller:

Name	Size	Purpose
Flash or program memory	8192 words of 14 bits	The program itself, or Lookup tables. Retained after power off.
Random Access Memory (RAM)	368 bytes of 8 bits	Variables used in the program. Lost after power off.
Electronically Erasable Programmable Read Only Memory (EEPROM)	256 bytes of 8 bits	Data storage used by the programmer. Retained after power off.

Figure 159. Memory overview of the 16F877A microcontroller.

Hardware

For this project a 16F877A PIC microcontroller is selected, with a Switch board on port A and an LCD on port B. Note that both boards need power so you need to connect the +Vin terminal of both boards to one of the +V terminals of the Programmer board

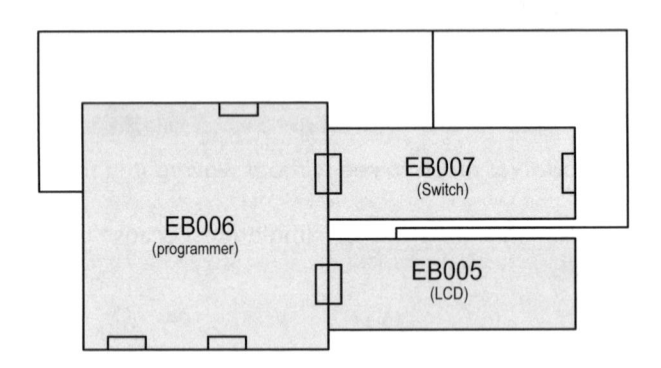

Figure 160. Schematic of the flash project hardware.

Connection summary:

Programmer	EB006 Switches to XTAL and Fast, LVP jumper on I/O port, J29 to PSU, J12-14 to USB, use external power supply.
Port A	EB007 Switch board.
Port B	EB005 LCD, jumper to default.

4   Advanced

Software

In the menu select Chip, then Configure and then switch to Expert Config Screen. In the section Configuration Word(s) make sure HEX is selected and then click on the Config1 button and enter: 0x3F3A.

There are no Flowcode commands to read and write to flash memory, but it does come with a C library with appropriate functionality. First of all the definitions and function declaration of this library needs to be added to the supplementary code:

   #include <flash.h>

The next step is to add the library to the linker. In the Chip menu open the Compiler options and add the library flash.pic16.lib to the parameter list in the Linker/Assembler options, as can be seen in the next Figure. Linker information is not project dependent but part of the general Flowcode settings. So remember to remove this library once the project is completed.

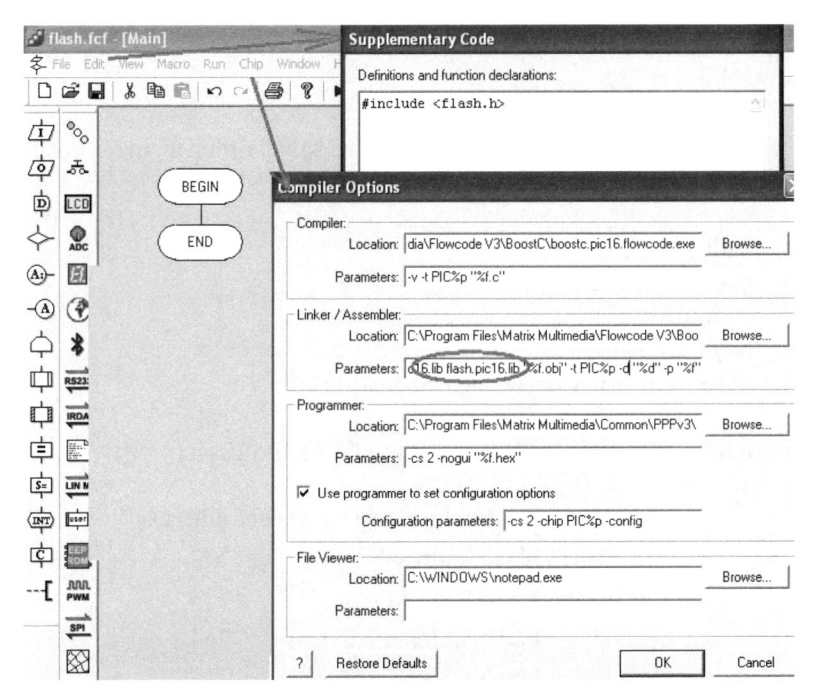

Figure 161. Adding the flash.pic16.lib library.

Since the microcontroller program itself is in flash memory too the first thing to do is check how much space is available, or rather what the first available memory location is.

4.9 Flash memory

The best way to approach this is to simply write the program, using a dummy start address for the data storage, and load it into the microcontroller. Once Flowcode is done a message is displayed which states how much memory is used.

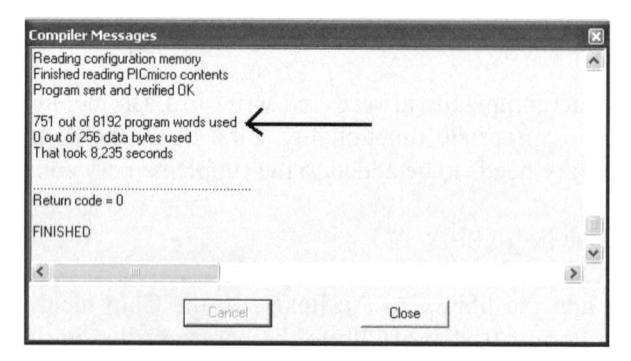

Figure 162. Used flash memory.

So in this example 751 bytes were used. That means data can be stored starting at memory location 752.

      FlashAddress = 752

The Flash_write function stores four bytes at the same time, in incrementing memory addresses. For example the numbers 1, 212, 63 and 40.

      flash_loadbuffer(1);
      flash_loadbuffer(212);
      flash_loadbuffer(63);
      flash_loadbuffer(40);
      flash_write(FCV_FLASHADDRESS);

The previous code (in a C-box) will store data to these addresses:

data	relative address	real address
1	FlashAddress	752
212	FlashAddress + 1	753
63	FlashAddress + 2	754
40	FlashAddress + 3	755

Figure 163. Data storage in flash memory.

The next Figure shows the Flowcode program section that stores the data including the C snippets shown before.

4   **Advanced**

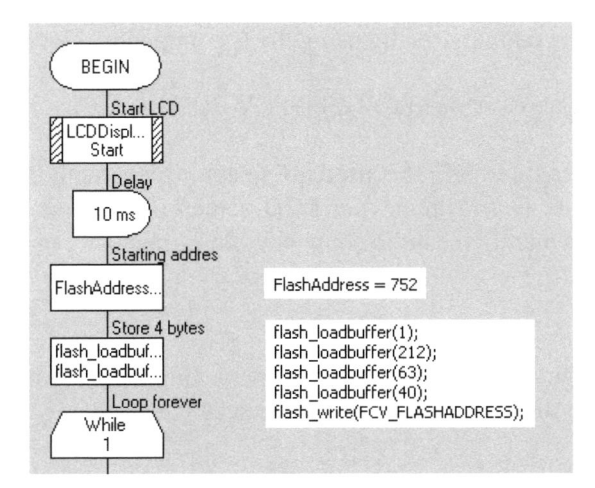

Figure 164. Storing data in flash memory.

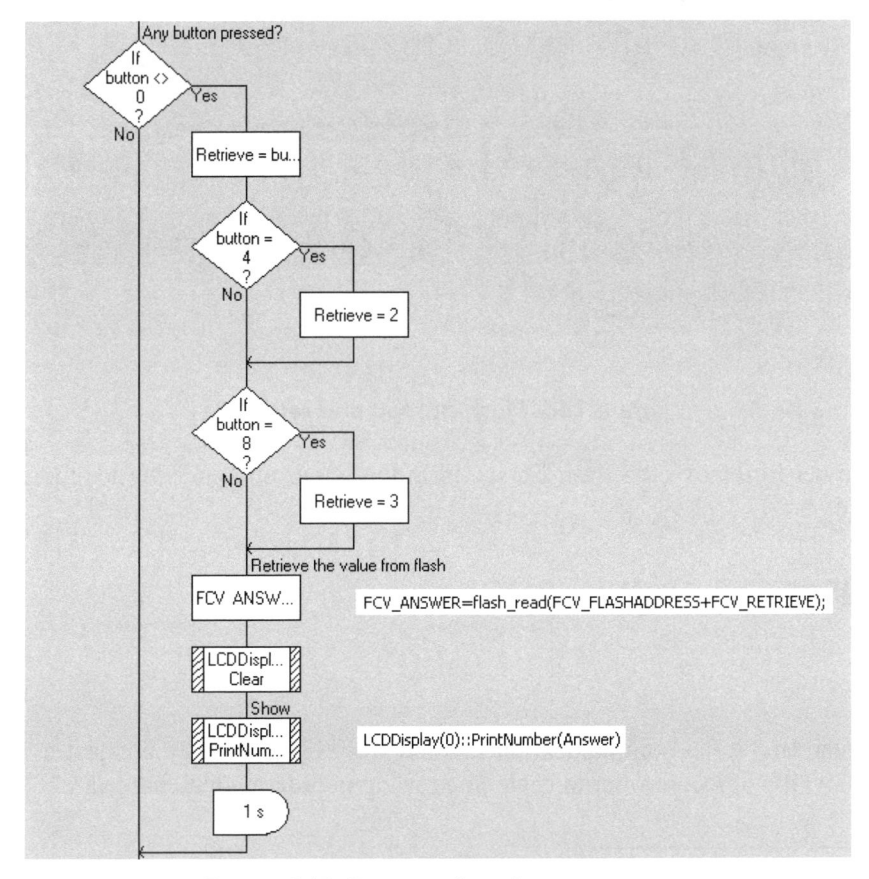

Figure 165. Retrieve data from memory.

143

4.10 USART connection

The bytes can be retrieved individually using the C command:

flash_read(FCV_FLASHADDRESS+FCV_RETRIEVE);

In this project four buttons will be used to select which memory address has to be retrieved, and the data is shown on the LCD screen. Of course this in itself has no practical purpose, it is merely meant to show how flash memory can be used.

Operational

Click on one of the first four buttons to retrieve a number from memory. As a simple debouncing technique the retrieve loop has a one second delay.

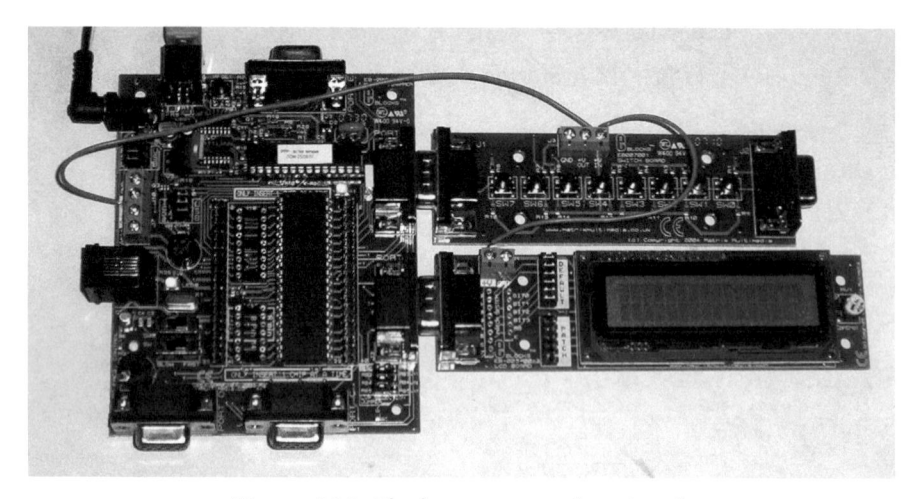

Figure 166. Flash storage and retrieval.

Do remember to remove the flash library from the linker options list once the project is completed!

4.10 USART connection

Concept

Use the standard serial communication module USART to directly connect a 16F877A and an ECIO40 microcontroller to each other, using no intermediate hardware[25].

---

[25] USART is the acronym for Universal Synchronous Asynchronous Receiver Transmitter, also known as the Serial Communications Interface or SCI.

4 Advanced

Hardware

For this project a 16F877A PIC microcontroller and an ECIO40 (18F4455) are selected. Two LED boards, a Switch board and an Application board are also required.

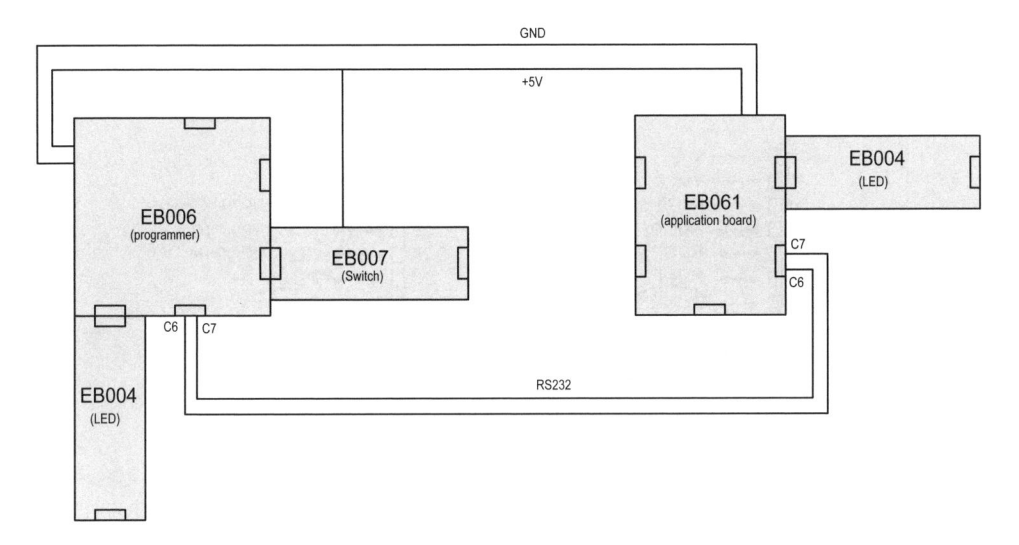

Figure 167. USART connection.

Connection summary:

Programmer	EB006 Switches to XTAL and Fast, LVP jumper on I/O port, J29 to PSU, J12-14 to USB, use external power supply.
Port B	EB007 Switch board.
Port C	Wire from C6 to C7 on the other unit.
	Wire from C7 to C6 on the other unit.
Port D	EB004 LED board.
Application	EB061 Application board with an ECIO40 (jumper to EXT).
Port B	EB004 LED board.
Port C	Wire from C6 to C7 on the other unit.
	Wire from C7 to C6 on the other unit.

Both the 16f877A and the ECIO40, which is in fact a regular 18F4455 with a built-in USB bootloader, have a built in USART communications module that allows them to communicate in a semi RS232 mode. It is not a real RS232 mode because that would require voltages ranging from -12 to +12 volt, while the microcontrollers can only operate

4.10 USART connection

in the 0 to +5 V range. So if the USART is to be connected to a PC a converter chip must be put in between with a charge pump to widen the voltage range, such as on the EB015 RS232 board.

In this project both USART modules are connected with cross-over wires, meaning the TX (transmit) pin of one is connected to the RX (receive) pin of the other[26]. Since both operate in the 0 to +5 V range the communication is flawless.

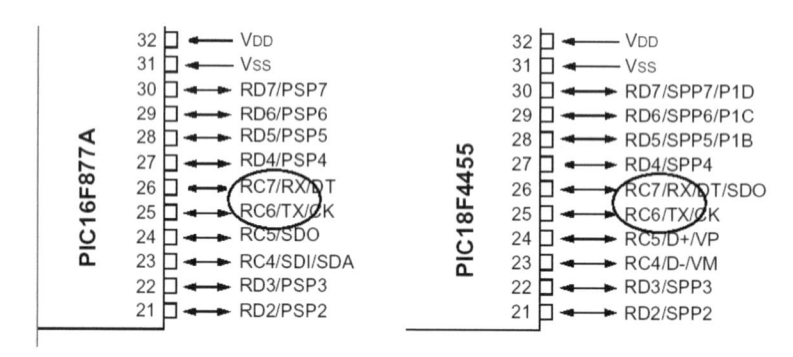

Figure 168. Pin configuration according to the datasheet.

The two C-ports should of course be connected with a proper D9 plug with the wires securely soldered in place. A more relaxed approach as seen in the next Figure is possible too, but not advisable.

Figure 169. The cross over connection using loose wire..

---

[26] Datasheets can be downloaded from the Microchip website.

4 Advanced

Software

For the 16F877A in the menu select Chip, then Configure and then switch to Expert Config Screen. In the section Configuration Word(s) make sure HEX is selected and then click on the Config1 button and enter: 0x3F3A.

The 16F877A runs a small program that checks which of the buttons on port B is pressed. The result of that check is send to the LED board on port D, and to the ECIO40 using an RS232 component. The ECIO40 receives this signal and sends it to the LED board connected to port B. See project 3.4 for more information on RS232 transmission and receipt.

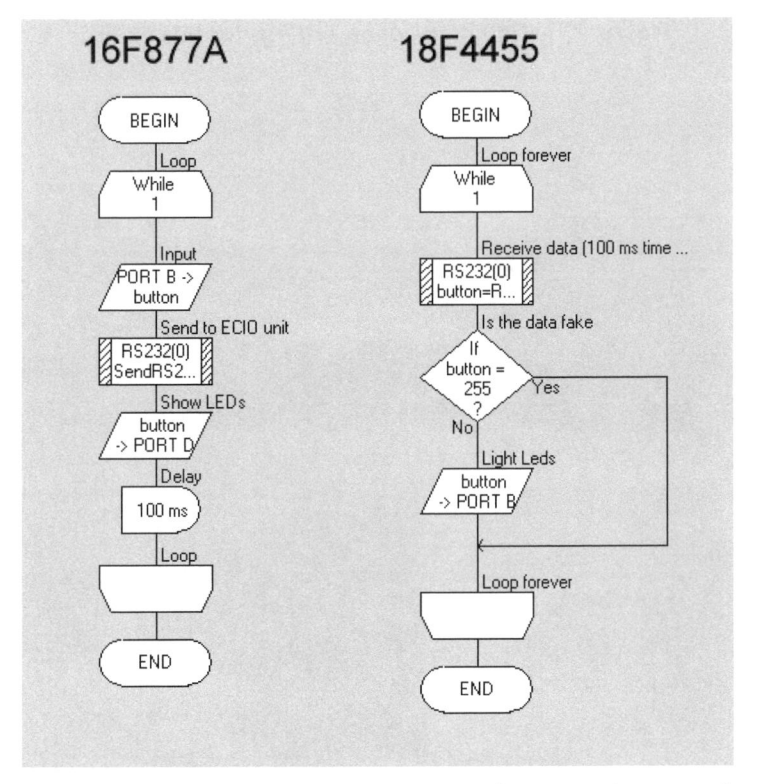

Figure 170. Software in the 16F877A and ECIO40 (18F4455).

It doesn't make much difference which settings are used for the RSR232 components in Flowcode, as long as they are the same in both programs.

147

4.10 USART connection

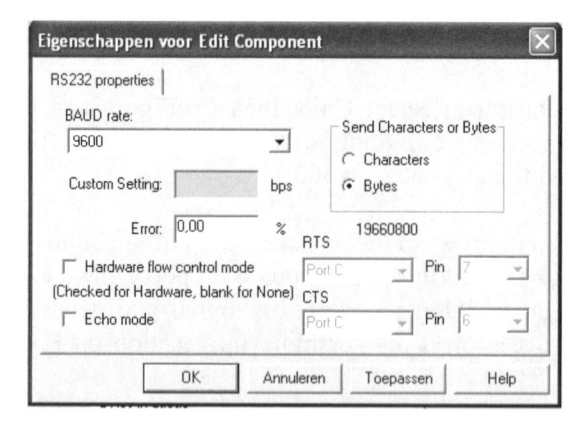

Figure 171. Communication settings for both units.

Operational

Figure 172. USART communication in action

Press one or more buttons on the Switch board, and the corresponding LEDs on both LED boards should light. It is best to use two D9 connectors with wires soldered to them rather than loose wires. Note that both units are powered by a single power supply.

4   Advanced

RS232 was designed for a maximum of 15 meters. The actual maximum distance between the two microcontrollers is very dependent on the circumstances. In a residential building the distance will be considerably longer than in an industrial environment.

4.11 GPS tracking

Concept

Use the NMEA protocol to read data from a handheld GPS and show the actual location on an LCD screen[27].

Hardware

For this project a 16F877A PIC microcontroller is selected with an RS232 board and an LCD board. A Garmin E-trex handheld GPS is connected to the RS232 board side connector.

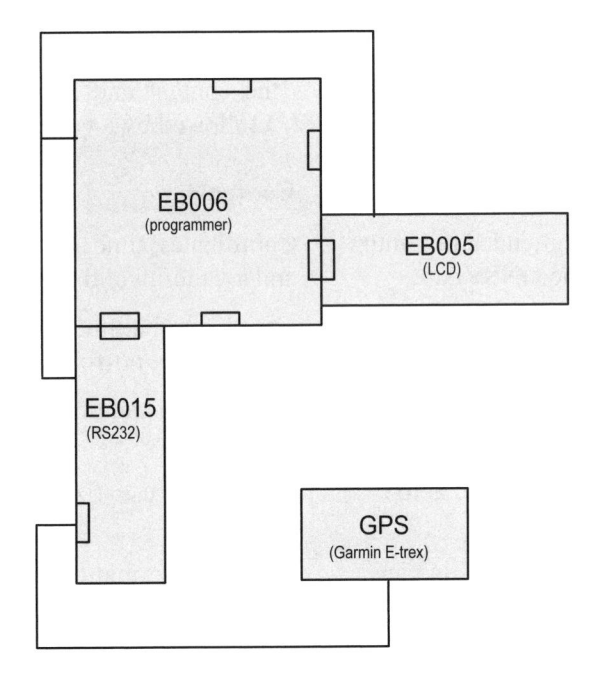

Figure 173. Schematic of the GPS hardware.

---
[27] GPS is an acronym for Global Positioning System.

4.11 GPS tracking

Connection summary:

Programmer	EB006 Switches to XTAL and Fast, LVP jumper on I/O port, J29 to PSU, J12-14 to USB, use external power supply.
Port B	EB005 LCD board, jumper to default.
Port C	EB015 RS232 board, jumpers to C and 2, Garmin E-trex connected to the side connector.

Software

In the menu select Chip, then Configure and then switch to Expert Config Screen. In the section Configuration Word(s) make sure HEX is selected and then click on the Config1 button and enter: 0x3F3A.

Most GPS units are capable of communicating in a standardized protocol called NMEA - 0183[28]. It is a serial protocol with a speed of 4800 BAUD specifically designed for maritime applications Transmission takes place in sentences.

Each sentence starts with a dollar sign ($) and a two letter abbreviation of the equipment sending this sentence: the talker id. For a GPS that would be GP. Next follows a sentence identifier of three letters, which determines the content and in fact the layout of the sentence. The sentence ends with an asterisk (*) followed by a two digit checksum.

Code	Name	Contents
$GPRMC	Recommended minimum specific GNSS data	Coordinates, time, date, speed, direction and a valid/invalid indicator
$GPGGA	Global positioning system fixed data	Coordinates, altitude, number of satellites, fix/no-fix indicator
$GPGLL	Geographic position - latitude / longitude	Coordinates and time.
$GPGSA	GNSS DOP and active satellites	Satellites in use, fix/no-fix. DOP values.
$GPGSV	GNSS satellites in view	Detailed information on satellites in view, may consist of up to three lines.
$GPVTG	Course over ground and ground speed	Heading and speed.

Figure 174. Some GPS NMEA-0183 sentences.

---

[28] National Marine Electronics Association. The protocol is for sale at their website.

4 Advanced

In this project the $GPRMC sentence will be used. This is an example of an actual sentence as send by the Garmin GPS with the fields separated by comma's:

$GPRMC,124226,A,5130.9624,N,00426.9466,E,0.0,0.0,110108,1.0,W,A*03

Explanation of the content:

Field	Description
$GPRMC	Sentence identifier.
124226	Time of the measurement.
A	GPS has a satellite fix.
5130.9624	Latitude: 51 ° (degrees). 30 ' (minutes). 60x.9624= 57 " (seconds).
N	Northern hemisphere.
00426.9466	Longitude: 004 ° (degrees). 26 ' (minutes). 60x.9466= 57 " (seconds).
E	Eastern hemisphere.
0	Speed.
0,0.0,110108,1.0, W,A*03	The program will ignore the rest of the fields.

Figure 175. $GPRMC used fields.

The software will read incoming data and cut it in separate fields by looking for the field delimiters ASCII 44 (comma) or ASCII 36 (dollar sign). These fields are compared to the target field $GPRMC. If this is correct a variable called Identifier is set to 1 to indicate that the next fields must be stored and analyzed[29].

---

[29] Make sure you use the Flowcode release 3.4.7.48 or later, earlier versions have a bug in the Compare$ statement which is invisible in simulation but not in real life.

4.11 GPS tracking

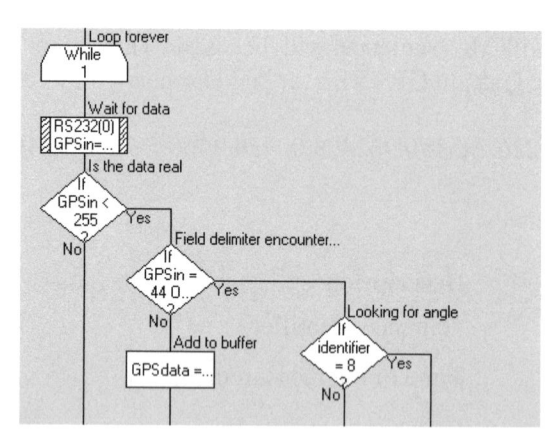

Figure 176. Cutting incoming data into separate fields using the delimiters.

With each new field the identifier is incremented until the angle field is detected. At that point the identifier is reset. The next Figure shows a small program snippet.

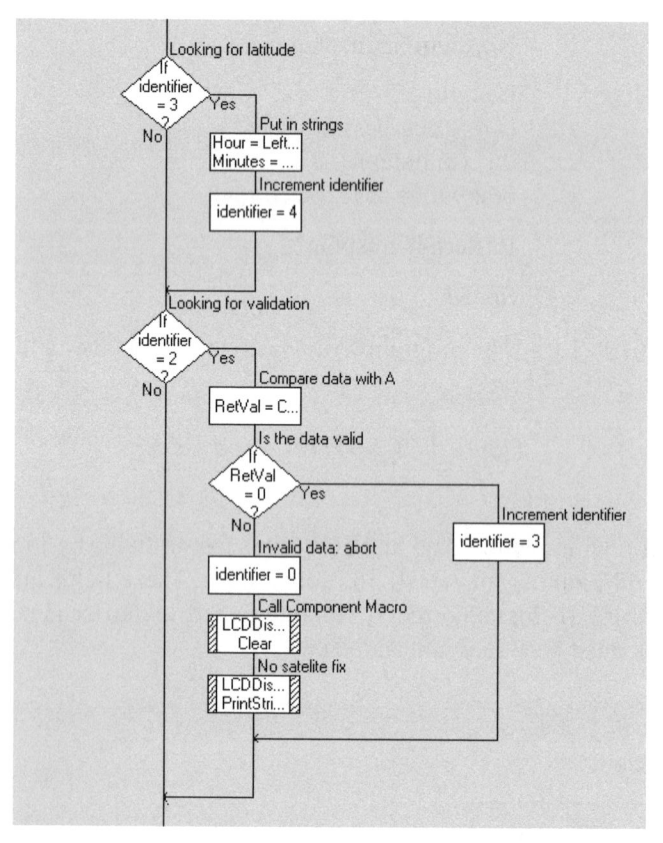

Figure 177. Example of field analyses and incrementing the identifier.

4   Advanced

Note that the fields are handled in reverse order so an increased identifier only affects the next field and not the current one.

Field three can contain either an A (GPS has satellite fix) or a V (GPS has no fix). If the field contains a V the analyses will be aborted and the message "GPRM rec no fix..." will be printed on the LCD.

Once the Angle field has been reached all relevant fields are converted and printed on the LCD.

The conversion of the location fields is done in three steps. First the field in split in three parts.

> Hour = Left$(GPSdata, 2)
> Minutes = Mid$(GPSdata, 2, 2)
> Seconds = right$(GPSdata, 4)

For 5130.9624 this would result in:

> Hour = 51
> Minutes = 30
> Seconds = 9624

Next the seconds are converted to a decimal value by getting each byte from the string, converting it from an ASCII string to a number by subtracting 48 and multiplying it by ten if it is in the position:

> SecByte = (Seconds[0] - 48) * 10
> SecByte = SecByte + Seconds[1] - 48

In reality this number is a fraction and needs to be multiplied by 0.6 to get the real seconds. Of course this is not possible so a fraction (60/100) will be used instead, see section 12.4 for more information on microcontroller mathematics.

> SecByte = (SecByte * 60) / 100

For 96 this would result in 57. Note that only two of the four available digits have been used, and that SecByte, despite its name, is declared as an integer, so it can easily hold 60 x 96.

Once all data has been printed to the LCD the program will wait for new data to arrive.

4.11 GPS tracking

Operational

Make sure the Garmin is set to NMEA protocol using the settings page. Shortly after power up the display will read "GPRM rec no fix". This means a valid record has been received but the GPS does not have a fix on sufficient satellites to determine the location.

After a while the LCD will display the location of the GPS and the speed with which it is moving.

After the picture of the project was taken the GPS was moved to my desk for its picture, and then lost the connection. This is why the GPS shows a different reading (no fix in fact) than the LCD screen.

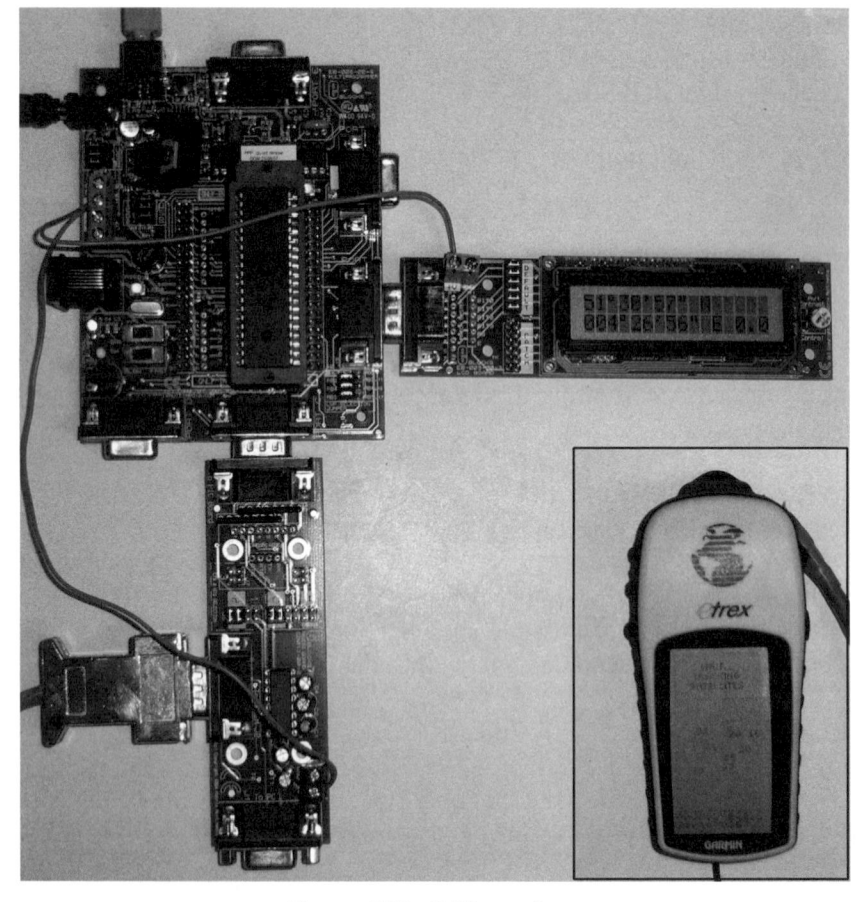

Figure 178. GPS reading.

4 Advanced

4.12 Use PPP to access EEPROM

Concept

Use PPP to view and edit microcontroller EEPROM as a proof of concept.

Hardware

For this project a 16F877A PIC microcontroller is selected, with a Switch board on port A and an LCD on port B. Note that both the Switch board and the LCD board need power so you need to connect the +Vin terminals of both boards to one of the +V terminals of the Programmer board

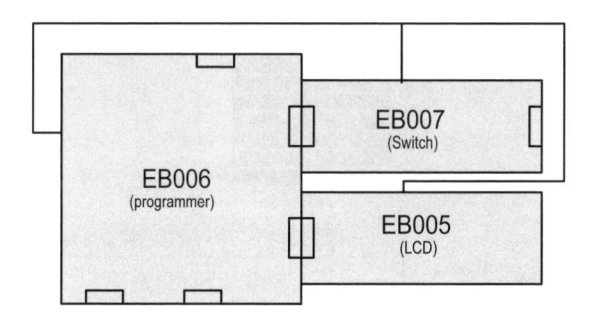

Figure 179. Schematic of hardware.

Connection summary:

Programmer	Switches to XTAL and Fast, LVP jumper on I/O port, J29 to PSU, J12-14 to USB, use external power supply.
Port A	EB007 Switch board.
Port B	EB005 LCD, jumper to default.

Note that the EB006 programmer must be connected to the PC using the USB cable to allow PPP access to the microcontroller.

Software

In the menu select Chip, then Configure and then switch to Expert Config Screen. In the section Configuration Word(s) make sure HEX is selected and then click on the Config1 button and enter: 0x3F3A.

155

4.12 Use PPP to access EEPROM

The 16F877A has 256 bytes of 8 bits EEPROM, which will maintain its content even during a power down. Flowcode allows access to EEPROM using the EEPROM component which shows its content on-screen, ideal during simulation.

This program checks the status of the Switch board and stores it in variable Button. If this variable is not equal to zero, meaning a button has been pressed, the value of that variable is stored in address 0 of EEPROM.

In the next step the value of address 0 is read from EEPROM and shown on the LCD screen. Note that this is not necessarily the value of the variable Button, it is the value of memory location one. An important difference as you will see in the next section of this project.

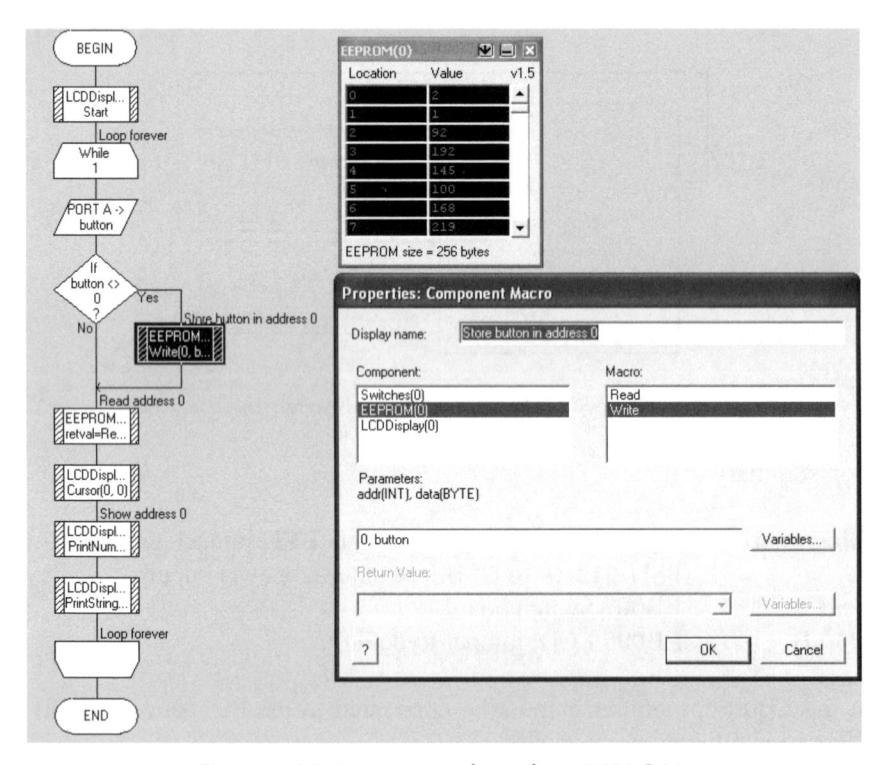

Figure 180. Writing and reading EEPROM.

Operational

When you run the program the value of the button pressed on the Switch board is shown on the LCD screen (note that since Switch board is on port A buttons 6 and 7 are not connected).

4 Advanced

EEPROM memory can be viewed using PPP, the software that controls the EB006 programmer. Take the following steps:

1. Press any of the buttons, for example SW2.
2. Take a note of the number on the LCD, for example 4.
3. Start PPP[30]
4. Select View and the View PIC Micro, make sure the programmer is connected using the USB cable. Optionally you could save the content of Program memory and EEPROM to disk (Save to file button) for future use[31].

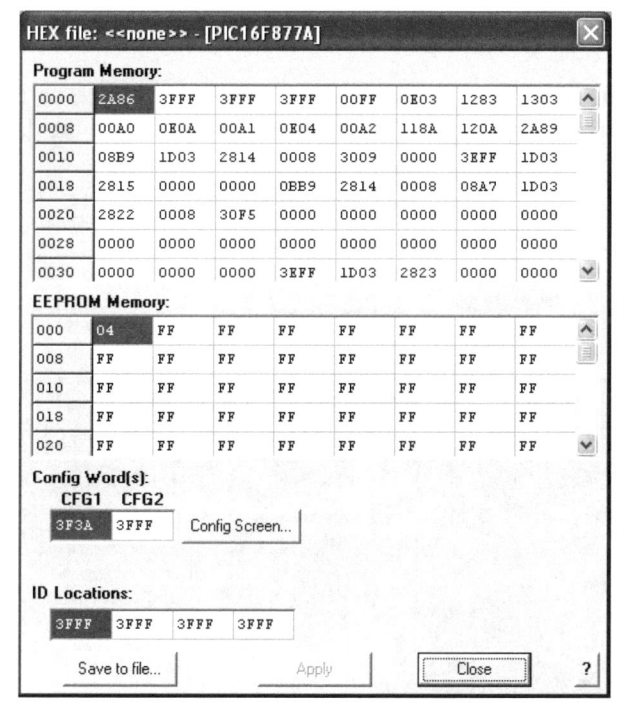

Figure 181. Editing the EEPROM content.

You will now see the content of program memory and EEPROM memory. EEPROM address 000 contains the value you noted in step 2, but in HEX.

---

[30] The default installation of Flowcode doesn't make a shortcut to PPP. The program can be found in the Matrix Multimedia directory, for example:
C:\Program Files\Matrix Multimedia\Common\PPPv3\PPPv3.exe

[31] To use the HEX file start PPP. Then use File and then Open. Select the correct HEX file. Now select View and then View HEX file. You are now back at the end of step 4.

157

4.12 Use PPP to access EEPROM

Interestingly enough it is possible to change these values and write them back to the microcontroller. If you mess with program memory it is rather likely that the program will not run anymore, but EEPROM is safe. Take the following steps:

1. Double click on EEPROM address 000. A window will pop up. Change the value, for example to 0x08. Note that you need to use HEX values!
2. Click on the Config screen button and then on the Ok button. This step doesn't do anything useful but skipping it will generate a warning regarding "the second config field", which by the way doesn't exist.
3. Click on the Apply button and then on Close.
4. Click on the Send to PICmicro button.

The program restarts after the memory has been rewritten. Since no button is pressed at this time the data read from EEPROM memory address 0 will be the data that was entered in step 5 (for example 8), but in decimal.

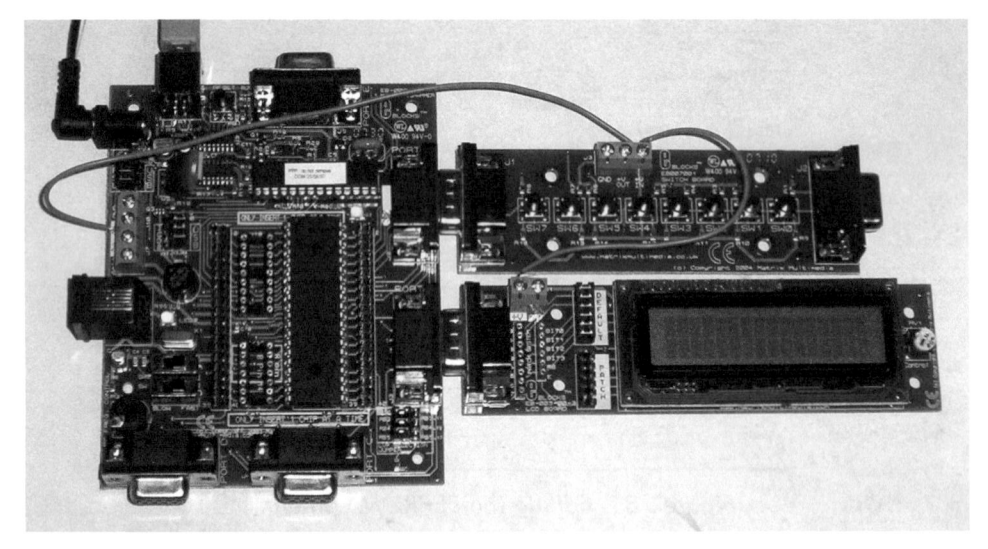

Figure 182. Using PPP the EEPROM can be viewed and modified.

4.13 Poetry box

It is assumed that you installed the drivers and software that are required for the ECIO boards. If you haven't now would be a good time to do so[32].

Concept

In an Objet d'art show a poem on an LCD screen. The poem should be on an MMC card so it can be changed regularly on a PC without having to move the Object d'Art.

Hardware

For this project the ICO40 is selected. To enable connection to the E-blocks an EB061 application board is used with an MMC board and an LED board. Note that both the MMC board and the LCD board need power so you need to connect the +Vin terminals of both boards to one of the +V terminals of the Application board. Beware of the unusual configuration of ports on the application board!

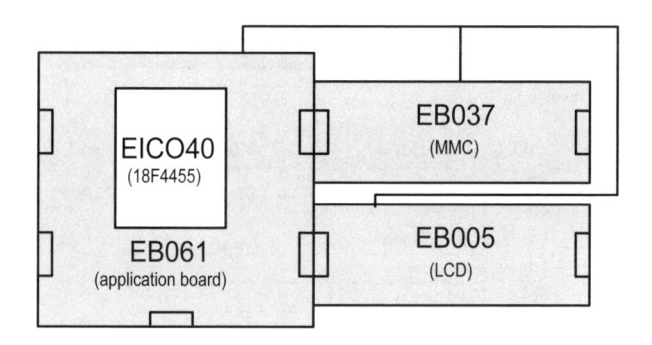

Figure 183. Schematic poetry box.

Connection summary:

        Programmer   None.
        Microcontroller ECIO40, jumper to EXT, on an EB061 application board.
        Port B   EB037 MMC board, jumpers on A and +5V.
        Port C   EB005 LCD board, jumper on default.

---

[32] You can download the required files from the Matrix Multimedia website http://www.matrixmultimedia.com/ECIO-X.php

4.13 Poetry box

Software

If you select the ECIO40 as target in Flowcode the configuration will be set automatically and cannot be changed by the user.

In this project a special FAT16 component will be used, which is in the project directory of this project in the download[33]. The file is called "custom_code.c" and needs to be copied into the components directory of Flowcode V3.

FAT, File Allocation Table, is the file system used by Microsoft Windows and many other operating systems. That means that files saved to the MMC card on a Windows operating system, such as WinXP, can be read by the microcontroller. Vice versa the files written by the microcontroller can be read on a PC. In this project we will only read from the MMC card.

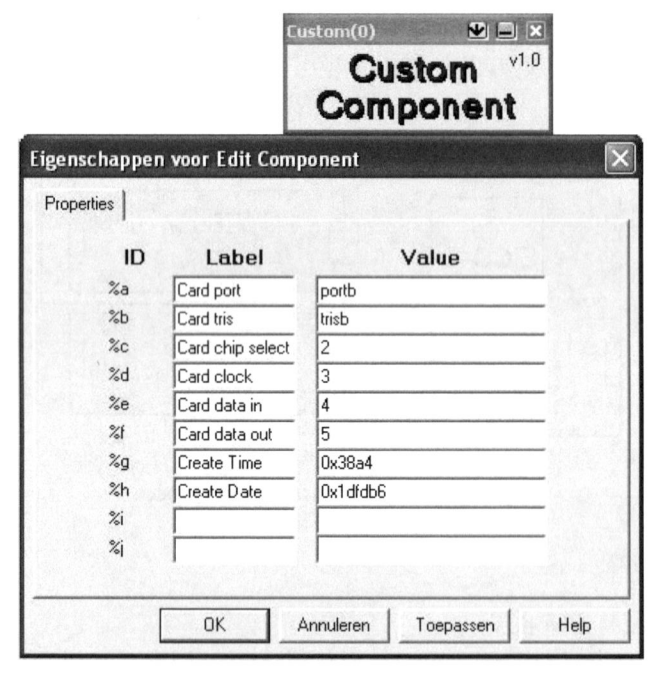

Figure 184. Custom component settings.

---

[33] This is a special test version supplied by Matrix Multimedia LTD. Recent versions of Flowcode may have an MMC FAT component built in by default. If that is the case you don't need this special version.

160

4 Advanced

Add the custom component (the little icon with "user" on it). Open the custom component and enter the following settings:

Card port	portb
Card tris	trisb
Card chip select	2
Card clock	3
Card data in	4
Card data out	5
Card time	0x38a4
Card date	0x1dfdb6

Due to the structure of the MMC cards read and write commands must be carried out with 512 bytes at the same time. This space is required in RAM memory, and is called the buffer[34]. So a read command will fill the buffer with 512 bytes from the MMC card file. If the file is shorter the read command will still return 512 bytes but the file length, which is really the length within that buffer rather than the length of the entire file, will be shorter than 512. Once that is the case you know a next read is not required.

To read a file in the root directory and display its content the following commands are necessary. The names between brackets are the macro commands that are automatically available once the custom component is loaded.

1. Initialize custom component (Init_FAT).
2. Goto root directory (Open_Folder "root").
3. Set file name (in this project mmctext.txt).
4. Open the file and read the first 512 bytes into memory (Open_File).
5. Get the file length within that buffer (Read_File_Length).
6. Show all bytes from the buffer (Read_byte_from_buffer).
7. If the buffer was completely full (file length = 512) then read the next sector from the file in the buffer (Move_To_Next_File_Sector) and go to step 5.
8. Else stop the program. There is no need to close the file, this is done automatically.

The next Figure shows the heart of the program In reality the flow is in a single column, it is split in two columns for space reasons.

---

[34] If you migrate this project to another microcontroller pay attention to the amount of RAM memory required. The 16F877A PIC microcontroller for example only has 368 bytes of RAM. The custom component doesn't use hardware SPI but software SPI. That means it can be used with any pin combination you like, and thus also on microcontrollers that do not even have SPI.

4.13 Poetry box

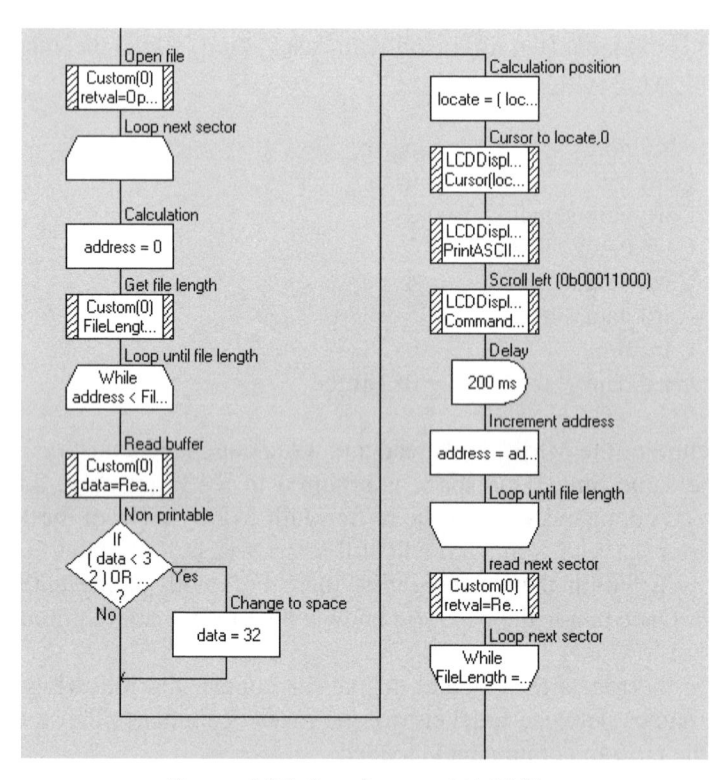

Figure 185. Reading an MMC file.

Since the text will not fit on the LCD it scrolls to the left. See project 3.4 (USB part) for more information on scrolling. Since the display is basically rotating around the text on the lower line "Art Exhibition 2008" is printed only once but visible every time the start of the display passes the view window.

Any non printable tokens in the file, such as CR and LF[35], are replaced by a space. Note the use of brackets: (data < 32) OR (data > 126). It is highly recommended to use brackets in decision such as these to make sure that Flowcode evaluates them as you intent it.

Operational

The file on the MMC card can be made with a normal ASCII text editor such as Microsoft Notepad. In the directory in the download you will find a beautiful poem by

---

[35] Carriage Return and Line Feed, common tokens at the end of a line to indicate that the next line starts. Carriage refers to typewriters where the whole paper was on a carriage and moved past the type bars. Line feed refers to the rubber roller that moved the paper upwards.

Charles Buchowski[36] called Layover for testing. Place this file (mmctext.txt) on your MMC card in the root directory.

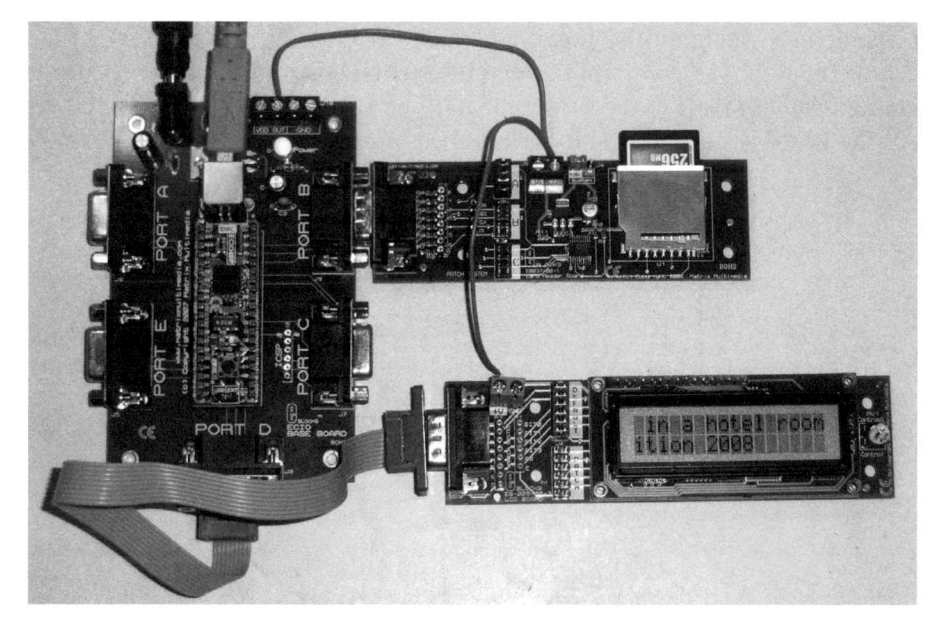

Figure 186. Poetry in motion.

Once the entire poem is displayed the text will stop and display the message "Press reset... to restart". In reality the LCD display should be part of an Objet d'art with the microcontroller hidden from view and a small button next to the LCD. The button is connected to the reset button, so each time an exhibition visitor pushes the button the microcontroller is reset and shows the poem.

The MMC card can be removed from the installation by the artist to change the poem (on a PC).

4.14 Voice command

Concept

Turn an LED on and off using voice commands such as "Light on" and "Light off". Make the technique memory independent so it can be used in small microcontrollers and/or with long sentences, though the latter is of course not recommended.

---

[36] Charles Bukowski (1920 – 1994) was an influential American poet and novelist.

4.14 Voice command

Hardware

For this project we will use the AT91SAM7S128 ARM microcontroller, in combination with a microphone pre-amplifier board, a switch (or button) board and an LED board. Note that the microphone pre-amplifier and the switch board need power so you need to connect the +Vin terminals to the +V terminal of the Programmer board. The microphone pre-amplifier board is a custom E-block described in section 9.1.

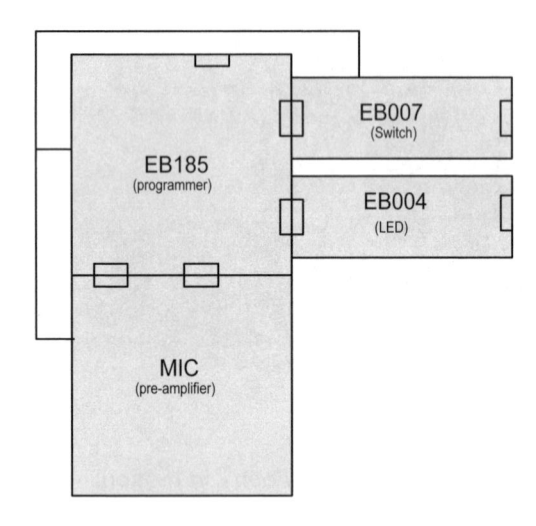

Figure 187. Voice command hardware.

Connection summary:

Programmer	EB185, use external power supply, jumpers J16 to PSU, J18 to USB, J15 to default.
Port A	EB007 Switch (or button), board
Port B	EB004 LED board.
Port D	Microphone pre-amplifier J1 first position (D0) J2 right (pre-amplifier)

Make sure the clock speed in the Chip menu is set to 47923200 Hz. Note that even though the microphone pre-amplifier is connected to port C and D at the same time only the connection on port D is in use.

4   Advanced

Software

The most likely method for voice command comparisons would be frequency analyses using a Fast Fourier Transformation (FFT). The ARM microcontroller in this project is certainly capable of achieving that. It would require a lot of memory though to store the received commands before they can be processed. Since the assignment was to develop a program that works on small microcontrollers as well, another solution must be used.

The next Figure shows a recording of two voice commands. The upper recording is "Light on" and the lower one is "Light off". The first part, "Light", is more or less identical, as it should be. The second part is quite different. An easy way to distinguish between these two commands is to add up all the values in the graph. This will give completely different results for the first and second commands. These results can be stored in memory. The microcontroller has now "learnt" these two commands.

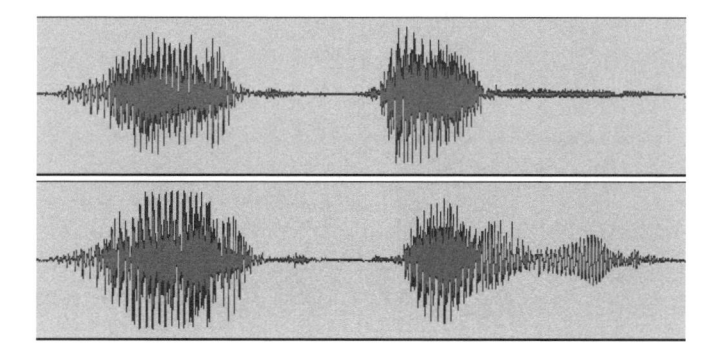

Figure 188. Light on (upper) and light off (lower).

You can do this by feeding the voice signal into an ADC (Analog to Digital Convertor) and adding up all recorded values into one sum. If ADC is recorded as a byte the maximum value will be 255. If a float is used to store the sum of all the ADC measurements, that means you can store $6.7 \cdot 10^{305}$ measurements. So you will run out of patience before you run out of space. It is best to eliminate noise so a threshold of 25 is used when recording the ADC measurements.

The program uses three switches. SW0 and SW1 are for recording the voice commands. SW2 is used for giving a voice command. Whenever you press a switch an LED will light to show that you can issue your command. LED D7 is the voice controlled LED. The next figure shows the recording loop for SW2, the actual command. The next step is to compare this recording with the learnt commands and choose the one that resembles this the most, meaning whichever value is closest.

165

4.14 Voice command

This is done by calculating the absolute difference with the fabs command.

ON = fabs(LEDon - LEDsound)
OFF = fabs(LEDoff - LEDsound)

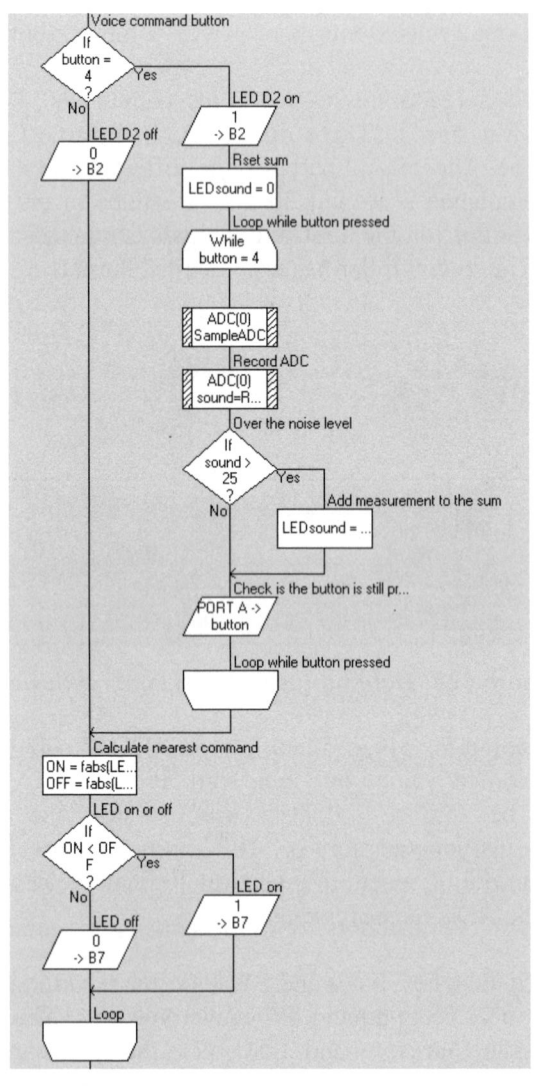

Figure 189. Recording the voice command and comparing it.

Note that we are looking for the smallest difference. If for example LEDon = 25378 and LEDoff is 33216 and the recorded command LEDsound = 31240 then:

LEDon - LEDsound = -5862
abs(LEDon - LEDsound) = 5862

LEDoff - LEDsound = 1976
abs(LEDoff - LEDsound) = 1976

Since 1976 is smaller than 5862 the recorded command must be LEDoff (turn LED D7 off).

If the switch bounces the loop will be exited and immediately entered again. At that point the sum will be reset to zero so your command will be cut in half. For that reason bouncing must be avoided. The Switch component in Flowcode has a debouncing variable as can be seen in the next figure. A value of 100 seems be sufficient. If your switches are old you may need to increase this value, the maximum value is 255.

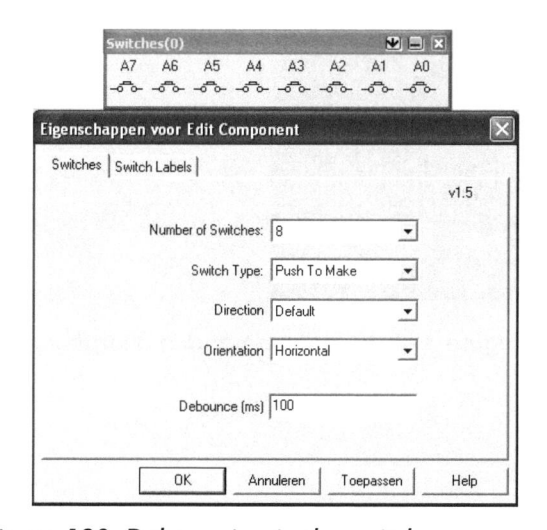

Figure 190. Debouncing in the switch component.

Operational

The technique is extremely simple. Surprisingly enough it works quite well, assuming you enter all commands at more or less the same volume. A small movie of this project in operation is posted on Youtube. Check out the support site www.boekinfo.tk for the current address.

4.14 Voice command

1. First press Sw0 (LED D0 will light) and enter the command to turn the LED on into the microphone, for example "Light on".
2. Then press SW1 (LED D1 will light) and enter the command to turn the LED off into the microphone, for example "Light off".
3. Now press SW2 (LED D2 will light) and enter one of these commands in the microphone. Based on what you said LED D7 will go on or off.

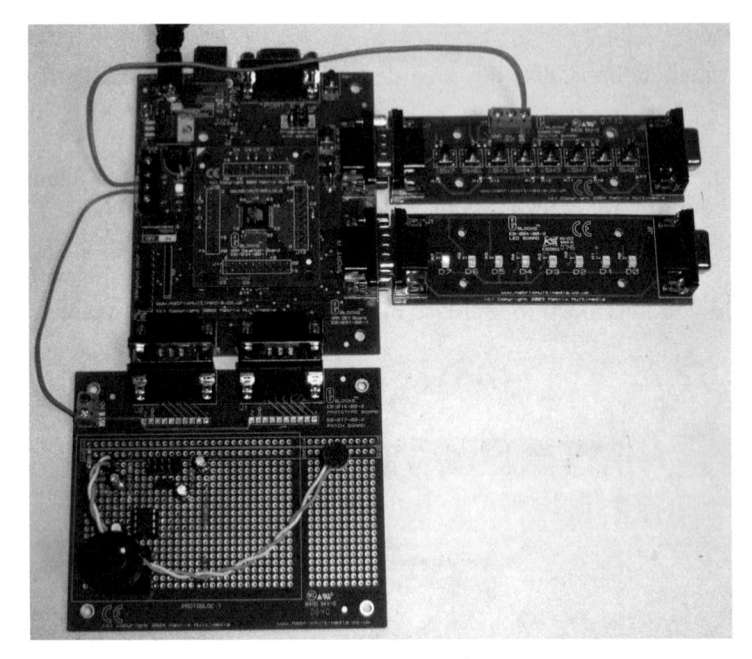

Figure 191. Voice command in operation.

5 Sensors

Sensors allow a microcontroller to react to its environment. They can be used for example to switch on lights when it gets dark, or control the temperature of a refrigerator. Sensors have been used in previous projects, for example an LDR (project 3.6). One might argue that a switch is also a sensor. This chapter covers a series of unusual sensors or more complicated use of sensors.

5.1 Infrared object detection

Concept

Infrared light is invisible to the human eye. Infrared sensors are often used as non-contact proximity sensors. In this project the Sharp GP2Y0D340K will be used as a proximity sensor to light an LED when an object is near.

Hardware

For this project we will use the ATMEGA 32 AVR microcontroller, in combination with an LED board. On the Proto board a Sharp GP2Y0D340K infrared object detector is mounted with support parts. Note that the Proto board needs power so you need to connect the +Vin terminal to one of the +V terminals of the Programmer board.

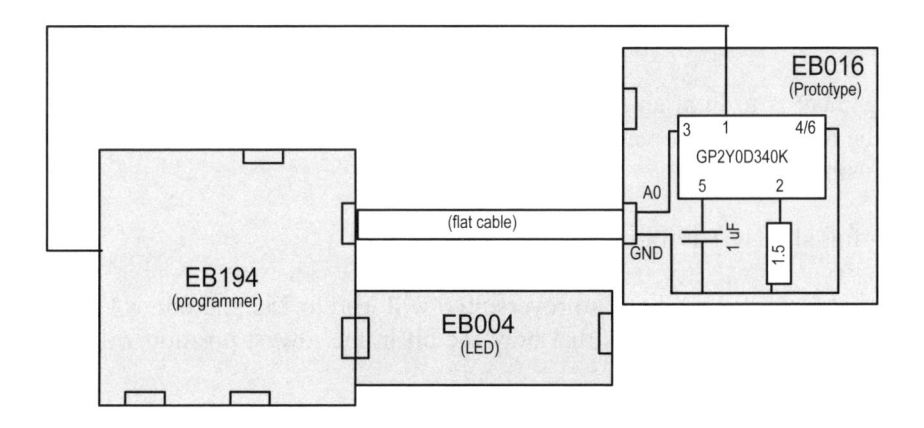

Figure 192. Infrared object detection.

5.1 Infrared object detection

Connection summary:

    Programmer   EB194 , jumper to default.
    Port A   EB016 Proto board. On the board a Sharp GP2Y0D340K infrared object detector. Connected the sensor pins as follows:
        Pin 1   to +5 Volt.
        Pin 2   1.5 ohm to GND.
        Pin 3   to ATMEGA 32 pin A0.
        Pin 4   GND.
        Pin 5   1 uF capacitor to GND.
        Pin 6   GND.
    Port B   EB004 LED board.

The software

If you haven't done so already first of all make sure that the fuses of the ATMEGA 32 are set correctly to 0x0,0xdf and 0x1,0xff. Select the "Chip" menu and "Configure". Enter the settings and remember to click on the Ok and Send button, because they will not be transferred by default. Of course the AVR programmer must be connected to the PC and powered on for this to work.

The sensor projects a beam of infrared light invisible to the human eye, and measures the reflected quantity. If an object is near the reflected quantity will be high and the sensor will cut the contact.

The assignment is to light an LED when an object is near, so the signal from the sensor needs to be reversed. After reading the status of pin A0 into a variable called Infrared it is reversed using

    infrared = NOT infrared

Unfortunately infrared is a byte, so reversing 0 will lead to 255 and not to 1. The solution is to AND with 1, which means that only the bit in the lowest position will be retained. This is because:

$$1 \text{ AND } 1 = 1$$
$$0 \text{ AND } 1 = 0$$
$$1 \text{ AND } 0 = 0$$
$$0 \text{ AND } 0 = 0$$

Figure 193. AND truth table.

5 Sensors

So these calculations

>infrared = NOT infrared
>infrared = infrared AND 1

Will yield this result:

measurement	infrared	NOT infrared	infrared AND 1	final result
0	00000000	11111111	11111111 AND 00000001	1
1	00000001	11111110	11111110 AND 00000001	0

Figure 194. NOT and AND on bit level.

Apart from this the program is rather straight forward. For simulation purposes a button component can be used as seen in the next Figure.

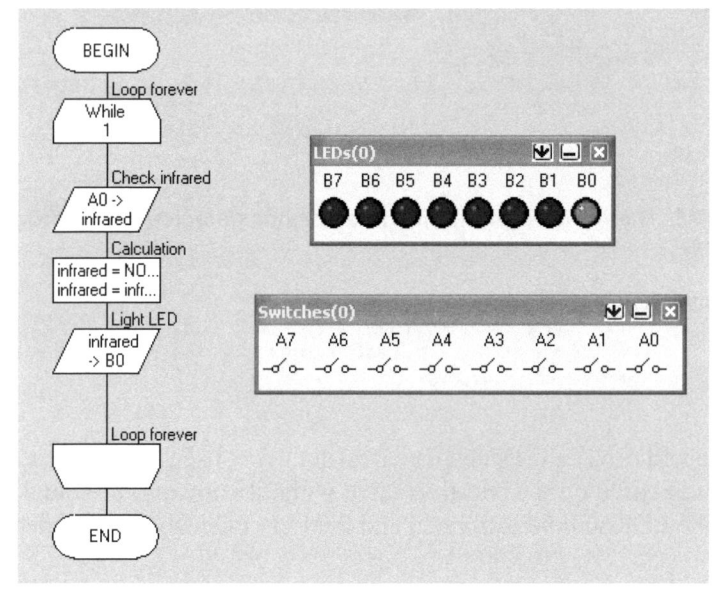

Figure 195. The software is simulated.

Operational

The performance of the proximity detector is highly dependent on the infrared reflective properties of the object in the beam. Whilst a white piece of paper was detected at 31 centimeters a black cup was detected at 20 centimeters.

5.2 Photometer

Note that the 1 uF capacitor and the 1.5 ohm resistor are hidden beneath the Sharp GP2Y0D340K infrared object detector and thus not visible in the next Figure.

Figure 196. The infrared proximity detector has detected the photographer.

5.2 Photometer

Concept

In project 3.6 an LDR (Light Dependent Resistor) was used in a dark activated switch. The threshold was based on the resistive value without knowing the actual light intensity. In this project the LDR will be calibrated and the light intensity will be measured in Lux.

Hardware

For this project we will use the AT91SAM7S128 ARM microcontroller, in combination with a Proto board and an LCD board. Note that both boards need power so you need to connect the +Vin terminals of the boards to the +V terminals of the Programmer board.

5 Sensors

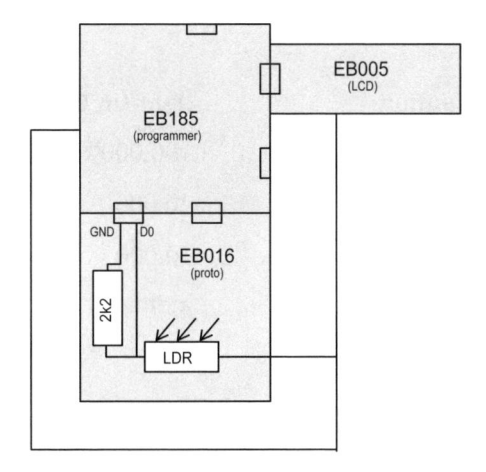

Figure 197. Hardware for the photometer.

Connection summary:

Programmer	EB185, use external power supply, jumpers J16 to PSU, J18 to USB, J15 to default.
Port A	EB005 LCD board, jumper on default.
Port D	EB016 Proto board .
D0	LDR and 2k2 resistor.
+V	LDR.
GND	2k2 resistor.

Make sure the clock speed in the CHIP menu is set to 47923200 Hz.

Software

The amount of light can be measured using an LDR. This is a resistor whose value is dependent on the amount of light that hits it. The relationship between the resistance and the amount of light is not linear and is usually something like this:

$$R = \frac{500}{L}$$

With R in k ohm and L in Lux.

5.2 Photometer

To get a feel for the meaning of Lux:

situation	light (in Lux)
direct sunlight	100,000
indirect sunlight	20,000
cloudy day	10,000
office	350
room with candle	50

Figure 198. Examples of Lux values.

Even "identical" LDRs can easily differ as much as 50%, so you'll need to calibrate it or use a variable resistor for fine adjustment. Keep in mind that the more light falling on the LDR the lower its resistance.

First the LDR needs to be calibrated. Since I don't have a photometer to calibrate it against, the resistance of the LDR was measured in direct sunlight, and in the shade (indirect sunlight), with these results:

Direct sunlight	37.2 ohms
Indirect sunlight	178 ohms

This means the formula for the LDR in this project is (with R in ohm):

$$L = \frac{3{,}630{,}000}{R} \qquad (1)$$

How accurate that is remains to be seen. Note that you need to calibrate your LDR as well, it will definitely not have the same resistance as the one used in this book.

The LDR has to be connected to the microcontroller as part of a voltage divider to convert the resistance into a voltage, as shown in the next Figure. Note that the ARM uses 3.3 volts as opposed to the PIC and AVR microcontrollers that generally run on 5 volts.

5 Sensors

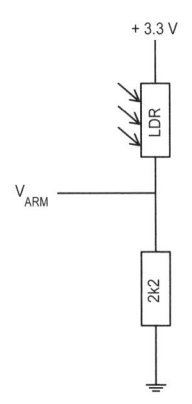

Figure 199. Voltage divider with an LDR.

For the voltage on the microcontroller input (V_{ARM}) the voltage divider yield this result:

$$V_{ARM} = \frac{2k2}{(R_{LDR} + 2k2)} * 3.3$$

Or:

$$R_{LDR} = \frac{2k2 * 3.3}{V_{ARM}} - 2k2 \qquad (2)$$

The analog to digital converter of the microcontroller will result in a value between zero and 255, where 255 is equivalent to 3.3 volts. In a formula:

$$V_{ARM} = 3.3 * \frac{ADC}{255}$$

By combining this with formula (2) we get:

$$R_{LDR} = \frac{2k2 * 3.3 * 255}{ADC * 3.3} - 2k2$$

Which can be simplified to:

$$R_{LDR} = \frac{561000}{ADC} - 2200$$

5.2 Photometer

Entering this in formula (1) results in:

$$L = \frac{3360000}{\frac{561000}{ADC} - 2200}$$

Which can be simplified to

$$L = \frac{3360}{\frac{561}{ADC} - 2.2}$$

Since the Flowcode for ARM supports floating point math this formula can be directly used in the program. If you use another microcontroller you need to use a Lookup table, see project 3.9 for an example.

After measuring the ADC value L is calculated as follows[37]:

L = 561.0 / ADC
L = L - 2.2
L = 3360 / L

Unfortunately printing a floating point variable such as L to an LCD is not possible. The solution is to use two special libraries: stdlib.h and OSstubs.c. These libraries need to be placed in the same directory as your program. In the supplementary code section place these lines in the Functions Implementations section:

#include <stdlib.h>
#include <OSstubs.c>
int errno;

Declare a variable called PrntBuff[20] as string. In a C-box the code

gcvt(FCV_L, 7, FCV_PRNTBUFF);

will convert variable L to string with 7 digits. Depending on the size of L these digits will partially be before the decimal point and partially after. This string can now be printed to the LCD. Note that since a C routine is used this program can not be simulated.

---

[37] If you haven't done so already it is highly recommended that you read section 12.4 on Microcontroller Mathematics which explains why 561.0 is used instead of just 561.

If ADC is 255 the denominator in the formula will be zero so in that case the program will show "Overflow" on the LCD. If ADC is 0 the program will show "Underflow" for similar reasons. In normal operations neither of these points should ever be reached.

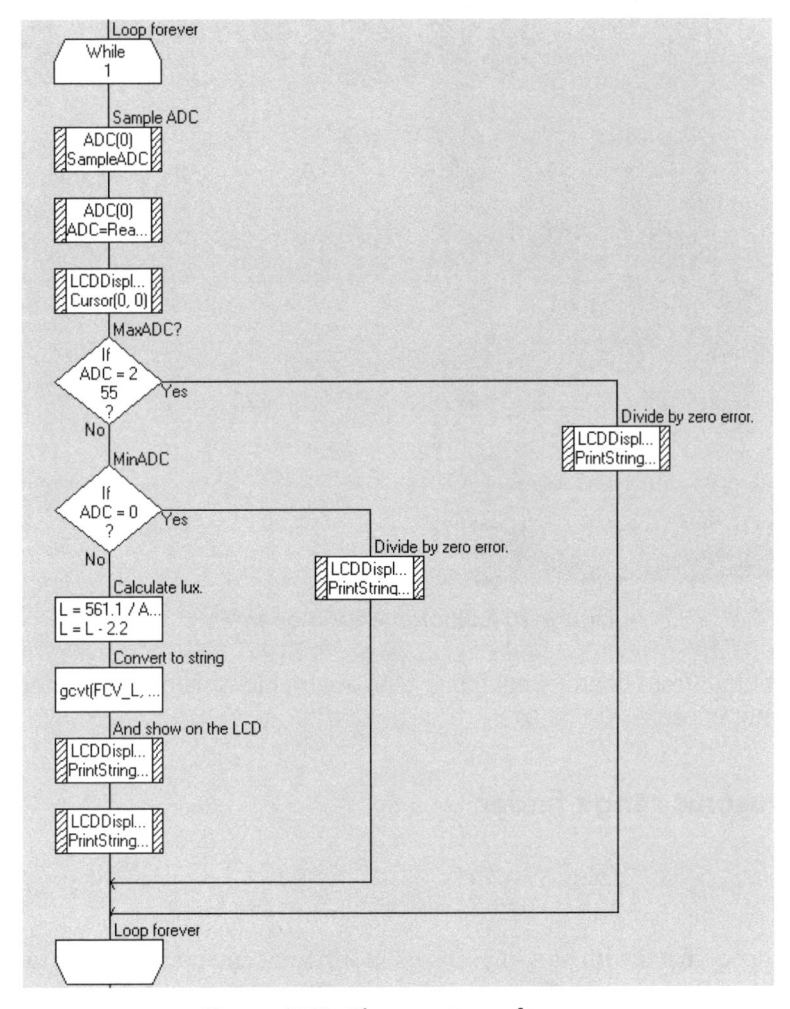

Figure 200. Photometer software.

Operational

Locate the project in the sun. The reading should be about 100,000 to 130,000 Lux. If you used the LCD board with a PIC or AVR microcontroller before this project you will need to adjust the brightness, since the ARM microcontroller runs off 3.3 volts whereas the other two use 5 volts.

5.3 Ultrasonic range finder

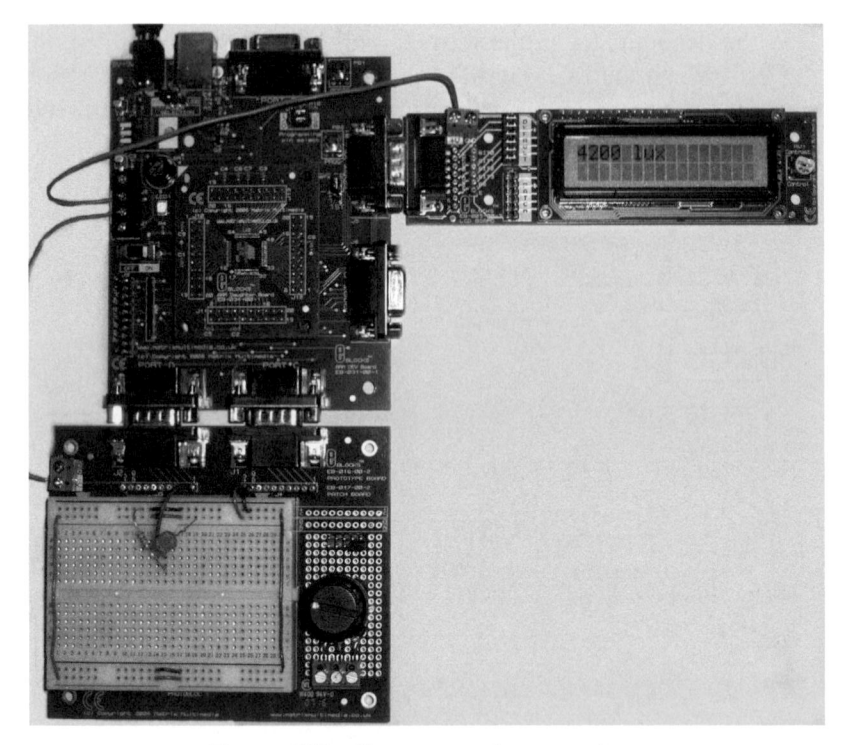

Figure 201. Photometer in operation.

In this project the Proto board is equipped with a variable resistor as described in section 9.1, but it is not in use.

5.3 Ultrasonic range finder

Concept

Many cars are equipped with parking sensors in the front and rear bumpers to help drivers park their car in tight spaces. These sensors use ultrasonic sound waves to measure the distance to the nearest object and alert the driver when an object is too close. The purpose of this project is to make such a sensor that displays the measured distance in centimeters.

Since the ultrasonic range finder doesn't depend on the light reflective properties of the objects, but on the ultrasonic sound reflective properties instead, this technique is much more accurate than the infrared object detection of project 5.1, though at a higher cost.

5 Sensors

Hardware

The SRF04 is a relatively cheap ultrasonic sensor that uses sound waves to measure the distance of objects. There is no E-block with this sensor so we will use a Proto board to connect the sensor to the microcontroller. Apart from the power connections it has a trigger line which is used to set the ultrasonic burst in motion, and a pulse line to relay the elapsed time to the microcontroller.

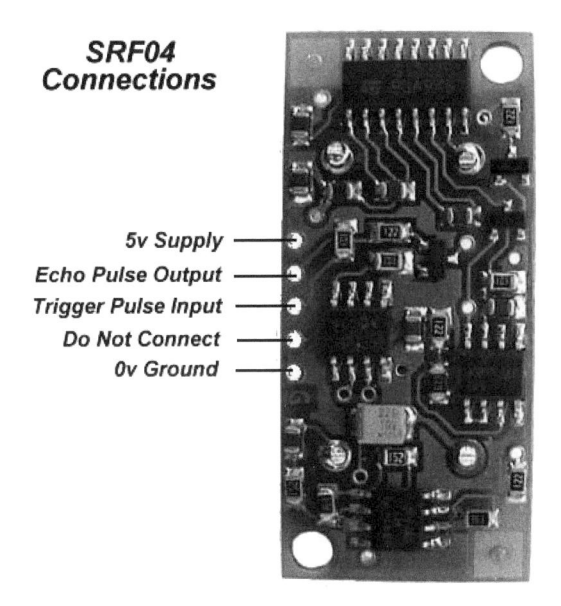

Figure 202. Connections of the SRF04.

For this project the PIC 16F877A has been selected. For the connections to the SRF04 port E will be used, bits 0 (pulse) and 1 (trigger). For the power that the SRF04 requires use the +V connection and the GND connection on the Proto board. An LCD connected to port B will be used to display the measurements. Note that both the Proto board and the LCD board need power so you need to connect the +Vin terminals of both boards to one of the +V terminals of the Programmer board

5.3 Ultrasonic range finder

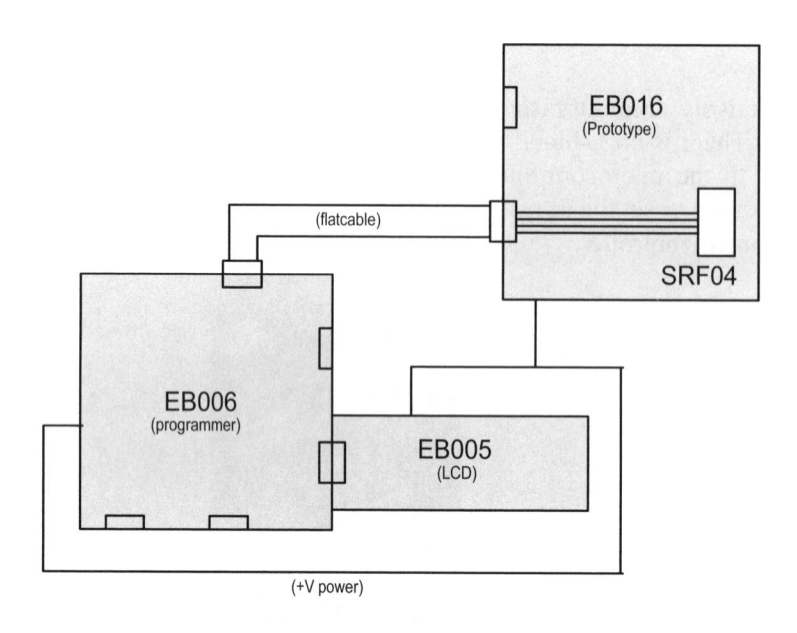

Figure 203. Schematic of the ultrasonic sensor project.

Connection summary:

Programmer	Switches to XTAL and Fast, LVP jumper on I/O port, J29 to PSU, J12-14 to USB, use external power supply.
Port B	LCD board, jumper to default.
Port E	E0 SRF04 pulse.
	E1 SRF04 trigger.
	+V SRF04 5V supply.
	GND SRF04 0V ground.

Software

In the menu select Chip, then Configure and then switch to Expert Config Screen. In the section Configuration Word(s) make sure HEX is selected and then click on the Config1 button and enter: 0x3F3A.

The detection cycle is started by the microcontroller with a pulse of 10 uS or more on the pulse trigger line. As soon as this line goes low again the ultrasonic module sends a burst of 8 pulses of 40 kHz sound. To avoid direct coupling between transmitter and receiver the unit waits a bit and then sets the echo line to high. This is the signal for the microcontroller to start a time measurement. The first ultrasonic echo to be received switches the echo line back to low again.

5 Sensors

SRF04 Timing Diagram

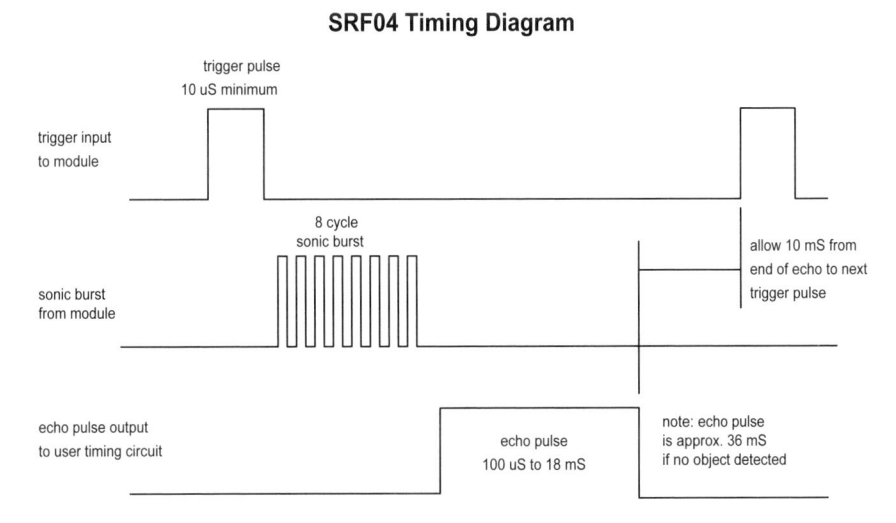

Figure 204. SRF04 timing diagram[38].

In the software this is a three part operation:

Step 1. Send the trigger pulse to the ultrasonic unit. This boils down to making the trigger line high for 20 uS.

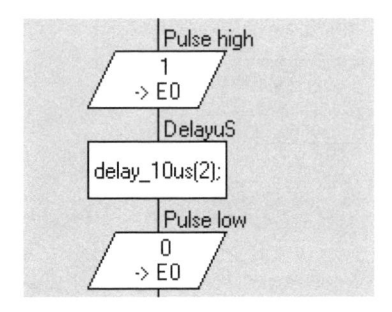

Figure 205. Send the trigger.

Step 2. Wait for the echo line to go high. This is done by checking the echo line in a small loop. As long as the line doesn't go high the program will remain in this loop.

---

[38] This picture is copyright Daventech and used with kind permission.

5.3 Ultrasonic range finder

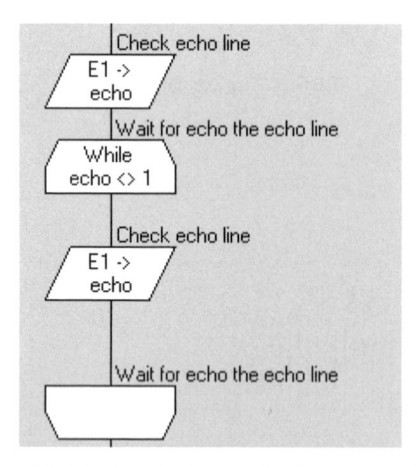

Figure 206. Wait for the echo line to go high.

Step 3. Wait for the echo line to go low again. This would mean an echo has been received. Meanwhile measure the elapsed time so the distance can be calculated.

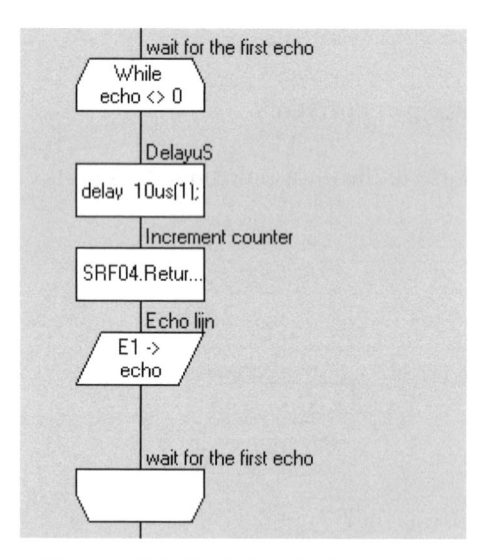

Figure 207. Wait for the first echo.

The distance can be calculated based on the elapsed time. There is quite a bit of difference between the measured elapsed time and the calculated elapsed time. If the distance between the object and the sensor is for example 10 centimeters the sound waves have to travel there and back, so a total of 20 centimeters. At the time of measurement the

5 Sensors

ambient temperature was 19 °C, so the speed of sound is 342 meters per second[39]. This means 20 centimeters takes about 580 uS. The time measured was 410 uS however, so a lot of time is lost in overheads in the While loop.

actual distance	measured elapsed time	calculated elapsed time
5	220	290
10	410	580
15	590	880

Figure 208. Measurements done with the SRF04.

Calibration shows that the distance can be calculated by dividing the number of 10 uS loops by 4. For a distance of 10 centimeters the calculated distance is 10.3 centimeters. Accurate enough for this application.

Operational

Figure 209. The completed project (Dutch version).

---

[39] The temperature in my office was about 19 degrees C. The formula is c = 20 * square root(T) where T is the air temperature (in Kelvin) and c is the estimated speed of sound at that temperature. Note that degrees Kelvin can be calculated by adding 273.15 to the temperature in degrees C.

5.4 Digital thermometer

When in use the sensor makes a very soft ticking noise. The newer version of this sensor, the SRF05 has a small indicator LED at the back that lights each time a sound burst is emitted.

The full source of this project is part of the download package and listed under this chapter number.

5.4 Digital thermometer

Concept

Temperatures can be measured using an NTC thermistor. The relationship between the resistance and the actual temperature is logarithmic, and may differ between different NTCs, even if they are the exact same type. If measurements with any kind of accuracy have to take place calibration will need to be done. Once that has taken place a simple program can be used to digitally display temperatures.

Hardware

For the first phase of this project, calibration, no microcontrollers are involved. The hardware consists of a tube thermometer and an NTC connected to a digital multimeter.

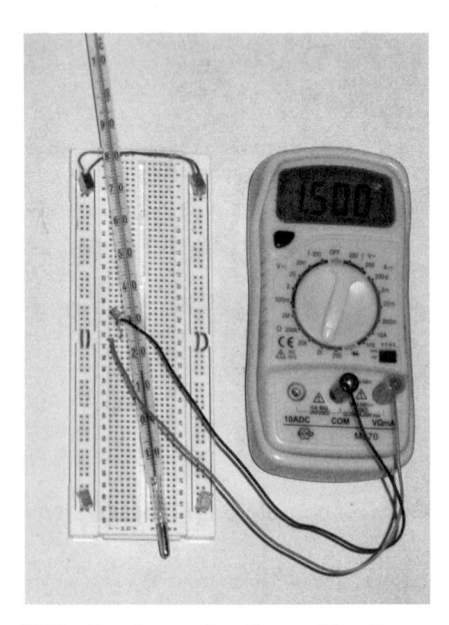

Figure 210. Hardware for the calibration process.

5 Sensors

In the second phase, temperature measurement, a 16F877A PIC microcontroller is selected. The NTC is connected to the microcontroller using a Proto board, and an LCD board is used to display the measured temperature. Note that the Proto board needs power so you need to connect the +Vin terminal to one of the +V terminals of the Programmer board.

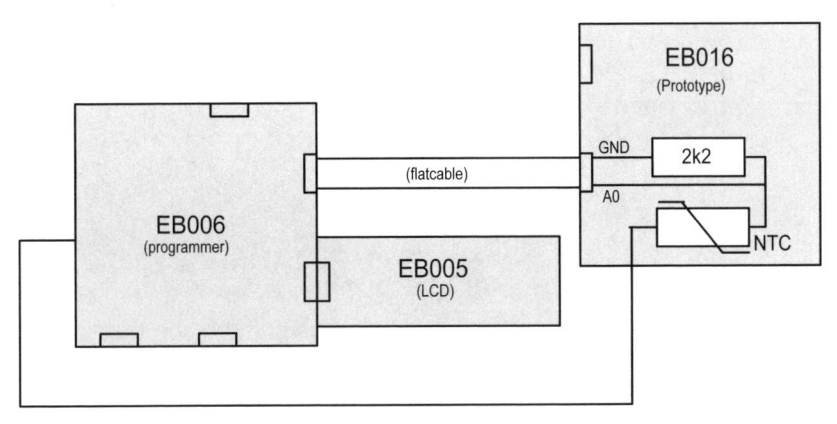

Figure 211. Schematic of the digital thermometer.

Connection summary:

Programmer	Switches to XTAL and Fast, LVP jumper on I/O port, J29 to PSU, J12-14 to USB, use external power supply.
Port B	LCD board, jumper to default.
Port A	A0 NTC and 2k2 resistor.
	+V NTC.
	GND 2k2 resistor.

Procedure

The first step is to take a series of measurements and record both temperature and NTC resistance.

resistance (ohm)	temperature (°C)
6890	-11
2100	9
1700	13
1530	15
1270	20

Figure 212. Calibration measurements.

5.4 Digital thermometer

The next step is to put these values in a graph and determine the relationship between temperature and resistance. A Microsoft Excel spreadsheet with these data and the associated graphs is included in the download package for your reference.

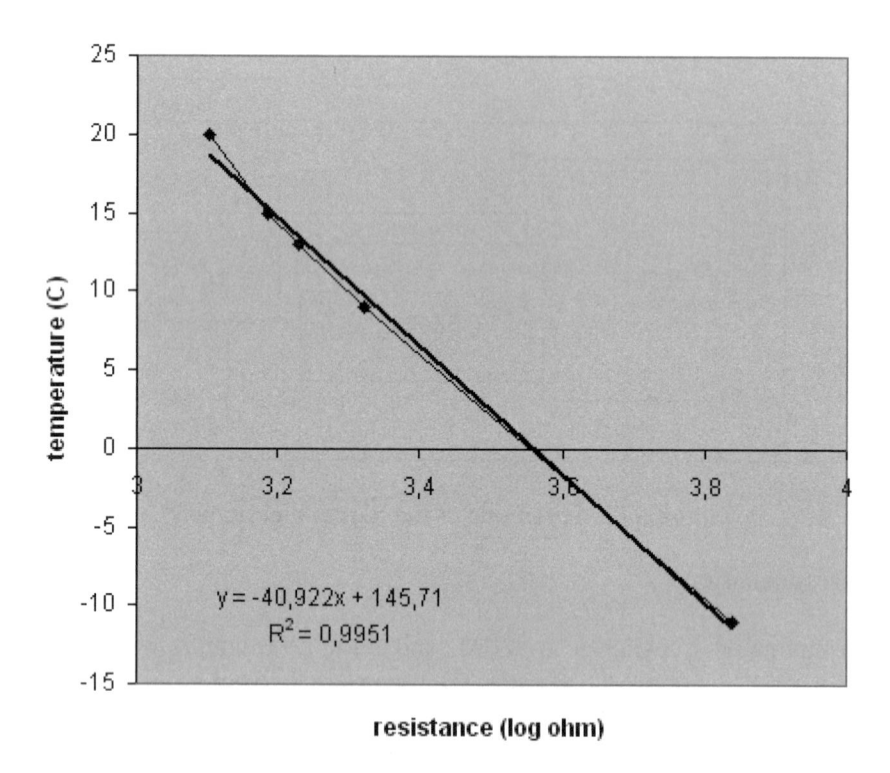

Figure 213. The relationship between T and R.

Note that the horizontal axis shows the resistance on a logarithmic scale.

So this is the formula:

$$T = 145{,}71 - 40{,}922 * \log(R_{NTC}) \qquad (1)$$

Where T is the temperature in °C and R_{NTC} the resistance of the NTC.

The NTC is connected to a microcontroller as part of a voltage divider to turn the resistance into a voltage, as shown in the next Figure.

5 Sensors

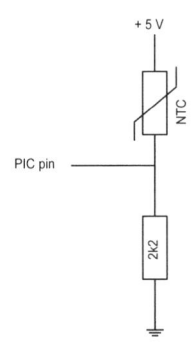

Figure 214. Voltage divider used with an NTC.

For the voltage on the microcontroller input (V_{pic}) the voltage divider yields this result:

$$V_{PIC} = 2k2/(R_{NTC} + 2k2) * 5$$

Or:

$$R_{NTC} = \frac{2k2 * 5}{V_{PIC}} - 2k2 \qquad (2)$$

The analog to digital converter of the microcontroller will result in a value between zero and 255, where 255 is equivalent to 5 volts. In a formula:

$$V_{PIC} = 5 * \frac{ADC}{255}$$

By combining this with formula (2) we get:

$$R_{NTC} = \frac{2k2 * 5 * 255}{ADC * 5} - 2k2$$

Which can be simplified to:

$$R_{NTC} = \frac{561000}{ADC} - 2200$$

5.4 Digital thermometer

Entering this in formula (1) yields the result we were looking for: the relationship between the ADC measurement and the actual temperature:

$$T = 145{,}71 - 40{,}922 * \log((561000/ADC)-2200)$$

Software

In line with the technique described in project 3.9 we will use this formula to store data in a lookup table, the microcontroller we selected for this project cannot handle logarithmic calculations. Unfortunately a lookup table can only handle bytes, and temperatures in the range that we are interested in are definitely going to be below zero.

The formula above shows that ADC values below 95 result in a negative temperature. The work-around is to store all temperatures in the lookup table as positive values. When we need to lookup an ADC value less than 95 we will add a minus sign to the result from the lookup table.

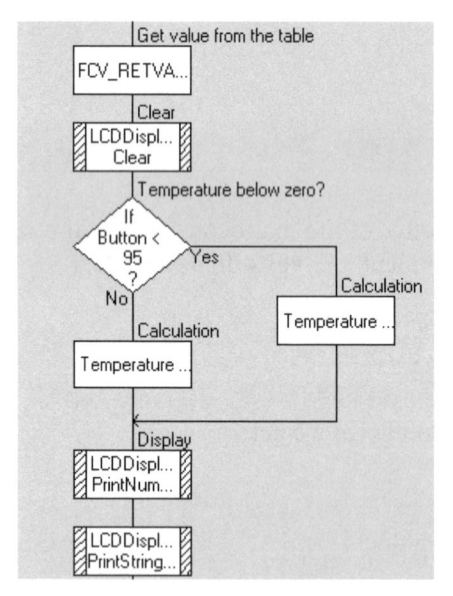

Figure 215. Adding the minus sign if needed.

In the menu select Chip, then Configure and then switch to Expert Config Screen. In the section Configuration Word(s) make sure HEX is selected and then click on the Config1 button and enter: 0x3F3A.

The full source of this project is part of the download package and listed under this chapter number. Note that if you use a different NTC in your projects you will need to do

5 Sensors

the calibration yourself. The ADC value below which temperatures are negative (95) may differ in your situation. So apart from using a different lookup table you most likely need to change this value too.

Operational

Figure 216. The digital thermometer.

5.5 Data sampling the fridge

Concept

Data sampling can be used to record data over a longer period of time in remote locations where a PC is not available. The data is stored in memory until the sampling is completed. Then the unit is moved to a base location and the data is transferred to a PC for analyses using for example a spreadsheet. In this project data sampling is used to record the temperature profile in a standard refrigerator after opening and closing the door, for a period of 10 minutes with a measurement every 0.1 seconds.

Hardware

In this project a 16F877A PIC microcontroller will be used. The data will be recorded in a 64 kbit FRAM memory accessible through an SPI interface, and transferred to the PC

5.5 Data sampling the fridge

using an RS232 connection[40]. A switch board and an LCD board will be used to control the operation. A Proto board will be used to connect the NTC thermistor to the microcontroller.

		RS232		SPI DAC	
pin D9	port C	description	jumper	description	jumper
1	C0			CS_{FRAM}	2(patch)
2	C1			CS_{DAC}	2(patch)
3	C2				
4	C3			SCK	A
5	C4			SDI	A
6	C5			SDO	A
7	C6	TX	c/2	**CS_{FRAM}**	**1**
8	C7	RX	c/2	**CS_{DAC}**	**1**
9	GND				

Figure 217. Connection overview of port C.

Both SPI and RS232 are on port C of the microcontroller. In the previous Figure all connections are shown in a table. The default settings for the SPI board indicate a conflict on C7 and C8. The FRAM chip select line is the same line as the RS232 transmit line. The solution is to set the jumper to position 2 and use the patch panel to reroute the chip select lines to C0 and C1.

Note that both the boards need power so you need to connect the +Vin terminals of all boards to one of the +V terminals of the Programmer board

---

[40] See project 3.12 for more information on SPI and project 3.4 for more information on RS232.

5 Sensors

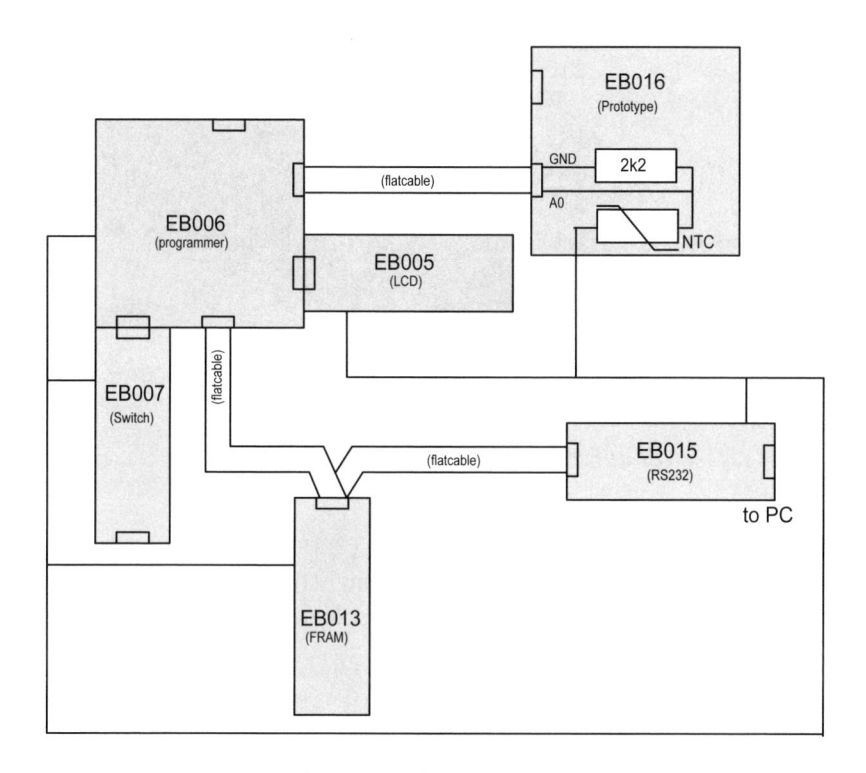

Figure 218. Schematic of the data sampling project.

Connection summary:

Programmer	Switches to XTAL and Fast, LVP jumper on I/O port, J29 to PSU, J12-14 to USB, use external power supply.
Port A	A0 NTC and 2k2 resistor.
	+V NTC.
	GND 2k2 resistor.
Port B	LCD board, jumper to default.
Port C	RS232 board.
	FRAM board patch FRAM to C0.
	patch DAC to C1 (see next Figure).
Port D	Switch board.

5.5 Data sampling the fridge

Figure 219. Patch panel of the EB013.

Software

In the menu select Chip, then Configure and then switch to Expert Config Screen. In the section Configuration Word(s) make sure HEX is selected and then click on the Config1 button and enter: 0x3F3A.

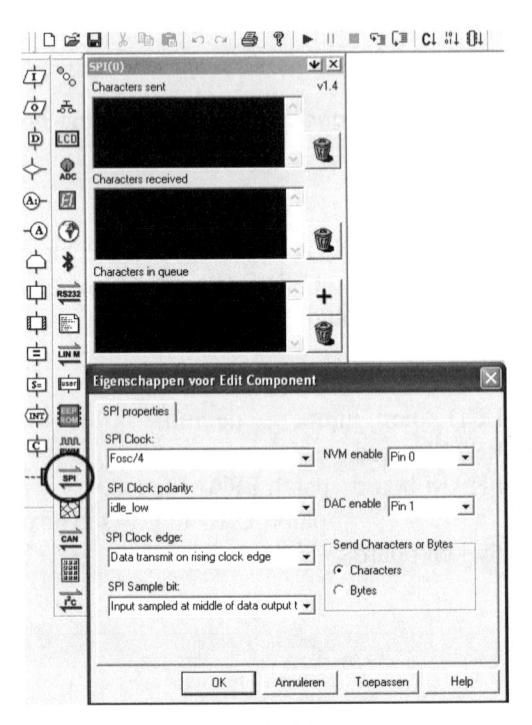

Figure 220. FRAM SPI settings.

5 Sensors

FRAM memory on the EB013 is an SPI device. Add an SPI device to the program and open it using the down arrow. Select the tab "SPI properties" and enter the following settings:

SPI clock	Fosc/4
SPOI clock polarity	idle_low
SPI clock edge	Data transmit on rising clock edge
SPI sample bit	Input sampled at middle of data output time
NVM enable	pin 0
DAC enable	pin 1
Send characters or bytes	Characters

Figure 221. FRAM SPI settings.

Note that the pin numbers used are the numbers of the pins on port C and not on the D9 connector.

First the program will perform an ADC conversion on pin A0 and convert that value to degrees centigrade using a lookup table as described in project 5.4, and display it on the LCD screen.

The target for this project is to store a measurement every 100 ms for a period of 10 minutes, which translates to a total of 6000 measurements. Since the FRAM in use has a capacity of 8000 bytes there is plenty of room. After the 10 minutes interval the program will continue to measure but refrain from storing the result. This means that even when the sampling is over you can still read the actual temperature on the LCD display.

The program uses an integer as a counter, but FRAM requires a high and low byte, which is calculated using this formula:

cHigh = counter / 255
cLow = counter - (cHigh * 255)

At the press of a button the entire content of FRAM is sent to a PC using an RS232 connection. Note that this does not clear memory, so if something went wrong during the transfer you can simply try again.

193

5.5 Data sampling the fridge

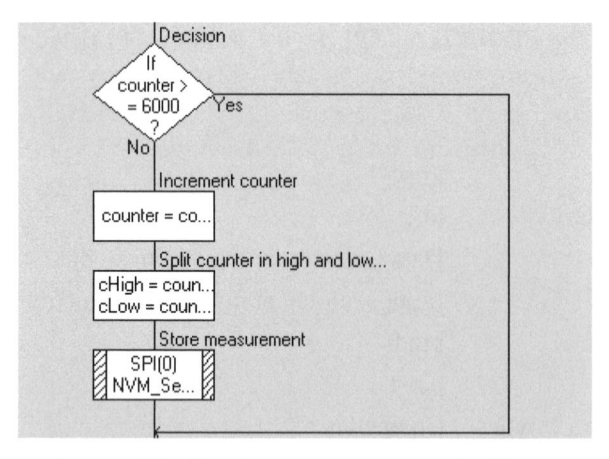

Figure 222. Storing measurements in FRAM.

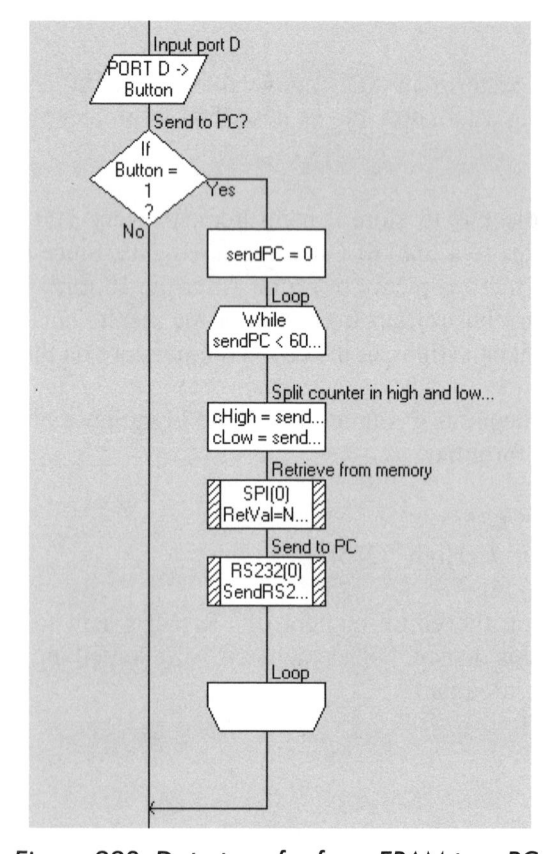

Figure 223. Data transfer from FRAM to a PC.

5   Sensors

In most cases sampling will not take place near a PC, otherwise one might sample with the PC itself. So once the program has started it waits five seconds before sampling starts. This should give the user enough time to press the button and initiate a transfer to the PC. For this reason the "send to PC" loop assumes the value of the counter to be incorrect (after all the program may just have been restarted) and simply sends the first 6000 memory locations from FRAM to the PC, whether they are in use or not.

The full source of this project is part of the download package and listed under this chapter number.

Operational

This is the finished project in operation on the kitchen floor. The white wire on the right top side is connected to a sensor inside the refrigerator. The data was recorded for about three minutes, and than transferred to a PC to be analyzed using Microsoft Excel.

Figure 224. Data sampling in progress.

5.5 Data sampling the fridge

After opening the door the temperature rises, and falls again when the door is closed as is to be expected. Interestingly enough the compressor didn't switch on so the entire drop in temperature is a result of the coldness of the products stored in the fridge. For that reason the final temperature is over a degree higher than when the experiment started.

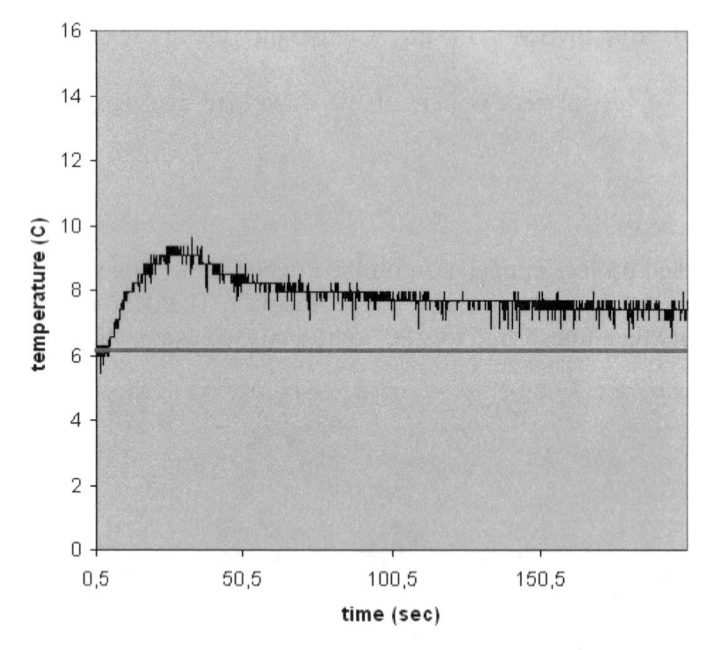

Figure 225. Temperature profile of opening and closing the door.

The purpose of the switches is:

None: *Perform data sampling:* Place the NTC is a suitable location. Switch the power on. Wait for ten minutes. The actual temperature is displayed on the LCD screen.

D0: *Transfer to the PC:* Connect the project to a PC using an RS232 connection. On the PC use a terminal program that can store received data in a file, for example MICterm. Switch the power on to the project. Press the D0 button within 5 seconds and keep it pressed until the data transfer starts. Use a tool such as Microsoft Excel to read the file and analyze it.

D7: *Erase memory:* Switch the power on to the project. Press the D7 button for ten seconds. Switch the power off and then back on again.

5.6 Heat loss in a residential building

Concept

With the ever increasing cost of oil and thus energy insulating a home has become big business. In this project the heat loss of a residential building will be measured in an attempt to assess the insulation level.

Theory

The setup consists of two NTC thermistors, one inside the house and one outside at some distance but sheltered against wind and direct sunlight. In this experiment the outdoor temperature is lower than the indoor temperature. If the temperature drops this means the house is losing heat to the outside. We will assume that anything on the inside of the insulation blanket is regarded as "indoors" and anything on the outside of the insulation is regarded as "outdoors".

The heat flow with the heater off is:

$$Q = m * c * dT/dt \qquad (1)$$

Where:
    c   relative thermal capacity (J/kgK)
    m   mass (kg)
    dT   temperature difference over time (K)
    dt   time difference (s)
    Q   heat flow in J/s (a.k.a. W)

We will ignore furniture and assume that only the air and the brick walls contribute to the thermal capacity. The total volume of this particular house is 338 m3, so the thermal capacity of the air is 437 kJ/K[41].

The volume of the inside of the outer wall, the interior walls and the floors is 22.95 m^3. The heat retention of brick is rather high and the experiment will only take a couple of hours, so it is estimated that only 35% of the walls and floors actually cool down during that period. That means the thermal capacity of the bricks is 9939,563 kJ/K.

---

[41] The relative thermal capacity of air is 1 kJ/kgK and of brick 750 kJ/kgK. The density of air is 1.293 kg/m^3 and of brick 1650 kg/m^3.

5.6 Heat loss in a residential building

So formula (1) becomes:

$$Q = 10376563 * dT/dt \quad (2)$$

Based on the heat flow the insulation index K can be calculated, because:

$$Q = K * s * dT \quad (3)$$

Where: K = insulation index (W/m²K)
s = wall surface area (m²)
dT = temperature difference between inside and outside (K)
Q = heat flow in J/s (a.k.a. W)

The surface area of the walls, windows and roof for this house is 206 m² so formula (2) becomes:

$$Q = K * 206 * dT \quad (4)$$

Hardware

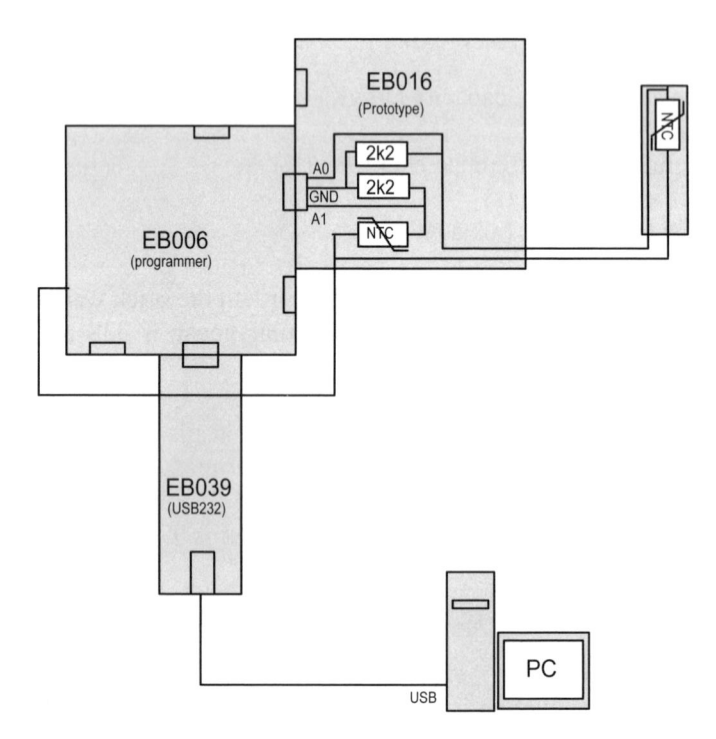

Figure 226. Schematic of the heat loss project.

5 Sensors

In this project a 16F877A PIC microcontroller will be used. The microcontroller will communicate with the PC using a USB interface. A Proto board is used for the connection to the NTCs.

Connection summary:

Programmer		Switches to XTAL and Fast, LVP jumper on I/O port, J29 to PSU, J12-14 to USB, use external power supply.
Port A	A0	NTC/2k2 resistor - outdoors.
	A1	NTC/2k2 resistor - indoor.
	GND	2k2 resistors.
	+V	NTCs.
Port C		USB board.

Software

In the menu select Chip, then Configure and then switch to Expert Config Screen. In the section Configuration Word(s) make sure HEX is selected and then click on the Config1 button and enter: 0x3F3A.

The microcontroller is in fact just an intelligent sensor. When it receives a "space" over the USB connection from the PC it samples both NTCs and sends the result back to the PC. Using this intelligent sensor and a portable PC with USB connection these measurements can easily be carried out on location. On the microcontroller side the USB board behaves like an RS232 connection. Use 38400 BAUD, send bytes.

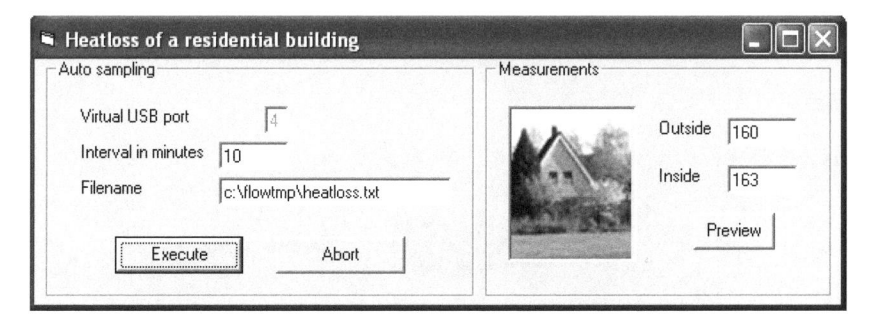

Figure 227.Sampling in progress.

On the PC side a small Visual Basic program, included in the download, sends a space at a regular interval, and stores the answers together with a date/time stamp in a file.

5.6 Heat loss in a residential building

```
Private Sub MSComm1_OnComm()

    'see if data is received
    If MSComm1.InBufferCount Then
        'store it and close the port
        Text1.Text = Asc(MSComm1.Input)
        Text2.Text = Asc(MSComm1.Input)
        MSComm1.PortOpen = False
    End If

    Open Text4.Text For Append As #1
    Print #1, Date$, Time$, Text1.Text, Text2.Text
    Close #1

End Sub
```

An sample of the data file:

03-21-2008	15:09:54	169	160
03-21-2008	15:10:15	160	160
03-21-2008	15:10:18	166	160
03-21-2008	15:10:21	170	160
03-21-2008	15:10:22	171	160
03-21-2008	15:10:25	171	160
03-21-2008	15:10:30	172	160
03-22-2008	14:30:22	158	160
03-22-2008	14:31:02	159	161

Operational

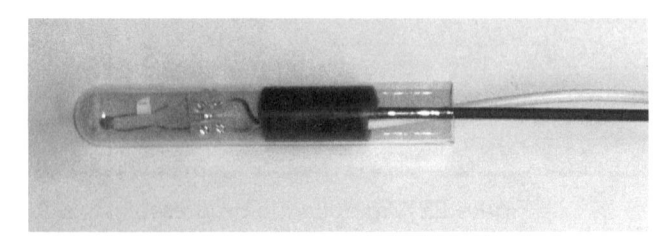

Figure 228. Outdoor sensor in a protective tube.

The outdoor sensor is placed inside a protective glass tube and located in the garden, about 1.5 meters from the house. The indoor sensor is mounted directly on the Proto board and located in the middle of the room near the PC. The sky was overcast with occasional minor drizzle and strong wind. The measurements started at 15:20 and were terminated at 20:10.

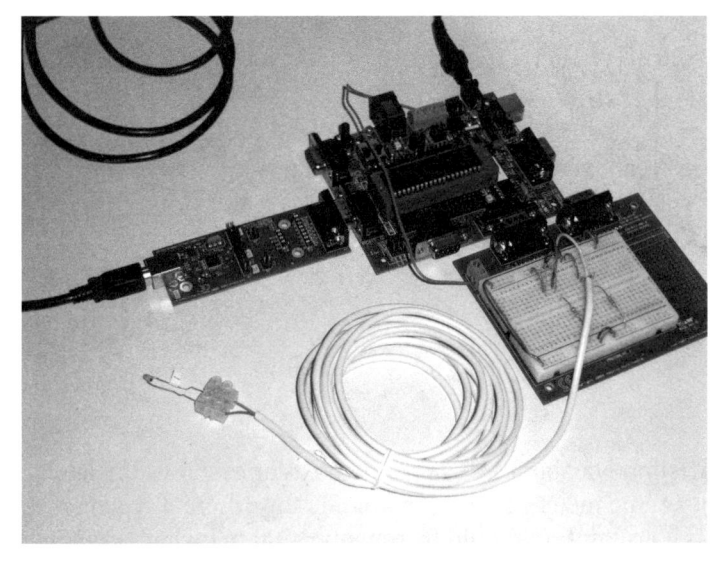

Figure 229. Heat loss sampling equipment.

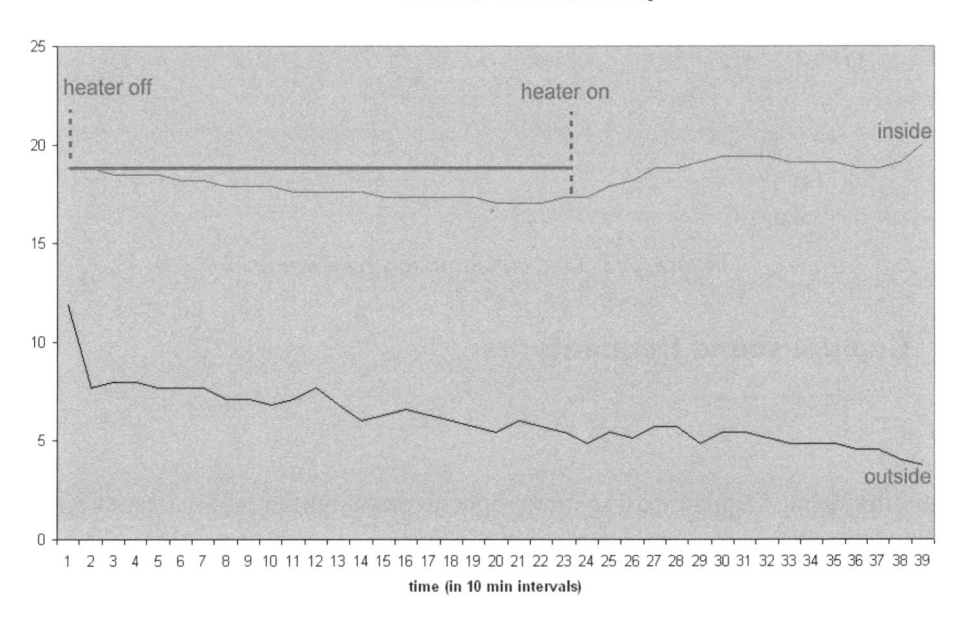

Figure 230. Actual measurements.

5.7 Capture sound frequency

During the temperature decline indicated in the graph with "heater off" the heat flow is 1170 W at an 11 degree temperature difference between the indoor and outdoor measurements, as calculated using formula (2)

$$Q = 10376563 * dT/dt$$
$$Q = 1170 \text{ W}$$

Now the value of K can be calculated using formula (4):

$$Q = K * 206 * dT$$
$$1170 = K * 206 * 11$$

That means that this house has a K = 0.52.

Reality check.

The house in question was built in 1987. The next table shows the average consumption of natural gas per cubic meter of building volume for different K values. Since this house is 338 m^3 the gas consumption should be roughly 1700 m3 which is about correct[42].

K (W/m2K)	Average consumption of natural gas used for heating (m^3 gas per m^3 building volume)
3.13	30
2.94	29
2.70	26
2.56	25
1.75	17
0.37	4
0.32	3

Figure 231. Gas consumption by K value.

5.7 Capture sound frequency

Concept

Measure the sound frequency using a microphone pre-amplifier and the capture mode of the microcontroller CCP1 pin. The incoming signal will need to be cleaned by using a Schmitt trigger such as the microcontroller comparator.

---

[42] The actual average usage over a period of 6 years was 1778 m^3/year, which includes cooking and hot water in the bathroom.

5 Sensors

Hardware

For this project a 16F877A PIC microcontroller is selected. You will need the microphone board from section 9.2. If you didn't build the board you can use the schematic given in that chapter to build the project on a Proto board. The Proto board is also needed for the comparator sensitivity adjustment. An LCD board is used to display the elapsed time.

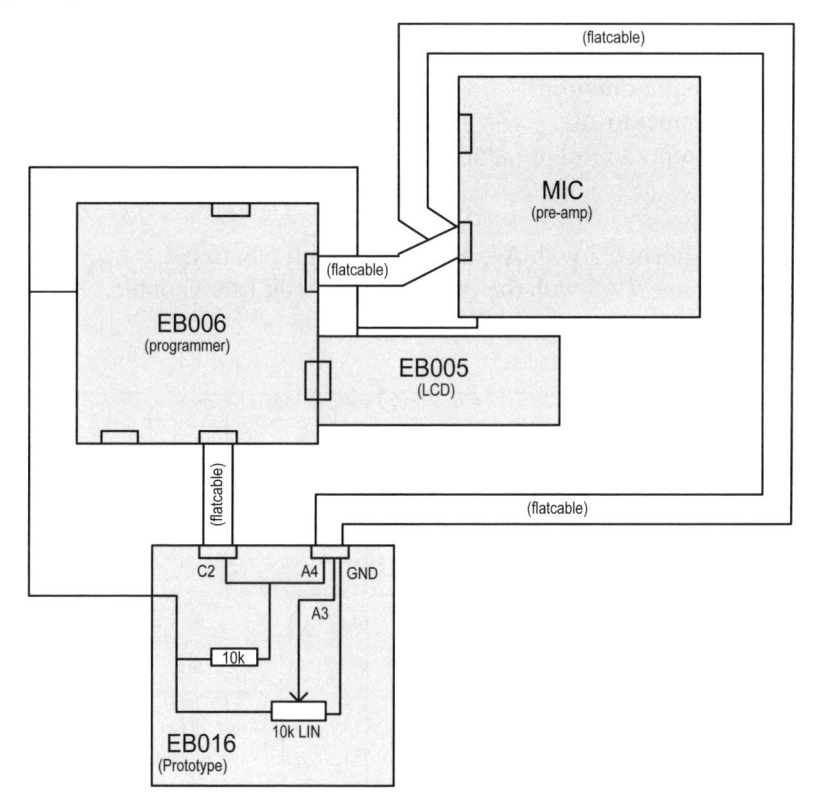

Figure 232. Schematic of the capture frequency project.

The setup is a bit complicated because both the microphone pre-amplifier as well as the Proto board need access to port A. For easier reference the next Figure shows the actual hardware.

5.7 Capture sound frequency

Connection summary:

    Programmer   Switches to XTAL and Fast, LVP jumper on I/O port, J29 to PSU, J12-14 to USB, use external power supply.
    Port A   Microphone pre-amplifier board
              Proto board
    Port B   LCD board, jumper to default.
    Port C   Proto board

    Microphone pre-amplifier:
        - jumper to A0.
        - jumper to full pre-amplifier.

    Proto board:
        - connect C2 with A4, and pull up with 10k to the +V.
        - connect A3 with the center pin of a 10k LIN variable.
        resistor between GND and +V.

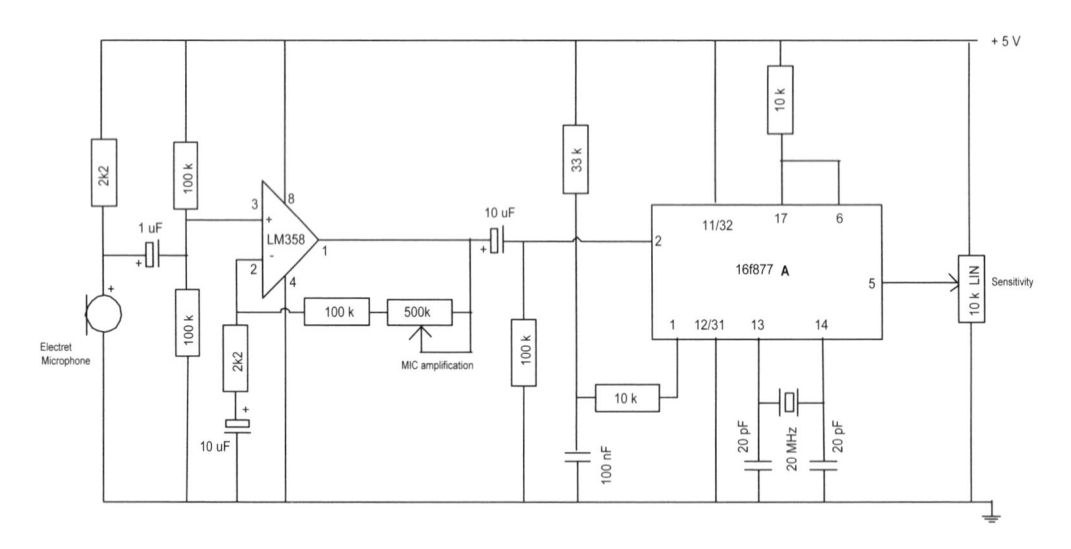

Figure 233. Actual schematic.

Software

In the menu select Chip, then Configure and then switch to Expert Config Screen. In the section Configuration Word(s) make sure HEX is selected and then click on the Config1 button and enter: 0x3F3A.

5   Sensors

According to the datasheet of the 16F877A *"In Capture mode, CCPR1H:CCPR1L captures the 16-bit value of the TMR1 register when an event occurs on pin RC2/CCP1. An event is defined as one of the following: every falling edge, every rising edge, every 4th rising edge, every 16th rising edge."* So if a wave is fed into the capture pin the time difference between two rising edges would indicate the frequency of the wave.

Flowcode doesn't allow direct access to CCP1 or the comparators so these need to be set manually using c blocks. We will use the datasheet to determine which steps need to be taken (the relevant sections are included in this book). First CCP1 needs to be set to capture mode.

REGISTER 8-1:   CCP1CON REGISTER/CCP2CON REGISTER (ADDRESS: 17h/1Dh)

U-0	U-0	R/W-0	R/W-0	R/W-0	R/W-0	R/W-0	R/W-0
—	—	CCPxX	CCPxY	CCPxM3	CCPxM2	CCPxM1	CCPxM0
bit 7							bit 0

bit 7-6   **Unimplemented:** Read as '0'

bit 5-4   **CCPxX:CCPxY**: PWM Least Significant bits
Capture mode:
Unused
Compare mode:
Unused
PWM mode:
These bits are the two LSbs of the PWM duty cycle. The eight MSbs are found in CCPRxL.

bit 3-0   **CCPxM3:CCPxM0**: CCPx Mode Select bits
0000 = Capture/Compare/PWM disabled (resets CCPx module)
0100 = Capture mode, every falling edge
0101 = Capture mode, every rising edge
0110 = Capture mode, every 4th rising edge
0111 = Capture mode, every 16th rising edge
1000 = Compare mode, set output on match (CCPxIF bit is set)
1001 = Compare mode, clear output on match (CCPxIF bit is set)
1010 = Compare mode, generate software interrupt on match (CCPxIF bit is set, CCPx pin is unaffected)
1011 = Compare mode, trigger special event (CCPxIF bit is set, CCPx pin is unaffected); CCP1 resets TMR1; CCP2 resets TMR1 and starts an A/D conversion (if A/D module is enabled)
11xx = PWM mode

Figure 234. CCP1CON register of the 16F877A.

Bits 3-0 of the CCP1CON register take care of this. We will select a capture every rising edge, so 0101. In C:

```
// set CCP1 to capture mode, every rising edge 0000_0101
ccp1con = 0x05;
```

5.7 Capture sound frequency

The next step is to set the speed of the timer used during capture: timer0.

REGISTER 6-1:   T1CON: TIMER1 CONTROL REGISTER (ADDRESS 10h)

U-0	U-0	R/W-0	R/W-0	R/W-0	R/W-0	R/W-0	R/W-0
—	—	T1CKPS1	T1CKPS0	T1OSCEN	T1SYNC	TMR1CS	TMR1ON
bit 7							bit 0

bit 7-6   Unimplemented: Read as '0'

bit 5-4   **T1CKPS1:T1CKPS0**: Timer1 Input Clock Prescale Select bits
11 = 1:8 Prescale value
10 = 1:4 Prescale value
01 = 1:2 Prescale value
00 = 1:1 Prescale value

bit 3   **T1OSCEN**: Timer1 Oscillator Enable Control bit
1 = Oscillator is enabled
0 = Oscillator is shut-off (the oscillator inverter is turned off to eliminate power drain)

bit 2   **T1SYNC**: Timer1 External Clock Input Synchronization Control bit
When TMR1CS = 1:
1 = Do not synchronize external clock input
0 = Synchronize external clock input
When TMR1CS = 0:
This bit is ignored. Timer1 uses the internal clock when TMR1CS = 0.

bit 1   **TMR1CS**: Timer1 Clock Source Select bit
1 = External clock from pin RC0/T1OSO/T1CKI (on the rising edge)
0 = Internal clock (FOSC/4)

bit 0   **TMR1ON**: Timer1 On bit
1 = Enables Timer1
0 = Stops Timer1

Figure 235. T1CON register of the 16F877A.

At this point it's not really important what the settings are as long as they are known, because we need them later to calculate the measured frequency. So we will set the prescaler to 1:1. The timer is left switched off as long as no capture is in progress. In C:

```
// set T1CON but leave the timer off, set timer to zero, prescaler to 1:1
t1con = 0x00;
```

The incoming signal from the microphone pre-amplifier will be a mixture of irregular sinusoidal waves, not at all the clean square wave that the capture function is expecting. So some sort of pre-processing is required, for example by using a Schmitt trigger. In the 16F877A that would mean using one of the comparators.

5 Sensors

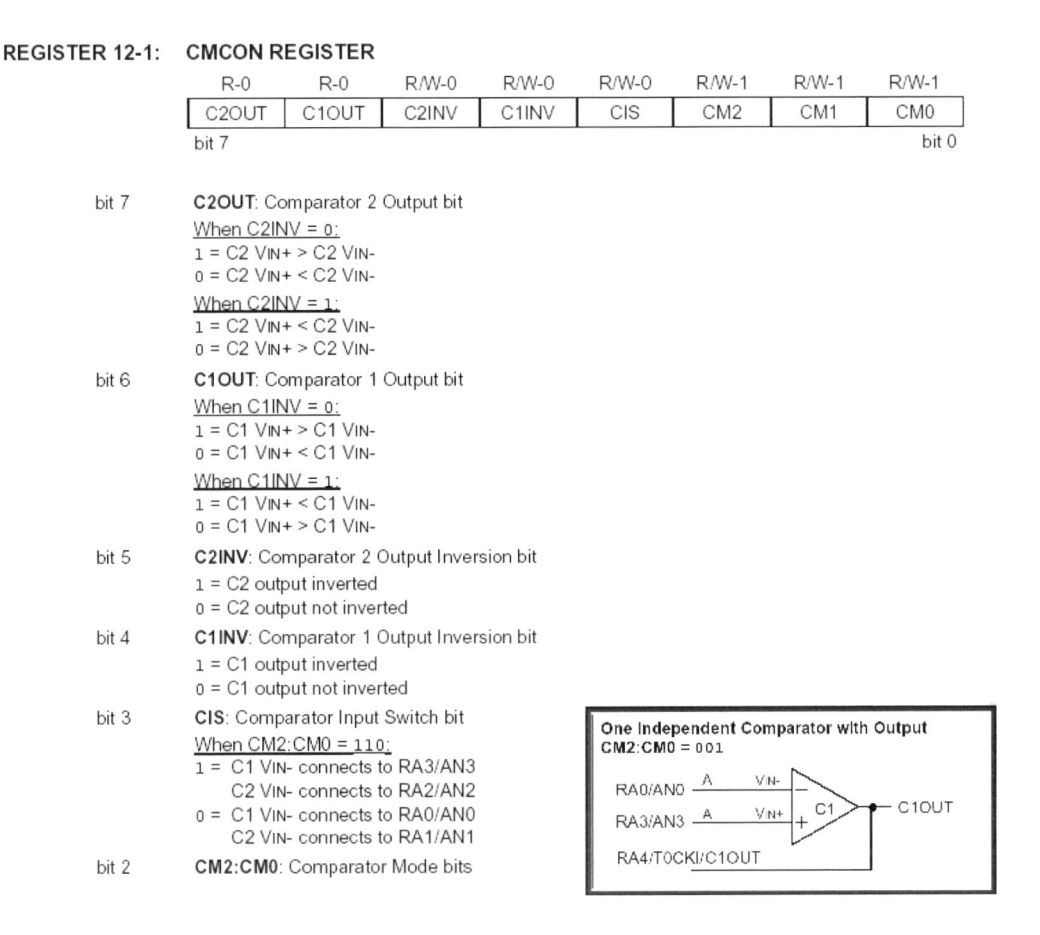

REGISTER 12-1: CMCON REGISTER

R-0	R-0	R/W-0	R/W-0	R/W-0	R/W-1	R/W-1	R/W-1
C2OUT	C1OUT	C2INV	C1INV	CIS	CM2	CM1	CM0

bit 7 .... bit 0

bit 7   **C2OUT**: Comparator 2 Output bit
When C2INV = 0:
1 = C2 V$_{IN+}$ > C2 V$_{IN-}$
0 = C2 V$_{IN+}$ < C2 V$_{IN-}$
When C2INV = 1:
1 = C2 V$_{IN+}$ < C2 V$_{IN-}$
0 = C2 V$_{IN+}$ > C2 V$_{IN-}$

bit 6   **C1OUT**: Comparator 1 Output bit
When C1INV = 0:
1 = C1 V$_{IN+}$ > C1 V$_{IN-}$
0 = C1 V$_{IN+}$ < C1 V$_{IN-}$
When C1INV = 1:
1 = C1 V$_{IN+}$ < C1 V$_{IN-}$
0 = C1 V$_{IN+}$ > C1 V$_{IN-}$

bit 5   **C2INV**: Comparator 2 Output Inversion bit
1 = C2 output inverted
0 = C2 output not inverted

bit 4   **C1INV**: Comparator 1 Output Inversion bit
1 = C1 output inverted
0 = C1 output not inverted

bit 3   **CIS**: Comparator Input Switch bit
When CM2:CM0 = 110:
1 = C1 V$_{IN-}$ connects to RA3/AN3
     C2 V$_{IN-}$ connects to RA2/AN2
0 = C1 V$_{IN-}$ connects to RA0/AN0
     C2 V$_{IN-}$ connects to RA1/AN1

bit 2   **CM2:CM0**: Comparator Mode bits

One Independent Comparator with Output
CM2:CM0 = 001

Figure 236. CMCON register of the 16F877A.

The insert in the previous Figure shows that a (one in fact) comparator will be enabled if bits 2-0 are set to 001. Since none of the other bits is relevant this translates to:

     // set the comparator on in mode 1
     cmcon = 0x01;

Only A0 and A3 are required to be inputs, the others are not connected to anything. Since unconnected, and thus floating, pins should never be inputs we will make them outputs. The TRISA register takes care of this. Each bit of that register represents a pin, and setting that bit to 1 makes that pin and input. So in this case TRISA should be 1001. In C:

     // set A0 and A3 to input others to output
     trisa = 0x09;

5.7 Capture sound frequency

This completes the settings. Now in a continuous loop the frequency can be captured by measuring the time that the capture flag is high.

REGISTER 2-5: PIR1 REGISTER (ADDRESS 0Ch)

R/W-0	R/W-0	R-0	R-0	R/W-0	R/W-0	R/W-0	R/W-0
PSPIF[1]	ADIF	RCIF	TXIF	SSPIF	CCP1IF	TMR2IF	TMR1IF

bit 7   bit 0

bit 7   PSPIF[1]: Parallel Slave Port Read/Write Interrupt Flag bit
            1 = A read or a write operation has taken place (must be cleared in software)
            0 = No read or write has occurred

bit 6   ADIF: A/D Converter Interrupt Flag bit
            1 = An A/D conversion completed
            0 = The A/D conversion is not complete

bit 5   RCIF: USART Receive Interrupt Flag bit
            1 = The USART receive buffer is full
            0 = The USART receive buffer is empty

bit 4   TXIF: USART Transmit Interrupt Flag bit
            1 = The USART transmit buffer is empty
            0 = The USART transmit buffer is full

bit 3   SSPIF: Synchronous Serial Port (SSP) Interrupt Flag
            1 = The SSP interrupt condition has occurred, and must be cleared in software before returning from the Interrupt Service Routine. The conditions that will set this bit are:
- SPI
  - A transmission/reception has taken place.
- I²C Slave
  - A transmission/reception has taken place.
- I²C Master
  - A transmission/reception has taken place.
  - The initiated START condition was completed by the SSP module.
  - The initiated STOP condition was completed by the SSP module.
  - The initiated Restart condition was completed by the SSP module.
  - The initiated Acknowledge condition was completed by the SSP module.
  - A START condition occurred while the SSP module was idle (Multi-Master system).
  - A STOP condition occurred while the SSP module was idle (Multi-Master system).

            0 = No SSP interrupt condition has occurred.

bit 2   CCP1IF: CCP1 Interrupt Flag bit
            <u>Capture mode:</u>
            1 = A TMR1 register capture occurred (must be cleared in software)
            0 = No TMR1 register capture occurred
            <u>Compare mode:</u>
            1 = A TMR1 register compare match occurred (must be cleared in software)
            0 = No TMR1 register compare match occurred
            <u>PWM mode:</u>
            Unused in this mode

bit 1   TMR2IF: TMR2 to PR2 Match Interrupt Flag bit
            1 = TMR2 to PR2 match occurred (must be cleared in software)
            0 = No TMR2 to PR2 match occurred

bit 0   TMR1IF: TMR1 Overflow Interrupt Flag bit
            1 = TMR1 register overflowed (must be cleared in software)
            0 = TMR1 register did not overflow
            Note 1: PSPIF is reserved on PIC16F873/876 devices; always maintain this bit clear.

Figure 237. PIR1 register of the 16F877A.

5 Sensors

The capture flag is bit 2 of the PIR1 register. So first set the timer0 to zero, wait for bit 2 of PIR1 to go high, start timer0, wait for bit 2 of PIR1 to go low again, stop timer0 and record the timer0 value.

Since this involves handling registers and systems variables this has to be done in C as well:

```
// clear the counter
tmr1h = 0;
tmr1l = 0;

// reset the capture flag ccp1if
pir1.2= 0;

// wait for the first capture to take place
while (pir1.2 == 0);

// start the capture and clear the capture flag
t1con.0= 1;
pir1.2 = 0;

// wait for the next capture
while (pir1.2 == 0);

// stop the timer and record the value
t1con.0 = 0;
FCV_PASSTIMELOW = ccpr1l;
FCV_PASSTIMEHIGH = ccpr1h;
```

Now all that is left to do is display the elapsed time on the LCD.

It is a great feature of Flowcode that it integrates so nicely with C to allow programs like this.

5.7 Capture sound frequency

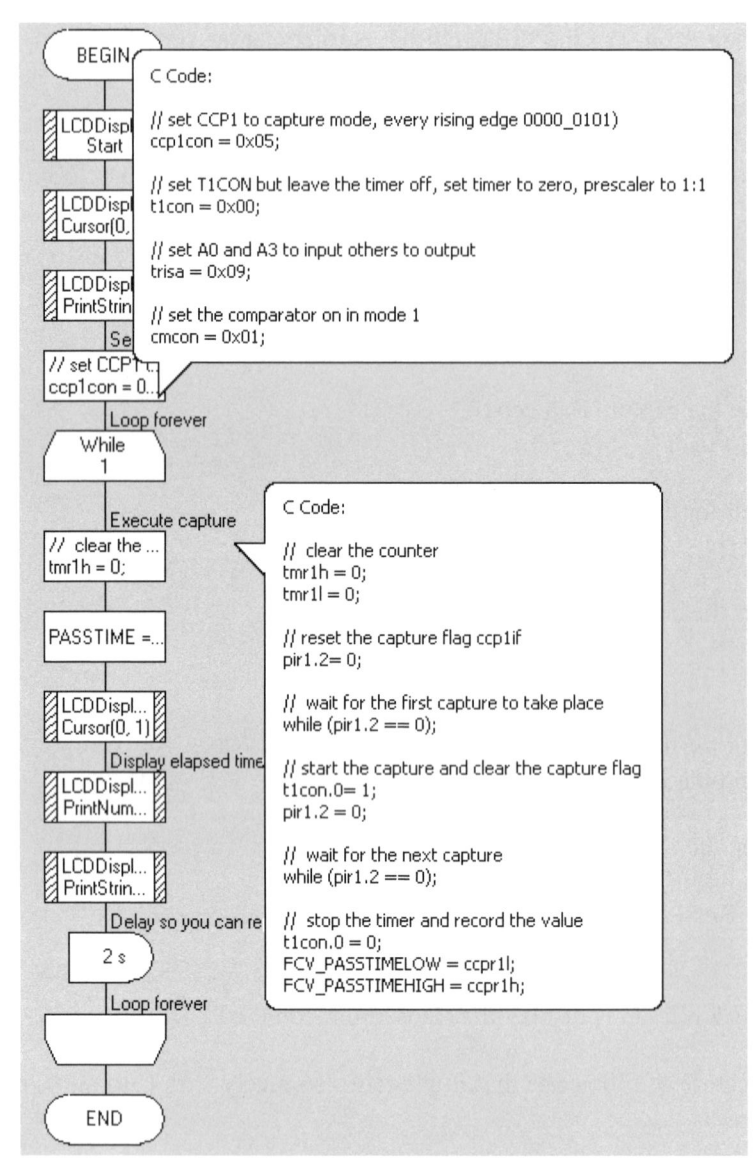

Figure 238. Capture sound frequency.

Flowchart contents:

BEGIN → LCDDispl Start → LCDDispl Cursor(0,...) → LCDDispl PrintStrin... → Set... → While 1 → Execute capture → PASSTIME =... → LCDDispl Cursor(0, 1) → Display elapsed time → LCDDispl PrintNum... → LCDDispl PrintStrin... → Delay so you can re... 2 s → Loop forever → END

C Code (initialization):
```
// set CCP1 to capture mode, every rising edge 0000_0101)
ccp1con = 0x05;

// set T1CON but leave the timer off, set timer to zero, prescaler to 1:1
t1con = 0x00;

// set A0 and A3 to input others to output
trisa = 0x09;

// set the comparator on in mode 1
cmcon = 0x01;
```

C Code (capture):
```
// clear the counter
tmr1h = 0;
tmr1l = 0;

// reset the capture flag ccp1if
pir1.2 = 0;

// wait for the first capture to take place
while (pir1.2 == 0);

// start the capture and clear the capture flag
t1con.0 = 1;
pir1.2 = 0;

// wait for the next capture
while (pir1.2 == 0);

// stop the timer and record the value
t1con.0 = 0;
FCV_PASSTIMELOW = ccpr1l;
FCV_PASSTIMEHIGH = ccpr1h;
```

Operational

A frequency generator is used to check the accuracy of this project. Use the 10k variable resistor to adjust the sensitivity of the comparator. Use the variable resistor on the microphone pre-amplifier to adjust the volume. If the settings are correct a value will be displayed at the LCD screen that is refreshed every two seconds.

At 1000 Hz the average measurement is 4874, see the next table. The crystal connected to the microcontroller is 19.66 MHz. Every clock tick requires four instructions so the frequency of the clock ticks is 19.66 MHz/4 = 4.92 MHz.

The timer0 prescaler is zero, so it will run at maximum speed. That means that one increment of timer0 takes:

$$\frac{1}{4.92 \text{ MHz}} = 2 \cdot 10^{-7} \text{ second}$$

On average 4874 increments were measured, so $4874 \times 2 \cdot 10^{-7} = 9.748 \cdot 10^{-4}$ second. So the measured frequency is $1/(9.748 \cdot 10^{-4}) = 1026$ Hz.

The next table shows a series of measurements at different frequencies. The deviation column shows the deviation in the measurements, not the deviation between actual and measured frequency.

Actual frequency (Hz)	Measurements	Average	Deviation (%)	Measured frequency (Hz)
1000	4760,4626,4846,4868,4904,4987, 4801,4990,4853,5074,4905	4874	7.4%	1026
2000	2520,2433,2509,2369,2395,2396, 2417,2344,2383,2469,2445,2389, 2441	2424	7.3%	2063
5000	970,985,984,988,974,970,976, 995,972	979	2.6%	5107
10000	484,486,485,487,489,491,498, 493,487	489	2.8%	10225

Figure 239. Measured frequency compared to actual.

The deviation assumes that my frequency generator is 100% stable, which it probably is not. Never the less the results are quite satisfactory.

5.8 Tow away alarm

Figure 240. Capture in progress.

5.8 Tow away alarm

Concept

An ignition- or starterdisabler, or a steering wheel clamp, may prevent car thieves from driving your vehicle, but it is not effective against towing your car away. This project covers a motion detection alarm. Once the alarm is armed any movement will set it off.

Hardware

For this project we will use the AT91SAM7S128 ARM microcontroller, in combination with a Proto board and an LED board. Note that the Proto board needs power so you need to connect the +Vin terminal to the +V terminal of the Programmer board. On the Proto

5 Sensors

board a Sharp GP1S036HEL "Photointerruptor for Detecting Tilt Direction" is used[43], mounted almost horizontally. When soldering wires to this component make sure it doesn't get too hot. The sensor uses a little plastic ball inside and if this ball melts the sensor will not work anymore.

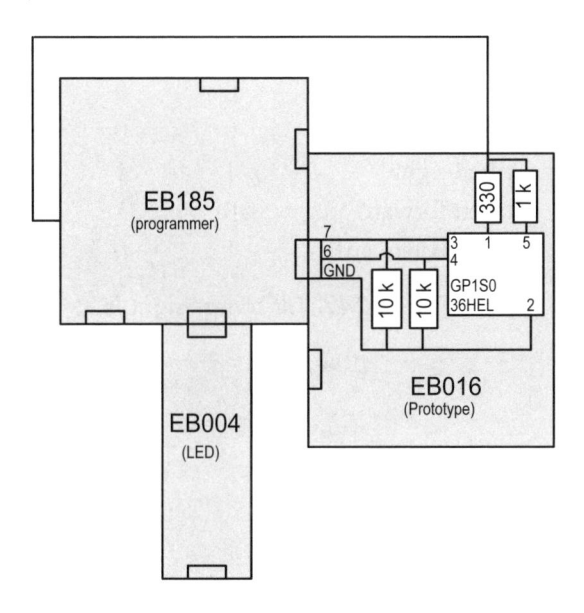

Figure 241. Hardware for the tow away alarm.

Connection summary:

Programmer	EB185, use external power supply, jumpers J16 to PSU, J18 to USB, J15 to default.
Port B	EB016 Proto board.
	B6 to pin 4 of the GP1S036HEL and with a 10K resistor to GND.
	B7 to pin 3 of the GP1S036HEL and with a 10K resistor to GND.
	GND to pin 2 of the GP1S036HEL.
	Pin 1 of the GP1S036HEL to a 330 ohm resistor and then to +V.
	Pin 5 of the GP1S036HEL to a 1k resistor and then to +V.
Port C	EB004 LED board.

Make sure the clock speed in the Chip menu is set to 47923200 Hz.

---

[43] The sensor has a LED on one side (on the inside) and four light sensitive resistors on the other side. A little plastic ball blocks the light to one or more of these resistors depending on the way the sensor is held.

5.8 Tow away alarm

Software

The Sharp sensor is mounted almost horizontally and connected to pins B6 and B7. Depending on its position one or more of these pins will be made high.

position	B6	B7
level	0	0
tilted left	0	0
tilted right	1	1
tilted forward	0	1
tilted backward	1	0

Figure 242. Tilt sensor signals.

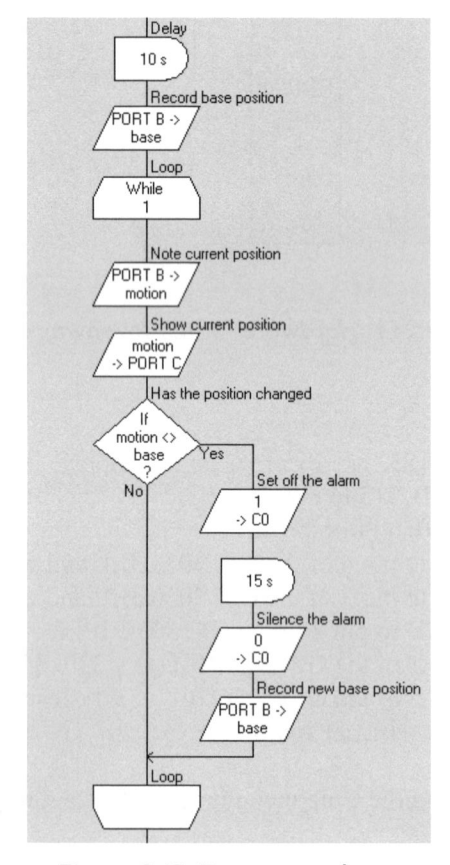

Figure 243. Tow away alarm.

5 Sensors

The program starts with a 10 second delay which allows you to get out of your car and close the door. At the start of the program the current sensor position is recorded. This is the base position, which will not result in an alarm. This will allow you to park your car on an incline in any direction. Any change on pin B6 and B7 will set the alarm (the LED on B0) to go off for a duration of 15 seconds. A limited alarm time is mandatory by law in most countries. Once these 15 seconds have passed the alarm switches off again, and the current position is used as the new base.

Operational

In the next Figure the tow away alarm is operational. Note the small inlay that shows how the sensor is connected to the microcontroller.

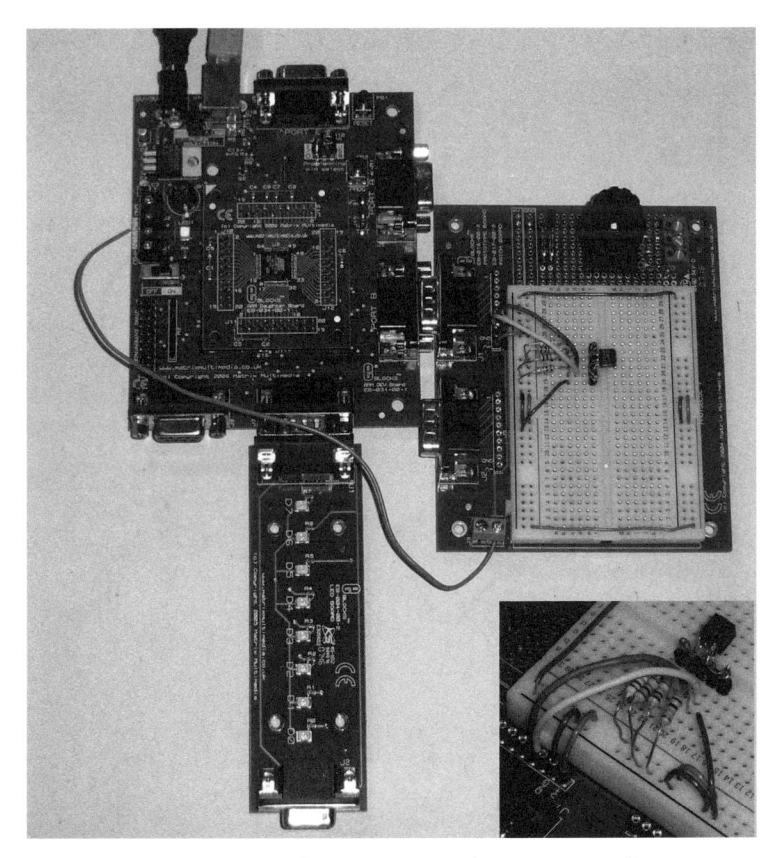

Figure 244. The tow away alarm is armed.

Hold the sensor in any position, then switch it on using the on/off switch on the programmer. After 10 seconds the alarm engages. The position is indicated using the LEDs on B6 and B7. If the sensor changes position the alarm LED on B0 will come on

215

5.8   Tow away alarm

for 15 seconds. Then the alarm resets itself accepting the current position of the sensor as base point. Any subsequent change in position will set the alarm off again.

In real life you may want to add a relay board and connect it to your car horn. That will probably deter thieves more than a small LED coming on.

Note that the Proto board is equipped with a variable resistor as described in chapter 9.1, but it is not used in this project.

6 Cell phone

Cell phones have become the modern communication tool of choice. This chapter covers a few projects that make use of cell phone technology using a special cell phone modem.

6.1 Send a text message

Concept

Use a microcontroller connected to a cell phone modem to send a text message to a cell phone. Both cell phone number and message are fixed in the program.

Hardware

For this project we will use the ATMEGA 32 AVR microcontroller. The cell phone modem is connected to the microcontroller using an RS232 board. Since the modem has a female D9 connector it needs to use the side connection on the RS232 unit.

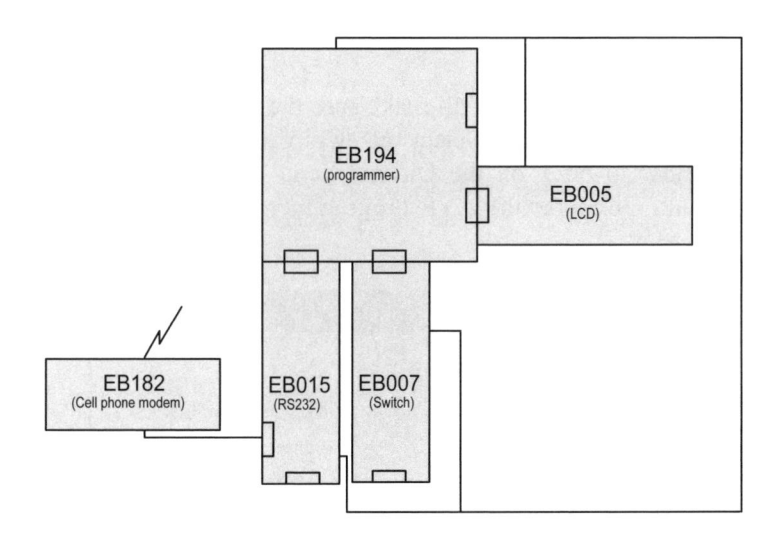

Figure 245. Schematic to send a text message.

Connection summary:

Programmer	EB194, jumper to default.
Port B	LCD board, jumper to default.
Port C	Switch board
Port D	RS232 board, Cell phone modem on side connector.

6.1 Send a text message

On the RS232 board use the patch system, jumper D, and route wires from pin 0 to RX and Pin1 to TX. You will also have to use Jumper (3) and patch wires from pin2 to RTS and pin 3 to CTS.

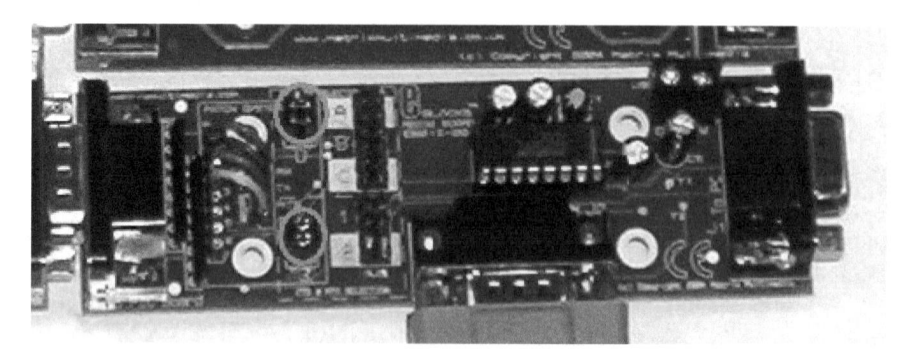

Figure 246. RS232 patch panel for ATMEGA32 port D.

Connect the cell phone modem to the side of the RS232 board. Insert a SIM card into the modem. Make sure the card is prepaid and has sufficient funds to send text messages.

Software

If you haven't done so already first of all make sure the fuses of the ATMEGA 32 are set correctly to 0x0,0xdf and 0x1,0xff. Select the "Chip" menu and "Configure". Enter the settings and remember to click on the Ok and Send button, because they will not be transferred by default. Of course the AVR programmer must be connected to the PC and powered on for this to work.

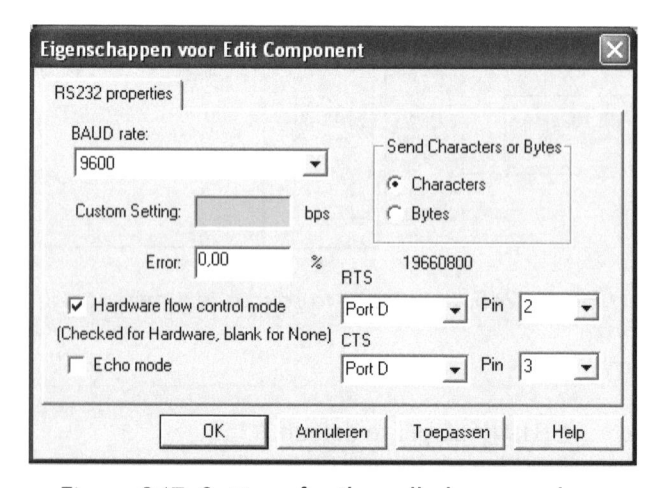

Figure 247. Settings for the cell phone modem.

6   Cell phone

The next step is to set the communications settings for the cell phone modem as follows:

Settings: BAUD rate: 9600
Send Characters
Enable Hardware flow control mode
RTS Port D pin2
CTS Port D pin3

Hardware flow control means that the modem and the microcontroller use pins to check if the other party is ready to receive data. If a party wants to send data it makes the RTS line high. RTS is an acronym for Request (permission) To Send. If the other unit is able to receive data it will respond by making the CTS line high. CTS is an acronym for (you are) Cleared To Send.

We will make use of two macros by Matrix Multimedia, one for sending a single character, and one for receiving a single character. Discussing the inner workings is outside the scope of this book so they will be used as is. These macros are included in the download package.

The first step we need to take is to enter a valid cell phone number into the program to send the text message to.

    NUMBER = "1234567890"

Then the modem needs a series of commands. First set the message format to text mode:

    COMMAND = "AT+CMGF=1"

Next set the new message indicator to mode 2, buffer text message when the modem-microcontroller link is busy and flush as soon as it is not busy any more, and mt 2, do not store text messages:

    COMMAND = "AT+CNMI=2,2"

Each command can be send to the cell phone modem using the send macro. Since the modem will give a reply, a receive macro is also needed. This reply should be "OK" but at this point we will simply ignore the reply and assume that all is well.

The program itself also shows relevant messages on the LCD screen so the user can keep track of progress. The full source of this program is included in the download package and listed under this chapter number.

6.1 Send a text message

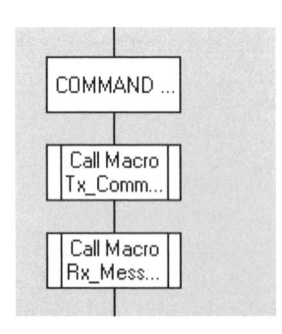

Figure 248. Send a command to the cell phone modem.

The next step is to send the text message.

>TEXT = "Greetings from your AVR"
>COMMAND = "AT+CMGS=" + mark + NUMBER + mark
>COMMAND = TEXT + ctrlZ

The variable "mark" is CHR$(34), the quotation mark, which cannot be included in a string otherwise.

The full source of this project is part of the download package.

Operation

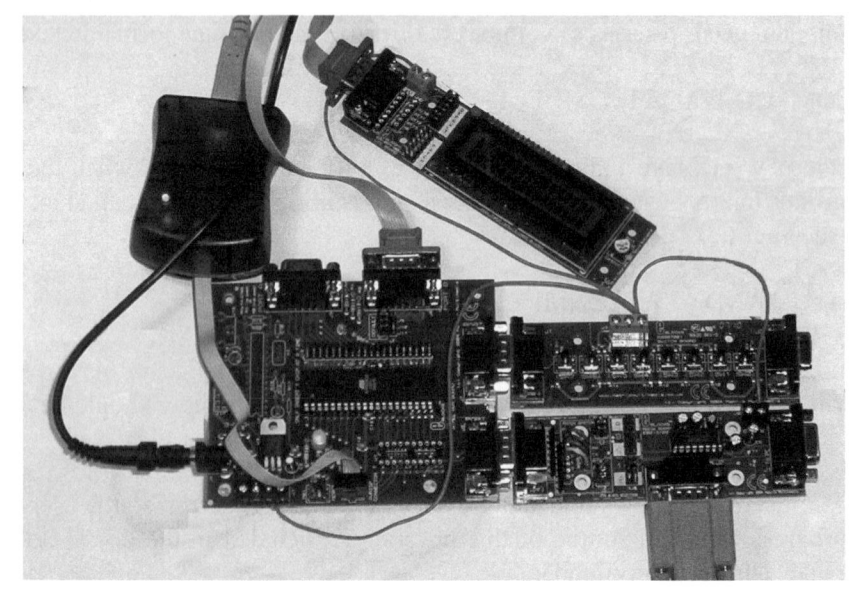

Figure 249. Project in operation.

6   **Cell phone**

Switch the power on and wait for the green LED in the cell phone modem to stop flashing. That means it has connected to the network and is ready to be used. If it doesn't stop flashing move the modem to a different location. If all else fails put the SIM card in you cell phone to check if the card is ok, and the network service is available.

Once the LED is steady press button C0. The modem will now be prepared and the text message sent. Progress is shown on the LCD screen. Note that text messages are not free, you need sufficient funds on the prepaid SIM card in the cell phone modem.

NOP

If you took a look at the macros the NOP at the end of the receive macro may have surprised you. This is because an AVR macro cannot terminate correctly after a jump. Oddly enough the NOP, and assembler command for "do nothing", seems to fix that.

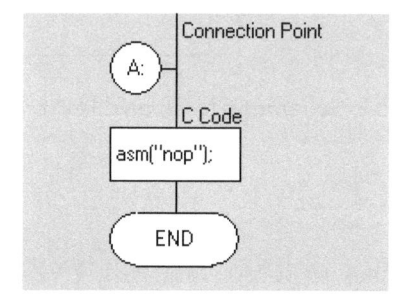

Figure 250. The NOP between the jump and the end of the macro.

6.2   Receive a text message

Concept

Use a microcontroller connected to a cell phone modem to receive a text message from a cell phone and display it on an LCD.

Hardware

In this project we will use a 16F877A PIC microcontroller. The cell phone modem is connected to the RS232 board which is connected to port C. The modem has a female D9 plug so it needs to be connected to the side D9 connector of the RS232 board. An LCD board is connected to port B. Note that both boards need power so you need to connect the +Vin terminals of both boards to one of the +V terminals of the Programmer board

221

6.2 Receive a text message

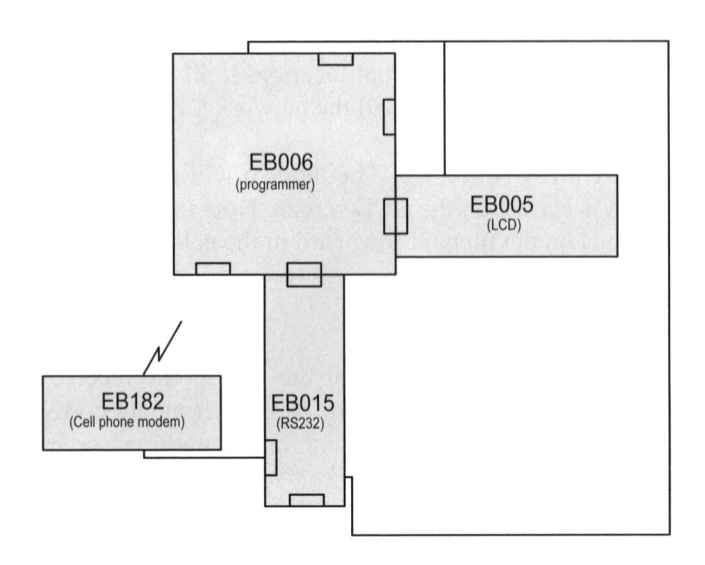

Figure 251. Schematic to receive text messages.

Connection summary:

Programmer	Switches to XTAL and Fast, LVP jumper on I/O port, J29 to PSU, J12-14 to USB, use external power supply.
Port B	LCD board, jumper to default.
Port C	RS232, Cell phone modem on side connector.

Software

In the menu select Chip, then Configure and then switch to Expert Config Screen. In the section Configuration Word(s) make sure HEX is selected and then click on the Config1 button and enter: 0x3F3A.

This program uses the same macros that were discussed in the project 6.1 for sending and receiving characters. The initial part of the program, setting up the cell phone modem for text messaging, is identical too. The communication settings are similar but the PIC uses a different port and pins.

6   **Cell phone**

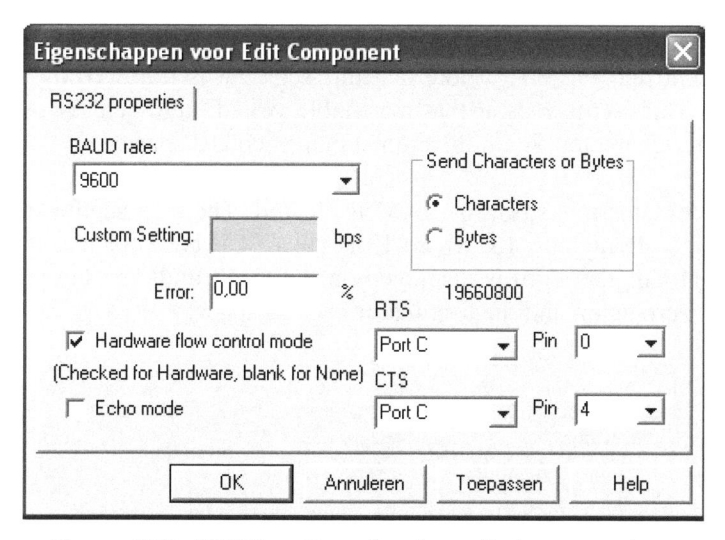

Figure 252. RS232 settings for the cell phone modem.

Settings: BAUD rate: 9600
Send characters
Hardware flow control enabled
RTS Port C pin 0
CTS Port C pin 4

Incoming text messages consist of three parts, for example:

+CMT: "+1234567890",,"08/02/12,10:06:43+04"
Greetings mate!

The first part indicates that a text message is received:

+CMT:

The second part contains the phone number that the text message originated from and a date/time stamp:

"+1234567890",,"08/02/12,10:06:43+04"

The third part contains the actual text message:

Greetings mate!

223

6.2 Receive a text message

So as soon as a segment is received the program must check if this segment contains the text message identifier "+CMT:". Note that this segment is followed by a space and not by a line feed. This is the reason that a variable called "term_ch" is used to store the current terminator character. So at this moment term_ch is a space.

If the segment contains this string the LCD is cleared. The next segments are terminated with a line feed, so term_ch = 13, where 13 is the ASCII code for line feed. The second segment is discarded. The third is displayed on the LCD, and then the message segment counter is set to zero again and the terminator back to space.

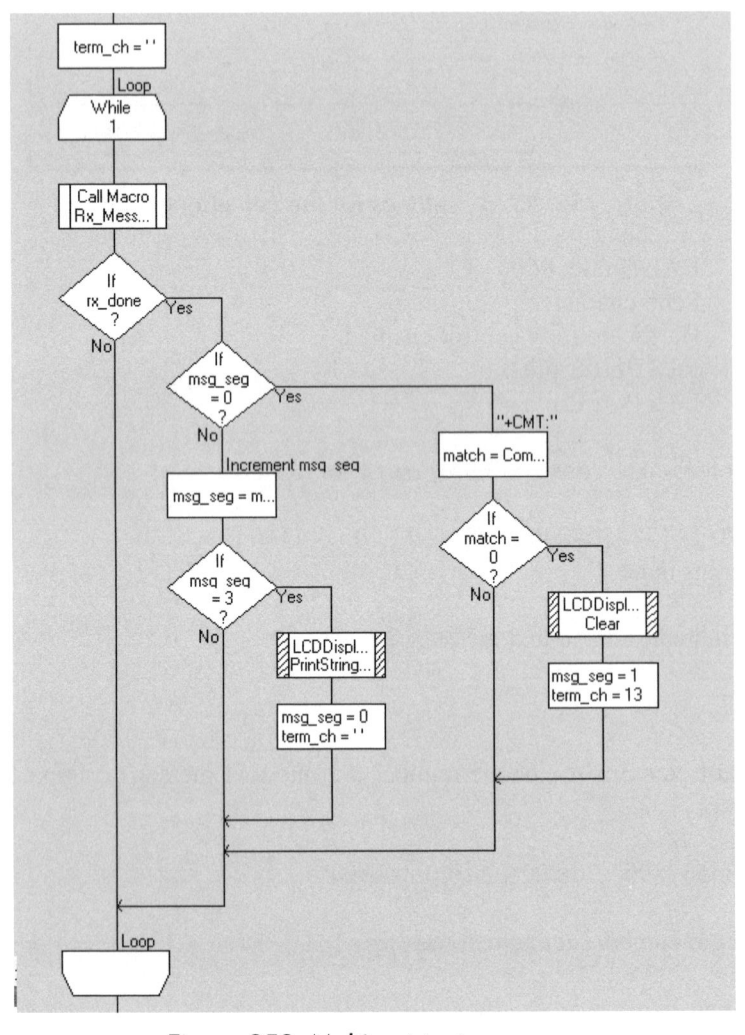

Figure 253. Multipart text message.

6 Cell phone

The full source of this project is part of the download package.

Operational

This is what the complete project looks like.

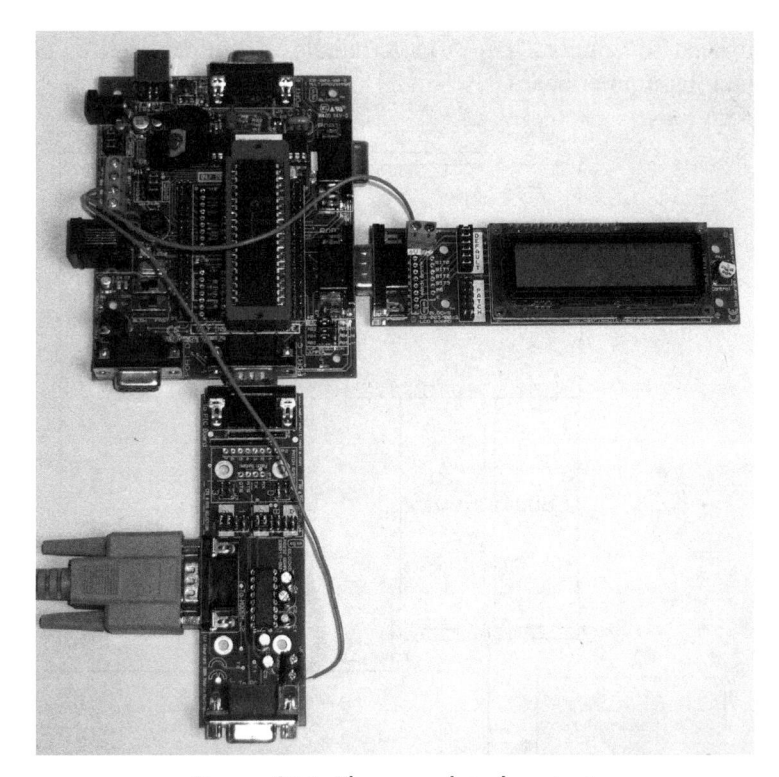

Figure 254. The completed project.

6.3 Remote control

Concept

In Japan vending machines selling soft drinks and other items are found in the most unlikely places, such a near the crater of the Nakadake volcano. It would be convenient if machines like these could be remotely controlled or serviced using text messages. In this project a microcontroller switches LEDs on and off based on received text messages. Instead of LEDs you could use relays and have your coffee waiting for you when you get home.

225

6.3 Remote control

Hardware

In this project we will use a 16F877A PIC microcontroller. The cell phone modem is connected to the RS232 board which is connected to port C. The modem has a female D9 plug so it needs to be connected to the side D9 connector of the RS232 board. An LCD board is connected to port B and a LED board to port D. Note that both boards need power so you need to connect the +Vin terminals of both boards to one of the +V terminals of the Programmer board

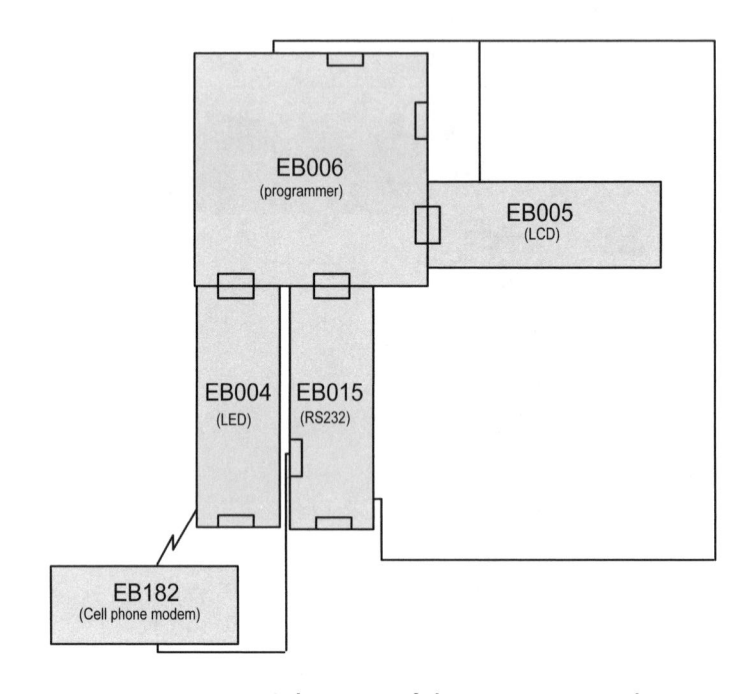

Figure 255,. Schematic of the remote control.

Connection summary:

  Programmer Switches to XTAL and Fast, LVP jumper on I/O port, J29 to PSU, J12-14 to USB, use external power supply.
  Port B LCD board, jumper to default.
  Port C RS232
    Cell phone modem on side connector
  Port D LED board

6 Cell phone

Software

In the menu select Chip, then Configure and then switch to Expert Config Screen. In the section Configuration Word(s) make sure HEX is selected and then click on the Config1 button and enter: 0x3F3A.

The software uses four steps:

1. Receive a text message
2. Decode the message
3. Send the decode message to the LED board
4. Send an SMS to confirm receipt.

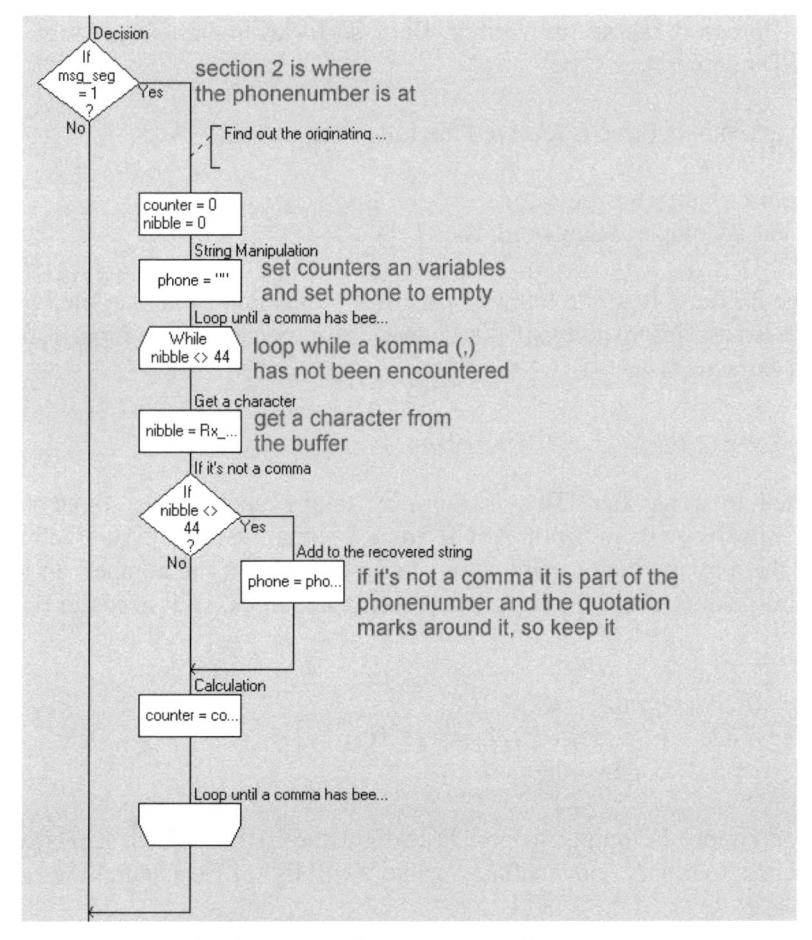

Figure 256. Phone number extraction from segment two.

6.3 Remote control

Receiving text messages has been discussed in the previous chapter. In that project message segment two was discarded, but in now we need to extract the originating phone number from this in order to send a confirmation text message. This is the content of segment 2:

"+1234567890",,"08/02/12,10:06:43+04"

The phone number will be extracted including the quotation marks since these will be needed later on to send a reply. The previous Figure shows an annotated section of the program where this extraction takes place.

The messages have the format "codeword number", where codeword is a secret word to prevent abuse, and number is a number between 0 and 255 that will be send to the LED board. In this program the secret word is "Bert" so for example text message "Bert 008" will light LED number 4.

Once message segment three is received the following snippet:

    keyword = left$(Rx_buffer, 4)
    RetVal = Compare$(keyword, "bert", 1)

checks to see if "Bert" is in the leftmost part of this segment (note that the ",1" indicates the compare is case insensitive). If the code word is correct the number following this codeword is extracted:

    codeword = Mid$(Rx_buffer, 5, 3)

and converted to a number. This is done by taking each of the three positions in codeword, converting them from ASCII to a decimal value by subtracting 48, and multiplying them by the factor that belongs to the location of the number. So if a number is on the third position from the right it represents hundreds, so it needs to be multiplied by 100.

    code = (codeword[0] - 48) * 100
    code = code + ((codeword[1] - 48) * 10)
    code = code + codeword[2] - 48

The code can simply be output to port D to light the LEDs. Which LEDs will light is simply a decimal to binary conversion, so value 9 will light LED D0 and D3.

The next step is to send a reply as described in project 6.1 with the content "Your message is confirmed".

6   Cell phone

Operational

Send text message "Bert 008" to the number of the SIM card in the cell phone modem. LED D3 will light and you will get a return message to confirm this.

Instead of a LED board you could also connect a relay board EB038, see project 3.3. This will allow you to switch on a coffee machine or your porch light while for example driving home.

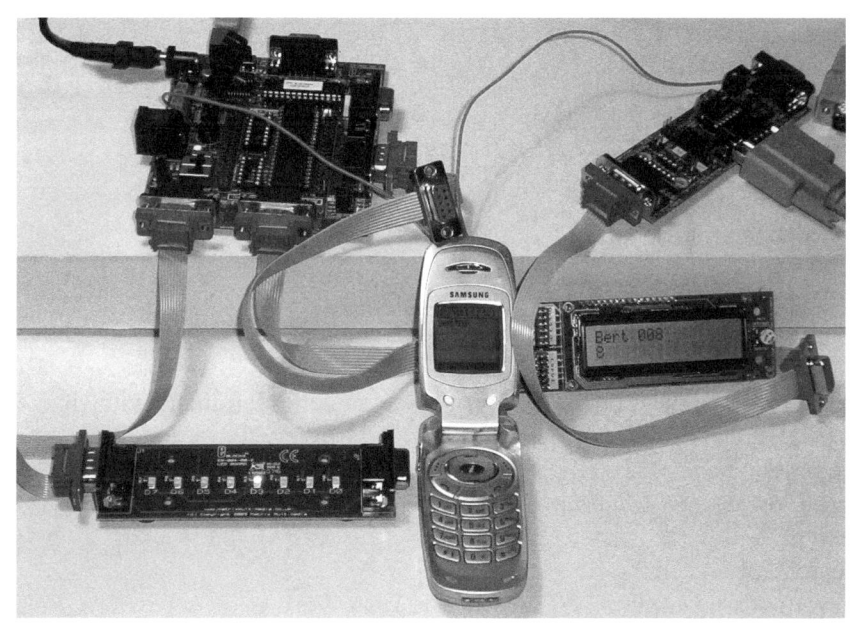

Figure 257. Remote control.

Optional

If you own a second cell phone modem you can connect it to your PC and control your own home from that PC. Switch on the porch light or make sure that your coffee is waiting for you when you get home.

Included in the download package is a Visual Basic program that allows you to mark the relays on the EB038 that you want switched on. Then click on the "Send SMS" button to send a text message to the microcontroller in your home.

The reply received from the microcontroller is decoded and shown in the green or red squares next to your check boxes. This means that rather than just a confirmation, the

6.3 Remote control

microcontroller also returns the number that it has received, with a different code word, so project 6.3 needs to be adapted a little bit.

The RS232 settings in Visual Basic are:

> *'Set the communication module, this is where you make changes if you*
> *'need another COM port or another speed. Note that the default speed is*
> *'115200 BAUD, but the E-block is set by Matrix Multimedia to 9600 BAUD*
> With GSMmodem
>   .CommPort = 1
>   .DTREnable = False
>   .Handshaking = 2
>   .NullDiscard = False
>   .RThreshold = 1
>   .RTSEnable = False
>   .Settings = "9600,n,8,1"
>   .SThreshold = 1
>   .InputLen = 1
> End With

Sending commands to the modem is easy, but remember to terminate with character 13 or control-Z and the end of the text message itself:

> *'see if the modem is online and operational*
> okreply = 0
> searchreply = "OK"
> GSMmodem.Output = "AT" + Chr$(13)

This time wait for the proper reply from the modem:

> *'wait for the proper reply*
> start = Timer
> Do While Timer < (start + 2)
>   DoEvents
>   If okreply = 1 Then Exit Do
> Loop
> If okreply = 0 Then GoTo modemproblem

The rest of the program is straight forward. The executable as well as the source of this Visual Basic program are part of the download package and listed under this chapter number. Note that in the next Figure the cell phone numbers have been removed for privacy reasons. In reality both local and remote numbers are visible and changeable.

6   Cell phone

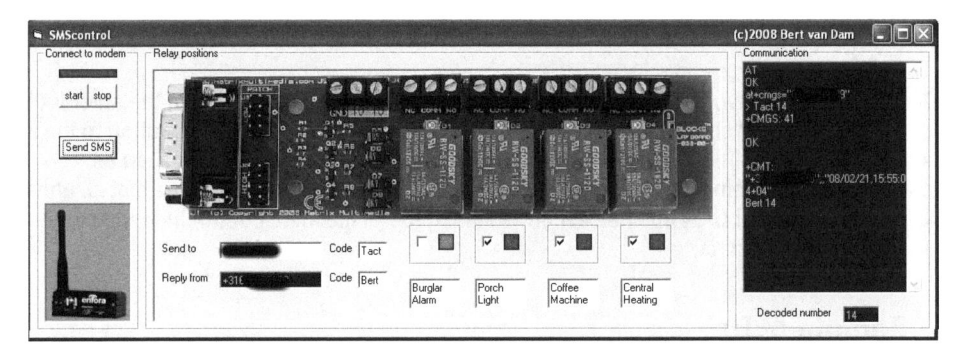

Figure 258. Remote control with text messages.

231

7.1 Remote LEDs

7 CAN bus

CAN (Controller Area Network) bus is a broadcast wiring system primarily used in the automotive industry to link intelligent controllers together. Bosch developed it in 1986 as a solution to the ever-increasing amount of cabling that went into new cars, with the associated issues such as incompatibility and problem solving. CAN bus consists of two simple twisted wires that all units tie into. Nowadays the use of CAN bus has expanded into general machine control in industrial as well as in automotive applications.

7.1 Remote LEDs

Concept

Use the buttons on the CAN bus board to control the LEDs on the CAN bus board connected to the other node.

Hardware (node A)

For this node we will use a 16F877A PIC microcontroller with a CAN bus board. Note that this board needs power so you need to connect the +Vin terminal to one of the +V terminals of the Programmer board.

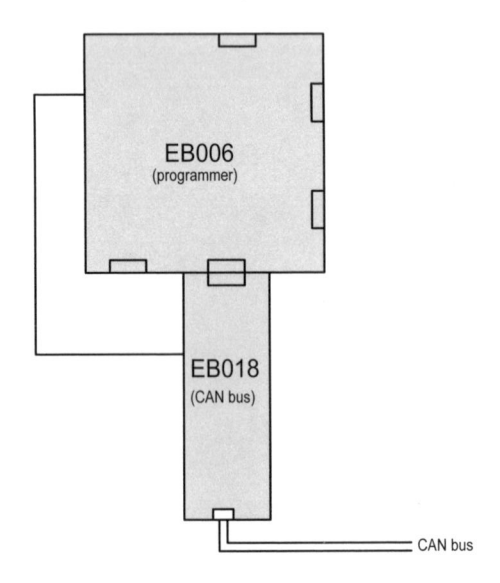

Figure 259. Schematic CAN bus node A.

7   CAN bus

Connection summary:

    Programmer   Switches to XTAL and Fast, LVP jumper on I/O port, J29 to PSU, J12-14 to USB, use external power supply.
    Port C   EB018 CAN bus board, jumpers to A, 1 and end node.

Software (node A)

In the menu select Chip, then Configure and then switch to Expert Config Screen. In the section Configuration Word(s) make sure HEX is selected and then click on the Config1 button and enter: 0x3F3A.

Since no jumpers were set on the CAN bus patch board the default General settings can be used as seen in the next Figure.

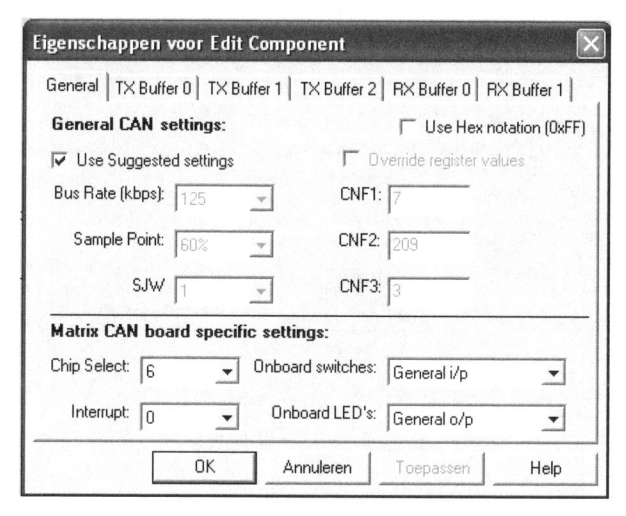

Figure 260. General CAN bus settings for node A.

All CAN bus messages have eight bytes and a message ID. All messages are broadcasted. A single node doesn't know who will be receiving this broadcast, nor does it get any receipt confirmation. Nodes on the CAN bus will read messages based on their ID number. Any message with an unknown ID number will be ignored. If the ID number is known the message will be copied into a buffer. The program in the microcontroller can read the buffer at its convenience. If a new message with the same ID is received the old one in the buffer is simply overwritten.

This means the CAN bus system is extremely flexible. Nodes can be added or removed without any impact on the existing structure. Any node can pick up and process any

7.1 Remote LEDs

message on the bus. This node will be receiving messages with ID 100, so this ID will be assigned to a receive buffer, in this case buffer zero.

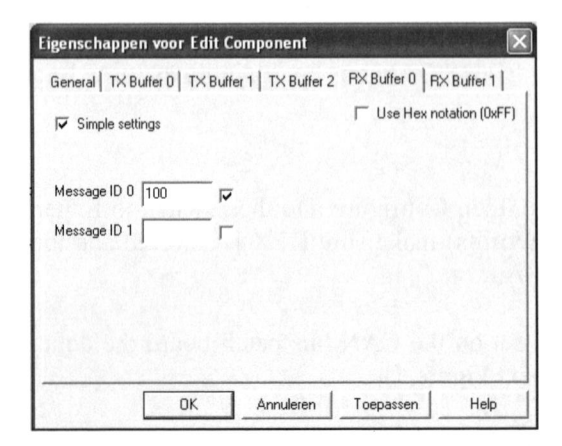

Figure 261. Message ID 100 assigned to RX buffer 0.

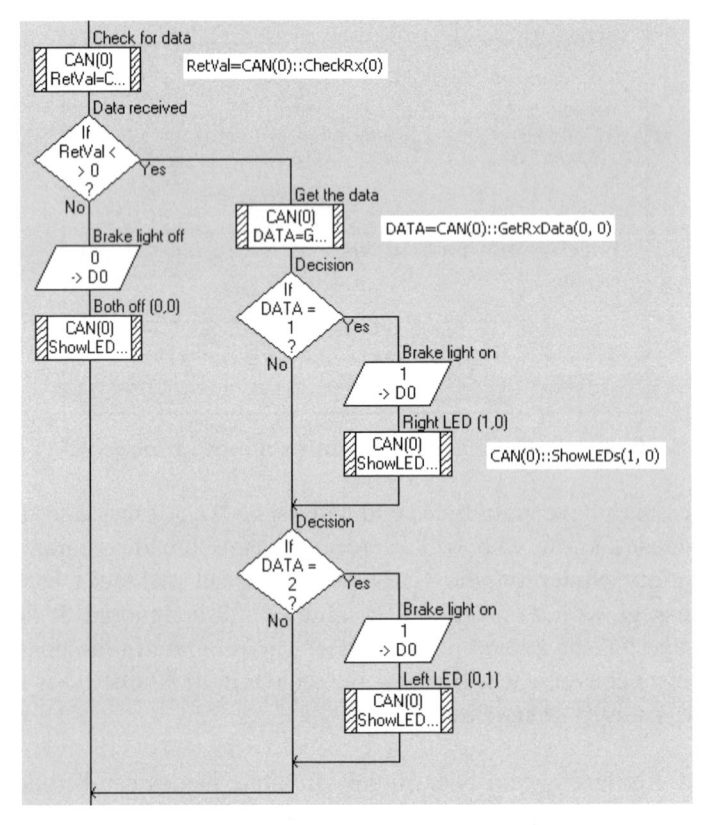

Figure 262. Processing incoming data.

7   CAN bus

After initializing the CAN bus component the program continuously polls for incoming data. If none is received both LEDs will be switched off. If data was received then byte zero from buffer zero will be read. Note that any other data in the message will be ignored. Depending on the value of byte 0 one of the LEDs will be switched on, see the previous Figure.

Hardware (node B)

For this node we will use the ATMEGA 32 AVR microcontroller with a CAN bus board. Note that this board needs power so you need to connect the +Vin terminal to one of the +V terminals of the Programmer board.

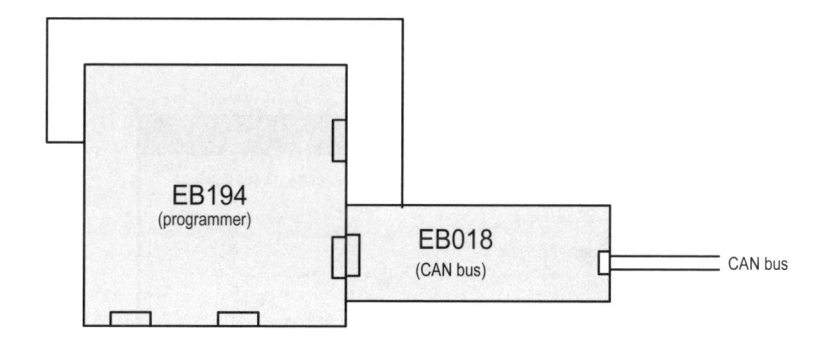

Figure 263. Schematic CAN bus node B.

Connection summary:

Programmer   EB194, jumper to default.
Port B   EB018 Can bus, jumpers to C, 2 and end node,
             Patch SDO to B5, SDI to B6, SCK to B7,
             INT to B4, CS to B3.

AVR uses different names for the SPI connections, and they are on also different pins:

E-block		AVR		Remarks
SDO	C5	MOSI	B5	master output
SDI	C4	MISO	B6	master input
SCK	C3	SCK	B7	clock
CS	C0			chip select
INT	C6			interrupt

Figure 264. E-block and AVR nomenclature.

235

7.1 Remote LEDs

This means the connections need to be patched. The pins for INT and CS can be chosen freely, so B3 and B4 are arbitrary choices.

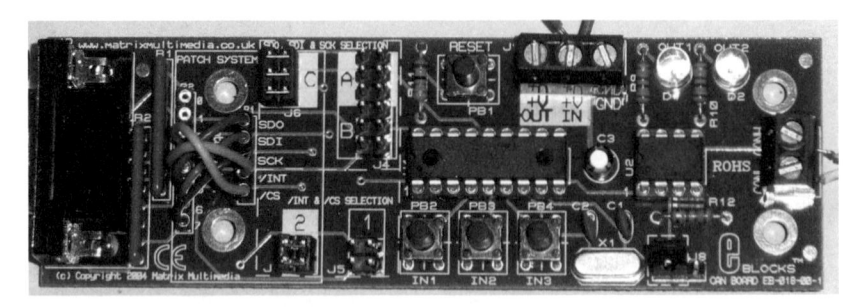

Figure 265. EB018 patched for node B.

Software (node B)

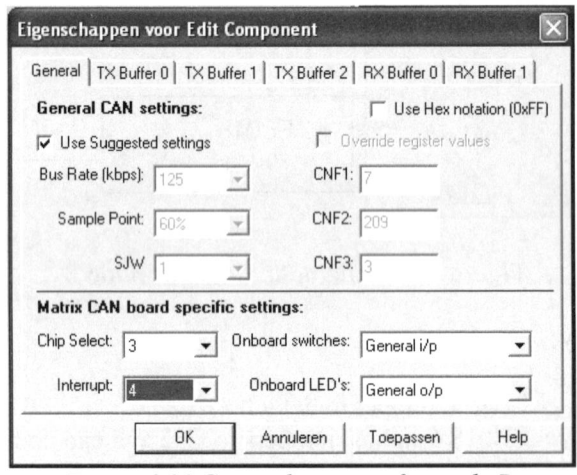

Figure 266 General settings for node B.

Since the patch panel has been used to move the CS and INT lines, this must be entered into the General settings of the CAN bus component. The other node expects a message with ID 100, so this ID will be assigned to a buffer for later use. In this project transmit buffer 0 is selected.

7   CAN bus

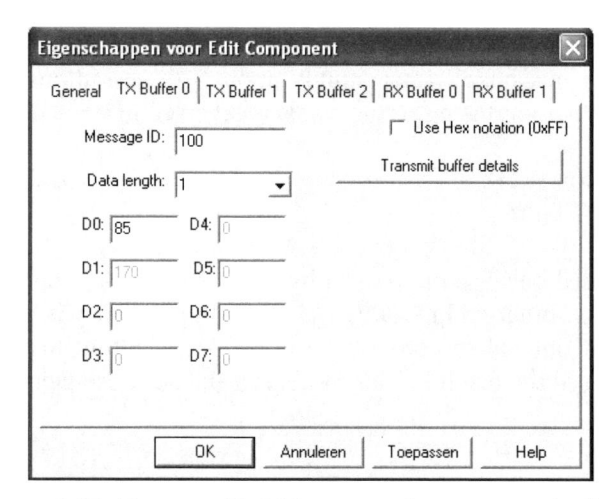

Figure 267. Message ID 100 assigned to transmit buffer 0.

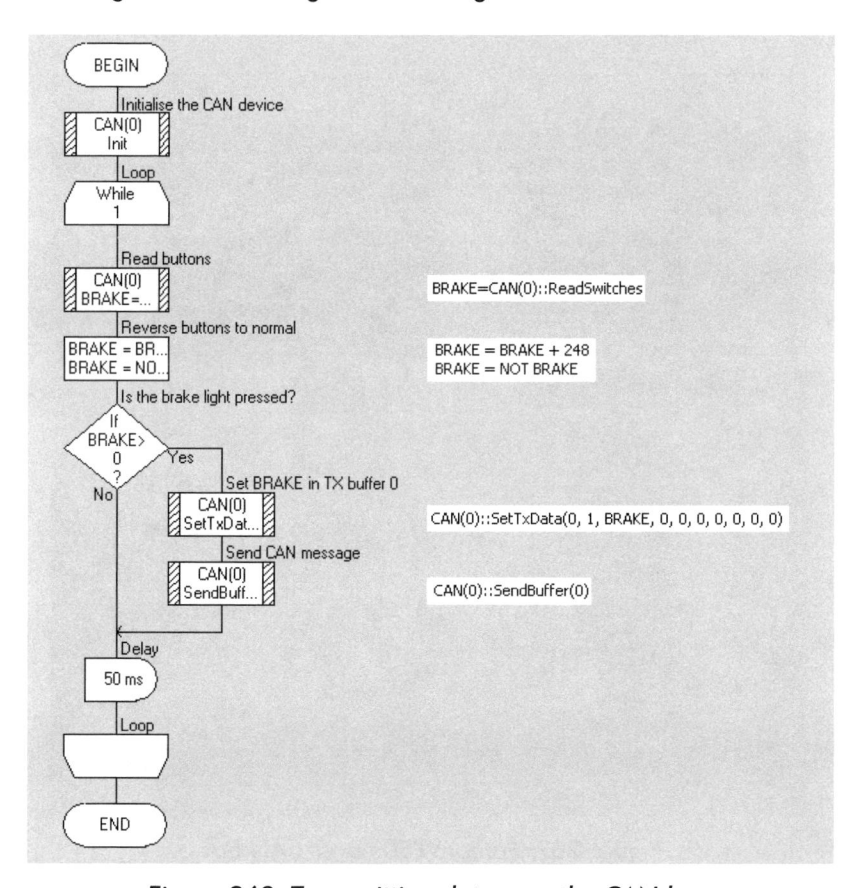

Figure 268. Transmitting data over the CAN bus.

237

7.1 Remote LEDs

After initializing the CAN bus component the program polls the status of the three buttons on the CAN bus board. Interestingly enough these buttons read one when <u>not engaged</u>, which is rather confusing so the status is reversed in a calculation component:

    button = button + 248
    button = NOT button

The first line is needed because button is a byte and NOT works on bit level by flipping each bit. Adding 248, binary 11111000, and then flipping bit wise the first 5 bits, sets them to zero so that only alterations of the other three button bits are monitored. If a button has been pressed the result is added to buffer 0, and subsequently sent.

Operational

In this project both nodes have their own power supply so the only connecting wires belong to the CAN bus.

Figure 269. Remote LEDs over CAN bus.

7 CAN bus

The nodes A and B must be connected together using the CANL (low) and CANH (high) connections at the end of the CAN bus board with ordinary twisted pair wire, shielding is not required. Note that all CANL connections need to be tied together and that all CANH connections need to be tied together. The wires do not cross!

On the CAN bus board connected to the AVR microcontroller button IN1 controls the red LED on the other unit, and button IN2 controls the yellow LED. When none of the buttons are pressed both LEDs will be off.

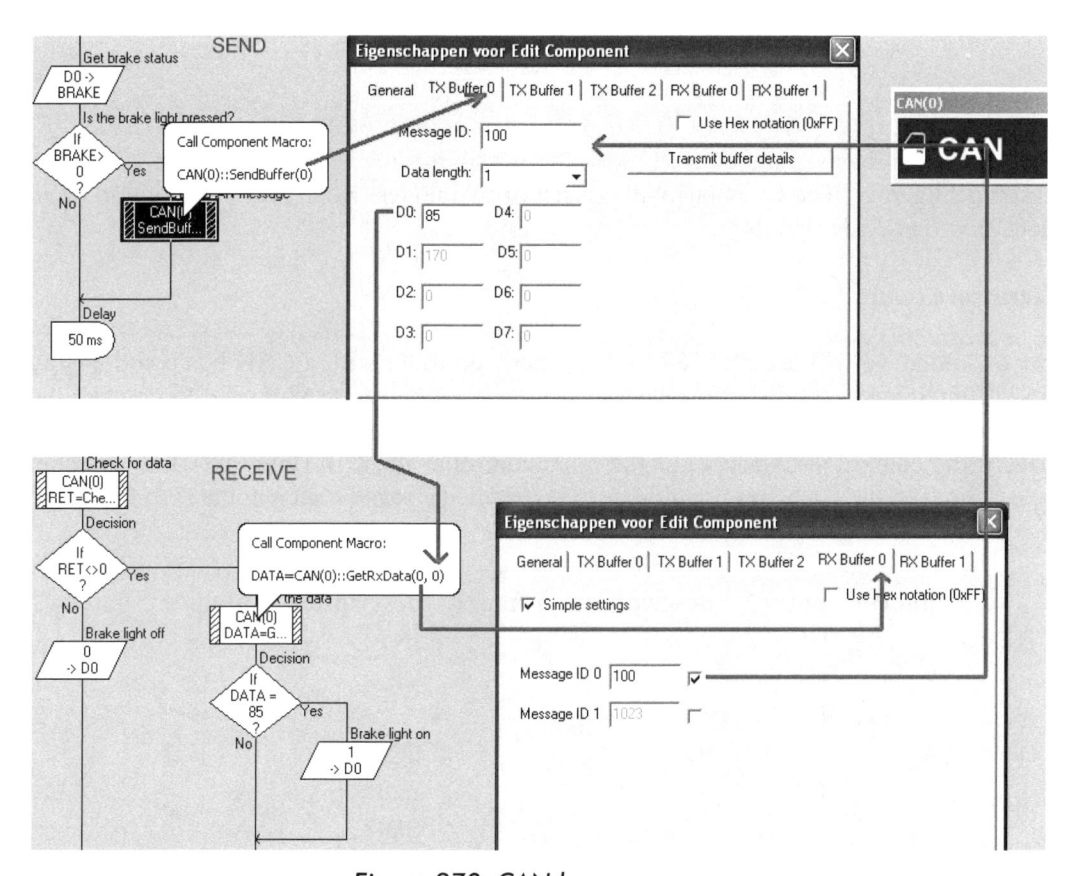

Figure 270. CAN bus messages.

This is an overview of the way the messages are tied together, see the previous Figure:

Transmitting side
1. Gather the data that needs to be sent.
2. Assign a transmit buffer and give it a message ID.
3. Add the data to that buffer (max eight bytes).
4. Send the buffer.

239

7.2 Monitor

Receiving side
1. Assign a receive buffer and give it that same message ID.
2. Regularly poll to see if any messages have come in.
3. Get the data from the buffer byte by byte.
4. Process the data.

It is possible to assign multiple message ID's to a single receive buffer. If that is the case you need to check first which ID the message has, prior to processing.

7.2 Monitor

Concept

Show all CAN bus signals on a PC with the possibility of viewing them in a graph, for easier debugging. The CAN bus will consist of two nodes. Node A is the monitor while node B will provide signals.

Hardware (node A)

For this node we will use a 16F877A PIC microcontroller with a CAN bus board and an RS232 interface to the PC. Note that all boards need power so you need to connect the +Vin terminal to one of the +V terminals of the Programmer board. Since both boards need to be connected to port C of the microcontroller the INT (interrupt) and CS (chip select) lines of the CAN bus board have to be patched as can be seen in the next Figure.

pin D9	port C	RS232 description	jumper	CAN bus description	jumper	patch
1	C0			INT	2	1
2	C1			CS	2	2
3	C2					
4	C3			SCK	A	
5	C4			SDI	A	
6	C5			SDO	A	
7	C6	TX	C/2	CS	1	
8	C7	RX	C/2			
9	GND					

Figure 271. Settings to combine CAN bus and RS232 on port C (appendix 12.5).

The CAN bus board is an SPI board, see project 4.2 for more information on SPI. Without patching CS would be on C6 and clash with RS232 TX (transmit).

7 CAN bus

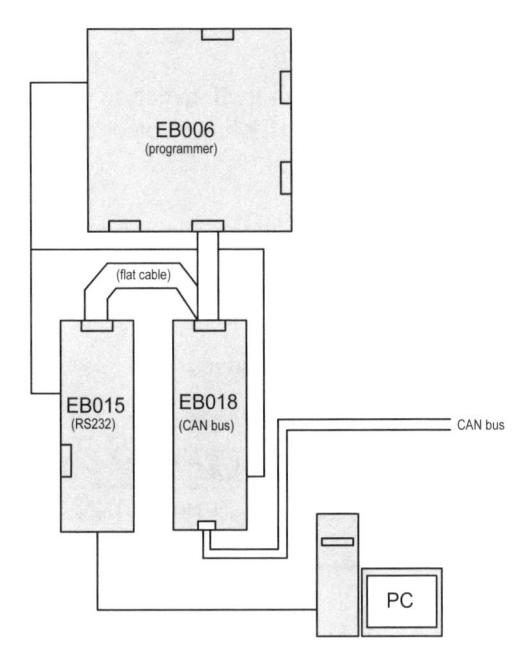

Figure 272. Schematic of the node A hardware.

Connection summary:

Programmer	Switches to XTAL and Fast, LVP jumper on I/O port, J29 to PSU, J12-14 to USB, use external power supply.
Port C	EB015 RS232 board, jumpers to C and 2. EB018 CAN bus board, jumpers to A, 2 and end node, patch INT to C0 and CS to C1, see next Figure.

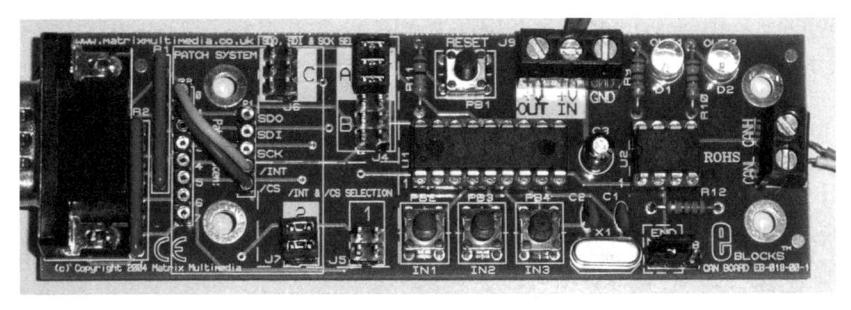

Figure 273. EB018 patched for node A.

7.2 Monitor

Software (node A)

In the menu select Chip, then Configure and then switch to Expert Config Screen. In the section Configuration Word(s) make sure HEX is selected and then click on the Config1 button and enter: 0x3F3A.

In this project node A will receive any message on the bus regardless of it's ID and send it to the PC for data processing. In the CAN bus component for this node the settings for buffer 0 must therefore be the following:

    Buffer settings   Accept all messages
    Buffer rollover   Disable

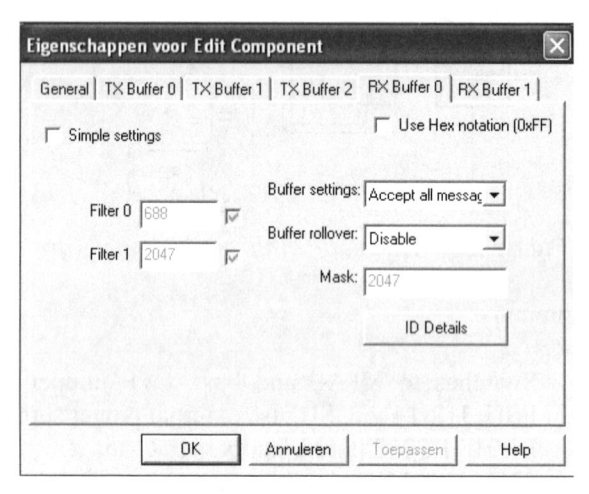

Figure 274. Buffer settings for node A.

Buffer rollover Disabled means that new data will overwrite old data. If this is set to Enable new data will be copied into buffer 1. We want all data to stay in buffer 0 because that is the only buffer we will read.

Since the patch panel was used to move the INT (interrupt) and CS (chip select) lines this must be copied into the general settings page of the CAN bus component. The program itself starts with initializing the CAN component. In a continuous loop the CAN component is polled for data. This is what the INT line is used for as SPI doesn't use interrupts. If this line is high it means that new data has arrived and is waiting in the appropriate buffer. If data is waiting a small loop extracts the eight bytes from the buffer and sends them to the PC.

7   CAN bus

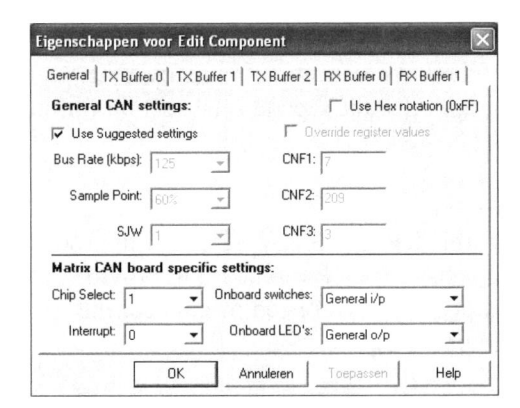

Figure 275. General CAN settings node A.

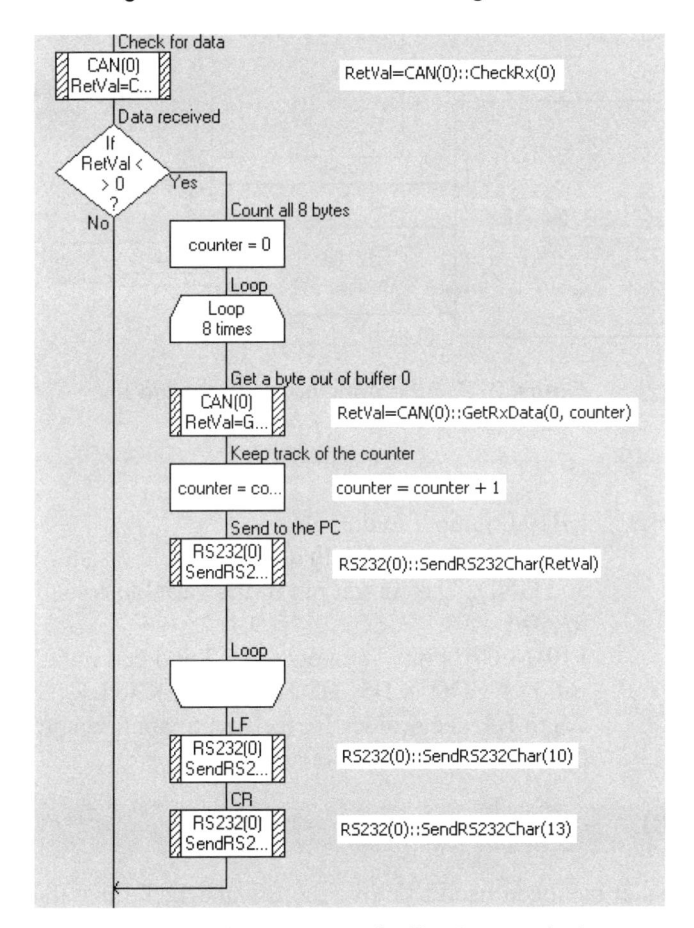

Figure 276. Processing buffer 0 at node A.

243

7.2 Monitor

The data to the PC is terminated with a Line Feed / Carriage Return combo. At the PC a Visual Basic program displays the data in columns by byte. Optionally a column can be selected and shown in a graph. See the Operational section for more details.

Hardware (node B)

For this project we will use the ATMEGA 32 AVR microcontroller with a CAN bus board and a 10 k variable resistor on a Proto board to provide data to be sent over the bus. Note that all boards need power so you need to connect the +Vin terminal to one of the +V terminals of the Programmer board.

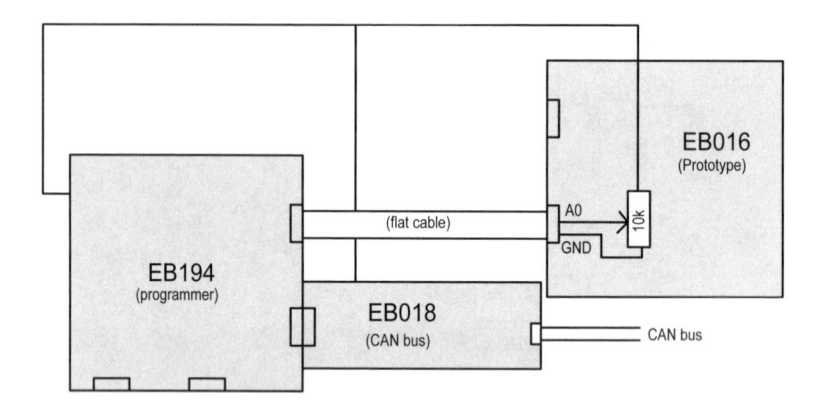

Figure 277. Schematic hardware node B.

Connection summary:

Programmer	EB194, jumper to default.
Port A	EB016 Proto board with a 10k variable resistor between +5V and GND. The central pin of the variable resistor is connected to A0.
Port B	EB018 CAN bus, jumpers to C, 2 and end node, patch as follows: SDO to B5, SDI to B6, SCK to B7, INT to B4, CS to B3, see project 7.1 for an explanation and a picture of the patched board.

Software (node B)

Since the patch panel has been used to move the CS and INT lines this must be entered into the General settings of the CAN bus component.

7 CAN bus

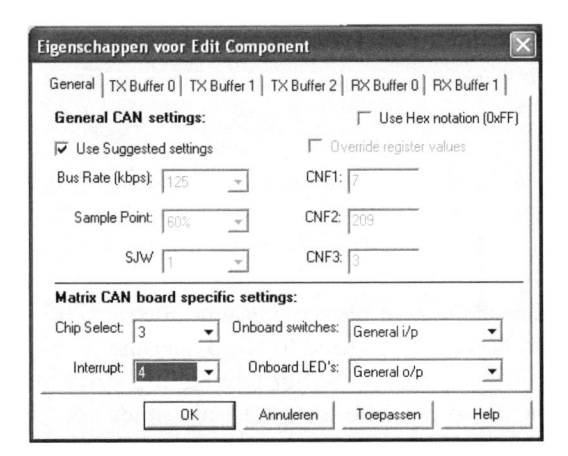

Figure 278 General settings for node B.

The program in this node first initializes the CAN bus component. In a continuous loop it checks the ADC value of pin A0. If the value deviates from the previous measurement a CAN bus message is sent: resist, button, 0, 0, 0, 0, 0, 0

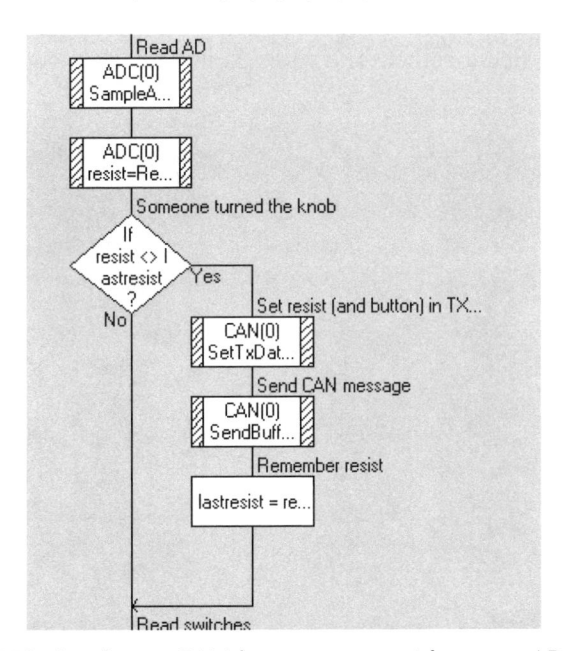

Figure 279. Sending a CAN bus message with a new ADC value.

In the same loop the status of the three buttons on the CAN bus board is checked. Interestingly enough these switches read one when not engaged, which is rather confusing so the status is reversed in a calculation component:

245

7.2 Monitor

```
button = button + 248
button = NOT button
```

The first line is needed because button is a byte and the NOT operation works on bit level by flipping each bit. Adding 248, binary 11111000, and then flipping bit wise the first 5 bits, sets them to zero so that only alterations of the other three button bits are monitored.

If the button situation has changed a message is sent, identical to the section before. Two variables, lastbutton and lastresist, are used to remember the previous status. The message ID for this message is 668, see the TX buffer page in the CAN bus component, which is completely irrelevant in this project because the only other node is the data monitor and this node is picking up everything.

Operational

The nodes A and B must be connected together using the CANL (low) and CANH (high) connections at the end of the CAN bus board with ordinary twisted pair wire, shielding is not required. Note that all CANL connections need to be tied together and that all CANH connections need to be tied together. The wires do not cross!

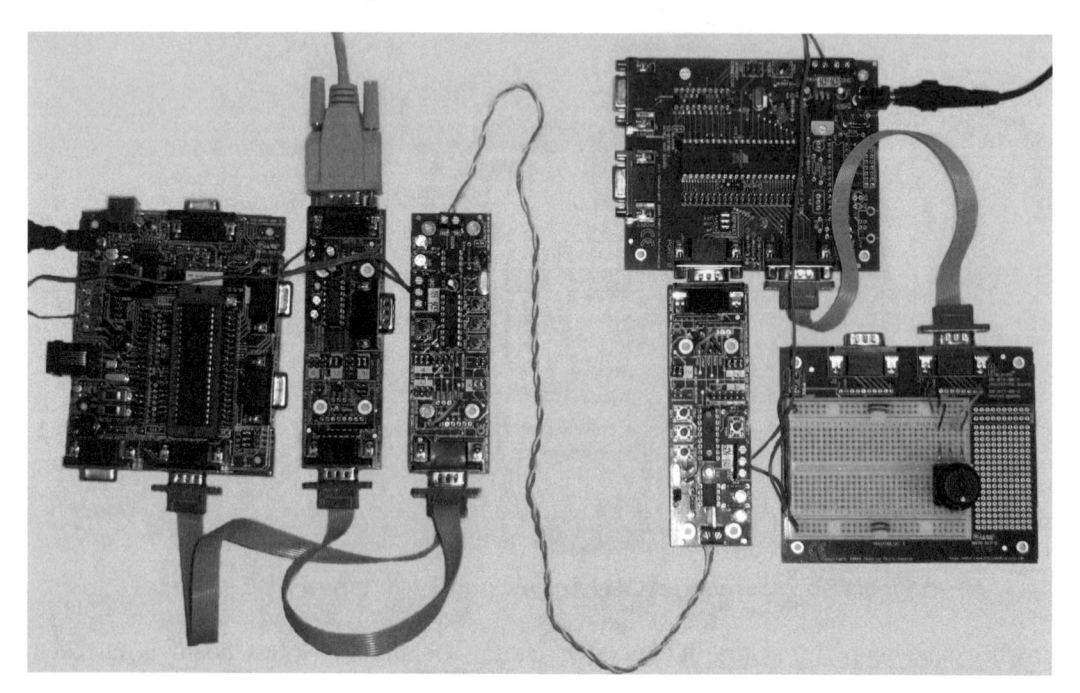

Figure 280. CAN bus in operation.

7   CAN bus

In this project both nodes have their own power supply so the only connecting wires belong to the CAN bus.

On the PC start the program CANmonitor.exe, the Visual Basic source is also included in the download package. Check the COM port that node A is connected to. The speed is correct by default unless you changed the speed in node A. Click on the start button.

Turn the variable resistor on node B. Rows of data will start coming in and be shown in the CAN bus traffic window, each byte in a column. Below the graph check Enable and select the byte you want to see displayed. In this project byte 0 would make sense. The speed of the graph can be controlled using the slider. The red line, white in the next Figure, is the actual data, the purple line is the average since the start. Click on the reset button to clear and thus restart the average.

The default display is in decimal, optionally select HEX to see the HEX values in the traffic window. If you use Microsoft Windows XP you can select data in the traffic window using your mouse and copy it into a spreadsheet for further processing. Note that the window will hold a maximum of about 100 messages.

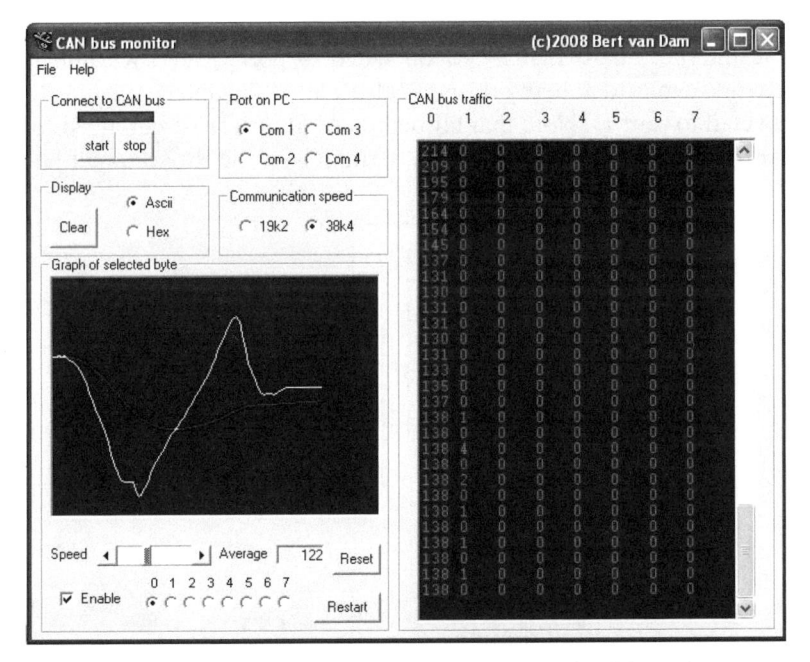

Figure 281. CAN bus monitor with graph of byte 0.

8.1 Ping (Are you there?)

8 Internet

This is a series of internet projects. This is definitely not a beginner's subject. It is highly recommended that you try some of the Basic and Advanced projects before starting on the internet. The first project, Ping, also describes how to set up your network. Since this is not repeated for subsequent projects it is probably a good idea to start with this project.

8.1 Ping (Are you there?)

Concept

Build internet hardware and make sure the components can ping ("see") each other. Since connection to the actual internet involves knowledge of your ISP, routers and security measures, which will be different for every reader, a local version of the internet will be used, a so called intranet.

Hardware

In this project we will use a 16F877A PIC microcontroller. An LCD board is connected to port B. The Internet board EB023 is connected to port C, and with an RJ45 CAT 5 crossover network cable to a network card, also called "adapter", in the PC. A Switch board is connected to port D. Note that all boards need power so you need to connect the +Vin terminals of all boards to one of the +V terminals of the Programmer board

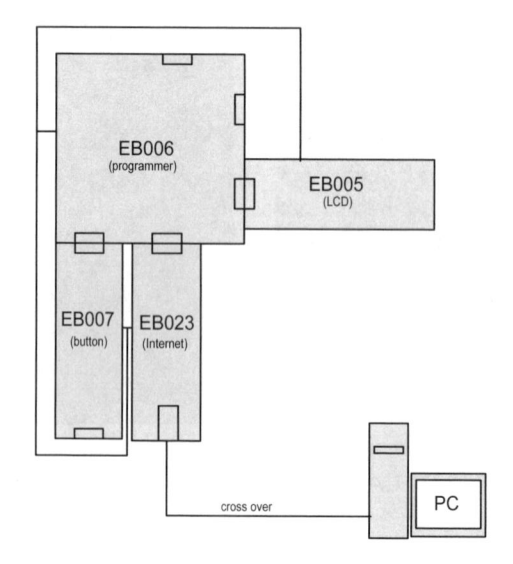

Figure 282. schematic of the ping hardware.

248

8 Internet

Connection summary:

Programmer	Switches to XTAL and Fast, LVP jumper on I/O port, J29 to PSU, J12-14 to USB, use external power supply.
Port B	LCD board, jumper on default.
Port C	EB023 Internet board, jumpers to A, +5V, address 1-1-1, an RJ45 CAT 5 crossover network cable to the network card in the PC.
Port D	EB007 Switch board.

Remove your current Internet cable from the PC and insert the crossover cable. Important: do not use a straight cable, only a crossover cable. The first step once the hardware is connected is to change the settings of the internet card that the EB023 Internet board is connected to.

Instructions for actions on the PC are based on Windows XP. If you use a different operating system you may need to follow slightly different steps. On most PCs an administrator account or administrator privileges are required. On your PC go to the Configuration screen, select Network and Internet connections, and select Network connection. Double click on the Internet connection that belongs to the network card.

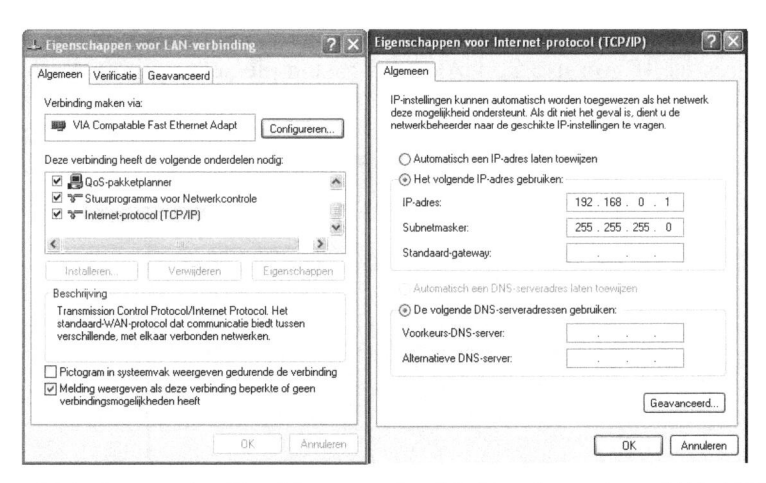

Figure 283. Setting the IP address on the PC (Dutch version of WinXP SP2).

Note the current settings so they can be reinstalled once the project is completed. Then enter the following data:

IP	192.168.0.1
Subnet	255.255.255.0

Leave the gateway address unchanged

8.1 Ping (Are you there?)

Make sure to select "Use this IP address". Then save the settings.

Next go to the Internet Options Control panel and ensure that "Use a proxy server" is not ticked, if it was note this and remember to change it back after this project is completed. At this point you may have to reboot the computer for these settings to become active.

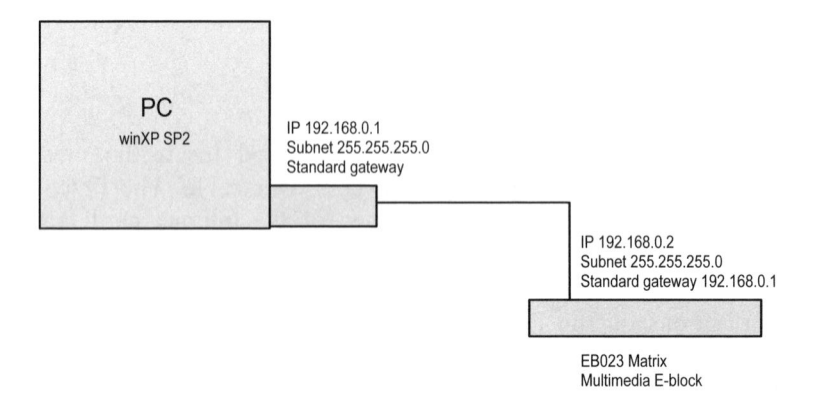

Figure 284. IP numbers.

If you use Firewall software add the IP address of the EB023 to the trusted zone or the list of trusted addresses. If you use ZoneAlarm for example select Firewall, then Zones and enter the data as seen in the next Figure.

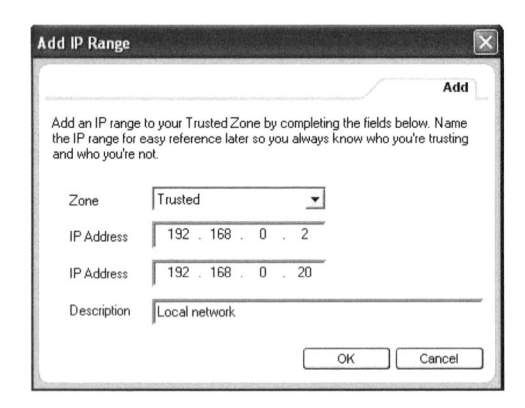

Figure 285. Trusted zone in ZoneAlarm.

Software

In the menu select Chip, then Configure and then switch to Expert Config Screen.

8   Internet

In the section Configuration Word(s) make sure HEX is selected and then click on the Config1 button and enter: 0x3F3A.

Internet communications use TCP/IP[44] to get messages from one component (PC, microcontroller) to another. That is a very loose term to describe a communication protocol that consists of nine layers, as shown in the next Figure.

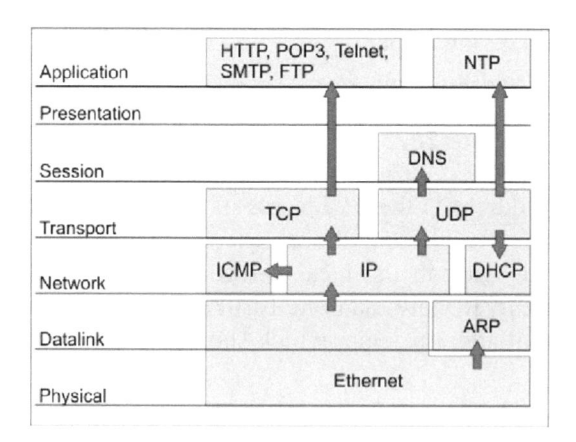

Figure 286. TCP/IP OSI model, courtesy Matrix Multimedia Ltd.

Ping is basically an "Are you there?" request from one component to another on network level, to test the physical and logical connection between the two. So the protocol required for ping is ICMP[45]. This program uses three macros by Matrix Multimedia which handle the actual sending and receiving data:

macro	function
receive_icmp_msg	Receive an ICMP message
send_ip_data	Send an ICMP ping request
checksum	Calculate the checksum of an ICMP ping request

Discussing the inner workings is outside the scope of this book so they will be used as is. Import the macros into the program.

---

[44] Transmission Control Protocol / Internet Protocol
[45] Internet Control Message Protocol

251

8.1 Ping (Are you there?)

Add a TCP/IP component and enter the following settings:

Gateway address	192.168.0.1
Subnet mask	255.255.255.0
IP address	192.168.0.2
Hardware address	0.8.220.0.0.0
I2C interrupt	0
Address setup	1-1-1

Figure 287. TCP/IP component settings.

Note that the gateway address is the IP address of the card in the PC that the EB023 is connected to, and that the IP address in the table is the address of this particular EB023. If more than one EB023 is used in the local net both need a different IP address and a different hardware address. If more than one EB023 is used on the same microcontroller both also need a different address setup, which should match the jumper settings on that particular EB023.

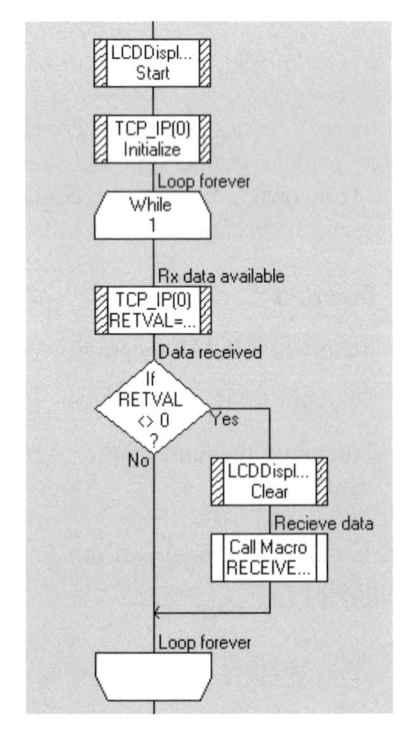

Figure 288. Checking for, and receiving, incoming data.

8   Internet

Use component macros to start the LCD and initialize TCP/IP. The program will continuously listen for incoming communications. If incoming data is detected Rx-data-available returns a non-zero, the LCD is cleared and the receive_icmp_msg is called. This macro will print incoming messages to the LCD. It will not scroll, so anything that doesn't fit is lost.

When the user presses a button a ping request will be send out to the only other component in the network: the PC. Sending a ping involves three steps:

1. Create an IP socket, this is basically a connection to the network on IP level.
2. Set the destination, this is the IP address that the ping has to go to.
3. Send the actual message.

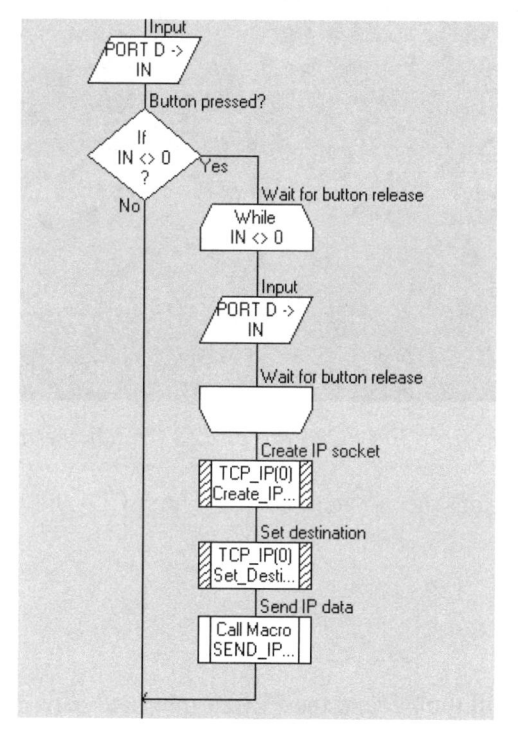

Figure 289. Sending a ping.

The complete program (the previous two sections put together) is part of the download package.

253

8.1 Ping (Are you there?)

Operational

On the PC open a DOS box. Click the "Start" button, select Execute and enter "Command", then click the OK button. You now have a window with a black background. Type the following text:

   ping 192.168.0.2

and press enter. If you get a reply with a list of times as in the following Figure, all connections are fine.

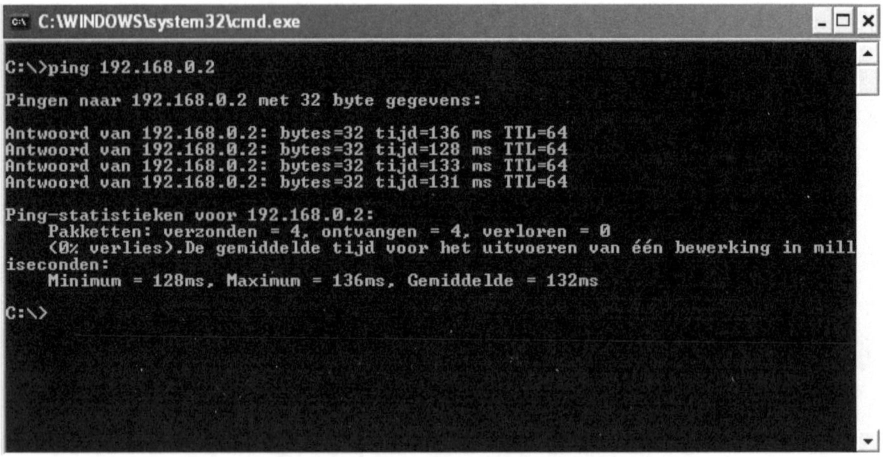

Figure 290. Ping from the PC to the EB023 (Dutch version WinXP SP2).

Now press any button on the Switch board. The LCD should show the following information:

   Ping received.
   Data: abcdefgh

If both tests are successful the PC and the EB023 Internet board can see each other which means the hardware and the settings are correct.

8　Internet

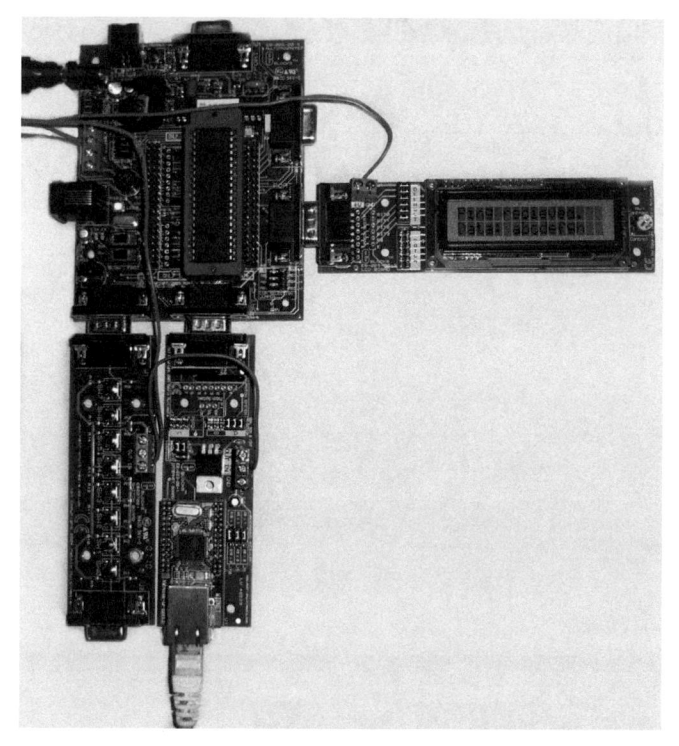

Figure 291. A successful ping to the network card in the PC.

Debugging

An important tool for debugging anything that has to do with the internet is Wireshark[46]. This is a free network packet analyzer that shows all traffic on internet adapters. You must use an administrator account or have administrator privileges in order to see the packets. Without these privileges the program will start but you will not see any traffic!

Start the Wireshark program, select Capture and then Interfaces. Click on the Start button of the interface that has IP address 192.168.0.1 listed next to it. Now click on a button on the microcontroller project. At least four lines should show up on the screen as can be seen in the next figure.

---

[46] http://www.wireshark.org/

255

8.1 Ping (Are you there?)

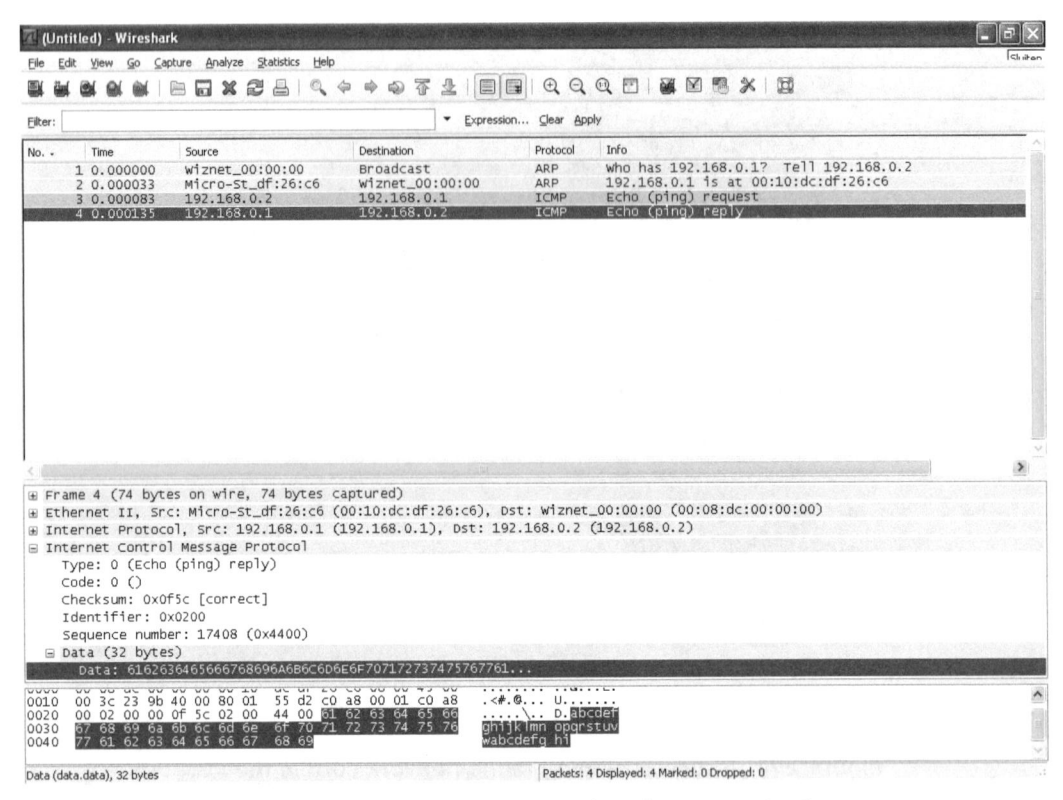

Figure 292. Ping request and reply in Wireshark

Each line represents a single packet send over the internet connection. Click on it to view the different layers in the packet shown in the lower half of the screen. By clicking on one of those layers it can be opened even further with the contents shown at the very bottom of the screen. These are the four important lines:

Source   *Destination*   *Protocol Info*
Wiznet_00:00:00   *Broadcast*   *ARP*   *Who has 192.168.0.1? Tell 192.168.0.2*

On the lowest level of the TCP/IP model messages are sent to a hardware address. So the first thing that needs to be done is to find out which hardware address belongs to a particular IP address. The EB023 (Wiznet_00:00:00) is sending a message to anyone (Broadcast) in a special protocol (ARP[47]) asking who has the IP address that the ping needs to be send to.

---

[47] Address Resolution Protocol.

Source   Destination   Protocol Info
Micro-St_df:26:c6   Wiznet_00:00:00   ARP   192.168.0.1 is at 00:10:dc:df:26:c6

In the next line the PC (Micro-St_df:26:c6) replies to the EB023 (Wiznet_00:00:00) using that same protocol. It confirms that it has IP address 192.168.0.1 and advises that it's hardware address: 00:10:dc:df:26:c6. So now the EB023 has all the information it needs to send messages directly to the PC.

Source   Destination   Protocol Info
192.168.0.2   192.168.0.1   ICMP   Echo (ping) request

This is the actual ping. Note that ping uses a higher level protocol than the previous communication, so as destination the IP address is used. An invisible lower level protocol is actually sending this message to the hardware address. Wireshark calls this "Ethernet II", and if you click on a line you will see that the actual addresses being used are 00:08:dc:00:00:00 and 00:10:dc:df:26:c6 (which are indeed the hardware addresses).

Source   Destination   Protocol Info
192.168.0.1   192.168.0.2   ICMP   Echo (ping) reply

At this point the PC sends a reply. Since the content of the reply, as well as the original ping message itself, is irrelevant the message consists of parts of the alphabet: abcdefghijklmnopqrstuvwabcdefghi

If your project doesn't work compare your Wireshark results with the explanation above and the previous Figure. The most likely cause of failure is a blockage between Wireshark and the EB023 caused by a firewall or other security software. This may happen on ARP level, so you never even see the "Who is..." request, or on ICMP level, so you only get the first two lines. Should you disable safety features of the PC in order to get these projects to work make a note of the settings and remember to restore them all prior to connecting to the internet again.

If you don't see any messages at all make sure you run Wireshark using administrator privileges or an administrator account. Next make sure all instructions at the beginning of this chapter were followed exactly. If that still fails load the HEX file[48] included in the download package to eliminate any errors in your Flowcode program.

---

[48] HEX files can be loaded using the PPP software which belongs to the EB006 Programmer board, the program can be found in the Matrix Multimedia subdirectory. Start the program, use File Open to locate the HEX file, the click on Send to PICmicro.

8.2 Webserver

8.2 Webserver

Concept

A small internet server that can be used to remotely view the status of the microcontroller and components attached to it. In this project the position of a 10k variable resistor can be observed using the Webserver.

Hardware

For this project we will use the ATMEGA 32 AVR microcontroller with a patched EB023 Internet board and a Proto board with a variable resistor.

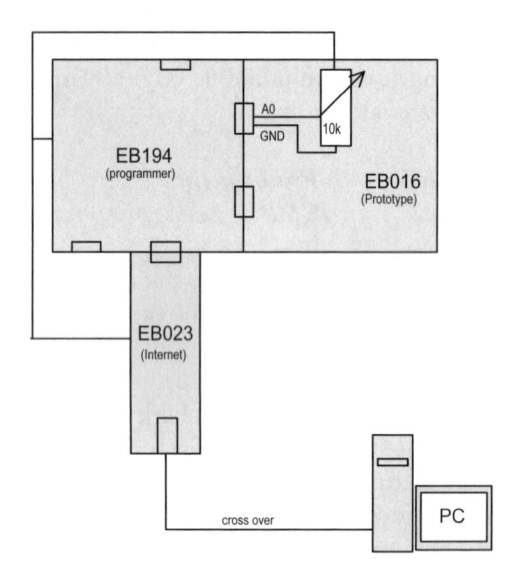

Figure 293. Schematic of the webserver hardware.

Connection summary:

    Programmer   EB194, jumper to default.
    Port A   Proto board, 10k resistor between GND and +V, center connected to A0.
    Port C   EB023 Internet Board, jumpers to C, +5V, address 1-1-1, an RJ45 CAT 5 crossover network cable to the network card in the PC, patched SDA to C0, SCL to C1, /INT to C2.

8 Internet

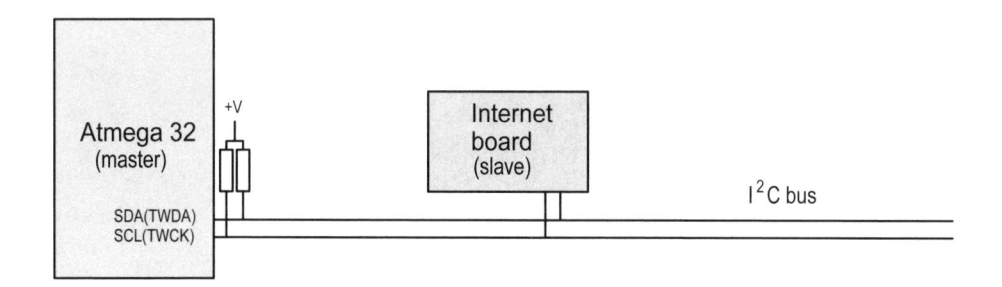

Figure 294. I²C bus.

TheEB023 board uses I²C to communicate with the microcontroller[49]. Atmel uses the term TWI in their datasheets[50], but technically it is the same thing. I²C uses two lines for communication, a data line SDA or TWDA and a clock line SCL or TWCK. Each I²C bus has one master and one or more slaves. The master controls the communication, and also the clock line. Interestingly enough both lines are pulled high by resistors, so when the bus is not busy both lines will be high, rather than the more common low.

Each slave on the bus has a three bit chip select code. The master uses the chip select code to selectively address the different slaves on the bus. Chip select is usually a hardware setting on the slaves. For the EB023 the chip select are the three jumpers labeled "Address set-up", and set to 111 by default.

I²C doesn't use an interrupt, so the INT line that has to be patched is not a real interrupt. The INT pin is polled by the software to check if the EB023 requires attention. This is handled automatically.

Searching the datasheet of the ATMEGA 32 reveals that SDA is on pin C0 and SCL is on pin C1. This means the patch panel must be used, so the jumper needs to be set to C. It doesn't matter where INT is patched to, so C2 will be used.

If you haven't done so already, follow the installation instructions for the Ping project. In fact it is highly recommended to do the Ping project first.

---

[49] Inter Integrated Circuit bus.
[50] Two Wire Interface.

8.2 Webserver

Figure 295. EB023 patched for the Atmega 32.

Software

If you haven't done so already first of all make sure that the fuses of the ATMEGA 32 are set correctly to 0x0,0xdf and 0x1,0xff. Select the "Chip" menu and "Configure". Enter the settings and remember to click on the Ok and Send button, because they will not be transferred by default. Of course the AVR programmer must be connected to the PC and powered on for this to work.

In this project the Webserver will have four pages. One menu, one with a measurement of the ADC on pin A0, and two brightly colored pages. These pages can be designed with any normal HTML[51] editor, with a few rules:

 1. Only straight HTML, no scripts.
 2. A maximum of four pages.
 3. No pictures or other embedded objects.
 4. Refer to other pages by their full URL.
 5. A maximum of four Flowcode variables per page.
 6. Flowcode variables must be enclosed in percentage signs (%).

It is customary that the menu page is called index.html. This is what web browsers will look for by default, so if no page is specified in the URL, index.html will be the one that is loaded.

---

[51] HyperText Markup Language.

This is the index.html file that is used in this project:

```html
<HTML>
<HEAD>
 <META NAME="GENERATOR" CONTENT="Adobe PageMill 3.0 Win">
 <TITLE>Main page</TITLE>
</HEAD>
<BODY>

<P><CENTER><B>Welcom to the AVR microcontroller Webserver</B></CENTER></P>

<P><CENTER><TABLE WIDTH="450" BORDER="1" CELLSPACING="2" CELLPADDING="2">
 <TR>
  <TD WIDTH="50%">
  <A HREF="http://192.168.0.2/">Index</A></TD>
  <TD WIDTH="50%">   Home</TD>
 </TR>
 <TR>
  <TD WIDTH="50%">
  <A HREF="http://192.168.0.2/page2">Page 2</A></TD>
  <TD WIDTH="50%">   See the variable resistor position.</TD>
 </TR>
 <TR>
  <TD WIDTH="50%">
  <A HREF="http://192.168.0.2/page3">Page 3</A></TD>
  <TD WIDTH="50%">   The red page.</TD>
 </TR>
 <TR>
  <TD WIDTH="50%">
  <A HREF="http://192.168.0.2/page4">Page 4</A></TD>
  <TD WIDTH="50%">   The blue page.</TD>
 </TR>
</TABLE></CENTER></P>

</BODY>
</HTML>
```

Note that all pages from this menu are referred to by their full URL, so page 2 is referred to as http://192.168.0.2/page2.

8.2 Webserver

This is the HTML for page two that includes a reference to the Flowcode variable B001.

```
<!DOCTYPE HTML PUBLIC "-//W3C//DTD HTML 4.0 Transitional//EN">
<html>
<head>
<title>Internet E-Block Component</title>
</head>
<body BGCOLOR="#FFFFFF">
<font face="arial">
  <H1>Variable resistor measurement = %BOO1%</H1>

</font>
</body>
</html>
```

Note that the Flowcode variable B001 is enclosed in percentage signs: %B001%

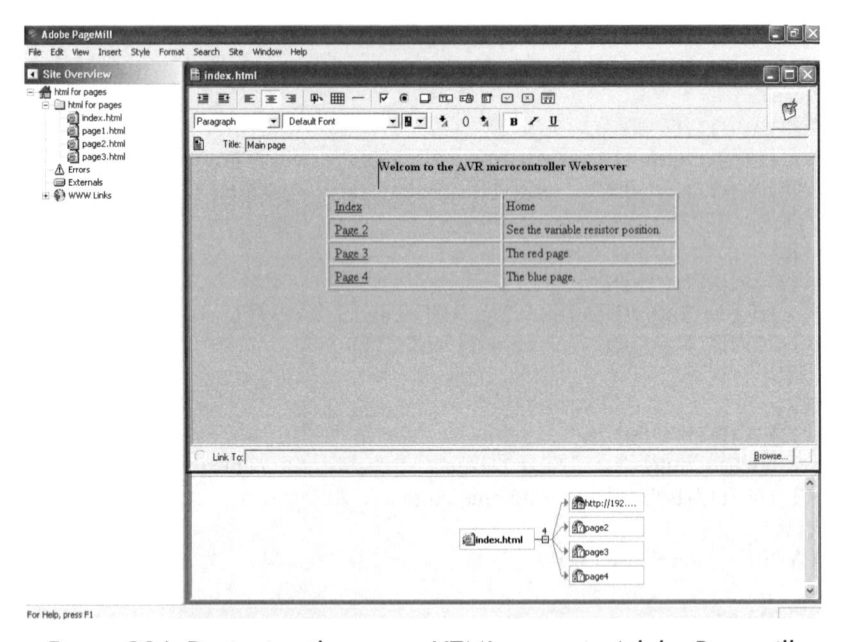

Figure 296. Designing the server HTML pages in Adobe Pagemill.

The Flowcode program itself is rather straight forward. This time a Webserver component is used instead of a TPC/IP component, with the following settings. Note that the I^{2}C interrupt is set to 2 because the INT line is patched to pin C2.

262

8 Internet

Gateway address	192.168.0.1
Subnet mask	255.255.255.0
IP address	192.168.0.2
Hardware address	0.8.220.0.0.0
I2C interrupt	2
Address setup	1-1-1
Maximum number of webpages	4

Figure 297. Webserver component settings.

In the next tabs of the Webserver component the HTML for each of the pages can be added. The full source of this project including all HTML can be found in the download package.

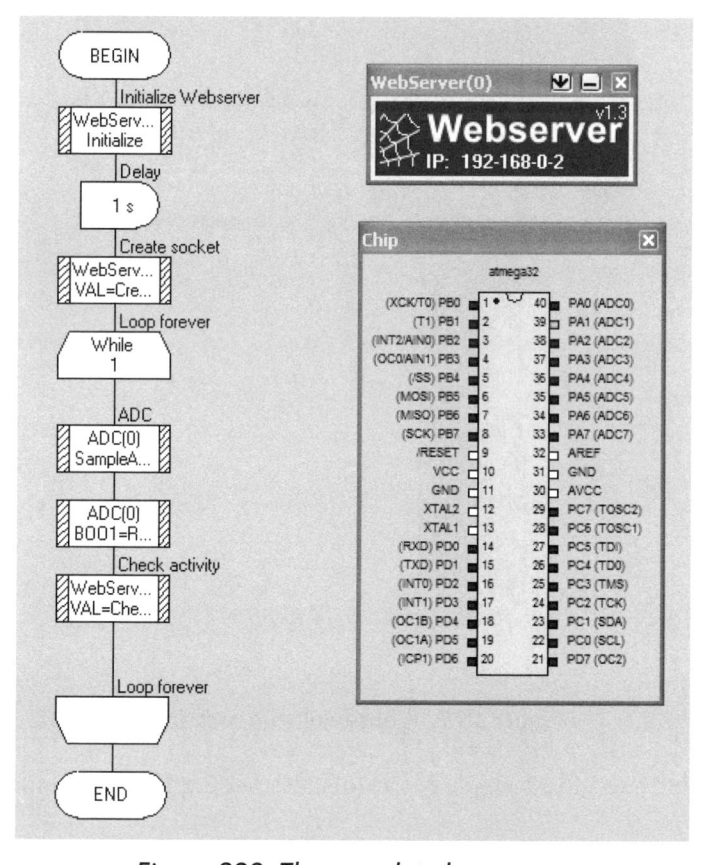

Figure 298. The completed program.

263

8.2 Webserver

The program itself consists of four steps:

1. Initialize the Webserver.
2. Create a server socket, this is basically a connection to the network on IP level.
3. Measure the ADC value of port A0 and put it in byte B001.
4. Check for activity on the server socket (if there is any activity the Webserver component will take further care of it).

Operational

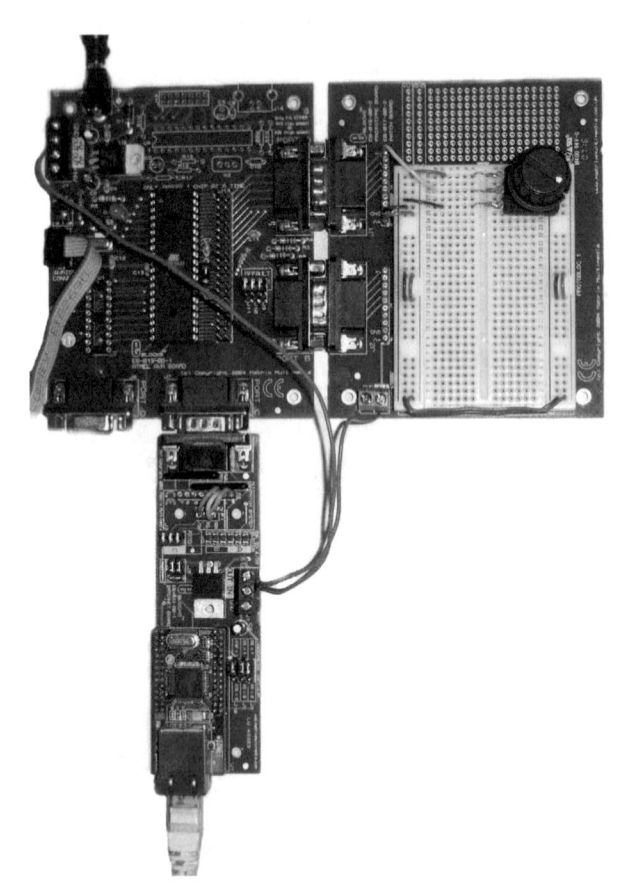

Figure 299. Webserver in operation.

Start your web browser, for example Microsoft Internet Explorer, and enter the following address:

http://192.168.0.2/

8 Internet

Your should now see the Webserver menu. Click on Page 2, which will bring up the page with the measurement of the variable resistor. Turn the variable resistor into a different position and press "refresh" on the browser. The page will refresh and a new value will be shown.

8.3 Send an alarm e-mail

Concept

A microcontroller measures the voltage on a pin. If the voltage exceeds a certain value the microcontroller will send an e-mail to alert a remote user.

Hardware

In this project we will use a 16F877A PIC microcontroller. An LCD board is connected to port B. The Internet board EB023 is connected to port C, and with an RJ45 CAT 5 crossover network cable to a network card, also called "adapter", in the PC. A Proto board is connected to port A. Note that all boards need power so you need to connect the +Vin terminals of all boards to one of the +V terminals of the Programmer board

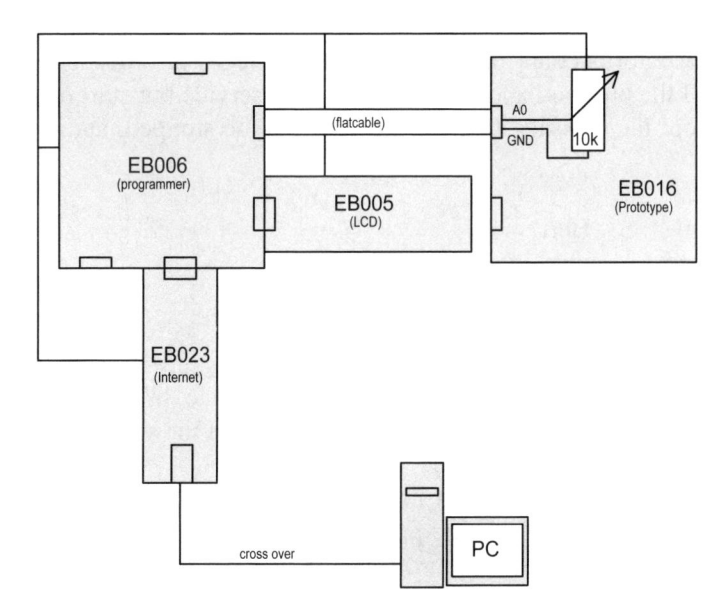

Figure 300. schematic of the alarm e-mail hardware.

8.3 Send an alarm e-mail

Connection summary:

    Programmer   Switches to XTAL and Fast, LVP jumper on I/O port, J29 to PSU, J12-14 to USB, use external power supply.
    Port A   Proto board with a 10 k variable resistor mounted between GND and +5 V. The center is connected to pin A0.
    Port B   LCD board, jumper on default.
    Port C   EB023 Internet board, jumpers to A, +5V, address 1-1-1, an RJ45 CAT 5 crossover network cable to the network card in the PC.

If you haven't done so already follow the installation instructions for the Ping project. It is highly recommended to do the Ping project first.

Software

In the menu select Chip, then Configure and then switch to Expert Config Screen. In the section Configuration Word(s) make sure HEX is selected and then click on the Config1 button and enter: 0x3F3A.

E-mail is processed by mail servers, so the first step is to install a mail server on the PC in the network. In this project we will use Tiny-Mail, a shareware program by Aptus[52]. You need an administrator account or administrator privileges in order to install and use this program. Install the program and select "Install as a service but start manually". Open the properties, accept the message that the services will be stopped, and enter the following information:

    username   Bert
    password   xxx
    name   Bert van Dam
    local e-mail   bert@localhost

Of course you can, and maybe should, use your own name, but remember to also change this in the Flowcode source. Once the data is entered start the service.

Start your e-mail program and add a new account. The following instructions apply for Microsoft Outlook Express. For other programs the steps to take may differ. Go to Extra, Accounts and click on the Add button. Call the account localhost and use the data you just entered into Tiny-Mail. At POP3 and SMTP servers enter IP address 127.0.0.1. This IP address refers to the machine that the software is running on, in this case your PC.

---

[52] http://www.aptuslab.com/software/tmail/

8 Internet

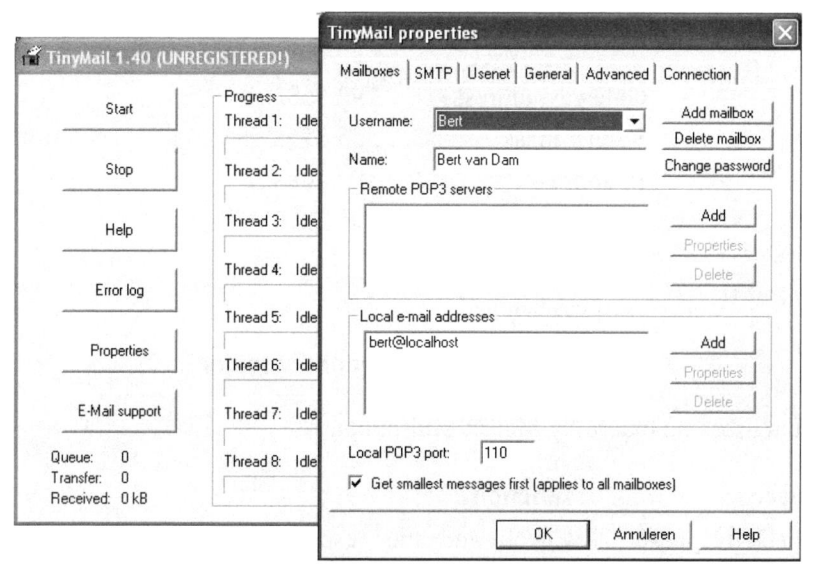

Figure 301. Tiny-Mail settings.

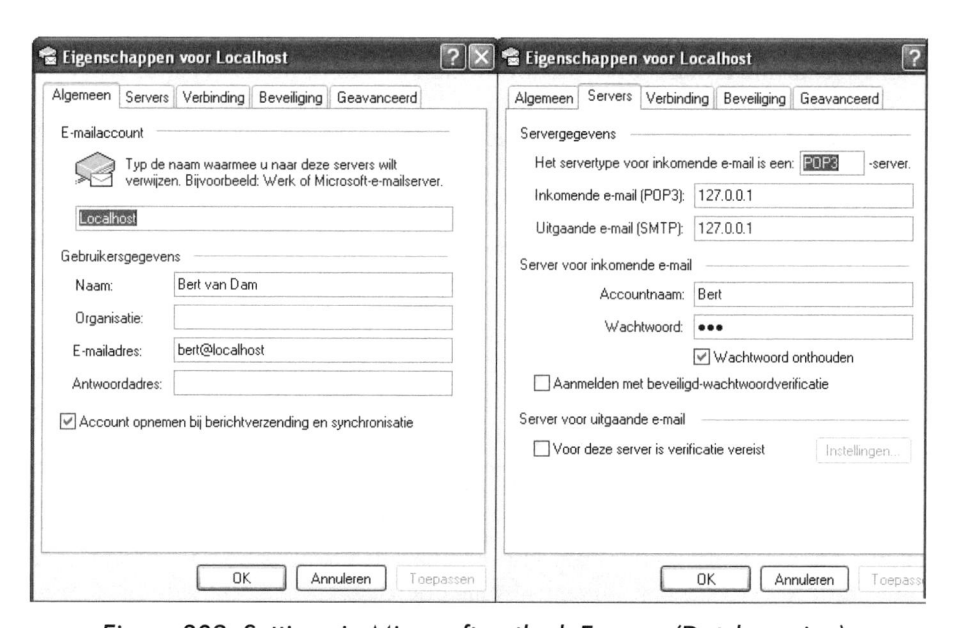

Figure 302. Settings in Microsoft outlook Express (Dutch version).

Once these settings have been entered try to collect mail from this account (In Outlook select Extra, Send and Receive, Localhost). There should not be any errors, nor mail for that matter. This completes the software installation on the PC side.

8.3 Send an alarm e-mail

In Flowcode the TCP/IP component will be used, with the following settings:

Gateway address	192.168.0.1
Subnet mask	255.255.255.0
IP address	192.168.0.2
Hardware address	0.8.220.0.0.0
I2C interrupt	0
Address setup	1-1-1

Figure 303. TCP/IP component settings.

This program uses one macro by Matrix Multimedia:

macro	function
check_response	Check and the response and extract the response code.

Discussing the inner workings is outside the scope of this book so it will be used as is. Import the macro into the program. The second macro that the program uses is the macro that actually sends the e-mail. Take the following steps to write this macro:

1. *Open a socket and connect to the server.*

   This is basically a connection to the network on IP level. Since multiple versions of this program may be running on the same network all guarding a particular machine a random local port is creating using the tmr0 value in a C-box:

   ```
   //create a "random" port from TMR0
   FCV_SRC_PORT = tmr0;
   ```

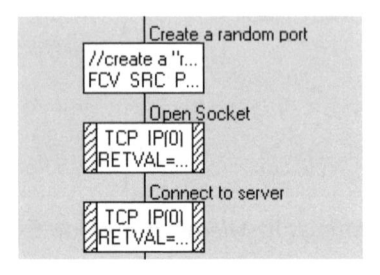

Figure 304. Open a socket.

8 Internet

The mail server will be expecting a connection to port 25, so this is the number that needs to be used as a remote port while connecting.

2. *Check to see if the response is 220 (meaning a mail server is present)*

    Calling the check_response macro and comparing the answer with the expected one does this. This section is the same for step 4, 6, 8 ,10, 12 and 14 with the exception that different answers are expected. If the response is incorrect the program jumps to connection point B, which basically informs the user that an unexpected reply has been received, and that the program consequently terminates.

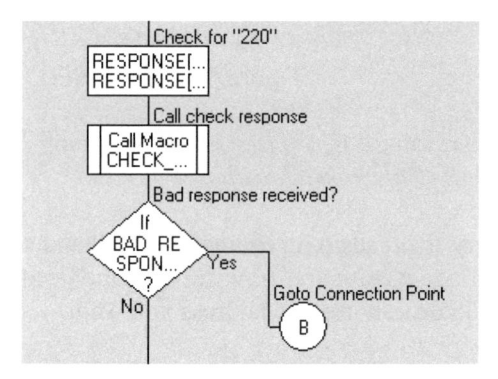

    Figure 305. Check response.

    This is an overview of the responses one would normally expect:

Response	Description
220 [server details]	Mail server present and introducing itself.
221 [server name]	Server closing connection
250 [message data repeated]	Acknowledgement
354	Ready to receive data

    Figure 306. E-mail server messages.

3. *Send: Helo followed by a name.*

    The HELO (yes, just one L) command is used to identify yourself to the server. In this project the server will accept just about anything so any name you fancy will be all right.

8.3 Send an alarm e-mail

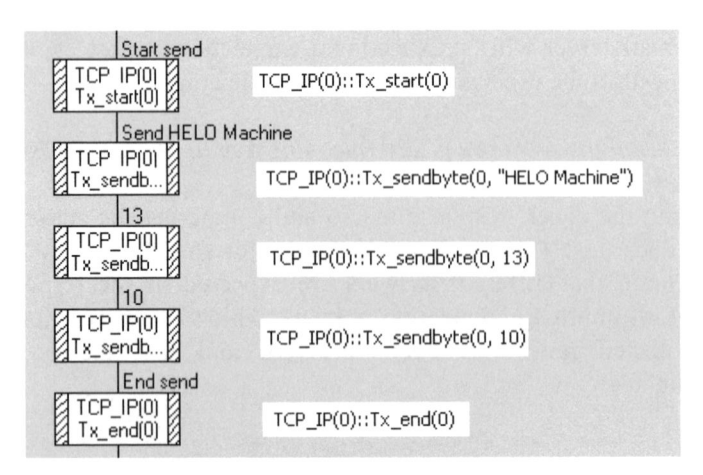

Figure 307. Send HELO.

4. Check to see if the response is 250 (acknowledgement)
5. Send: MAIL FROM:<flowcode@localhost>

   Note that every line ends with character 13, 10 and an end(0) command, where 13 is ASCII Carriage Return and 10 is ASCII Line Feed. Since nobody is going to be returning mail you can use any address you want.

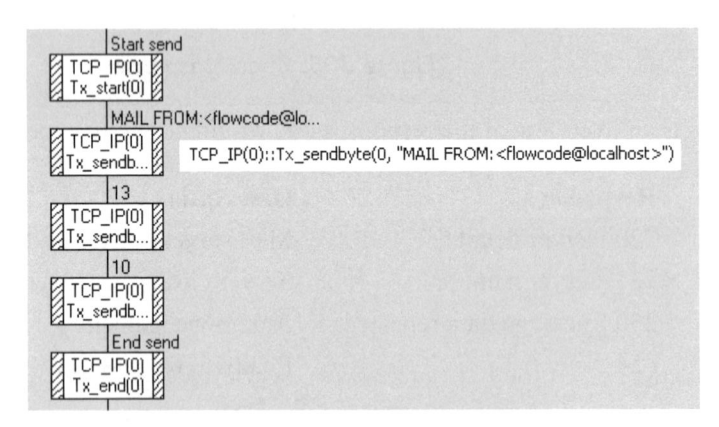

Figure 308. Mail from address.

6. Check to see if the response is 250 (acknowledgement)
7. Send: RCPT TO:<bert@localhost>
8. Check to see if the response is 250 (acknowledgement)
9. Send: data
10. Check to see if the response is 354 (ready to receive data)

8 Internet

These steps are very similar to the previous steps.

11. Send the entire message (header + content)

First the header needs to be send. The header consists of the From address, the To address and the Subject line. It is terminated by the command

> 0, "X-Mailer: Machine SMTP"

Followed by a double ASCII 13/10 combo.

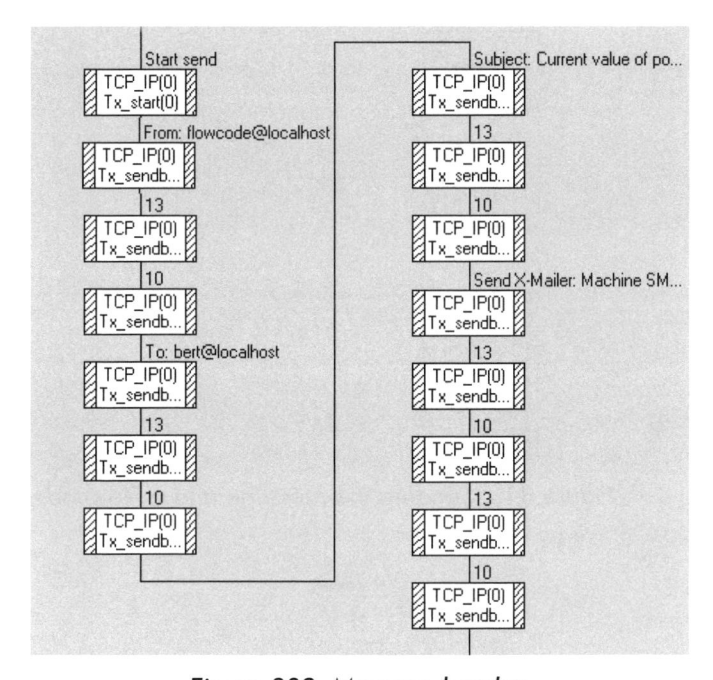

Figure 309. Message header.

After the header the message itself is sent. Note that in the Figures for this step the program in reality is a single line down, for space reasons the program is presented in two columns.

The most interesting part is how the Flowcode variable ends up embedded in the message. After Sending the line:

> 0, "Warning: the potmeter value is over the alarm value. Value at e-mail transmission time : "

271

8.3 Send an alarm e-mail

The measurement itself is first converted into a string:

RS = ToString$(SendMail.ResistorValue)

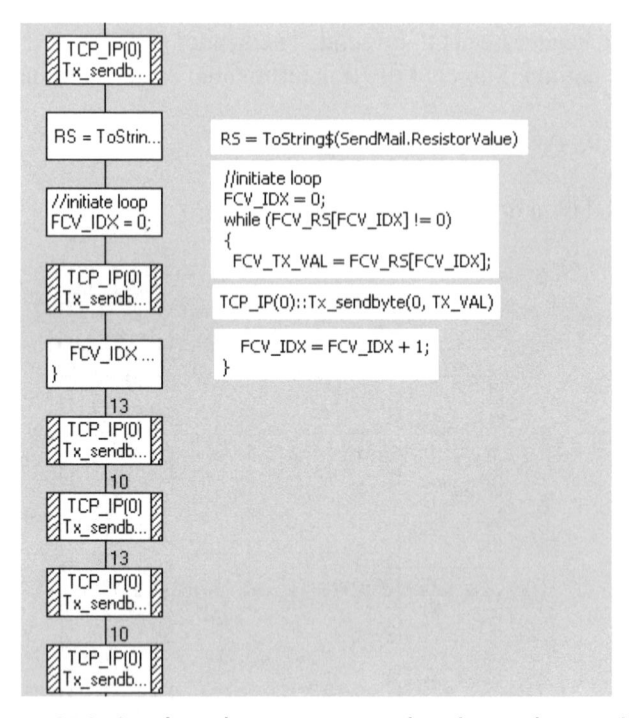

Figure 310. Sending the message and a Flowcode variable.

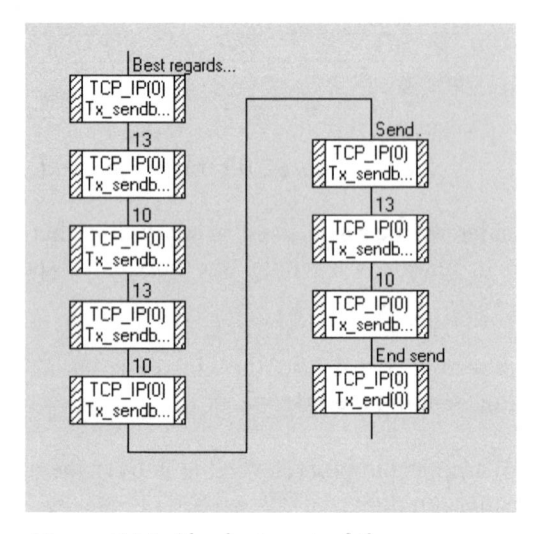

Figure 311. The last part of the message.

8 Internet

The next step is to send this string byte by byte in a curious combo of two C-boxes and a macro symbol, which surprisingly enough actually works.

The message is terminated with ASCII 13/10 followed by a dot and yet another ASCII 13/10 combo.

12. Check to see if the response is 250 (acknowledgement)
13. Send: quit
14. Check to see if the response is 221 (server closing connection).

These steps are very similar to the previous steps.

The main program itself is rather simple. After starting the LCD and initializing TCP/IP the program loops forever reading the voltage on pin A0. If this exceeds a certain value an e-mail is send to alert the remote user. To prevent sending a continuous stream of e-mails variable AlertGiven is used to remember that an alert has been mailed. If the measured value drops below the threshold the program resets itself by making AlertGiven zero again.

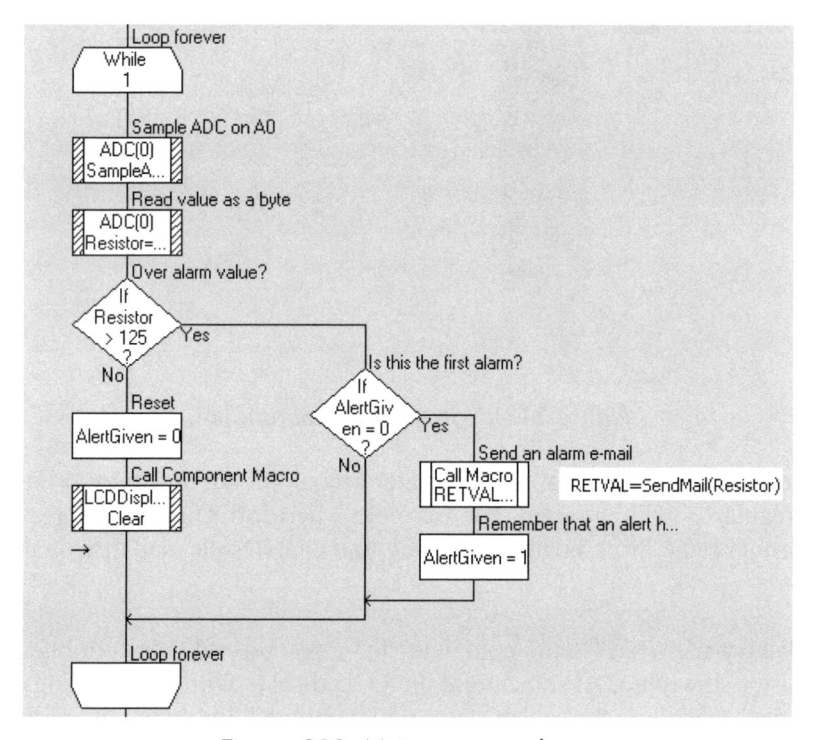

Figure 312. Main program loop.

273

8.3 Send an alarm e-mail

The program can be simulated in Flowcode but it will always give a "Bad response" because sending e-mails is obviously not part of the simulation.

Operational

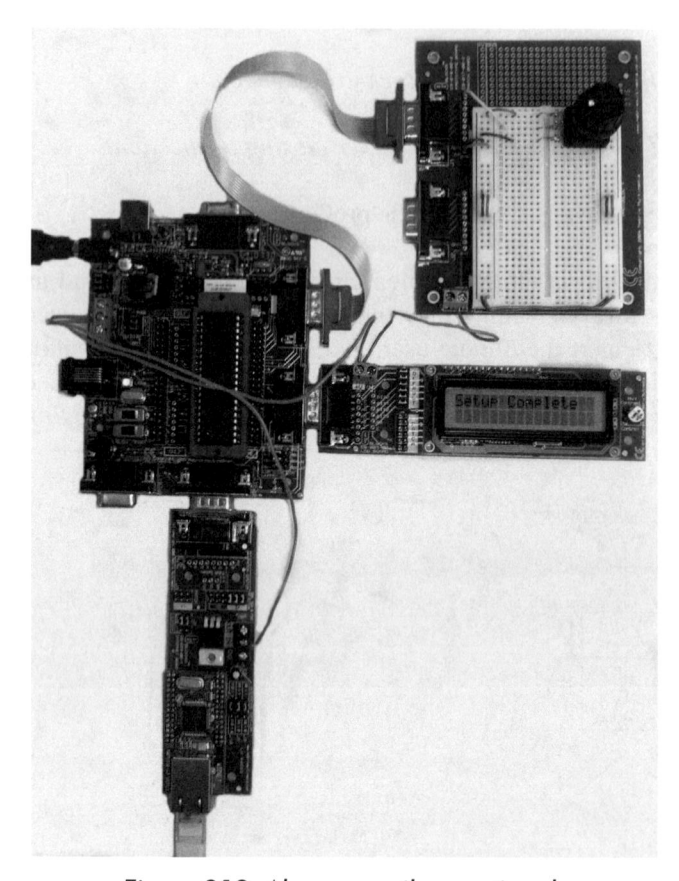

Figure 313. Alarm e-mail operational.

Start the Tiny-Mail server with an administrator account or administrator privileges. Then start your regular e-mail program, for example Microsoft Outlook Express. Turn the variable resistor on the Proto board all the way to the GND side, and turn on the power to your project.

The LCD display will read "Setup complete" for 1 second and then turn blank. Turn the variable resistor slowly up. At some point the LCD display will say "Sending..." and then "done". On the second line the socket status will be printed, this is purely informational. .

8   Internet

In your e-mail program collect the mail from the Localhost account. You should now have a new message waiting for you.

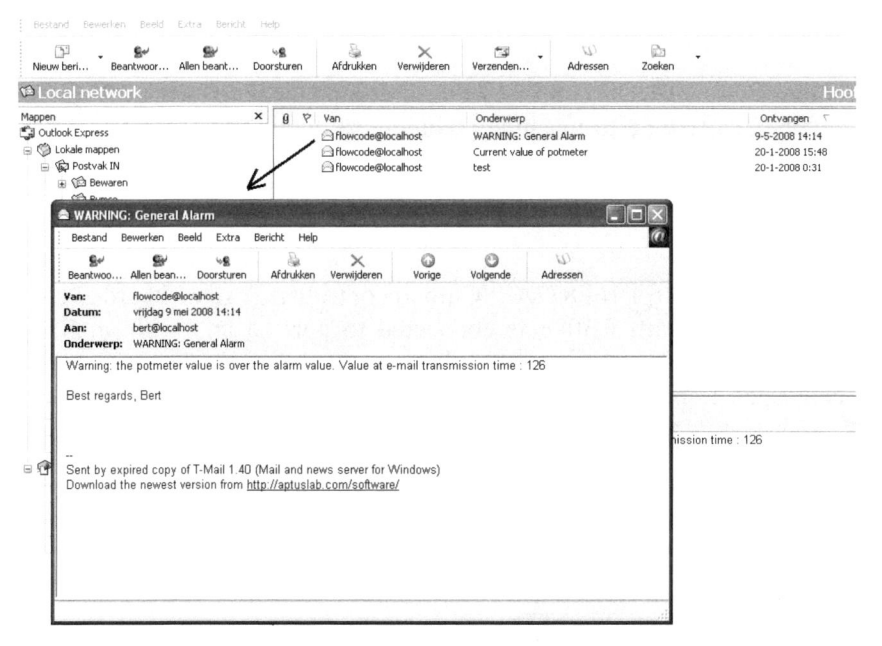

Figure 314. The message is received.

In Wireshark the different steps that were taken in order to send an email can quite easily be checked. Note that on ARP level the EB023 first inquires where the server is.

Figure 315. Wireshark example of an e-mail transfer.

275

8.4 UDP remote control

8.4 UDP remote control

Concept

User Datagram Protocol UDP is a fast form of communication between known systems and used often for machine to machine communications in factories. In this project we will use an UDP connection over an Intranet to remotely control a set of relays.

Hardware

In this project we will use a 16F877A PIC microcontroller. A relay board is connected to port B. The Internet board EB023 is connected to port C, and with an RJ45 CAT 5 crossover network cable to a network card, also called "adapter", in the PC. A Switch board is connected to port D. All boards need power so you need to connect the +Vin terminals of all boards to one of the +5V terminals of the Programmer board. Note that the relay board needs a higher voltage than the other ones, so it needs to be connected to the +14V terminal of the programmer board.

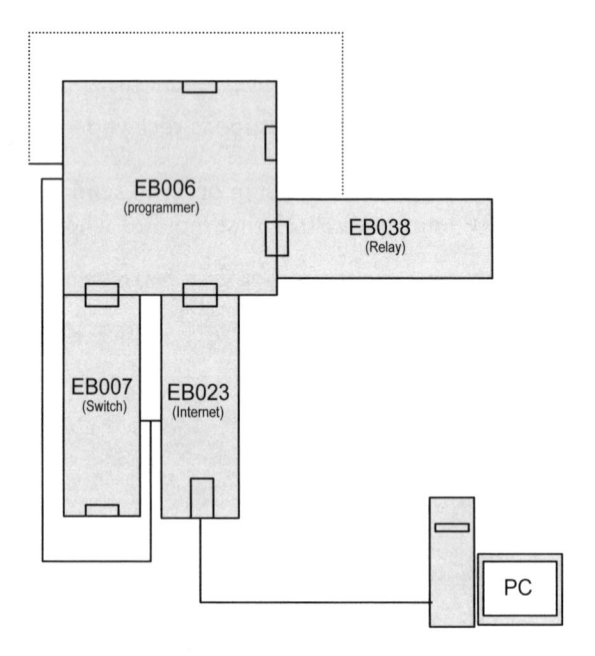

Figure 316. UDP remote control schematic.

8 Internet

Connection summary:

Programmer	Switches to XTAL and Fast, LVP jumper on I/O port, J29 to PSU, J12-14 to USB, use external power supply.
Port B	EB038 Relay board, jumper on low.
Port C	EB023 Internet board, jumpers to A, +5V, address 1-1-1, an RJ45 CAT 5 crossover network cable to the network card in the PC.
Port D	EB007 Switch board.

According to the documentation of the relay board the relays can handle mains, but it recommends not to exceed 24 volts. The relays themselves are stamped 7A / 250 V (Song Chuan, type 812BH-1C-CE)[53].

If you haven't done so already follow the installation instructions for the Ping project. In fact it is highly recommended to do the Ping project first.

Software

In the menu select Chip, then Configure and then switch to Expert Config Screen. In the section Configuration Word(s) make sure HEX is selected and then click on the Config1 button and enter: 0x3F3A.

UDP (User Datagram Protocol) is a transport protocol, on the same level as TCP, see project 6.1 for an overview of the TCP/IP layers, but it doesn't have any error checking. If the applications themselves do not contain any feedback mechanism UDP may be referred to as "send and prey".

In Flowcode the TCP/IP component will be used with the following settings:

Gateway address	192.168.0.1
Subnet mask	255.255.255.0
IP address	192.168.0.2
Hardware address	0.8.220.0.0.0
I2C interrupt	0
Address setup	1-1-1

Figure 317. TCP/IP component settings.

---

[53] Should you use mains remember that high voltages can kill. Take all necessary safety precautions and follow local safety rules and guidelines. Proceed at your own risk.

8.4 UDP remote control

Sending an UDP message requires the following steps, after initializing the TCP/IP component:

1. Create an UDP socket at port 5.
2. Set the IP address that the message has to go to (192.168.0.1).
3. Start the transmission.
4. Send the status of the Switch board.
6. End the transmission.

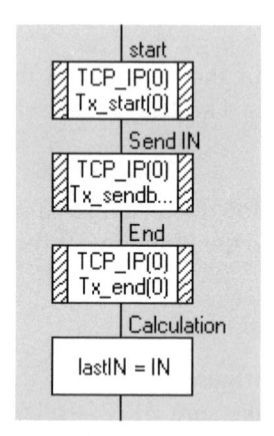

Figure 318. Send a byte over UDP.

Receiving the UDP message from the PC is simple because only one byte will be received, so anything else can be ignored:

1. Check if data is available.
2. Read the very first byte, and send it to port B.
3. Flush the buffer.

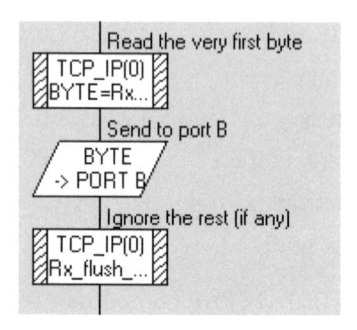

Figure 319. Receive a byte over UDP.

8 Internet

The next piece of software is in Visual Basic and runs on the PC. You can find the executable in the download package. If you own Visual Basic 5 you could modify the source (also in the download) to your own needs, else skip forward to the "operational" section. The core is the Microsoft Winsock Component 6.0 (SP4) which needs to be loaded using Projects and then Components.

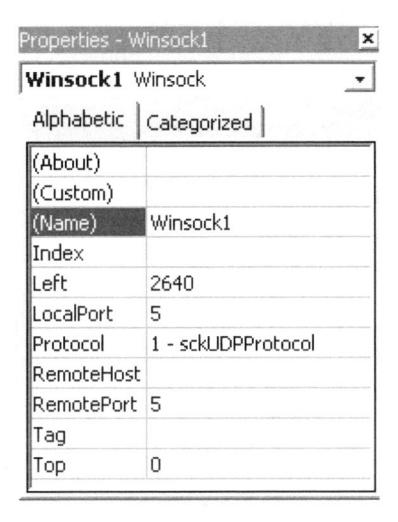

Figure 320. Winsock settings.

At startup the program creates a socket with the information from the component and data the user entered on the screen:

```
If connect = 1 Then
    Winsock1.Close
    connect = 0
End If
Winsock1.RemoteHost = Text1.Text
Winsock1.RemotePort = Text2.Text
Winsock1.LocalPort = Text3.Text
Winsock1.Bind Text3.Text
connect = 1
```

Where text1 is the IP address of the microcontroller, text2 is the UDP port on the microcontroller and text3 is the UDP port on your PC.

Once the socket is created data can be send using the Winsock1.SendData Chr$(ToSend) command. If new data is available on the socket the call Winsock1_DataArrival(ByVal

279

8.4 UDP remote control

bytesTotal As Long) will automatically be initiated, and your program should the use Winsock1.GetData MSG, vbString to get the data from the buffer for further processing.

Operational

Start the Visual Basic program first, click on the Open UDP connection button, and then power up the microcontroller.

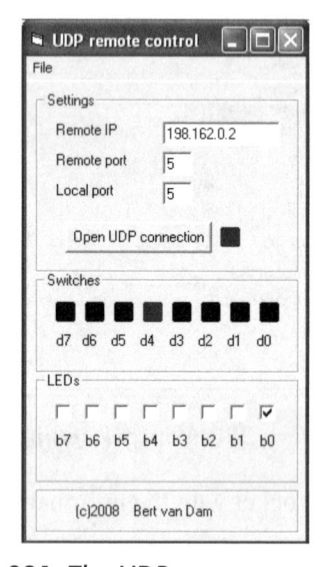

Figure 321. The UDP remote control unit.

If you push a button on the EB007 an alert from your firewall will probably pop up, even if the IP address has been added to the secure zone. If you use ZoneAlert the alerts will be something like "Do you want to allow Visual Basic to act as a server" or "Do you want to allow Visual Basic to accept connections from the local network", or "Do you want to allow Visual Basic to access the internet".

Verify that the request is indeed from the local net and allow this message and future ones. If your application doesn't work chances are a firewall or other protective software is silently blocking access. Should you disable safety features of the PC in order to get this project to work, make a note of the settings and remember to restore them all prior to connecting to the internet again.

If you check or uncheck any of the LEDs this information is send to the microcontroller. If you use an LED board the checkmarks correspond to LEDs. If you use a relay board

8   Internet

only four checkmarks apply (the board only has four relays). With the jumper on low as per the instructions the applicable numbers are 0 to 3.

Figure 322. Security warning from ZoneAlert.

Figure 323.Relay engaged by UDP remote control.

9 Design your own E-block

Even though the selection of available E-blocks is quite impressive you may at some point need blocks that simply do not exist. If you need this particular block only once you can built it on a Proto board. But if you need it more often a more robust solution is advisable.

9.1 Analog test signal

Concept

For testing programs that use or process analog signals a variable resistor is an ideal tool. With a simple knob the full voltage range from GND to +V can be supplied. You can insert one into the breadboard area of an EB016 Proto board, and in fact many projects in this book do it this way. For a more permanent solution the small patch section on the Proto board is an ideal location.

Hardware

A 10k linear variable resistor is mounted between the +V and the ground. The center pin is connected to one of the D9 connector pins, using a small jumper section for flexibility. The jumper can be used to connect the variable resistor to one of the first five pins (0 through 4).

Sensory components such as an NTC of LDR may be connected partly in series with the variable resistor. For that reason a three screw terminal will be used. One of the leads must always be connected to the center terminal, and thus the center pin of the variable resistor. The other pin can be connected to the GND (left screw when the openings are facing you) so a reduction in resistance will cause a reduction in voltage, or to the +V for the reverse effect.

It is easy to remember which terminal is GND and which is +V. If you turn the knob "low" (all the way to the left) the indicator is pointing to the GND. If you turn the knob to "high" (all the way to the right) the indicator is pointing to the +V.

9 Design your own E-block

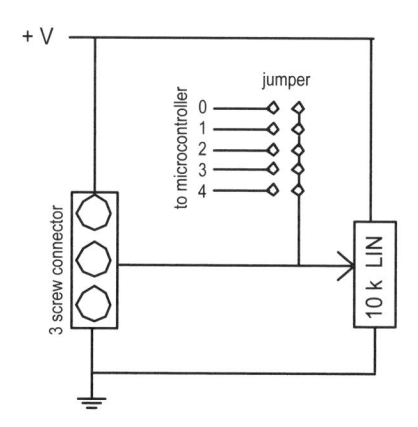

Figure 324. Schematic analog test signal.

No PCB design has been made, the schematic is simple enough to solder directly onto the patch area. The variable resistor is mounted upright for easier control, and glued to the patch board. In the next Figure the jumper is set to pin 0.

Figure 325. The extension to the Proto board.

Note that the breadboard area is wired to GND and +V. It is advisable to do this and leave it in place between projects. You wouldn't be the first to wonder why a project isn't working only to find out that part of it simply is not powered.

Operational

You can see this extension in operation in for example project 3.6.

283

9.2 Microphone pre-amplifier

9.2 Microphone pre-amplifier

Concept

For sound applications a high quality microphone pre-amplifier would be a handy E-block. In this project we will take a design by Christopher Hunter[54], shown in the next Figure, and turn that into a new E-block using the EB017 Patch board.

Hardware

The design is based on the LM358, an operational amplifier specifically targeted for sound applications.

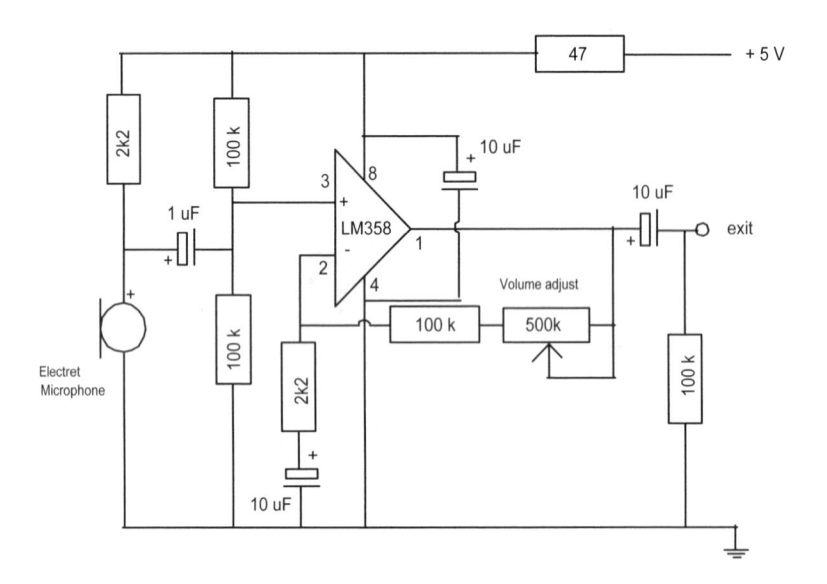

Figure 326. Microphone pre-amplifier by Christopher Hunter.

The electret microphone is encapsulated in a traditional network, and fed into the non-inverting input of the OPAMP. The two 100k resistors set the nominal voltage at 2.5 volt allowing for a maximum voltage swing. The inverting input is DC blocked by the 10 uF capacitor. The feedback loop enables a gain between 46 and 273 depending on the position of the 500k variable resistor. The gain is very high, which is possible because the LM358 can swing rail to rail even with a non-symmetrical power supply such as used in

---

[54] Christopher is an electronics engineer. He works for a company that designs, builds, installs and maintains traffic signal controller equipment. The design is used with his kind permission.

284

9 Design your own E-block

this case. The 100k resistor to ground at the exit prevents the microcontroller input from floating.

The first step is to build this schematic on a Proto board and test the performance in an actual application. This resulted in the addition of the 47 ohm resistor in the power line and the 10 uF capacitor directly over the OPAMP, which originally were not in the schematic. These parts filter microcontroller noise on the power lines. The pre-amplifier has an excellent sound quality, crisp and clear. This is an ideal design for any application, not just microcontrollers.

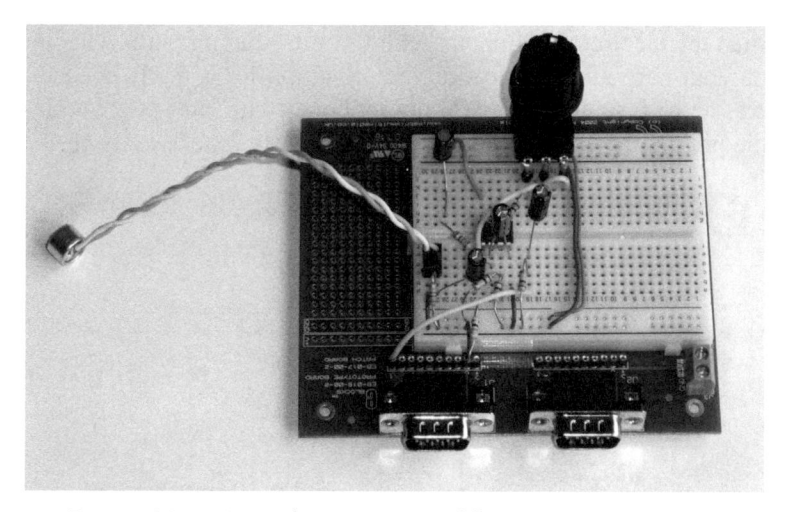

Figure 327. Microphone pre-amplifier on a Proto board.

Printed circuit board

The next step is to feed the schematic into a printed circuit board (PCB) design program. We will use the Eagle CAD design program[55].

Since the goal is to build the project on a Patch board the holes are already present, so the proper grid of these holes (2.531) needs to be invoked. This is done by issuing the command "grid dots on mm 2.531 alt mm 0.1" The alternative grid (0.1 mm) can be used to place text on the PCB (hold the ALT key to get this grid). Of course you can use the exact same design for a "real" printed circuit board.

There are a few important deviations from the original design on the Proto board, which have been incorporated to maximize flexibility.

---

[55] With kind permission of CadSoft Computer GmbH, http://www.cadsoft.de

9.2 Microphone pre-amplifier

Port pins (jumper J1)

Between the connector and the pre-amplifier itself a set of five jumpers is mounted so the output can be connected to any of the first five pins of the port that the board is connected to. This means multiple boards can be connected to the same port.

Divert signal (jumper J2)

The second jumper is less obvious. It is located between the two 100k resistors and the non inverting input of the OPAMP. This jumper allows one to either use the entire pre-amplifier, or just the electret microphone with the surrounding parts. This means you can test whether in your particular application the pre-amplifier is really needed. Perhaps you can get away with just the electret microphone with its peripheral components. Eliminating the pre-amplifier, if possible, would seriously reduce mass production cost.

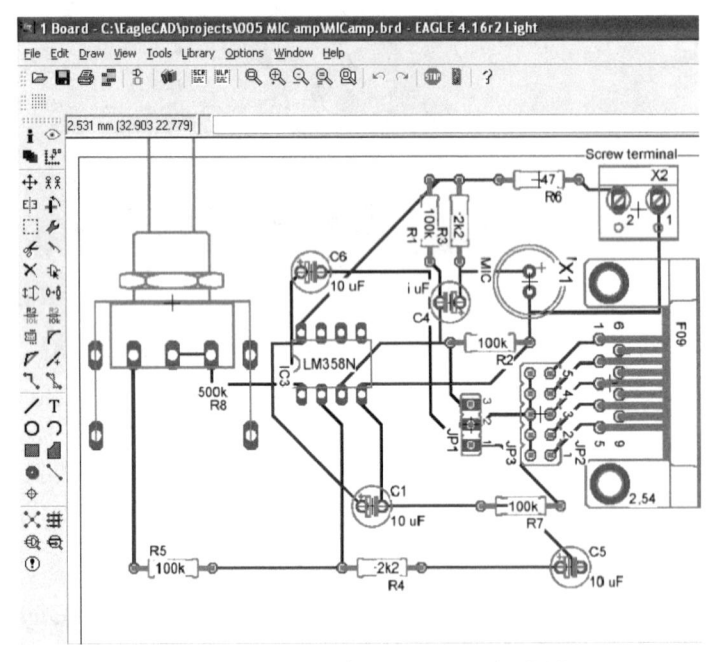

Figure 328. PCB design in Eagle CAD.

9 Design your own E-block

In the finished project the microphone is mounted on a wire, the PCB however has plenty of space for a surface mounted microphone. The size of the design can be seriously reduced if the variable resistor is mounted vertically on one side. The Patch board has plenty of space however so the resistor is mounted flat and glued down for ease of use.

Figure 329. Finished project on a patch board.

Operation

You can see this new board in operation in for example projects 3.6, 3.8, 4.2, 4.14 and 5.7. This board is designed to operate at 5 volts, but it will also work at 3.3 volts, see project 4.14.

10.1 Software

10 Migration between PIC, AVR and ARM

In this book three different microcontroller families are used. The advantage of using an advanced high level language such as Flowcode is that programs can quite easily be transferred from one microcontroller family to the other.

10.1 Software

Flowcode software written for a particular microcontroller can be imported in Flowcode for another microcontroller family by using File and then Import. During loading Flowcode will advise you for which microprocessor the program was originally written, and prompt you to select a new target.

In order to make that decision it is important to know what functionality is required in the project. Does it need special features such as I²C, SPI or PWM? In that case the new target should have that functionality too. So compare the features of the original target and select an appropriate new target.

In this book the following microcontrollers are used[56], which have more or less the same features, meaning programs written for one can usually be migrated to the other quite easily:

```
PIC    16F877A
EICO   40 (PIC 18F4455)
AVR    ATMEGA32
ARM    AT91SAM7S128
```

Note that for the PIC 16F877A this is not the default microcontroller that came with the EB006 multi programmer board but a much larger PIC instead.

Once a new target has been selected the program will be converted and shown on the screen. You will see no difference compared to the original program!

Flowcode for AVR has a minor bug that doesn't allow you to jump to an end. Of course you should try to avoid jumps anyway because they make the program less readable. Adding a small NOP as shown in the next Figure will solve the bug.

---

[56] With the exception of chapters 2 (PIC 16F88) and 11 (PIC 12F675).

10   Migration between PIC, AVR and ARM

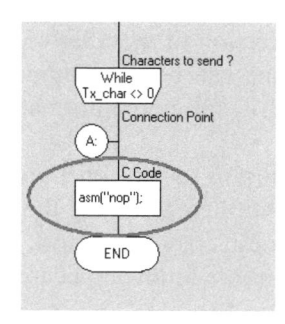

Figure 330. NOP between a jump and an end in an AVR program.

Flowcode for ARM is the only version that has floating point math support, see for example project 5.2. Migrating a project that contains floating point requires a re-write of that particular section.

Only PIC microcontrollers use Lookup Tables, so this also has to be re-written in case of migration.

Some projects contain assembler or C code, or direct access to registers. These programs usually cannot even be directly migrated to other microcontrollers of the same family, let alone to a different family. So in these cases a re-write of these sections will be required.

After a migration make sure to check the configuration and clock speed settings and adapt them to your needs.

10.2 Hardware

Obviously you need a programmer that can handle your new target microcontroller.

Microcontroller family	Programmer
EICO	Self programming
PIC	EB006
AVR	EB194
ARM	EB031 (or EB185)[57]

---

[57] EB185 is a combination of the EB031 programmer board and an EB034 daughter board with an AT91SAM7S128 ARM processor.

10.2 Hardware

The ECIO40 units are a special version of the 18F4455 PIC microcontroller, since they are equipped with a bootloader and can be programmed without the need for a regular EB006 programmer. See chapter 3.12 for more information.

E-blocks that make use of general port or pin functionality do not need to be converted when used on a different microcontroller, assuming the ports and pins actually exist. The AVR ATMEGA32 for example doesn't have an E port, the PIC 16F877A doesn't have an A7 pin etc. Within those restrictions the following boards that are used in this book do not need conversion:

EB004	LED board
EB005	LCD board
EB007	Switch (button) board
EB014	Keypad board
EB038	Relay board

The ARM microcontroller programmer uses pins B5 and D4 for programming. This means that these pins are not available for use unless you move J18 from USB to I/O. Remember to put it back before programming. So if you don't move the jumper the LCD board can only be used on ports B and D if you use the patch panel.

Note that the ARM microcontroller runs on 3.3 volts, whereas PIC and AVR run on 5 volts. That means on several boards the power jumper needs to be changed. For the LCD board it means that the brightness resistor at the end of the board needs a different position.

The other boards use a specific communication between the board and the microcontroller, such as SPI, or functionality only available at certain ports and pins. The following tables show the differences in pin layout between the four microcontrollers used in this book. If you use other microcontrollers use the datasheets to add these settings to the table. In appendix 12.5 an overview is given of the connections of all E-blocks used in this book. Combining these two will show you exactly how to set the jumpers, patch the patch board and which data to enter in the Flowcode component.

Note that a star (*) means that you can choose the pin freely, however your choice must be reflected in the settings of the component in Flowcode. The port names refer to the D9 connectors on the programmer boards, the numbers refer to the pins on these ports. So for example B5 would be bit 5 at port B.

10 Migration between PIC, AVR and ARM

SPI pins

SPI pin name	Description	16F877A	ATMEGA32	AT91SAM7S128	ECIO40 18F4455
SDO / MOSI	Master output	C5	B5	B5	C7
SDI / MISO	Master input	C4	B6	B4	B0
SCK	Clock	C3	B7	B6	B1
CS	Chip select	*	*	*	*
/INT	Interrupt	*	*	*	*

Figure 331. SPI pin overview (means free choice).*

This table applies to SPI boards:

EB013	SPI memory and D/A board
EB037	MMC board
EB018	CAN bus board

If you use the ARM microcontroller, which runs off 3.3 volts, note that the EB013 board is 3.3 volt compatible, except for FRAM memory. Jumper J18 on the ARM programmer board EB185 needs to be set on I/O in order to use SPI, remember to set it back to USB before re-programming.

I^{2}C pins

I^{2}C pin name	Description	16F877A	ATMEGA32	AT91SAM7S128	ECIO40 18F4455
SDA/TWD	Data	C4	C1	A3	B0
SCL/TWCK	Clock	C3	C0	A4	B1
/INT	Interrupt	*	*	*	*

Figure 332. I^{2}CI pin overview (means free choice).*

This table applies to I^{2}C board:

| EB023 | Internet board |

291

10.2 Hardware

USART pins

USART pin name	Description	16F877A	AT MEGA32	AT91SA M7S128	ECIO40 18F4455
RX	Receive	C7	D0	C7	C7
TX	Transmit	C6	D1	C6	C6
RTS	Request to send	*	*	*	*
CTS	Clear to send	*	*	*	*

Figure 333. USART pin overview (* means free choice).

This table applies to USART boards:

    EB015   RS232 board
    EB039   USB board

PWM pins

PWM pin name	Description	16F877A	AT MEGA32	AT91SA M7S128	ECIO40 18F4455
PWM 1	PWM	C2	D5	A0	C2
PWM 2	PWM	C1	D4	A1	C1
PWM 3	PWM	n/a	D7**	A2**	n/a
PWM 4	PWM	n/a	B3**	n/a	n/a

Figure 334. PWM pin overview (n/a means not available, ** means not directly supported by Flowcode.).

This table applies to PWM board:

    EB022   Motor driver board

When all these pins are taken care of make sure specialty components on a patch board, Proto board or custom designed hardware are connected the proper way. Consult the datasheets of the components and the microcontroller if in doubt.

10   Migration between PIC, AVR and ARM

10.3 Example

As an example let's migrate the Internet Webserver (project 8.2) from AVR to PIC.

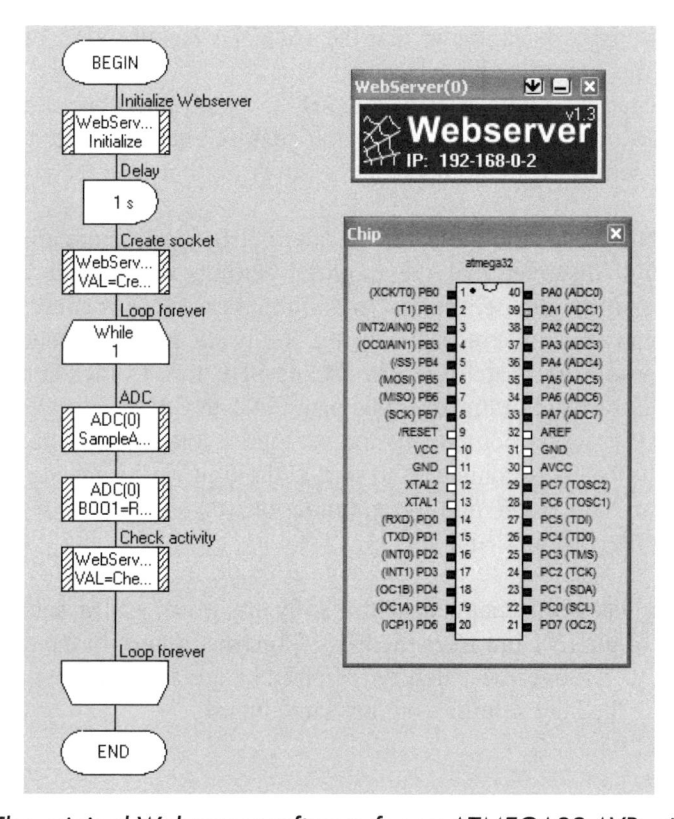

Figure 335. The original Webserver software for an ATMEGA32 AVR microcontroller.

The migration process requires just eight simple steps:

1. Start Flowcode for PIC, and click on the cancel button when the Flowchart selection window pops up.
2. Use File and then Import to select the AVR Flowcode file and load it. Set Filetypes to "Flowcode for AVR files (*.fcf_avr)" if you can't find the correct file.
3. At the notification "Imported file uses the [ATMEGA32] chip" click the OK button. A "Choose a target" window appears, select the 16F877A as target.
4. Save the imported program.
5. Use View and then Attached components to verify that all components are shown.

293

10.3 Example

6. The ADC component is connected to ADC0. Select View and then Chip to view the pin lay out of the 16F877A. Run the simulation for a few seconds. Pin A0 is now green, indicating that the ADC component is connected to pin A0. So this is where the variable resistor needs to be connected.
7. The Webserver component uses the EB023 Internet board. Consultating the I²C table a few pages back shows that the 16F877A has the SDA pin at C4 and SDC at C3. At this point you have three options:
   1. You check the datasheet of the EB023 board and check the connections. If you do you will discover that the required settings are in fact the default board settings if the jumpers are set to A. In that case INT is connected to pin C0.
   2. You can check the table for the internet board in appendix 12.5. If you do you will discover that the required settings are in fact the default board settings if the jumpers are set to A. In that case INT is connected to pin C0
   3. You can't be bothered so you use the patch panel no matter what. Set the jumper to C and patch SDA to C4 and SDC to C3. Pick something, anything in fact, for INT. In this example patch INT to C0.
8. Open the Webserver component and set the I²C interrupt in the properties box to 0 (since the board is connected to port C the 0 in reality means C0). Connect the hardware to the EB006 multi programmer board.
9. Download the program and test it.

Note that nothing has been changed in the software itself, just a setting to reflect the different location of the INT pin from the EB023 Internet board. In the hardware itself the only change was to remove the patch wires and change a jumper, or change the patch wires if you choose the lazy solution, on that same board.

10 Migration between PIC, AVR and ARM

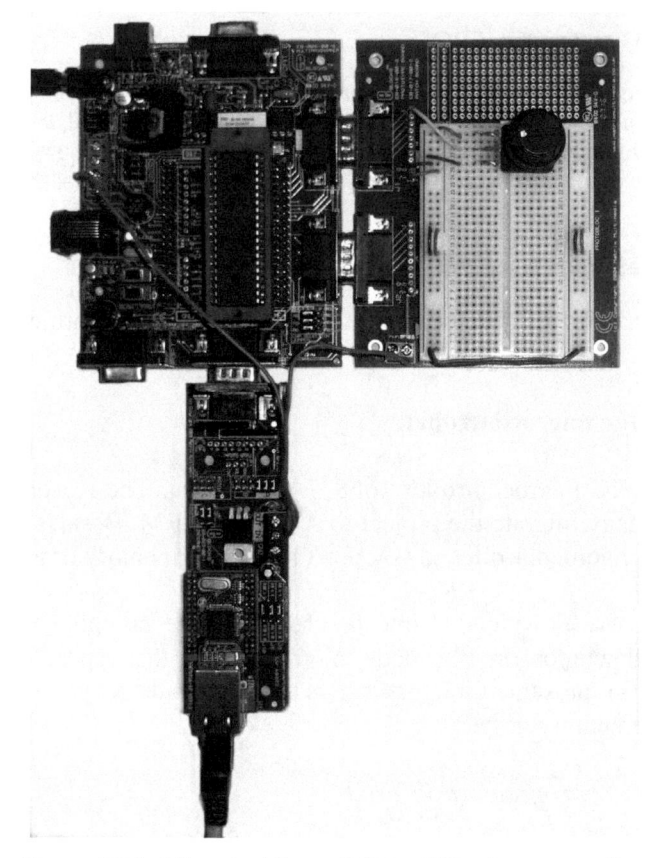

Figure 336. Migrated from AVR to PIC microcontroller.

11.1 Youth deterrent (continued)

11 Going into production

The projects in this book all end with a working prototype. How to proceed from there depends on your purpose. Are you doing that project just for fun, or with the intent to sell. If you want to sell a product you need to turn your prototype into a real product. In this chapter we will take a prototype project and show you which steps you need to take to turn it into an actual sellable product.

11.1 Youth deterrent (continued)

We will start where project 3.7 left off, so if you haven't done this project now would be a good time to do so.

Step 1: Optimize the microcontroller.

In project 3.7 the PIC microcontroller 16F877A was used. The reason for this was that this allows us to easily migrate the project to AVR and ARM. Besides it is convenient to develop on a "big" microcontroller so you don't run out of memory or pins.

When this project was downloaded into the 16F877A the compiler made an extensive report in the small window in Flowcode. You will find this report also in a file with extension .msg.txt in the same directory where the Flowcode program is located. Part of this report was the memory usage.

> *83 out of 8192 program words used*
> *0 out of 256 data bytes used*
> *That took 1,407 seconds*

So in effect this program almost took no memory. By the way I like the proud "That took 1,407 seconds" remark. Because it is very fast indeed.

Anyway, apart from the power connections in total three pins were used:

> pin 13 crystal
> pin 14 crystal
> pin E0 loudspeaker

It would be nice if we could get rid of the crystal but since the frequency of the sound is very important, and high, the crystal needs to stay.

The cheapest option would be to use a PIC microcontroller with 3 pins, excluding the power pins, and 83 bytes of program memory. Comparing the possible microcontrollers

11   Going into production

on the Microchip[58] website with the types supported by Flowcode and the types that my supplier can deliver the most sensible option is the 12F675 priced at 0.73 US$ in bulk quantities.

The tiny 8 pin 12F675 has these properties:

Item	Specification
Program memory	1024 words (14 bit)
RAM	64 bytes
EEPROM	128 bytes
I/O pins	6
A/D pins	4 (of 8 or 10 bits wide)
Speed	5 mips

Step 2: Migrate to that microcontroller.

Load the project from chapter 3.7 into Flowcode. Select Chip and then Target and select the 12F675 from the list. You will get an alert that one of the commands in the program cannot be run on that target, with a question asking if you would like to see the offending command. Click on yes.

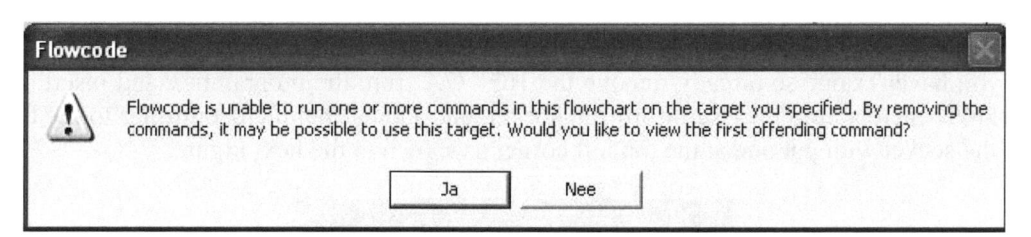

Figure 337. Flowcode alert for offending command.

Flowcode will highlight the command in the interrupt macro where the pin on port E is set. The 12F675 only has port A, so change port E to port A. There are no further alerts.

In the menu select Chip, then Configure and then switch to Expert Config Screen. In the section Configuration Word(s) make sure HEX is selected and then click on the Config1 button and enter: 0x3F82.

---

[58] Microchip is the manufacturer of PIC microcontrollers. The website URL is www.microchip.com

297

11.1 Youth deterrent (continued)

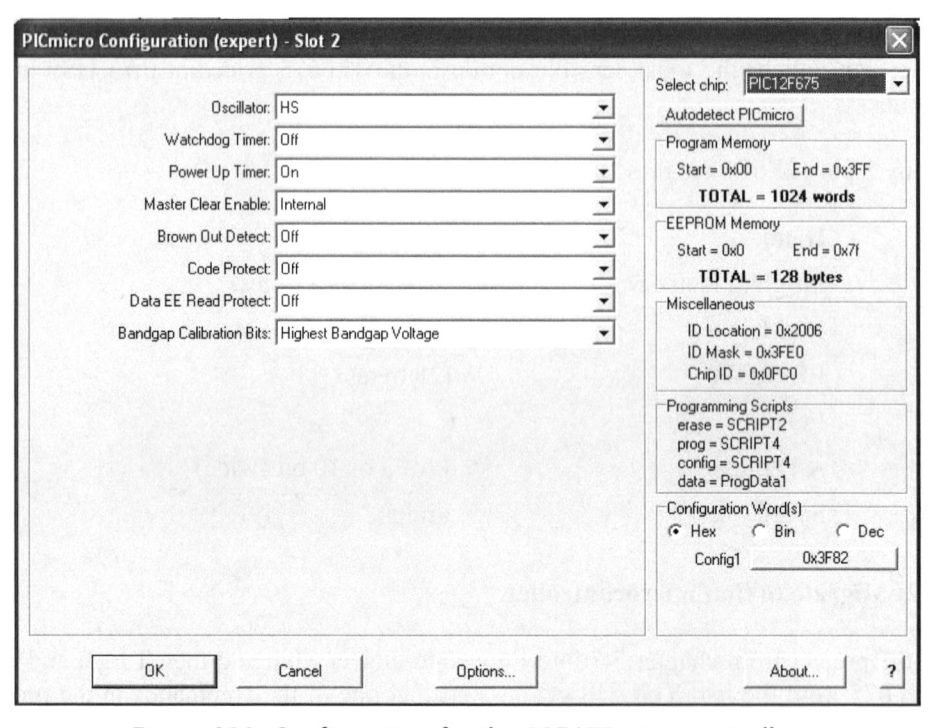

Figure 338. Configuration for the 12F675 microcontroller.

Step 3: Test the hardware.

If you haven't done so already remove the 16F877A from the programmer and insert the 12F675 microcontroller. Use the 14 pin socket, and mount the microcontroller to the top of the socket with pin one at the top left corner as shown in the next Figure.

Figure 339. Mounting the 12F675 in the 14 pin socket.

11   Going into production

Since we just changed the pin to A0 you might expect that this would also be the pin in use on the EB006 programmer board. This is not the case however since the 12F675 only uses half the socket. The datasheet of the EB006 programmer states that pin GP0, the official name for A0 in this microcontroller, is mapped to B7 so this is where the loudspeaker is connected to.

Download the program and use a teenager or a spectrum analyzer to verify that is it working as it should.

Figure 340. Youth deterrent with a 12F675 in the EB006 programmer.

Step 4: Determine the circuit.

Now that everything works as it should, the actual circuit that is used must be extracted from the prototype. Consult the datasheet of the EB006 programmer to find out how the 12F675 is connected to the power and the crystal.

pin	connection
1	+V
2	20 MHz crystal and 10 pF capacitor to GND
3	20 MHz crystal and 10 pF capacitor to GND
7	loudspeaker, other side to GND
8	GND

Figure 341. 12F675 connections.

299

11.1 Youth deterrent (continued)

I prefer to use 20pF capacitors to tie the crystal to ground, so these will be used in the next steps. Based on this a schematic will be drawn with the actual parts to be used. Since step 5 will be to design a PCB it is advisable to draw the schematics diagram into PCB design software. We will use the Eagle CAD design program[59].

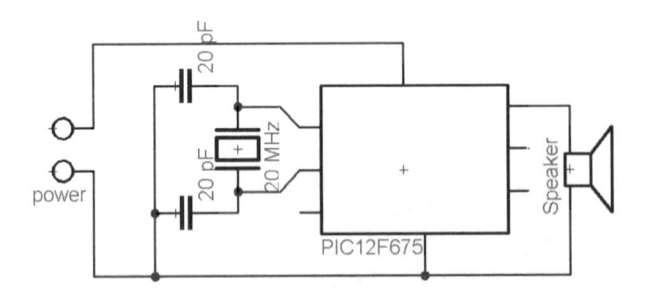

Figure 342. Actual schematic.

Step 5. Design a PCB.

Use the same program to turn the schematic into a PCB. Make sure to leave enough room for the speaker!

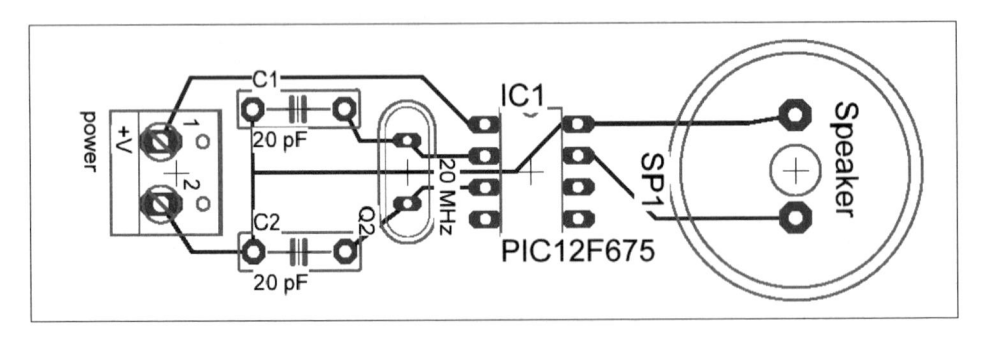

Figure 343. PCB for the youth deterrent.

---

[59] With kind permission of CadSoft Computer GmbH, http://www.cadsoft.de

11 Going into production

Step 6. Built the completed project.

The power consumption is 15 mA, so a set of 2100 mAh rechargeable batteries should last about 80 hours. Of course the effective range is rather small, just a few meters[60].

Distance	Effect
5 m	Somewhat annoying when in a quiet environment. Switching it on does get instant attention.
3 m	Annoying, don't want to hang around here.
1 m	Extremely irritating, can feel the inside of the ears vibrate, want to cover ears.

Figure 344. The effect on teenagers.

Note that in some countries this device may be illegal if operated on or near public places, even when located on private premises.

---

[60] One meter is 3.28 ft.

301

12.1 ASCII table

12 Appendix

Answers to questions you didn't even know you had.

12.1 ASCII table

ASCII	Character	ASCII	Character	ASCII	Character
0	ctl@	43	+	86	V
1	ctlA	44	,	87	W
2	ctlB	45	-	88	X
3	ctlC	46	.	89	Y
4	ctlD	47	/	90	Z
5	ctlE	48	0	91	[
6	ctlF	49	1	92	\
7	ctlG	50	2	93	]
8	ctlH	51	3	94	^
9	ctlI	52	4	95	_
10	ctlJ	53	5	96	`
11	ctlK	54	6	97	a
12	ctlL	55	7	98	b
13	ctlM	56	8	99	c
14	ctlN	57	9	100	d
15	ctlO	58	:	101	e
16	ctlP	59	;	102	f
17	ctlQ	60	<	103	g
18	ctlR	61	=	104	h
19	ctlS	62	>	105	i
20	ctlT	63	?	106	j
21	ctlU	64	@	107	k
22	ctlV	65	A	108	l
23	ctlW	66	B	109	m
24	ctlX	67	C	110	n
25	ctlY	68	D	111	o
26	ctlZ	69	E	112	p
27	ctl[	70	F	113	q

ASCII	Character	ASCII	Character	ASCII	Character
28	ctl\	71	G	114	r
29	ctl]	72	H	115	s
30	ctl^	73	I	116	t
31	ctl_	74	J	117	u
32	Space	75	K	118	v
33	!	76	L	119	w
34	"	77	M	120	x
35	#	78	N	121	y
36	$	79	O	122	z
37	%	80	P	123	{
38	&	81	Q	124	|
39	'	82	R	125	}
40	(	83	S	126	~
41	)	84	T	127	DEL
42	*	85	U		

12.2 Visual Basic communications

Writing your own software is the most fun, because you can fit it exactly to your own needs. Any programming language that can communicate with the COM port can be used. Microsoft often has special offers where simple versions of their development software can be downloaded for free such as Visual Basic or Visual C++.

All PC programs in this book were written in Microsoft Visual Basic 5.0. A few snippets of these programs may be of interest to you.

Read incoming data

Add the component Microsoft Comm. Control 6.0 to your project and drag the phone symbol onto the form. The default name is MSComm1.

Give MSComm1 the following settings, for example in form load subroutine:

```
MSComm1.CommPort = 1
MSComm1.DTREnable = True
MSComm1.EOFEnable = False
```

12.2 Visual Basic communications

```
MSComm1.InputLen = 1
MSComm1.InputMode = comInputModeText
MSComm1.NullDiscard = False
MSComm1.ParityReplace = 0
MSComm1.RThreshold = 1
MSComm1.RTSEnable = False
MSComm1.SThreshold = 0
MSComm1.Settings = "9600,N,8,1"
MSComm1.ParityReplace = 0
```

Open the port with these settings using:

```
MSComm1.PortOpen = True
```

To collect incoming data a special routine is used that is automatically called whenever something happens on the COM port. That "something" doesn't necessarily have to be new data, so first we check the buffer:

```
If MSComm1.InBufferCount Then
```

If there is something in the buffer we will read it character by character. The entire routine looks like this:

```
Private Sub MSComm1_OnComm()

    If MSComm1.InBufferCount Then

        datapresent = MSComm1.Input
        For Counter = 1 To Len(datapresent)

            'put all data one by one in variable reading
            reading = Mid$(datapresent, Counter, 1)

            'this is where the rest of your program goes

        Next Counter
    End If

End Sub
```

The incoming characters are one by one put into the *reading* variable, so that you can process them. This variable is a string and can contain all characters up to

12 Appendix

ASCII code 255, and includes control characters. If you want to print the received data you must remove the control characters and replace them with, for example, a star:

> If Asc(reading) < 32 Then NewText = "*"

Optionally convert to the ASCII value:

> NewText = Asc(reading)

Or to hex:

> NewText = Hex(Asc(reading))

Send data

> Use the MSComm1 setting from the previous snippet. If you want to send a string the characters must be extracted and send one by one in a small loop:
>
> ```
> For counter = 1 To Len(mytext)
>     MSComm1.Output = Mid$(mytext,counter, 1)
> Next counter
> ```

12.3 Tips and tricks

A selection of tips and tricks to help you improve your microcontroller programs.

0. Installation

> If you purchase Flowcode you get a CD and a serial number. Do not use the CD but use a downloaded version instead[61]. Your serial number will still work, and you will get the latest version that may have more functionality and bug fixes. Note that no matter what you do, you do need to validate your version with Matrix Multimedia following the instructions when installing the software.
>
> The instructions enclosed in the Flowcode CD are very clear. But if you initially install from a downloaded trial version you won't see any of it. A few small tips to get you started. On most computers you need administrative privileges or an administrator account in order to install Flowcode and the programmer drivers.

---

[61] If you do use the CD go to the Matrix Multimedia website regularly to look for upgrades.

12.3 Tips and tricks

PIC

- On WinXP the computer will complain that the drivers have no Microsoft Certificate. Ignore this warning.
- During the installation of PPP, the programmer software, make sure to also select the pport driver, even if you don't need it.

ECIO40

- On WinXP the computer will complain that the drivers have no Microsoft Certificate. Ignore this warning.

AVR

- On WinXP the computer will complain that the drivers have no Microsoft Certificate. Ignore this warning.
- The EB194 is in fact equipped with the "AVRdude" so select "yes" when asked if you want to use AVRISP mkll.
- The first time you use the programmer the computer will not recognize it. Insert the "Technical Library CD" and let the computer search for the driver itself.

ARM

- On WinXP the computer will complain that the drivers have no Microsoft Certificate. Ignore this warning.
- Remember to switch the programmer board on using the on/off switch located near the power connector strip.
- When the board is first plugged in the computer needs the location of the driver. DO NOT let the computer search but point to the proper directory manually.

1. Converting a number into a string

Use the standard Flowcode command ToString$, for example:

stringvariable = ToString$(variable)

Example project: 8.3. This is perhaps a very obvious tip but you will need it for the next tip.

12 Appendix

2. Sending a string byte by byte

You can do this by using a C-code loop to extract the byte from the string:

```
//initiate loop
FCV_IDX = 0;
while (FCV_RS[FCV_IDX] != 0)
{
  FCV_TX_VAL = FCV_RS[FCV_IDX];

//* send the byte TX_VAL*//

FCV_IDX = FCV_IDX + 1;
}
```

At the location of the remark insert a Flowcode symbol to do the actual sending. This may be a symbol for sending the byte over and RS232 connection, or a TCP/IP connection, as seen in the next Figure.

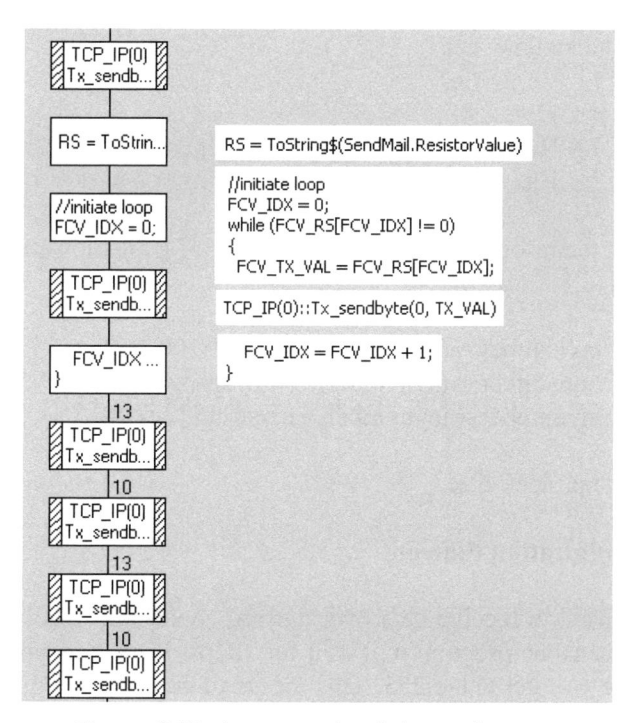

Figure 345. An example of this technique.

307

12.3 Tips and tricks

Note that in Flowcode the variables IDX and TX_VAL need to be declared as bytes, and RS as string.

Example project: 8.3.

3. Convert a string to byte

Extract the different digits and multiply them by their location denominator. If the string is for example mystring = "274" extracting the digit at position 0 of this string is done like this:

firstdigit = mystring[0]

This gives you firstdigit as an ASCII value. To get the actual number subtract 48, so the first digit as an actual number is done like this:

firstdigit = mystring[0] - 48

Extracting all three digits would yield 2, 7 and 4. To get the actual number multiply like this:

4 x 1 = 4
7 x 10 = 70
2 x 100 = 200

Adding them together results in the byte 274. In Flowcode this can be done as follows:

mynumber = (mystring[0] - 48) * 100
mynumber = mynumber + ((mystring [1] - 48) * 10)
mynumber = mynumber + mystring [2] - 48

Example project: 6.3.

4. Serial communication time-out

If you want to receive data over a serial connection a good time-out value is 10. This means the program will wait for 10 ms. If no data has arrived the "received" variable will get value 255. This means of course that you cannot send the value 255 over a serial connection this way because you don't know if you received the time-out value or the actual value.

An alternative is to set the time-out to 255. This effectively disables the time-out altogether, so any value including 255 can now be received. The draw back is that the program will wait for data over the RS232 connection forever. Literally!

Example project: 3.11.

5. Variable declaration

If you make a new variable and start using it in your program it will not necessarily be zero! The new variable name points to a memory location and anything that just happened to be there becomes the value of that variable. So at the start of your program set variables to zero or any other value you prefer.

Since variables in simulation do initialize at zero this can be an ugly cause for deviation between the simulation and real life operation.

6. Replace standard routines

Occasionally you may find that the Flowcode routines don't do exactly what you want. The easiest way to fix this is to compile the program to C. Then use Chip and View C to view the generated C-code. Copy the routine you want to change into a C-box, and modify as you like.

This way you don't have to write a complete C routine but just make some small changes. Note that the C-box is a procedure so you don't need to copy the procedure headings themselves.

Example project: 4.1.

7. Angles in Flowcode for ARM trigonometry

The trigonometry functions in Flowcode for ARM use radians (rad) instead of degrees. Conversion:

$$1 \text{ radial} = 180/\pi = 57.29577951 \text{ degrees.}$$
$$1 \text{ degree} = \pi/180 = 0.017453292 \text{ radians.}$$

Where $\pi = 3.141592654$.

12.3 Tips and tricks

8. Flowcode variables in a C-box

If you want to use Flowcode variables in a C-box precede them with FCV_ and change the variable name to capitals. For example a variable declared in Flowcode as myvar would be accessible in a C-box as FCV_MYVAR.

Example project: 8.3.

If you want to use Flowcode variables in assembler precede them with yet another underscore, so myvar in Flowcode would be _FCV_MYVAR in assembler.

9. Direct access to registers

Registers can be addressed by their names as used in the datasheet, but they must be in a C-box, so remember the semi-colon at the end of each line! Setting ADCON1 to 1 in a C-box is done as follows:

   adcon1 = 0x01;

Some register bits are known to Flowcode as well, for example TMR1H can be reset using:

   tmr1h = 0;

If the bit is not known by its name it can be addressed by its location in the register. For example resetting the capture flag CCP1IF, which is bit two of PIR1, can be done as follows:

   pir1.2= 0;

Example project: 5.7.

10. EB037 card reader card types

The default examples for the card reader are applicable only for MMC cards. Note that this is not the same as the more common SD card which use a different access protocol and have an extra connection.

12 Appendix

Figure 346. SD card (left) and MMC card (right).

The FAT routines used in project 4.13 work on both MMC and SD.

11. Print floating point numbers on an LCD

Flowcode for ARM allows floating point math. Unfortunately printing these numbers to an LCD is not possible. The solution is to use two special libraries: stdlib.h and OSstubs.c. These libraries need to be placed in the same directory as your program[62]. In the supplementary code section place these lines in the Functions Implementations section:

```
#include <stdlib.h>
#include <OSstubs.c>
int errno;
```

Declare a variable called PrntBuff[20] as string. In your program use

```
gcvt(FCV_MYVAR, 6, FCV_PRNTBUFF);
```

in a C-code box where MYVAR is the name of the float variable in your Flowcode program (in capitals) and the number is the total number of digits you want to display. Print variable PrntBuff to the LCD using a LCDPrintString in a stardard macro box.

If for example MyVar in Flowcode contains 1234.56789 and you use the above function to print it to an LCD the result will be 1234.56 (6 digits).

Make sure to read the Microcontroller Mathematics section in the appendix if your calculations yield unexpected results.

Example project: 5.2

---

[62] You will find these files in the download package in chapter 12, section 12.3, as well as in project 5.2

311

12.3 Tips and tricks

12. Flip bits in bytes

The NOT operator can be used to flip variables, which means a zero will become a one, and a one will become a zero. So for example if 5 is a byte then NOT 5 = 250 because on bit level 5 is 00000101 so NOT 5 is 11111010 which is equal to 250. If 5 was an integer[63] however then NOT 5 would be -32762 (integers are signed so the first bit indicates if it is a positive or negative number).

It is also possible to flip just one bit out of a byte, if you AND the result with the bit you want to flip. For example 1 is a byte and you want to flip only bit 0. First do a NOT (the result is 254) and then an AND with 1 (the result is 0). In binary:

```
1                0000 0001
NOT 1            1111 1110
NOT 1 AND 1      0000 0000
```

Example project: 5.1.

13. Debouncing switches

When you press a switch the metal contacts inside approach and then glide over each other. During this time contact is made and lost, back and forth many times. You won't see any of this, but the microcontroller will. It will see this as a series of on/off switching. This is called bouncing.

There are several ways to cope with this problem ("debouncing"), for example in projects 3.3, 3.9, 3.10, 3.11 and 4.14. As switches get older bouncing gets worse so don't debounce "just enough" but be rather generous instead.

14. ZIF socket

Inserting small microcontrollers in the programmer sockets (PIC and AVR) is doable, but the big 40 pins microcontrollers are a real hassle. The solution is to insert a DIL socket and on top a ZIF socket. ZIF is an acronym for Zero Insertion Force and that is exactly what it does. Make sure the ZIF socket has its pins rotated the right way, or even better: round pins[64]. Apparently this brand has: http://www.rapidonline.com

---

[63] An integer is 15 bit plus 1 sign bit. If the 16th bit is zero the number is positive, if the 16th bit is one the number is negative.
[64] Apparently Aries has round pins, available here: http://www.rapidonline.com

12 Appendix

Figure 347. ZIF socket with 16F877A inserted.

15. ARM clockspeed

If you use the ARM microcontroller make sure the clock speed (in the Chip menu) is set to 47923200 Hz.

16. Resistor color table

The value of resistors is color coded using three bands around the resistor. Use this table to determine the color code for the resistors used in this book. Make sure the gold or silver band is on the right, then read the color from left to right.

Resistor value (ohm)	Color code (left to right)
1.5	brown-green-gold
47	yellow-violet-black
330	orange-orange-brown
1 k (1000)	brown-black-red
2k2 (2200)	red-red-red
10k (10,000)	brown-black-orange
100k (100,000)	brown-black-yellow

Figure 348. Resistor color codes.

The resistor values in this book are not very critical, however it is recommended that you use resistors with a 5% accuracy (the rightmost band is gold) rather than 10% (the rightmost band is silver).

12.4 Microcontroller Mathematics

17. Changing PIC microcontroller.

If you want to use a different PIC than you have used in a previous project the PPP software sometimes has difficulty switching over, and will complain that the PIC in the programmer is incorrect, even though the configuration is set correctly. This is a work-around:

1. Insert the "new" PIC in the programmer.
2. Go to Chip, Configure and open the expert screen.
3. Click on autodetect PICmicro.
4. Click on OK.

12.4 Microcontroller Mathematics

If you divide 255 by two and then multiply the result by two the answer should be 255 again. If you do the same thing in a microcontroller the answer is 254. This is by far the most likely cause for unexpected mathematical results in your microcontroller programs.

The problem is caused by the way microcontrollers store numbers in their memory. When a variable is defined a certain amount of space is allocated for that variable. Normally this would be a space of 8 bits, called a byte. Bits can either be zero or one. Depending on their position in a byte these zero's and ones have a different value.

bit position	7	6	5	4	3	2	1	0
value	128	64	32	16	8	4	2	1

So for example 00000001 would have value 1, and 00000101 would have value 1 + 4 = 5. For easier reading a space is often added in the middle, like this 0000 0011. This has no impact on the value. The biggest number would be 1111 1111 which has a value of 255. So a byte can have a value from 0 to 255. Decimals are not possible, so these values need to be whole numbers, called integers.

A byte is the standard variable type for microcontrollers. All microcontroller and microcontroller related peripherals use, or can use, bytes. That means external communications using RS232, SPI and I^{2}C for example all use bytes. The same applies to internal functions such as PWM and registers.

12 Appendix

Flowcode can handle the following types:

Type	Range
byte	0 to 255, integers only
integer	-32768 to 32767, integers only
floating point[65]	$-1.7\ 10^{308}$ to $1.7\ 10^{308}$, real

Note that Flowcode doesn't use single bit variables. See tip 9 in the Tips and Tricks section on how to access single bits in registers. Note that since bytes take the least amount of memory limiting yourself to bytes as much as possible is certainly advisable.

Bytes

If variable MyByte is a byte then the calculation:

  MyByte = 255 / 2

will result in 127. The real answer would be 127.5 but since a byte must be an integer the decimals are chopped off. Multiply this answer by 2 and you get 254, the answer from the introduction to this section.

Bytes can never be smaller than 0, and never be larger than 255. If you go outside the range the value will "roll over" meaning it will start again. So the calculation:

  MyByte = 255 + 1

Will result in 0, and en the calculation:

  MyByte = 250 + 20

will result in 14. By the same token subtracting will also cause a roll over, but in the other direction:

  MyByte = 0 - 1

will result in 255.

---

[65] ARM microcontrollers only. The float variables are 64-bit variables that have 1 sign bit, 11 exponent bits, and 52 mantissa bits - giving the range $+/-1.7\ 10^{+/-308}$ with approximately 16 decimal digits of accuracy.

315

12.4 Microcontroller Mathematics

Since bytes are integers you cannot use decimals in your calculations, so you need to use fractions instead. If for example you want to multiply MyByte by 0.6 simply convert 0.6 to fractions which is 6/10. This can be reduced to 3/5 by dividing numerator and denominator by the greatest common divisor of the two, which would result in this calculation:

> MyByte = (MyByte * 3) / 5

Dividing or multiplying by two, or in fact powers of two, can be done very easily and thus extremely fast, by the microcontroller. To divide by two for example you need to move all bits in a byte one position to the right. So six (0000 0110) divided by two is three (0000 0011).

This means that the previous calculation can be made faster if a power of two is used as denominator, like this:

> MyByte = (MyByte * 19) / 32

Of course this is not exactly the same since 19/32 is 0.594. On a range of 0 to 255 the maximum error this causes is 2, a 0.8% error. Weather you need accuracy over speed depends on the application.

The microcontroller will ignore decimals when doing calculations. That means that a result of for example 12.9 will be truncated to 12, where we would probably feel that 13 would be more appropriate.

The solution is to add 0.5 to the result of the calculation. You can do this by multiplying the result by ten, adding five, and the dividing by ten again: ((12.9 * 10) + 5) /10 = 13.4 which will be truncated to 13.

Another way to handle decimals is by using scaling. This means that a decimal value is represented by a non decimal value. If your program needs to use values ranging from 0.10 to 0.90 you could scale them up by a factor of one hundred, so they will now be in the range from 10 to 90. Prior to printing them on an LCD you can scale them down again. See project 3.9 and 5.4 for examples.

If calculations start to get complicated and the results are important carefully check the calculations step by step, paying attention to roll over and truncation. Use the rules of

12 Appendix

mathematical operations[66] to determine which steps the microcontroller will take and in which order.

Another operation which can cause an unexpected result is the NOT operation, which will flip all bits. That means that NOT 1 will not result in 0 but in 254. This is because a byte with value 1 is in reality 0000 0001. If you use the NOT operator on this the result is 1111 1110, which is 254 in decimal.

Integers

This is a bit of a confusing name. Integer means whole number, while microcontroller Integers certainly don't cover all whole numbers. Flowcode integers are 16 bit, where 1 bit is the sign and 15 bits the value. This means that the range is -32768 to 32767.

bit position	15	14	13	12	11	10	9	8	7	6	5	4	3	2	1	0
value	+/-	16384	8192	4096	2048	1024	512	256	128	64	32	16	8	4	2	1

As far as calculations go integers behave the same as bytes, with the exception that Integers can be negative. When the largest negative number is reached the Integer will roll over to the largest possible integer, and vice versa.

For example:

    MyInt = -32768 - 1

will result in 32767.

Using the NOT operator means that all bits are flipped, including the sign bit. That means that NOT 1 will result in -32766.

Apart from this the calculation techniques discussed in the Bytes section are applicable to Integers as well.

---

[66] Resolve in this order: anything between brackets, exponents, multiplication, division, roots, addition, subtraction.

12.4 Microcontroller Mathematics

Floating point (or float)

This variable, which is available in Flowcode for ARM only, can contain real numbers from $-1.7 \cdot 10^{308}$ to $1.7 \cdot 10^{308}$, so it is rather unlikely that you calculation results will not fit. If variable MyFloat is a float and has the value 255 then the calculation:

    MyFloat = (MyFloat / 2) * 2

will result in 255. Note that if you want to print a float to an LCD screen you have to use the technique described in Tips and Tricks number 11.

Constants

Constants are not variables but numbers that do not change while a program is running. If for example you want to divide a variable by two then the number two would be a constant. Constants will be stored in the most efficient memory location. So if you use the number 2 it will be stored as a byte, if you use number -2 it will be stored as an integer, and if you use the number 2.7 it will be stored as a float if you have an ARM microcontroller.

Mixing types

Since the microcontroller has no idea what you are trying to achieve when you mix variable types in a calculation you have to be very careful in how you set them up. The base rule is that the compiler, that turns the Flowcode program into something that the microcontroller understands, tries to minimize its operations. This means it will attempt to use the smallest possible variable types. Take this example:

    MyByte = 255
    MyFloat = MyByte / 2

You would expect the result to be 127.5 since the answer will be in a float. The compiler however will first resolve MyByte / 2 which is 255/2. Since MyByte is a byte and 2 is a constant which fits into a byte and thus is actually a byte, the compiler will treat the entire calculation as a byte operation, so the result is 127. This result is then placed into the variable MyFloat but by then the decimal is already lost. So even though MyFloat could easily hold the decimal the result is still wrong.

The solution is to force the compiler to use a float for the first part of the operation by dividing by 2.0 instead of 2. The reason that this works is that 2.0 has a decimal and is thus a float, even if the decimal is zero. So the correct calculation is:

12   Appendix

>   MyByte = 255
>   MyFloat = MyByte / 2.0

And this will indeed result is 127.5.

Unfortunately the Flowcode simulator does not take this into account. It uses the calculation capabilities of your PC which doesn't try to save on resources. So you need to be careful when evaluating simulation results.

Interestingly enough Flowcode will let you get away with an attempt to store a large type variable into a small one. For example:

>   MyFloat = 923.4567
>   MyByte = MyFloat

The result will be that MyByte is 155 (923 causes three roll overs, the result is 155 as a remainder). You can use this to your advantage. Since most external peripheral components and several internal functions use bytes you can turn a float back into a byte at the end of a calculation. You do need to make sure that the end result is between 0 and 255 because it is rather difficult to predict the byte-size answer after multiple roll overs. Note that attempting to store negative numbers into a byte results in zero. So:

>   MyFloat = -923.4567
>   MyByte = MyFloat

means MyByte is now zero.

To avoid getting into trouble take the following steps if you want to mix variable types.

1. Break the calculation up into very small parts so it is easy to understand (for you, not for the microcontroller).
2. Use the rules of mathematical operations[67] to determine which steps the microcontroller will take and in which order.
3. In each step look only at the right side of the equation. The compiler will use the largest variable type used in that part of the equation to store the intermediary result.
4. If that largest variable type is smaller than the variable type on the left side of the equation modify a constant to make it match.

---

[67] Resolve in this order: anything between brackets, exponents, multiplication, division, roots, addition, subtraction.

12.5 E-block connections

5. If that largest variable type is larger than the variable type on the left side of the equation change the variable type on the left side. Unless you want the end result to be for example a byte, but be very careful to avoid a roll over and negative numbers.
6. Do not rely on the simulation. If you want to verify your calculation set the variables temporarily to known values so you can calculate the expected end result on a calculator. Then download the program to the microcontroller. Print the result on the LCD screen[68] and compare with your predictions.

See project 5.2 for an example of mixed variable types in a calculation.

12.5 E-block connections

This appendix contains the connections of the E-blocks used in this book. These are the standard connections that can be made using jumpers. Non-standard connections can be made using the patch panel if applicable, which allows you to use any pin combination you may require.

EB004 LED board

This board has no jumpers and can only be used in the default configuration.

| | | EB004 LED board | |
| | | Default | |
pin D9	port	description	jumper
1	0	D0	
2	1	D1	
3	2	D2	
4	3	D3	
5	4	D4	
6	5	D5	
7	6	D6	
8	7	D7	
9	GND		

---

[68] Note that if you want to print a float to an LCD screen you have to use the technique described in Tips and Tricks number 11.

12 Appendix

EB005 LCD board

If you don't see anything on the LCD, or just black squares, adjust the brightness with the little variable resistor. To patch you need to place jumper at "patch".

		EB005 LCD board	
		Default	
pin D9	*port*	*description*	*jumper*
1	0	Data	Default
2	1	Data	Default
3	2	Data	Default
4	3	Data	Default
5	4	RS	Default
6	5	Enable	Default
7	6		
8	7		
9	GND		

EB007 Switch (button) board

This board has no jumpers and can only be used in the default configuration.

		EB007 Switch (button) board	
		Default	
pin D9	*port*	*description*	*jumper*
1	0	SW0	
2	1	SW1	
3	2	SW2	
4	3	SW3	
5	4	SW4	
6	5	SW5	
7	6	SW6	
8	7	SW7	
9	GND		

12.5 E-block connections

EB013 SPI memory and D/A board

To patch you need to place the jumpers at C and 2. Jumper J11 allows you to select between EEPROM and FRAM memory. Jumper J2 allows you to select DAC output or amplified output, used for sound. Note that this board is 3.3 volt compatible, except for FRAM memory.

| | | EB013 SPI memory and D/A board ||||
| | | Default || Alternative ||
pin D9	port	description	jumper	description	jumper
1	0				
2	1			SDI	B
3	2			SDO	B
4	3	SCK	A		
5	4	SDI	A	SCK	B
6	5	SDO	A		
7	6	$CS_{FRAM/EEPROM}$	1		
8	7	CS_{DAC}	1		
9	GND				

EB014 Keypad board

This board has no jumpers and can only be used in the default configuration.

| | | EB014 Keypad board ||
| | | Default ||
pin D9	port	description	jumper
1	0	Column 1	
2	1	Column 2	
3	2	Column 3	
4	3		
5	4	Row A	
6	5	Row B	
7	6	Row C	
8	7	Row D	
9	GND		

12   Appendix

EB015 RS232 board

Jumper at 2 means no flow control. To patch you need to place the jumpers at D and 3.

pin D9	port	Default description	jumper	Alternatives description	jumper	description	jumper
1	0	RTS	1				
2	1			RX	B		
3	2	RX	A	TX	B		
4	3						
5	4	CTS	1				
6	5	TX	A				
7	6					TX	C
8	7					RX	C
9	GD						

EB018 CAN bus board

To patch you need to place the jumpers at C and 2. Note that this board is not 3.3 volt compatible and can therefore not be used with an ARM microcontroller.

pin D9	port	Default description	jumper	Alternatives description	jumper
1	0	INT	1		
2	1			SDI	B
3	2			SDO	B
4	3	SCK	A		
5	4	SDI	A	SCK	B
6	5	SDO	A		
7	6	CS	1		
8	7				
9	GND				

12.5 E-block connections

EB022 Motor driver board

These are the settings for the lower D9 connector. To patch you need to place jumper J10 at "patch". Consult project 4.7 for an extensive explanation of the upper D9 connector, which takes care of sensory feedback.

		EB022 Motor driver board	
		Default	
pin D9	*port*	*description*	*jumper*
1	0	In 1 (motor A or 1)	Default
2	1	In 2 (motor A or 1)	Default
3	2	In 3 (motor B or 2)	Default
4	3	In 4 (motor B or 2)	Default
5	4	Optional Enable A	Default
6	5	Optional Enable B	Default
7	6		
8	7		
9	GND		

EB023 Internet board

To patch you need to place the jumper at C. Note that jumper J5 needs to be placed according to the voltage you are using: 5 volts for PIC and ARV and 3.3 volts for ARM microcontrollers. Always make sure that the address jumpers J8-J10 are set according to the address in the Flowcode component.

		EB023 Internet board			
		Default		*Alternative*	
pin D9	*port*	*description*	*jumper*	*description*	*jumper*
1	0	INT	A	INT	B
2	1			SDA	B
3	2				
4	3	SCK	A		
5	4	SDA	A	SCK	B
6	5				
7	6				
8	7				
9	GND				

324

12 Appendix

EB037 MMC board

To patch you need to place the jumpers at C. Note that jumper J4 needs to be placed according to the voltage you are using: 5 volts for PIC and ARV and 3.3 volts for ARM microcontrollers.

		EB037 MMC board			
		Default		*Alternatives*	
pin D9	*port*	*description*	*jumper*	*description*	*jumper*
1	0				
2	1			SDI	B
3	2	CS	A	SDO	B
4	3	SCK	A		
5	4	SDI	A	SCK	B
6	5	SDO	A		
7	6				
8	7			CS	B
9	GND				

EB038 Relay board

Note that this board runs off 14 volts.

		EB038 Relay board			
		Default		*Alternative*	
pin D9	*port*	*description*	*jumper*	*description*	*jumper*
1	0	RLY1	Low		
2	1	RLY2	Low		
3	2	RLY3	Low		
4	3	RLY4	Low		
5	4			RLY1	High
6	5			RLY2	High
7	6			RLY3	High
8	7			RLY4	High
9	GND				

12.5 E-block connections

EB039 USB board

To patch you need to place the jumpers at D and 3.

| pin D9 | port | EB039 USB board ||||||
| | | Default || Alternatives ||||
		description	jumper	description	jumper	description	jumper
1	0	RTS	1				
2	1			RX	B		
3	2	RX	A	TX	B		
4	3						
5	4	CTS	1	RTS	2		
6	5	TX	A	CTS	2		
7	6					TX	C
8	7					RX	C
9	GD						

Miscellaneous

The EB016 Proto board and the EB017 Patch board are of course not listed because these are "empty" boards with no pre-made connections. The EB186 is a cell phone modem that connects into the EB015 RS232 board, so settings need to be made on that board and not on the modem itself.

Index

$GPRMC 151
12F675 297
16F877A 39; 46; 58; 63; 71; 78; 81; 101; 106; 112; 125; 129; 135; 140; 145; 150; 155; 180; 185; 191; 199; 204; 222; 226; 233; 241; 249; 266; 277; 293; 296
16F88 18
ACII table 302
ADC 165
ADC component 64
ADCON1 101
AND 85; 170
Application board 96; 159
ARP 256
Array 42
AT91SAM7S128 .... 20; 92; 164; 213
ATMEGA32 ....21; 33; 52; 67; 88; 119; 170; 217; 235; 244; 258; 293
AVRdude 306
Bitrate 112
Bootloader 96
Bouncing 49; 89; 93; 167
Byte 315
C symbol 74
Calculation symbol 41
CAN bus and RS232 240
CAN bus board . 233; 235; 241; 244; 323
CAN bus buffers 242
CAN bus component 233
CAN bus monitor 247
CCP1 205
CCP1CON 205
Cell phone modem 218; 226
CHARmaker 120
CMCON 207
CMT 223
Compare$ 151
Comperator 205

Component macro symbol 48
Configuration word(s) 40
Constant 318
Custom_code.c 160
DAC 111
Decision symbol 27
Delay symbol 28
Devmgmt.msc 59
Eagle CAD 285
Echo 60
ECIO40 145
EEPROM 25LC640 106
EEPROM component 156
EEPROM memory 155
EICO40 .... 96; 159
Electret microphone 284
Fabs 166
Fan 128
FAT 160
Firewall 250
Flash memory 86; 140
Flash.h 141
Flatcable 14
Float 318
Float print 311
Flowchart 9
Fractions 316
FRAM FM25640 106
Fuses 22
Garmin E-trex 149
GP1S036HEL 213
GP2Y0D340K 170
GPS 149
Heat flow 197
HTML 261
I^2C 259; 291
ICMP 251
Input symbol 25
Integer 317

327

Index

Internet board....249; 258; 266; 277; 324
Interrupt symbol 72
IP settings 249
K value... 202
Keypad board................. 46; 52; 81; 322
LCD ASCII.. 37
LCD board 33; 46; 52; 58; 63; 81; 88; 101; 119; 125; 129; 140; 150; 155; 159; 173; 180; 185; 191; 204; 217; 222; 226; 249; 266; 321
LCD commands.................................. 60
LCD component 34
LCD custom character 120
LDR 67; 173
LED board 18; 20; 21; 39; 78; 92; 96; 106; 135; 145; 164; 170; 213; 226; 320
LED component................................. 24
LM358 284
Lookup Table (LUT) 80
Loop symbol...................................... 23
Loudspeaker 116
Lux.. 68; 173
MIC pre-amp 78; 106; 164; 204; 284
MICterm 57
MMC board 159; 325
MOD... 60
Motor board 129
Motor driver board.......................... 324
MSComm 303; 304
NMEA 0183 150
NOP 221
NOT 75; 170; 238; 317
NTC 184
OPAMP 284
OR... 162
Output symbol 27
Patch 52
PCB 285
PIR1 209
Port and pin....................................... 40
PPP 155

Prescaler 73
Proto board 63; 67; 71; 101; 117; 173; 180; 185; 191; 199; 204; 213; 244; 258; 266; 277; 282; 284
PWM component..............................117
PWM frequency 133
PWM pins..292
Radians 309
Rand.pic16.lib 125
Random 124
Register bit 310
Relay board 46; 67; 277; 325
Resistor color code 313
RJ45 CAT 5.....................................249
RS232 and CAN bus 240
RS232 and SPI 190
RS232 board 52; 94; 150; 191; 217; 222; 226; 241; 323
RS232 component 54
Scroll text on LCD 60
SKYwriter 136
software oscilloscope 15
Speed of sound 183
SPI and RS232 190
SPI bus 107; 240
SPI component 108
SPI pins 291
SPI/DAC board 106; 112; 191; 322
SRF04..179
String manipulation symbol 84
Switch board 18; 20; 21; 88; 92; 106; 125; 129; 140; 145; 155; 164; 217; 249; 321
Switch component 24
T1CON 206
TCP/IP 251
TCP/IP component 252
Tiny Mail server 266
TMR0 interrupt 72
TMR0 offset 74
Torque 80
ToString$() 84

328

Index

TRISA	207
TWI	259
UDP	277
USART	146
USART pins	292
USB board	326
USB RS232 board	58; 199
Variable Manager	26
Visual Basic	303
Voice command	163
Voltage divider	174
Vref	100
WAVconvert	112
Webserver component	260
Winsock	279
Wireshark	255
Youtube	167
ZIF	312